Mathematical Techniques for Competitive Examinations

Mathematical Techniques for Competitive Examinations

Soudeep Deb
PhD (Statistics)
Assistant Professor, Indian Institute of Management Bangalore,
Bengaluru, Karnataka, India

Debangan Dey
PhD (Biostatistics)
Visiting Fellow, National Institute of Mental Health,
Bethesda, Maryland, USA

All rights reserved. No part of this book may be modified, reproduced or utilised in any form, or by any means, electronic or mechanical, including photocopying, recording or by any information storage and retrieval system, in any form of binding or cover other than in which it is published, without permission in writing from the publisher.

MATHEMATICAL TECHNIQUES FOR COMPETITIVE EXAMINATIONS

UNIVERSITIES PRESS (INDIA) PRIVATE LIMITED

Registered Office
3-6-747/1/A & 3-6-754/1, Himayatnagar, Hyderabad 500 029, Telangana, India
info@universitiespress.com; www.universitiespress.com

Distributed by
Orient Blackswan Private Limited

Registered Office
3-6-752 Himayatnagar, Hyderabad 500 029, Telangana, India

Other Offices
Bengaluru / Chennai / Guwahati / Hyderabad / Kolkata
Mumbai / New Delhi / Noida / Patna / Visakhapatnam

© Universities Press (India) Private Limited 2023
First published 2023

Cover and book design
© Universities Press (India) Private Limited 2023

ISBN: 978-93-93330-10-9

Typeset in NimbusRom 11 pt by 13 pt *by*
Mohan Boda, Hyderabad

Printed in India by
B.B. Press, Noida 201 301

Published by
Universities Press (India) Private Limited
3-6-747/1/A & 3-6-754/1, Himayatnagar, Hyderabad 500 029, Telangana, India

Care has been taken to confirm the accuracy of the information presented in this book. The authors and the publisher, however, cannot accept any responsibility for errors or omissions or for consequences from application of the information in this book, and make no warranty, express or implied, with respect to its contents.

Preface

In high school, students often struggle with challenging mathematical problems. In fact, according to a survey conducted by Cuemath, a multi-format maths learning program, at least 89% of Indian parents agree that Mathematics is the toughest subject for their kids while 77% of them believe that the subject is not taught well in schools. Quite naturally, even if students aspire to pursue undergraduate studies from prestigious institutes like the Indian Statistical Institute or Chennai Mathematical Institute, their preparations often fall short during the entrance examinations, without proper guidance.

Over the years, we have come across numerous students who are apprehensive of tackling complex problems and try to avoid challenging mathematic problems if they can. As we dig deeper, we realize that the natural fight-or-flight response either leads students to take up the struggle with the challenging problems or to avoid mathematics with a passion. Our aim in this book is to enable students to do the former. It is well known that one tends to like things that one is naturally good at. One would love something if there is visible and continuous success. Such success comes with dedication, hard work, as well as appropriate learning modules. This book is meant to help students in designing a well-planned pathway to tackle complicated problems from different branches of high-school mathematics. We earnestly believe that the problem-solving strategies and tricks of the subject described here will help students become confident in mathematics and subsequently pave the way to greater successes over time.

One must remember that this is not a typical textbook. Thus, before going through the problems here, the reader must study the basic mathematics related to every topic from any standard textbook. Only then will the student be able to get the best out of this book in preparing for competitive exams.

In every chapter of this book, we start with the most important formulae, definitions and results. Subsequently, an extensive set of solved examples are given. On the one hand, these examples show direct application of the concepts learnt in the chapter while on the other, relevant notes and tips are provided to help readers realize how they should approach such problems. Furthermore, throughout the book, we maintain continuity in describing the topics and results to show how maths topics are connected. Several problems are discussed in more than one chapter to indicate how different concepts can be used to solve the same problem. We also include interesting examples where a combination of multiple topics can help in designing an elegant solution to a challenging problem.

In light of the above, although each chapter of the book can be studied independently, students must remember that the book is constructed to reinforce patterns developed in stages throughout the book. Thus, it will be most useful for students who have covered the basics of all topics. Our suggestion is to first read the key concepts described at the beginning of every chapter. If the reader is comfortable with them, they can then try to solve each problem without looking at the given solution. For any hard problem, often it is key to find an auxiliary condition that is not a part of the problem but which will help in finding a solution in a couple of steps. In this book, we point out such ideas so that students can gain experience and become experts soon.

We promise that this book will make the reader more adept in problem solving. Remember that it is never too late to become an expert in any topic. For instance, Archimedes himself became a mathematician only at the age of 54. Last but not least, one must also keep in mind the adage from the great American inventor, Thomas Edison, "Genius is one percent inspiration, ninety-nine percent perspiration." In other words, one cannot become a math-genius without hard work and continuous practice; but with that, anything is possible.

Good luck!

Soudeep Deb
Debangan Dey

Acknowledgements

First and foremost, we want to thank all our students over the years who have always inspired us to be better teachers. It is their continuous appreciation that has motivated us to take up the challenge of writing this book. We also want to thank our families, who have been pillars of support, through thick and thin. And finally, we are grateful to the entire team of Universities Press (India) Private Limited for their invaluable support in this endeavour.

Soudeep Deb
Debangan Dey

Contents

Preface   *v*
Acknowledgements   *vi*

Chapter 1: Number Theory   1.1
Chapter 2: Combinatorics   2.1
Chapter 3: Algebra   3.1
Chapter 4: Calculus   4.1
Chapter 5: Euclidean Geometry   5.1
Chapter 6: Coordinate Geometry   6.1
Chapter 7: Probability and Statistics   7.1
Chapter 8: Miscellaneous   8.1
Appendix: Previous Years' Subjective Questions and Solutions   *A.1*

To

My father,

the first and most important

mathematics teacher I ever had

—Soudeep Deb

To

Football,

the beautiful game

—Debangan Dey

1
Number Theory

"God created the natural numbers, and all the rest is the work of man."

These words by the famous German mathematician Leopold Kronecker show the beauty that lies in the study of natural numbers or integers in general. Number theory, the common term for the study of the properties of integers, is in fact one of the most crucial topics for different examinations.

In this chapter, we shall discuss a few important results and formulae related to numbers and explore how they can help us in solving different problems.

KEY RESULTS

> Throughout this chapter, the following notations are used:
> $\mathbb{N}$ = the set of natural numbers $\qquad$ $\mathbb{Z}$ = the set of integers
> $\mathbb{R}$ = the set of real numbers $\qquad$ $\mathbb{Q}$ = the set of rational numbers
> $\mathbb{C}$ = the set of complex numbers

Definition 1.1 (Greatest Integer Function): For any $x \in \mathbb{R}$, the greatest integer function $[x]$ is defined as the largest integer m satisfying $m \leqslant x$. An alternative notation for $[x]$ is $\lfloor x \rfloor$, commonly known as the floor function. The fractional part of x is usually denoted by $\{x\} = x - [x]$.

> **Useful Tip:** An effective trick while solving a problem related to the greatest integer function is to remember that $[x] \leqslant x < [x] + 1$ and $0 \leqslant \{x\} < 1$.

Definition 1.2 (Divisor): Let $a, b \in \mathbb{Z}$. We say that a divides b or a is a divisor (or factor) of b if there exists some $q \in \mathbb{Z}$ such that $b = qa$. This is denoted as $a \mid b$.

Definition 1.3 (Primes and Composite Numbers): Let $n \in \mathbb{N}$ with $n > 1$. Then n is called prime if its only positive divisors are 1 and n. It is called composite otherwise. Equivalently, n is composite if and only if it can be written in the form $n = ab$, where $a, b \in \mathbb{Z}$ and $|a| > 1, |b| > 1$.

Theorem 1.1: Let $n \in \mathbb{N}$ with $n > 1$. Then n is prime if and only if n is not divisible by any prime p with $p \leqslant \sqrt{n}$.

Lemma 1.1 (Euclid's Lemma): If $a, b \in \mathbb{Z}$ and p is prime such that $p \mid ab$, then $p \mid a$ or $p \mid b$. More generally, if $a_1, ..., a_n \in \mathbb{Z}$ and p is prime such that $p \mid a_1, \cdots, a_n$, then there exists an i with $1 \leqslant i \leqslant n$ such that $p \mid a_i$.

Theorem 1.2 (Fundamental Theorem of Arithmetic): Every integer greater than 1 has a unique factorization into primes; that is, every integer $n > 1$ can be represented in the form

$$n = \prod_{i=1}^{r} p_i^{\alpha_i},$$

where the p_i are distinct primes, and the exponents α_i are positive integers. Moreover, this representation is unique except for the ordering of the primes p_i.

> **Useful Tip:** It is often helpful to write an integer n using its prime factorization, in which case, the known properties of prime numbers can be applied to solve challenging problems.

Definition 1.4 (Greatest Common Divisor): Let $a, b \in \mathbb{Z}$, with a and b not 0. The greatest common divisor (gcd) of a and b, denoted by $gcd(a,b)$, or simply (a,b), is the largest among the common divisors of a and b. That is

$$(a,b) = gcd(a,b) = \max\{d : d \mid a \text{ and } d \mid b\}$$

If $(a,b) = 1$, then a and b are called relatively prime or coprime.

Definition 1.5 (Least Common Multiple): Let $a, b \in \mathbb{Z}$, with a and b non-zero. The least common multiple (lcm) of a and b, denoted by $[a,b]$, is defined as the smallest positive integer that is divisible by both a and b. That is

$$[a,b] = \min\{m \in \mathbb{N} : a \mid m \text{ and } b \mid m\}$$

Definition 1.6 (Rational Number): We define r to be a rational number if and only if it can be written as $r = p/q$, where p, q are integers, $q \neq 0$ and $(p,q) = 1$. A number that is real but not rational is called irrational.

Theorem 1.3 (Bezout's Identity): Let $a, b \in \mathbb{Z}$ with a and b not 0, and let $d = (a, b)$. Then there exist $n, m \in \mathbb{Z}$ such that $d = an + bm$; that is, d is a linear combination of a and b with integer coefficients. Moreover, the set of all such linear combinations is exactly equal to the set of integer multiples of d, and d is the least positive element of this set.

$$\{an + bm : n, m \in \mathbb{Z}\} = \{dq : q \in \mathbb{Z}\}, \; d = \min\{an + bm : n, m \in \mathbb{Z}, an + bm > 0\}$$

Definition 1.7 (Euler's ϕ-function): For a natural number $n \geq 2$, Euler's ϕ-function is defined as the number of positive integers less than n and relatively prime to n. That is

$$\phi(n) = |\{k \in \mathbb{N} : k \leq n, \; (k, n) = 1\}|$$

Theorem 1.4: For Euler's ϕ-function defined as above, if $n = p_1^{\alpha_1} p_2^{\alpha_2} \ldots p_r^{\alpha_r}$, then

$$\phi(n) = n \prod_{i=1}^{r} \left(1 - \frac{1}{p_i}\right)$$

Theorem 1.5 (Division Algorithm): Given $a, b \in \mathbb{Z}$ with $b > 0$, there exist unique $q, r \in \mathbb{Z}$ such that $a = qb + r$ and $0 \leq r < b$. Moreover, q and r are given by the formulae $q = [a/b]$ and $r = a - [a/b]b$. We can also rewrite the above statement as $a \equiv r \pmod{b}$. In words, we say that a is congruent to r modulo b.

> **Useful Tip:** Division Algorithm leads to Euclid's Algorithm to find (a, b), which relies on the fact that if $a = qb + r$, where $q, r \in \mathbb{Z}, 0 \leq r < b$, then $(a, b) = (b, r)$.

Definition 1.8 (Residue Class): In number theory, a residue of an integer a in modulo b is the unique value r satisfying $a \equiv r \pmod{b}$. A residue class in modulo b is a complete set of integers that is congruent to r modulo b for some integer $0 \leq r \leq b - 1$. Clearly, in modulo b, there are exactly b different residue classes, and each residue class contains all integers in the form $kb + r$, where $k \in \mathbb{Z}$ and r is the corresponding residue.

A related concept is that of complete residue system. In modulo b, it is defined as a set of integers that satisfies the condition that every integer is congruent to a unique member of the set in modulo b. In other words, a complete residue system in modulo b contains exactly one member of each residue class in modulo b.

Theorem 1.6 (Chinese Remainder Theorem): Let m, n be relatively prime. Then each residue class in modulo mn is equal to the intersection of a unique residue class in modulo m and a unique residue class in modulo n. The converse is also true.

In other words, let $d_1, d_2, \ldots, d_n$ be relatively prime and suppose we want to find the least number K which leaves a remainder y_i when divided by d_i, for $i = 1, 2, \ldots, n$. Let $M = d_1 d_2 \ldots d_n$, and $b_i = M/d_i$. Now, if the numbers a_i satisfy $a_i b_i \equiv 1 \pmod{d_i}$ for every i, then the solution for $K = \sum_{i=1}^{n} a_i b_i y_i \pmod{M}$ is the solution we seek.

Theorem 1.7 (Fermat's Little Theorem): Let p be a prime and $a \in \mathbb{Z}$ not divisible by p. Then $a^{p-1} \equiv 1 \pmod{p}$.

Theorem 1.8 (Generalization of Fermat's Little Theorem): If a is an integer and m is a positive integer coprime to a, then $a^{\phi(m)} \equiv 1 \pmod{m}$, where ϕ is the above-mentioned Euler's ϕ-function.

Theorem 1.9 (Wilson's Theorem): For an integer $p > 1$, $(p-1)! + 1$ is divisible by p if and only if p is prime.

Theorem 1.10 (Lagrange's Theorem): Consider an odd prime number p, and let $x \in \mathbb{R}$. Suppose that

$$(x-1)(x-2)\ldots(x-(p-1)) = x^{p-1} - a_1 x^{p-2} + \ldots - a_{p-2} x + a_{p-1},$$

for some positive integers $a_1, \ldots, a_{p-1}$. Then, $a_{p-2} \equiv 0 \pmod{p^2}$, $a_{p-1} \equiv -1 \pmod{p}$.

Theorem 1.11 (Well Ordering Principle): Any non-empty subset of non-negative integers has a smallest element. In other words, if $S \subset \mathbb{N} \cup \{0\}$, then there exists $s_0 \in S$ such that $s_0 \leqslant s$ for all $s \in S$.

Many number theoretic proofs rely on the above and the principle of mathematical induction, which is a logical consequence of the well ordering principle.

Theorem 1.12 (Mathematical Induction): If a subset S of positive integers contains 1, and contains $n+1$ whenever it contains n, then S contains all positive integers.

In the *strong form* of the above theorem, if a subset S of positive integers contains 1, and contains $n+1$ whenever it contains $1, 2, \ldots, n$, then $S = \mathbb{N}$.

> **Useful Tip:** Mathematical induction is one of the most popular techniques to solve problems not only related to number theory, but also for other topics.

As the last key result of this section, we recall the definition of arithmetic function, various examples of which will be discussed in the solved examples below.

Definition 1.9 (Arithmetic Function): A function from $\mathbb{N}$ to the set of real numbers is called an arithmetic function. For example, Euler's ϕ-function introduced above is an arithmetic function. Another popular arithmetic function is the number of positive divisors of $n \in \mathbb{N}$. It is commonly denoted as $d(n)$. If the prime factorization of n is given by $p_1^{\alpha_1} \ldots p_r^{\alpha_r}$, then $d(n) = (\alpha_1 + 1) \ldots (\alpha_r + 1)$.

Solved Examples

1. Prove that for every $n \in \mathbb{N}$, $\sqrt{n}$ is either an integer or an irrational number.

Solution: Suppose $\sqrt{n}$ is not an integer, but a rational number. Then, there are relatively prime integers p and q such that $\sqrt{n} = p/q$. Thus, $p^2 = nq^2$, implying that q^2 is a factor of p^2. However, p, q are relatively prime and so, the only possibility is that $q = 1$, which further implies that $\sqrt{n} = p/q$ is essentially an integer. Hence, $\sqrt{n}$ is either an integer or an irrational number.

> **Useful Tip:** This technique is known as *proof by contradiction*, where we assume the converse of what we have to prove, and then show that the given assumption cannot be true in that case. In set theoretic notation, it is the same as saying $A \subset B$ is equivalent to $B^c \subset A^c$.

2. Let $x, n \in \mathbb{N}$. If $1 + x + x^2 + \ldots + x^{n-1}$ is a prime number, show that n is a prime number as well.

Solution: Using the concept of geometric progression, $1 + x + x^2 + \ldots + x^{n-1} = (x^n - 1)/(x - 1)$. This is a prime number, say p. Thus, we have $x^n - 1 = p(x - 1)$.

Suppose n is not a prime number. Then, $n = rs$ for integers r, s, both greater than 1. Subsequently, $x^n - 1 = (x^r - 1)(1 + x^r + (x^r)^2 + \ldots + (x^r)^{s-1})$. This can be further factorized as $(x - 1)(1 + x + x^2 + \ldots + x^{r-1})(1 + x^r + (x^r)^2 + \ldots + (x^r)^{s-1})$, which implies that

$$p = (1 + x + x^2 + \ldots + x^{r-1})(1 + x^r + (x^r)^2 + \ldots + (x^r)^{s-1})$$

The above clearly contradicts the assumption that p is prime. Hence, n must be a prime number.

3. For $k, n \in \mathbb{N}$, prove that $(k \cdot n)!$ is divisible by $(k!)^n$.

Solution: First, we prove that the product of any consecutive k positive integers is divisible by $k!$ for any natural number k. For this, let us consider the integers $r + 1, r + 2, \ldots, r + k$. Note that the product of these integers is

$$(r+1)(r+2)\ldots(r+k) = \frac{(r+k)!}{r!} = k! \binom{r+k}{r}$$

$\binom{r+k}{r}$ is a binomial coefficient denoting the number of ways of choosing r objects from $r+k$ objects, and so, it must be a positive integer. Thus, the product of those k integers is an integral multiple of $k!$, implying that it is divisible by $k!$.

Now, we can write

$$(k.n)! = (1.2.\ldots.k)((k+1)\ldots 2k)\ldots((k(n-1)+1)\ldots(kn)) = b_1 b_2 \ldots b_n$$

Note that each b_i, for $i = 1, 2, \ldots, n$, is a product of k consecutive integers, and thus, each of them is divisible by $k!$. Hence, $(k.n)!$ must be divisible by $(k!)^n$.

> **Useful Tip:** Remember that the product of k consecutive positive integers is divisible by $k!$ for any natural number k. This can be handy in solving many problems.

4. Let $D = a^2 + b^2 + c^2$, where a and b are consecutive positive integers and $c = ab$. Show that $\sqrt{D}$ is an odd integer.

Solution: We have $b = a+1$ and $c = ab = a(a+1)$. Simple algebraic manipulations give us $D = a^2 + a^2 + 2a + 1 + a^4 + 2a^3 + a^2 = \left(a^2 + a + 1\right)^2$. Since a and $a+1$ are consecutive integers, their product $a^2 + a$ is even, and hence, $\sqrt{D} = a^2 + a + 1$ is an odd positive integer.

5. For $n \in \mathbb{N}$, let $a_n = n^2 + 20$. If d_n is the gcd of a_n and a_{n+1}, prove that d_n is a factor of 81.

Solution: Since d_n is the greatest common divisor of $n^2 + 20$ and $(n+1)^2 + 20$, d_n divides their difference $2n+1$, and therefore, $n(2n+1) = 2n^2 + n$. Further, it means that d_n divides $(2n^2 + n) - 2(n^2 + 20) = n - 40$, which combined with $d_n | 2n+1$, implies that d_n is a divisor of 81.

6. Let $n \geqslant 2$ be an integer and let m be the largest integer which is $\leqslant n$ and a power of 2. If l_n denotes the least common multiple of $1, 2, \ldots, n$, prove that l_n / k is an integer for all integers $k \leqslant n$. Further, show that l_n / k is odd if and only if $k = m$. Using it or otherwise, prove that

$$1 + \frac{1}{2} + \frac{1}{3} + \ldots + \frac{1}{n}$$

is not an integer.

Solution: Since l_n is the least common multiple of $1, 2, \ldots, n$, it is of the form $l_n = p_1^{\alpha_1} p_2^{\alpha_2} \ldots p_r^{\alpha_r}$, where $p_1, p_2, \ldots, p_r$ are primes less than n. Also, α_r is the highest possible integer such that $p_r^{\alpha_r} \leqslant n$ but $p_r^{\alpha_r + 1} > n$. It is straightforward to see that l_n must be a multiple of all integers $k \leqslant n$, which proves the first part.

Now, since 2 is the only even prime, we can write that $l_n = mq_n$, where q_n is odd and m is the highest power of 2 that is less than n. Clearly, l_n/m is odd, and for any other integer $k \leqslant n$, l_n/k is even.

To prove the last part, observe that

$$1 + \frac{1}{2} + \frac{1}{3} + \ldots + \frac{1}{n} = \frac{l_n/1 + l_n/2 + l_n/3 + \ldots + l_n/n}{l_n}$$

In the numerator, only one term (l_n/m) is odd and the rest are even. Thus, the numerator is odd and the denominator is even, which implies that the quantity can never be an integer.

7. Prove that 9 divides $2^{2n} - 3n - 1$ for all $n \geqslant 1$.

Solution: For $n = 1$, $2^{2n} - 3n - 1 = 0$, and the result is trivially true. For $n \geqslant 2$, using the binomial expansion

$$2^{2n} - 3n - 1 = (1+3)^n - 3n - 1 = \sum_{r=0}^{n} \binom{n}{r} 1^{n-r} 3^r - 3n - 1 = \sum_{r=2}^{n} \binom{n}{r} 1^{n-r} 3^r$$

Since for all $r \geqslant 2$, each term in the above summation is an integer divisible by $3^2 = 9$, we can say that the whole expression is divisible by 9 for all $n \geqslant 1$.

> **Useful Tip:** Another way to solve this problem is to use mathematical induction. This is left as an exercise to the student.

8. Let F_n denote the nth non-square positive integer. For example, $F_1 = 2$, $F_2 = 3$, $F_3 = 5$, and so on. If $m^2 < F_n < (m+1)^2$, show that m is the integer closest to $\sqrt{n}$.

Solution: It is easy to check that $F_n = m^2 + r$, where $0 < r < 2m+1$ implies that $n = m^2 - m + r$. Now, using $\frac{1}{4} < r < 2m + \frac{1}{4}$, one can argue that $m^2 - m + \frac{1}{4} < n < m^2 - m + (2m + \frac{1}{4})$ and hence, $m - \frac{1}{2} < \sqrt{n} < m + \frac{1}{2}$. Thus, m is the integer closest to $\sqrt{n}$.

9. Let $n \in \mathbb{N}$ be greater than 1. If $3n + 1$ is a perfect square, prove that $n + 1$ is the sum of three perfect squares.

Solution: Any positive integer is of the form $3k$, $3k+1$ or $3k-1$. Since $3n+1$ is a perfect square, its square root is of the form $3k+1$ or $3k-1$. Writing $3n+1 = (3k \pm 1)^2$, we get that $3n+1 = 9k^2 \pm 6k + 1$, which implies $n = 3k^2 \pm 2k$.

Clearly, $n+1 = 3k^2 \pm 2k + 1 = k^2 + k^2 + (k \pm 1)^2$, and hence, it is the sum of three perfect squares.

> **Useful Tip:** For dealing with perfect squares, often it is helpful to consider the residue classes in modulo a, for some appropriate $a \in \mathbb{N}$. For example, in the above case, we considered $a = 3$, as we know that a perfect square must belong to the residue classes corresponding to $0 \pmod{3}$ or $1 \pmod{3}$. Think about what can be stated about perfect squares in modulo $4, 5, 6, 7, 8, 10$, etc.

10. Let $n \in \mathbb{N}$. Show that n is a perfect square if and only if n has an odd number of divisors.

Solution: Let the prime factorization of n be $n = p_1^{\alpha_1} p_2^{\alpha_2} \ldots p_k^{\alpha_k}$. Then, any divisor of n is of the form $p_1^{\beta_1} p_2^{\beta_2} \ldots p_k^{\beta_k}$, where $0 \leq \beta_i \leq \alpha_i$ for all $i = 1, 2, \ldots, k$. Thus, we have $(\alpha_i + 1)$ choices for β_i, and so, the total number of divisors of n, that is, $d(n)$, is $(\alpha_1 + 1) \ldots (\alpha_k + 1)$. Note that we have included both 1 (for $\beta_1 = \ldots = \beta_k = 0$) and n (for $\beta_1 = \alpha_1, \ldots, \beta_k = \alpha_k$).

Now, n is a perfect square if and only if each α_i is even, which, in turn, implies that the quantity $(\alpha_1 + 1) \ldots (\alpha_k + 1)$ is odd. In other words, we get n as a perfect square if and only if n has an odd number of divisors.

> **Useful Tip:** This result is extremely useful in other applications as well, and has appeared in entrance tests in various forms. We shall see some examples in the following chapters.

11. Let $a, b \in \mathbb{Q}, a, b \neq 0$. If the equation $ax^2 + by^2 = 0$ has non-zero solutions in $\mathbb{Q}$, show that for any rational number t, there is a rational solution to the equation $ax^2 + by^2 = t$.

Solution: Since $ax^2 + by^2 = 0$ has rational solutions, it is evident that exactly one of a and b is positive. Without loss of generality, let us assume that $b < 0$. For convenience, denote it as $-b$, in which case, we have to show that for $a, b > 0$, if $ax^2 - by^2 = 0$ has a rational solution, so does $ax^2 - by^2 = t$, for any $t \in \mathbb{Q}$.

Let $x_0, y_0 \in \mathbb{Q}$ be such that $ax_0^2 - by_0^2 = 0$, which implies that $x_0/y_0 = \sqrt{b/a}$. As x_0, y_0 are rational, $\sqrt{b/a}$ or $\sqrt{ab}$ are also rational. Now, for $x_1 = x_0 + z$ and $y_1 = y_0 - z\sqrt{a/b}$,

$$\begin{aligned} ax_1^2 - by_1^2 &= a(x_0^2 + 2x_0 z + z^2) - b\left(y_0^2 - 2y_0 z \sqrt{\frac{a}{b}} + \frac{az^2}{b}\right) \\ &= (ax_0^2 - by_0^2) + 2z\left(ay_0\sqrt{b/a} + y_0\sqrt{ab}\right) + (az^2 - az^2) \\ &= 4zy_0\sqrt{ab} \end{aligned}$$

Number Theory

Hence, if we choose $z = t/(4y_0\sqrt{ab})$, we get $ax_1^2 - by_1^2 = t$. Since t, y_0 and $\sqrt{ab}$ are all rational numbers, it is evident that z is rational as well. Therefore, $x_1, y_1 \in \mathbb{Q}$, satisfy $ax_1^2 - by_1^2 = t$. This completes the proof.

12. Let S_n denote the set of all positive integers $k \leqslant n$ such that $gcd(k,n) = 1$. Compute the arithmetic mean of the integers in S_n.

Solution: First, observe that if an integer r is relatively prime to n, then so is $(n-r)$. This is because any common prime divisor of r and n will always divide both $(n-r)$ and n, and vice versa.

Thus, for any n, the set S_n of all integers relatively prime to n can be divided into pairs of the form $(r, n-r)$, unless $r = n-r$ for some $r \in S_n$. However, that means $r = n/2$ is relatively prime to n and it is only possible if $n = 2$.

Clearly, if $n \geqslant 3$, we can partition S_n into different pairs of the form $(r, n-r)$. Note that each of these pairs has sum n. Now, if the cardinality of S_n is m, there are $m/2$ such pairs and the sum of all these elements is $mn/2$. Therefore, the arithmetic mean of the integers in S_n is $n/2$.

To complete this problem, consider the special cases of $n = 1$ and $n = 2$. In both cases, $S_n = \{1\}$, implying that the mean is 1. Hence, the arithmetic mean of the integers in S_n is 1 if $n = 1, 2$ and is $n/2$ otherwise.

> **Useful Tip:** A common mistake is to forget the special cases of $n = 1, 2$. However, without that, the solution is incomplete.

13. Prove that for all $n \in \mathbb{N}$, the number $11\ldots1$ with 3^n digits is divisible by 3^n.

Solution: We use mathematical induction to prove the result. Let us use a_n to denote the number $11\ldots1$ with 3^n digits. To start with, observe that

$$a_n = 1 + 10 + 10^2 + \ldots + 10^{3^n - 1} = \frac{1}{9}\left(10^{3^n} - 1\right)$$

For $n = 1$, $a_1 = 111 = 3 \times 37$, and thus, is divisible by 3^1. Next, assume that a_k is divisible by 3^k. Then

$$\frac{a_{k+1}}{a_k} = \frac{\left(10^{3^{k+1}} - 1\right)}{\left(10^{3^k} - 1\right)} = 10^{2 \cdot 3^k} + 10^{3^k} + 1$$

Since 10 leaves remainder 1 when divided by 3, any power of 10 also leaves remainder 1 when divided by 3, and hence, $(10^{2 \cdot 3^k} + 10^{3^k} + 1)$ is divisible by 3. Further, a_k is a multiple of 3^k, and hence, a_{k+1} is divisible by 3^{k+1}. Hence, by the principle of mathematical induction, the number $11\ldots 1$ with 3^n digits is divisible by 3^n.

14. Consider a set of n numbers $a_1, a_2, \ldots, a_n$ such that each a_i is either 1 or -1. If
$$a_1 a_2 a_3 a_4 + a_2 a_3 a_4 a_5 + \ldots + a_n a_1 a_2 a_3 = 0,$$
show that 4 divides n.

Solution: Note that each summand in the above equation is either 1 or -1. Since the sum of these n terms is 0, there must be an equal number of 1s and -1s, making n an even number. Let $n = 2k$. So, there are k number of 1s and k number of -1s in the sum.

Now, if we multiply all the terms in the above sum, we get $(-1)^k$. However, observe that each a_i appears in exactly four summands, and so, the product must be $\prod_{i=1}^{n} a_i^4$. Since each a_i is either 1 or -1, this product must be 1. Clearly, $(-1)^k = 1$, implying that k is even, say $2m$. Hence, $n = 4m$ and we get the answer that 4 divides n.

15. Let $n \in \mathbb{Z}$ such that
$$\frac{1}{1} + \frac{1}{2} + \ldots + \frac{1}{23} = \frac{n}{23!}.$$
What is the remainder if n is divided by 19?

Solution: Let us multiply both sides of the above equation by $23!$. It implies the following:
$$n = \frac{23!}{1} + \frac{23!}{2} + \ldots + \frac{23!}{23}.$$
Now, observe that 19 divides $(23!/k)$ for all $k \neq 19$. Thus, $n \equiv 23!/19 \pmod{19}$. It is easy to see that $23!/19 = (18!)(20)(21)(22)(23)$. Using Wilson's Theorem, we know that $18! \equiv -1 \pmod{19}$. Then
$$n \equiv (-1)(1)(2)(3) \pmod{19},$$
which implies that the required remainder is 13.

16. Suppose S is the set of all sequences $(a_1, a_2, \ldots)$ such that

(i) $a_i \in \mathbb{N} + \{0\}$;

(ii) $a_1 \geqslant a_2 \geqslant \ldots$; and

(iii) there exists $m \in \mathbb{N}$ such that $a_n = 0$ for all $n \geqslant m$.

Let us define the complement of the sequence $(a_1, a_2, \ldots) \in S$ to be another sequence $(b_1, b_2, \ldots)$, such that for $m \geq 1$, b_m is the number of a_ns that are $\geq m$.

(a) Prove that the complement of a sequence in S also belongs to S.

(b) Prove that the complement of the complement of $A \in S$ is A itself.

(c) Prove that the complements of distinct sequences in S must be distinct.

Solution:

(a) Suppose $(b_1, b_2, \ldots)$ is the complement of a sequence $(a_1, a_2, \ldots) \in S$. b_1 denotes the number of a_ns in the sequence that are greater than or equal to 1, b_2 denotes the number of a_ns that are greater than or equal to 2, and so on. Evidently, each b_j is a non-negative integer, and since a_ns are in decreasing order, it is also clear that $b_1 \geq b_2 \geq b_3 \geq \ldots$. On the other hand, the maximum element in the sequence $(a_1, a_2, \ldots)$ is a_1, which is a non-negative integer. Thus, $b_m = 0$ for $m \geq a_1 + 1$. Hence, all the properties of S are satisfied for the sequence $(b_1, b_2, \ldots)$, implying that the complement of a sequence in S belongs to S.

(b) Suppose the complement of a sequence $A = (a_1, a_2, \ldots)$ is the sequence $B = (b_1, b_2, \ldots)$ and suppose the complement of B is $C = (c_1, c_2, \ldots)$. b_1 denotes the number of elements in A that are greater than or equal to 1 and c_1 denotes the number of elements in B that are greater than or equal to 1. Thus, b_1 denotes the number of non-zero elements in A and c_1 denotes the number of non-zero elements in B. However, from the previous part, we know that $b_m = 0$ for all $m \geq a_1 + 1$. So, the number of non-zero elements in B is a_1, and hence, $c_1 = a_1$.

Now, b_2 denotes the number of a_ns that are greater than or equal to 2. So, we have $a_1 \geq a_2 \geq \ldots \geq a_{b_2} \geq 2$ and $a_{b_2+1}, a_{b_2+2}, \ldots < 2$. Similarly, $b_1 \geq \ldots \geq b_{c_2} \geq 2$ and $b_{c_2+1} < 2$.

Note that if $a_1 = a_2 = \ldots = a_k > a_{k+1}$, then

$$b_m \begin{cases} = 0 & \text{for } m \geq a_1 + 1, \\ = k & \text{for } k \geq 1, m = a_{k+1}+1, \ldots, a_1, \\ > k & \text{for } k \geq 1, m \leq a_{k+1}. \end{cases}$$

So, $k = 1$ tells us that b_m is greater than 1 for $m \leq a_2$ and is ≤ 1 for $m > a_2$. Combining this with what we obtained earlier, it is clear that $c_2 = a_2$.

Proceeding in a similar fashion, we get the answer that $a_i = c_i$ for all i, and hence, the complement of the complement of a sequence is the original sequence itself.

(c) Consider two sequences $A, B \in S$ and let their complements be A_d, B_d, respectively. Using the previous part, we can say that the complements of A_d, B_d are A, B, respectively. So, if we assume $A_d = B_d$, we must obtain $A = B$, and vice versa. Hence, the complements of distinct sequences must be distinct.

17. Consider a set G along with an operation $*$ which maps every element of $G \times G$ to a unique element of G. We say that G is a group under $*$, if

   (i) $(a*b)*c = a*(b*c)$ for all $a, b, c \in G$;

   (ii) there is an element $e \in G$ satisfying $a*e = e*a = a$ for all $a \in G$; and

   (iii) for each $a \in G$, there exists $a' \in G$ such that $a*a' = a'*a = e$.

Now, consider that G is the power set of a set X; that is, G consists of all subsets of X. Define $*$ as $A*B = (A \cup B)\setminus(A \cap B)$, for $A, B \subset X$. Prove that G is a group under $*$.

Solution: Using the definition $C\setminus D = C \cap D^c$, where D^c is the complement of D,

$$A*B = (A \cup B) \cap (A^c \cup B^c) = ((A \cup B) \cap A^c) \cup ((A \cup B) \cap B^c) = (B \cap A^c) \cup (A \cap B^c)$$

Thus, $A*B$ denotes the set of elements that are in exactly one of A and B. We now check the three properties in order to prove that G is a group under $*$.

   (i) Suppose $A, B, C \subseteq X$. Then, based on a previous result, $(A*B)$ denotes the set of elements that are in exactly one of A, B. Let us call it D. Now we consider $D*C$. This would denote the set of elements that are in exactly one of D and C. So, if there is an element in $D*C$, then either it is in D (which means it is in exactly one of A and B) and not in C or it is not in D and is in C. Clearly, $D*C$ denotes the set of all elements that are in exactly one of the three sets A, B, C.

   Similarly, $(B*C)$ denotes the set of elements that are in exactly one of B, C and when we take $A*(B*C)$, using similar arguments as before, we can say that it would describe the set of all elements that are in exactly one of the three sets A, B, C. Hence, $(A*B)*C = A*(B*C)$.

   (ii) If we consider the null subset ϕ, we can write that $A \cup \phi = \phi \cup A = A$ and $A \cap \phi = \phi \cap A = \phi$. Using these, we get that $A*\phi = \phi*A = A$ for any $A \in G$. So, ϕ acts as the identity element with respect to the operation $*$.

(iii) For any subset A of X, note that

$$A * A = (A \cup A) \setminus (A \cap A) = A \setminus A = A \cap A^c = \phi$$

Hence, A is the inverse of itself.

Clearly, all three properties are satisfied, and therefore, G is a group under $*$.

18. Let $n \in \mathbb{N}$ and consider the expression $(1+\sqrt{2})^n + (1-\sqrt{2})^n$. If $[\cdot]$ denotes the greatest integer function, show that the integers $[(1+\sqrt{2})^n]$ are alternatively even and odd as n takes values $1, 2, \ldots$

Solution: Let us denote $(1+\sqrt{2})^n$ by u_n and $(1-\sqrt{2})^n$ by v_n. Using binomial expansion, we get

$$u_n + v_n = \sum_{r=0}^{n} \binom{n}{r} 1^{n-r}(\sqrt{2})^r + \sum_{r=0}^{n} \binom{n}{r} 1^{n-r}(-\sqrt{2})^r = 2 \sum_{r \text{ is even}} \binom{n}{r} 2^{r/2}$$

As the above sum is taken over all even integers, $2^{r/2}$ are integers, and hence, $u_n + v_n$ is an even integer for all n. Now, observe that $|v_n| = \left|\sqrt{2}-1\right|^n < 1$ for all n. Also, v_n is negative if n is odd and positive otherwise.

Thus, when n is odd, $u_n + v_n$ is an even integer (say, $2k_n$), and so, $u_n = 2k_n - v_n$. Since v_n is a negative real number in $(-1, 0)$, the greatest integer less than or equal to u_n is $2k_n$. On the other hand, if n is even, v_n lies in $(0, 1)$, and hence, $[u_n] = 2k_n - 1$.

Therefore, the integers $[(1+\sqrt{2})^n]$ are alternatively even and odd as n takes the values $1, 2, \ldots$

19. For a real number x, let $\{x\}$ denote $x - [x]$, where $[\cdot]$ is the greatest integer function. How many solutions does the equation $13[x] + 25\{x\} = 271$ have?

Solution: It is trivial to note that x must be greater than 1. Since $[x]$ denotes the greatest integer less than or equal to x, we can say that $x - 1 < [x] \leqslant x$, and so, $0 \leqslant \{x\} < 1$. Therefore

$$13(x-1) < 13[x] + 25\{x\} = 271 < 13x + 25 \implies 246 < 13x < 284$$

Thus, x is a real number between $246/13$ and $284/13$, meaning that $[x]$ can be an integer between 18 and 21. However, if $[x] = 18$, we get $25\{x\} = 37$, which is not possible since $25\{x\}$ must be less than 25. Similarly, if $[x] = 21$, we get $25\{x\} = -2$, which is also impossible. Thus, $[x]$ can be either 19 or 20.

If $[x] = 19$, we get $25\{x\} = 24$, and so, $\{x\} = 24/25$, implying that a possible value of x is $19 + 24/25 = 19.96$.

For $[x] = 20$, we get $25\{x\} = 11$, and so, $\{x\} = 11/25 = 0.44$.

Hence, the possible solutions to the given equation are 19.96 and 20.44.

20. Let $p > 5$ be a prime number, and let the decimal expansion of $1/p$ be $0.\overline{a_1 a_2 \ldots a_r}$, where the line above the terms indicates a recurring decimal. Show that $10^r \equiv 1 \pmod{p}$.

Solution: The number with the above decimal expansion can be expressed as

$$\sum_{i=1}^{r} a_i \left(10^{-i} + 10^{-r-i} + 10^{-2r-i} + \ldots\right) = \sum_{i=1}^{r} a_i \times \frac{10^{-i}}{1 - 10^{-r}} = \frac{10^r}{10^r - 1} \sum_{i=1}^{r} \frac{a_i}{10^i}$$

Equating the above with $1/p$, we get

$$10^r - 1 = p \sum_{i=1}^{r} a_i 10^{r-i}$$

It is obvious that the right-hand side is divisible by p, and thus, 10^r leaves a remainder of 1 on being divided by p.

21. Let $a, b, c, d \in \mathbb{Z}$ such that $ad - bc \neq 0$. If b_1, b_2 are integer multiples of $ad - bc$, show that there exist $x, y \in \mathbb{Z}$ satisfying both the equations $ax + by = b_1, cx + dy = b_2$.

Solution: Observe that the equations $ax + by = b_1, cx + dy = b_2$ are simultaneously satisfied by

$$x = \frac{db_1 - bb_2}{ad - bc}, \quad y = \frac{ab_2 - cb_1}{ad - bc}$$

Since both b_1, b_2 are multiples of $ad - bc$, we can find integers k_1, k_2 such that $b_1 = (ad - bc)k_1, b_2 = (ad - bc)k_2$. Hence, $x = dk_1 - bk_2, y = ak_2 - ck_1$ are both integers and they satisfy the given equations. This completes the proof.

22. Let $J = \{0, 1, 2, 3, 4\}$. For $x, y \in J$, let $s_5(x, y)$ denote the remainder of $x + y$ after division by 5 and $p_5(x, y)$ denote the remainder of xy after division by 5. Find $x, y \in J$ satisfying the following equations:

$$s_5(p_5(x, 3), p_5(y, 2)) = 2, \quad s_5(p_5(x, 2), p_5(y, 4)) = 1$$

Solution: For the given conditions, $3x + 2y$ leaves remainder 2 when divided by 5 and $2x + 4y$ leaves remainder 1 after division by 5. To write it using mathematical notation

$$3x + 2y \equiv 2 \pmod{5}, \quad 2x + 4y \equiv 1 \pmod{5}$$

Thus, $2(3x+2y) - (2x+4y) = 4x \equiv 3 \pmod 5$. We can now simply check the elements in J to obtain $x = 2$. Using this value, $2y \equiv -4 \pmod 5$, that is, $2y \equiv 1 \pmod 5$. That means y must be 3.

Hence, the required solution is $x = 2, y = 3$.

23. Everyone knows the superstition involving *Friday the thirteenth*. Prove that every year, the 13th day of some month has to occur on a Friday.

Solution: To begin with, note that if the 13th of some month occurs on a Friday, then the month must start on a Sunday. So, if we can show that there is always a month starting on a Sunday in every year, the proof is complete.

Suppose the first day of January is the ith day of the week, where i is in $\{0,1,2,3,4,5,6\}$, with 0 corresponding to Sunday and 6 corresponding to Saturday. Now, there are 31 days (4 whole weeks and 3 more days) in January, and so, the first day of February is on the $(i+3)$th day of the week. We can proceed similarly and show that the first days of the first nine successive months are $i, i+3, i+3, i+6, i+1, i+4, i+6, i+2, i+5, i$ for a normal year, and $i, i+3, i+4, i+0, i+2, i+5, i+0, i+3, i+6, i+1$ for a leap year, all calculations being carried out in congruent modulo 7.

Interestingly, we see that every day of the week appears at least once as the first day of some month in a year. Hence, there must be some month starting on a Sunday, proving that the 13th day of some month will occur on a Friday.

> **Useful Tip:** One can focus only on the months from May through November, both inclusive, and show that the indexes corresponding to the 13th days of these seven months form a complete residue system in modulo 7.

24. Prove that for any $n \in \mathbb{N}$, the sum of $8n+4$ consecutive positive integers cannot be a perfect square.

Solution: If the first of $8n+4$ consecutive integers is $(a+1)$, then the sum of those integers is
$$A = \frac{1}{2}\left((8n+4+a)^2 + (8n+4+a) - (a^2+a)\right)$$

This can be simplified to obtain $A = 2(2n+1)(8n+2a+5)$. Clearly, 2 divides A but 4 does not, and hence, A cannot be a perfect square.

25. Let a, b, c, d be integers between 0 and 9, both inclusive. Consider the two-digit numbers formed by the expressions ab (a in the tens place and b in the units place) and cb (c in the tens place and b in the units place). If the product of these two numbers is of the form ddd (a three-digit number with every digit equal to d), what are the possible values of $a+b+c+d$?

Solution: To differentiate between the product ab and a two-digit number with digits a, b, let us use $\overline{ab}$ to denote the latter. Here, we have $\overline{ab} \cdot \overline{cb} = \overline{ddd}$ and the product's value is equal to $100d + 10d + d = 111d$.

Now, $111 = 3 \times 37$. Since $3, 37$ are primes, we deduce that each of them divides at least one of the numbers between $\overline{ab}$ and $\overline{cb}$. Observe that if one of them is divisible by both 3 and 37, then it must be $\geq \text{lcm}(3, 37) = 111$, contradicting the fact that the number has two digits. Now, suppose without loss of generality that 3 divides $\overline{ab}$ and 37 divides $\overline{cb}$. Since the only multiples of 37 having two digits are 37 and 74, we only need to check two cases.

First, $\overline{cb} = 37$, which implies $c = 3, b = 7$ and $\overline{ab} = 3d$. Further, because $\overline{ab}$ has two digits and d is a digit as well, $\overline{ab} \in \{12, 15, ..., 27\}$. Since $b = 7$, 27 is the only value that is suitable. Hence, $a = 2, d = 9$, and $a+b+c+d = 2+7+3+9 = 21$.

Second, $\overline{cb} = 74$, suggesting $c = 7, b = 4$ and $2(\overline{ab}) = 3d$. Since $\overline{ab}$ is even, d must be divisible by 4. However, $d = 4$ implies $\overline{ab} = 6$, an impossible situation. For $d = 8$, on the other hand, we obtain $\overline{ab} = 12$, but it contradicts the assumption $b = 4$.

Hence, the only possible value of $a+b+c+d$ is 21.

26. Find all solutions $x \in \mathbb{N}$ to the equation $[x/5] - [x/7] = 1$.

Solution: Let us consider that $[x/7] = k$ ($k \geq 0$). Then $[x/5] = k+1$. Now, because of the property of the greatest integer function, we can say that $k \leq x/7 < k+1$; that is, $7k \leq x < 7k+7$. Similarly, we obtain $5k+5 \leq x < 5k+10$. Combining these two, we get

$$\max\{7k, 5k+5\} \leq x < \min\{7k+7, 5k+10\}$$

Observe that as soon as k is bigger than 2, we can see that $7k > 5k+5, 7k+7 > 5k+10$. Thus, if $k > 2$, we must have $7k \leq x < 5k+10$ and that tells us k must be less than 5. So, we can check these cases separately:

$$k = 0 \ : \ 5 \leq x < 7,$$
$$k = 1 \ : \ 10 \leq x < 14,$$
$$k = 2 \ : \ 15 \leq x < 20,$$

$$k = 3 \ : \ 21 \leqslant x < 25,$$
$$k = 4 \ : \ 28 \leqslant x < 30.$$

Hence, the list of positive integers that satisfies the given condition is

$$\{5, 6, 10, 11, 12, 13, 15, 16, 17, 18, 19, 21, 22, 23, 24, 28, 29\}$$

27. Find a four-digit number A such that $B = 4A$ is also a four-digit number, and B has the same digits as A but in the reverse order.

Solution: Consider that the digits (from left to right) of A are a, b, c, d, respectively. Then, $A = 1000a + 100b + 10c + d$, and thus, $B = 4000a + 400b + 40c + 4d$. As B is a four-digit number, we must have $a = 1$ or $a = 2$.

Now, to satisfy the second condition, we get $1000d + 100c + 10b + a = 4000a + 400b + 40c + 4d$, which implies $3999a + 390b - 60c - 996d = 0$. Clearly, a must be even, and hence, $a = 2$. This again suggests that $7998 - 996d$ must be divisible by 10, and it is an easy deduction that the only possible values for d are 3 and 8.

If $a = 2, d = 3$, we get $390b - 60c + 5010 = 0$, which does not have a solution for $0 \leqslant b, c \leqslant 9$.

Using $a = 2, d = 8$, $390b - 60c + 30 = 0$, that is, $2c - 13b = 1$. Since c cannot be more than 9, the only possible solution is $c = 7, b = 1$. Hence, the required four-digit number is 2178.

28. If $n \in \mathbb{N}$, show that $4^n + n^4$ is a prime number if and only if $n = 1$.

Solution: It is obvious that $4^n + n^4$ can never be a prime number if n is even. Consider n to be odd and denote it as $2k + 1$, where $k \geqslant 1$. Recall that a natural number is not prime if and only if it can be expressed as a product of two integers greater than 1. Observe that the expression we have can be written as $n^4 + 4^n = (2k+1)^4 + 4 \cdot 4^{2k} = a^4 + 4b^4$, where $a = (2k+1)$, $b = 2^k$.

This can be further expressed as $(a^2 + 2b^2)^2 - 2 \cdot a^2 \cdot 2b^2 = (a^2 + 2b^2)^2 - (2ab)^2$. It is easy to note that the expression factorizes as $(a^2 + 2b^2 + 2ab)(a^2 + 2b^2 - 2ab)$, and hence

$$n^4 + 4^n = \left((a+b)^2 + b^2\right)\left((a-b)^2 + b^2\right)$$

Since $a \neq b$ and b is greater than 1, both the factors in the above expression are greater than 1. Hence, we can say that $4^n + n^4$ is not prime whenever n is greater than 1. For $n = 1$, it is easy to verify that $n^4 + 4^n = 5$, a prime number.

Useful Tip: The most straightforward way to show that a number is composite is to express it as a product of two numbers and to argue that both are greater than 1. However, a common mistake is to carry out the factorization but not to show that the factors are greater than 1. Keeping this in mind, try to find all $n \in \mathbb{N}$ for which $n^4 + 4$ is a prime number.

29. Consider the following array of numbers:

1	3	6	10	15	21	⋯
2	5	9	14	20	⋯	⋯
4	8	13	19	⋯	⋯	⋯
7	12	18	⋯	⋯	⋯	⋯
11	17	⋯	⋯	⋯	⋯	⋯
16	⋯	⋯	⋯	⋯	⋯	⋯
⋮	⋮	⋮	⋮	⋮	⋮	⋱

Identify the pattern in which the numbers are arranged in the above array, and then find the row and column at which the number 20096 appears.

Solution: Here, all natural numbers are arranged consecutively along reverse diagonals. Denote the number in the (i,j)th position of the arrangement by $t_{i,j}$. Note that the kth term in the first row is the sum of the integers from 1 to k. Thus, $t_{1,k} = k(k+1)/2$. On the other hand, the first term in the nth row is the nth term of the sequence $\{1, 2, 4, 7, 11, \ldots\}$, where the differences are in arithmetic progression $\{1, 2, 3, \ldots\}$. One can then find that $t_{n,1} = 1 + (1 + 2 + \ldots + n - 1) = 1 + n(n-1)/2$.

Now, observe that the gaps in which the numbers in the nth row are placed are $n+1, n+2, n+3, \ldots$. So, $t_{i,j} = t_{i,1} + (i+1) + (i+2) + \ldots + (i+j-1)$. Using the above, it can be simplified as

$$t_{i,j} = 1 + \frac{i(i-1)}{2} + i(j-1) + \frac{j(j-1)}{2}$$

Now, $t_{1,199} = 19900$ and $t_{1,200} = 20100$. Thus, 20096 lies in the 200th reverse diagonal and four terms before 20100 in that diagonal. So, if we move four rows down and four columns to the left, we get 20096. That is, 20096 lies in the 196th column and 5th row. To confirm this, note that $t_{i,j} = 20096$ for $i = 5, j = 196$.

Number Theory

30. For $n \in \mathbb{N}$, let $\langle n \rangle$ denote the integer nearest to $\sqrt{n}$. Given some $k \in \mathbb{N}$, find out the set of integers m for which $\langle m \rangle = k$. Further, compute the value of

$$\sum_{n=1}^{\infty} \frac{2^{\langle n \rangle} + 2^{-\langle n \rangle}}{2^n}$$

Solution: To begin with, in order to avoid confusion, let us follow the rule that the integer nearest to $k + 0.5$ (where k is an integer) is k and not $k+1$. Now, $\langle n \rangle$ denotes the integer nearest to $\sqrt{n}$. So, if $\langle n \rangle = k$, then $\sqrt{n} \in (k-0.5, k+0.5]$, implying that

$$k^2 - k + \frac{1}{4} < n \leqslant k^2 + k + \frac{1}{4} \implies k^2 - k + 1 \leqslant n \leqslant k^2 + k$$

Hence, all positive integers in the interval $[k^2 - k + 1, k^2 + k]$ satisfy the condition $\langle n \rangle = k$.

To work out the second part, observe that for a positive integer n, the term $\langle n \rangle$ is always a positive integer, and we have seen that it is equal to k (for $k = 1, 2, 3, \ldots$) for all n in $[k^2 - k + 1, k^2 + k]$. Also note that $(k+1)^2 - (k+1) + 1 = k^2 + k + 1$. Thus, we can divide $\mathbb{N}$ in sets of the form $\{k^2 - k + 1, k^2 - k + 2, \ldots, k^2 + k\}$ for all $k \in \mathbb{N}$, and write the following:

$$S = \sum_{n=1}^{\infty} \frac{2^{\langle n \rangle} + 2^{-\langle n \rangle}}{2^n} = \sum_{k=1}^{\infty} \sum_{n=k^2-k+1}^{k^2+k} \frac{2^{\langle n \rangle} + 2^{-\langle n \rangle}}{2^n} = \sum_{k=1}^{\infty} \sum_{n=k^2-k+1}^{k^2+k} \frac{2^k + 2^{-k}}{2^n}$$

It is easy to see that the inner summation (sum over n) in the above expression is a geometric series and its sum can be computed in the following way:

$$\left(2^k + 2^{-k}\right) \sum_{n=k^2-k+1}^{k^2+k} 2^{-n} = \left(2^k + 2^{-k}\right) 2^{-k^2+k-1} \left(\frac{1 - (1/2)^{2k}}{1 - 1/2}\right) = 2^{-k^2-2k}\left(2^{4k} - 1\right)$$

Substituting this in the previous equality, we obtain

$$S = \sum_{k=1}^{\infty} \left[\left(\frac{1}{2}\right)^{k^2 - 2k} - \left(\frac{1}{2}\right)^{k^2 + 2k}\right] = 2 \sum_{k=1}^{\infty} \left[\left(\frac{1}{2}\right)^{(k-1)^2} - \left(\frac{1}{2}\right)^{(k+1)^2}\right]$$

Now, using $k = 1, 2, 3, \ldots$ for the summands, we obtain the following terms:

$$k = 1 \; : \; \left(\frac{1}{2}\right)^{0^2} - \left(\frac{1}{2}\right)^{2^2},$$

$$k = 2 \; : \; \left(\frac{1}{2}\right)^{1^2} - \left(\frac{1}{2}\right)^{3^2},$$

$$k = 3 \; : \; \left(\frac{1}{2}\right)^{2^2} - \left(\frac{1}{2}\right)^{4^2},$$

and so on. Thus, all terms except the first terms for $k = 1, 2$ will be cancelled out. Hence, combining all these terms, we can finally say that the required sum is equal to

$$\sum_{n=1}^{\infty} \frac{2^{\langle n \rangle} + 2^{-\langle n \rangle}}{2^n} = 2\left(1 + \frac{1}{2}\right) = 3$$

Multiple Choice Questions

1. What is the remainder when $2^{20} + 3^{30} + 4^{40} + 5^{50} + 6^{60}$ is divided by 7?

   (a) 0   (b) 1   (c) 2   (d) 3

Solution: (a)

According to Fermat's Theorem, for any natural number a not divisible by a prime number p, the term a^{p-1} leaves remainder 1. Thus, writing $2^{20} = (2^6)^3 \times 2^2$, we can argue that $2^{20} \equiv 4 \pmod{7}$. Similarly

$$3^{30} \equiv 1 \pmod{7}, \; 4^{40} \equiv 4 \pmod{7}, \; 5^{50} \equiv 4 \pmod{7}, \; 6^{60} \equiv 1 \pmod{7}$$

Combining the above, we obtain that

$$2^{20} + 3^{30} + 4^{40} + 5^{50} + 6^{60} \equiv 0 \pmod{7}$$

2. What is the smallest positive integer n such that $50!/24^n$ is not an integer?

   (a) 14   (b) 22   (c) 12   (d) 16

Solution: (d)

We note that $24^n = 2^{3n}3^n$. Thus, $50!/24^n$ is not an integer if $3n$ is bigger than the power of 2 in 50! or if n is bigger than the power of 3 in 50!. We know that the power of a prime number p in 50! can be obtained through the formula

$$\sum_{k=1}^{\infty} \left[\frac{50}{p^k}\right]$$

Using the above, we get that $50!/24^n$ is not an integer if $3n \geqslant 47$ or if $n \geqslant 22$. Thus, the smallest possible such value is 16.

3. Let $x_1, x_2, \ldots, x_{50}$ be 50 integers such that the sum of any six of them is 24. Then,

(a) the largest x_i is equal to 6;
(b) the smallest x_i is equal to 3;
(c) $x_{13} = x_{39}$;
(d) none of the foregoing statements is true.

Solution: (c)

Since the sum of any six of the numbers is 24, choosing them properly, we can show that $x_i = x_j$ for all i, j. Thus, all numbers must be equal and it is easy to argue that all of them must be exactly equal to 4. Hence, (c) is the correct choice.

4. The sum of all integers in $\{1, 2, \ldots, 1000\}$ that are divisible by 2 and 5, but not divisible by 4, is

(a) 24500   (b) 25000   (c) 49500   (d) 50050

Solution: (b)

If an integer $\leqslant 1000$ is divisible by 2 and 5, and not divisible by 4, then it is of the form $10(2k+1)$, for $k = 0, 1, 2, \ldots, 49$. Thus, the required sum is

$$\sum_{k=0}^{49}(20k+10) = 20 \times \frac{49 \times 50}{2} + 500 = 25000$$

5. What is the remainder if the integer a is divided by 13, where

$$1 + \frac{1}{2} + \frac{1}{3} + \ldots + \frac{1}{25} = \frac{a}{25!}?$$

(a) 1   (b) 6   (c) 7   (d) 12

Solution: (a)

Multiplying both sides of the given equation by 25!, we get

$$a = 25! + \frac{25!}{2} + \frac{25!}{3} + \ldots + \frac{25!}{25}$$

It is easy to argue that 13 divides $23!/k$ for all $k \neq 13$. Thus

$$a \equiv (12!)(14 \times 15 \times \ldots \times 25) \pmod{13} \implies a \equiv (12!)^2 \pmod{13}$$

Using Wilson's Theorem, $12! \equiv -1 \pmod{13}$, and thus, the required answer is 1.

6. The number of pairs of positive prime integers (a,b) such that $a^2 - 2b^2 = 1$ is

(a) 0   (b) 1   (c) 2   (d) 8

Solution: (b)

Since $(a-1)(a+1) = 2b^2$, we can argue that a must be odd and that both $(a-1)/2$ and $(a+1)/2$ must be divisors of b. However, b is a prime number. Therefore, the only possibility is $a-1 = 2$, which leads to the solution $a = 3, b = 2$.

7. The number of ordered pairs of integers satisfying the equation $x^2 + 6x + y^2 = 4$ is

(a) 2   (b) 4   (c) 6   (d) 8

Solution: (d)

The given equation can be rewritten as $(x+3)^2 + y^2 = 13$. Since x, y are integers, the only possibilities are
$$x+3 = \pm 2, y = \pm 3 \text{ or } x+3 = \pm 3, y = \pm 2$$

Clearly, there are 8 possible solutions in total.

8. How many zeros are there at the end of 2022!?

(a) 404   (b) 484   (c) 503   (d) 601

Solution: (c)

The number of zeros at the end of 2022! is the same as the highest power of 5 in the expression $1 \times 2 \times \ldots \times 2022$. Using $[\cdot]$ to denote the greatest integer function, we can argue that the highest power of 5 in 2022! is

$$\sum_{k=1}^{\infty} \left[\frac{2022}{5^k}\right] = \left[\frac{2022}{5}\right] + \left[\frac{2022}{25}\right] + \left[\frac{2022}{125}\right] + \left[\frac{2022}{625}\right] = 404 + 80 + 16 + 3 = 503$$

9. The numbers $12n+1$ and $30n+2$ are relatively prime for

(a) any positive integer n;
(b) infinitely many, but not all, integers n;
(c) for finitely many integers n;
(d) none of the above.

Solution: (a)

If d is a common divisor of $12n+1$ and $30n+2$, then d divides $6n$. Subsequently, one can show that d must divide 1, and thus, the two numbers must be relatively prime.

10. Let A be the set of all prime numbers, B denote the set of all prime numbers and 4, and C be the set of all prime numbers and their squares. If D is the set of all positive integers k for which $(k-1)!/k$ is not an integer, then

(a) $D = A$ (b) $D = B$ (c) $D = C$ (d) $B \subset D \subset C$

Solution: (b)

If k is a prime number, then by Wilson's Theorem, we know that $(k-1)!+1$ is divisible by k, and hence, $(k-1)!/k$ is not an integer. On the contrary, if k is a composite number, then there are integers $a, b < k$ such that $ab = k$. Now, if $a \neq b$, then $(k-1)!$ is divisible by ab. Thus, we only need to consider the case where k is of the form p^2, where p is a prime. In this scenario, we can easily argue that for all $p > 2$, $(p^2 - 1)!$ must be divisible by p^2. For $p = 2$, however, we see that $(k-1)!/k = 6/4$, not an integer. That provides the required solution.

Exercises

1. For a prime number p, if $p \equiv r \pmod{30}$, then show that r is either prime or is 1.

2. Show that among any five consecutive positive integers, there must be one integer that is relatively prime to all of the other four integers.

3. Let $\alpha, \beta \in \mathbb{Q}$ satisfy the equation $x^2 + px + q = 0$, where p, q are integers. Prove that α, β are integers as well.

4. Prove that for each $n \in \mathbb{N}$, 7 divides $3^{2n+1} + 2^{n+2}$.

5. Prove that if $n > 1$ is an odd integer, then $80 \mid n^5 - n$.

6. If $k \in \mathbb{N}$ is odd, then show that for any $n \in \mathbb{N}$, $1^k + 2^k + \ldots + n^k$ is divisible by $n(n+1)/2$.

7. Prove that there do not exist integers $n_1, n_2, \ldots, n_8$ such that
$$n_1^4 + n_2^4 + \ldots + n_8^4 = 1993$$

8. Let $X = \{0, 1, 2, \ldots, 99\}$. For $a, b \in X$, we define $p_{100}(a, b)$ to be the remainder obtained by dividing the product ab by 100. Let $x \in X$. An element $y \in X$ is called the inverse of x if $p_{100}(x, y) = 1$. Find out which of the elements $1, 2, 3, 4, 5, 6, 7$ have inverses and write down their inverses.

9. If p is a prime number and $a \in \mathbb{N}$ is greater than 1, then prove that the greatest common divisor of $a - 1$ and $\frac{a^p - 1}{a - 1}$ is either 1 or p.

10. (i) If $k, l \in \mathbb{N}$ such that $k \mid l$, show that for every $m \in \mathbb{N}$, the gcd of $1 + (k+m)l$ and $1 + ml$ is 1.

    (ii) Prove that the arithmetic mean of the smallest numbers of the $\binom{n}{r}$ subsets (of size r) of $S = \{1, 2, \ldots, n\}$ is $(n+1)/(r+1)$.

11. Prove that there cannot exist $n, x \in \mathbb{Z}$ such that $x^3 + 7x - 14(n^2 + 1) = 0$.

12. If a, b, c are odd integers, prove that $ax^2 + bx + c = 0$ cannot have a solution $x \in \mathbb{Q}$.

13. (a) Can there be three prime numbers, each greater than 3, which are in arithmetic progression with a common difference less than 5?

    (b) Let $k \in \mathbb{N}$ be greater than 3. Prove that it is impossible to find k prime numbers, each greater than k, to be in an arithmetic progression with a common difference less than or equal to $k + 1$.

14. For $n \in \mathbb{N}$, consider the equation $n^2 + (n+1)^4 = 5(n+2)^3$.

    (a) Show that an integer k cannot be a solution of this equation if $k \equiv \pm 1 \pmod{3}$.

    (b) Does the equation have any solution?

15. Let us call function $f(n)$ defined on $\mathbb{N}$ multiplicative if $f(mn) = f(m)f(n)$ whenever m and n are coprime. Find out if the following functions are multiplicative:

    (a) $g(n) = 5^k$, where k is the number of distinct prime factors of n.

    (b) $h(n) = \begin{cases} 0 & \text{if } k^2 \mid n \text{ for some integer } k > 1, \\ 1 & \text{otherwise.} \end{cases}$

16. Prove that the sum of any 12 consecutive positive integers cannot be a perfect square. Is it true for 11 consecutive positive integers as well?

17. In number theory, Fermat numbers are those of the form $F_n = 2^{2^n} + 1$. Show that the last digit of F_n, for $n \geqslant 2$, is 7.

18. Is there any $n \in \mathbb{N}$ such that $n(n - 101)$ is a perfect square?

19. If m is an integer containing only 0 and 6 as digits, prove that it cannot be a perfect square.

20. Let $A \subset \mathbb{N}$ such that for all $m, n \in A$, $m + n \in A$; and assume that there is no prime number that divides all elements of A.

    (a) Let $n_1, n_2 \in A$ such that $n_2 - n_1 > 1$. Show that there exist $m_1, m_2 \in A$ such that $0 < m_2 - m_1 < n_2 - n_1$. Use it to argue that there are two consecutive integers in A.

    (b) Assume that n_0 and $n_0 + 1$ are two consecutive integers belonging to A. Prove that all $n \geqslant n_0^2$ are elements of A.

Hints

1. Write $p = 30k + r$, where $0 \leq r \leq 29$. Then, r cannot have any common factor with 30. Now, find the minimum possible value of r.

2. For any two positive integers $m < n$, any common divisor must be less than or equal to $n - m$. Use this fact to show that there is one odd integer among five consecutive positive integers such that it is not divisible by 3 and it is therefore relatively prime to all the other integers.

3. The roots of the equation are $(-p \pm \sqrt{p^2 - 4q})/2$. Show that $p^2 - 4q$ must be a perfect square and that the parity of $\sqrt{p^2 - 4q}$ and p are the same.

4. Use mathematical induction to prove this.

5. Note that $n^5 - n = n(n^4 - 1) = n(n^2 + 1)(n^2 - 1)$. Then, show that for any odd integer n, $n(n^2 - 1)(n^2 + 1)$ is divisible by 5, $n^2 - 1$ is divisible by 8, and that $n^2 + 1$ is divisible by 2. Now, combine these results to complete the proof.

6. It can be shown that for any $0 \leq r \leq n$ and for an odd integer k, $(n-r)^k + (r+1)^k \equiv 0 \pmod{n+1}$. Then, combine all such pairs (for different r) to argue that $1^k + 2^k + \ldots + n^k$ is divisible by $(n+1)$ when n is even, and by $(n+1)/2$ when n is odd. Next, use similar arguments with n instead of $(n+1)$, that is, $r^k + (n-r)^k \equiv 0 \pmod{n}$ for all $1 \leq r \leq n-1$.

7. Following the solution in Problem 5, one can show that any integer, when divided by 16, leaves remainder 1 or 0. Thus, $n_1^4 + n_2^4 + \ldots + n_8^4$, when divided by 16, leaves a remainder of at most 8. However, $1993 \equiv \pmod{9}$ and leads to a contradiction.

8. Note that an integer $x \in X$ has an inverse y if $xy \equiv 1 \pmod{100}$. Subsequently, argue that x has an inverse if and only if it is relatively prime to 100. Bezout's Identity can be used in this part.

9. Using $a^p - 1 = (a - 1)(1 + a + a^2 + \ldots + a^{p-1})$, one can show that $a \equiv 1 \pmod{d}$ implies that $1 + a + a^2 + \ldots + a^{p-1} \equiv p \pmod{d}$. Therefore, d divides p, and hence, it is either 1 or p.

10. If a prime p divides both $1 + (k+m)l$ and $1 + ml$, then p divides kl. Using the fact that k divides l, show that p must divide l. That leads to a contradiction, as it implies that p divides both ml and $1 + ml$. For the second part, observe that there are $\binom{n-k}{r-1}$ subsets for $k = 1, 2, \ldots, n - r + 1$, where k is the smallest number. Combinatorial arguments can be used to show that the sum $\sum_{k=t}^{n-r+1} \binom{n-k}{r-1}$ is equal to $\binom{n-t+1}{r}$. Use this identity to simplify the sum $\sum_{k=1}^{n-r+1} k \binom{n-k}{r-1}$ and show that it is equal to $\binom{n+1}{r+1}$. The required arithmetic mean can be computed directly from this.

11. If an integer d is a root of the equation, then show that 7 divides d^3, and thereby, $7 \mid d$. Let $d = 7k$ for some integer k. It implies that $n^2 + 1 \equiv 0 \pmod{7}$, which is impossible as a perfect square cannot leave remainder 6 when divided by 7.

12. The discriminant of the equation $ax^2 + bx + c = 0$ is $D = b^2 - 4ac$, where a, b, c are odd integers. The square of an odd integer is $1 \pmod 8$, and so $D \equiv 5 \pmod 8$. Clearly, D cannot be a perfect square, and hence, the equation cannot have a rational solution.

13. For the first part, use congruence modulo 3 to show that one of the three odd integers that are in an arithmetic progression with a common difference less than 5 must be divisible by 3. Apply a similar argument, considering congruent modulo $d - 1$, where d is the common difference, for the second part.

14. Use congruent modulo 3 to show the first part. Next, take $n + 1 = a$ to show that $a^2 - 2a + a^4 - 5a^3 - 15a(a+1) = 4$, which implies $a|4$. It is then easy to argue why no possible solution exists for the given equation.

15. Let m and n be two positive integers with no common factor. If m and n have k_m and k_n distinct prime factors, respectively, then mn has $k_m + k_n$ distinct prime factors. Thus, g is a multiplicative function. For part (b), note that if $h(m)$ is 0, then there is some integer $k > 1$ such that k^2 divides m. Evidently, k^2 divides mn as well, and so $h(mn) = 0$. If $h(m) = h(n) = 1$, then there is no prime k such that $k^2 \mid m$ or $k^2 \mid n$. As m and n are relatively prime, one can argue that mn is not divisible by k^2 for any $k > 1$. Hence, $h(mn) = 1$, implying that h is a multiplicative function.

16. The sum of 12 consecutive integers of the form $m+1, m+2, \ldots, m+12$ is $12m + 78$. In order to prove that this cannot be a perfect square, consider divisibility by 4. On the other hand, the sum of consider 11 consecutive integers $m+1, m+2, \ldots, m+11$ is $11m + 66 = 11(m+6)$, and it is a perfect square if $(m+6)$ is of the form $11k^2$. One example is $m = 5$.

17. Use the principle of mathematical induction on n to prove the required result.

18. Consider the equation $n^2 - 101n - t^2 = 0$. As n is a natural number, $101^2 + 4t^2$ must be a perfect square. Let $101^2 + 4t^2 = k^2$, which implies $(k-2t)(k+2t) = 101^2$. 101 being a prime, the only possible solution can be found out to be $n = 2601$.

19. Consider the last two digits of the number and they can be: $\{06\}, \{66\}, \{60\}$ or $\{00\}$. Use congruent modulo 4 to show that none of this allows m to be a perfect square.

20. Using the assumptions, one can argue that if $m \in A$, then for any positive integer k, $km \in A$. Further, $m, n \in A$ and $a, b \in \mathbb{N}$ imply that $am + bn \in A$. First, we want to show that for any $a \in A$, there exists $b \in A$ such that b is relatively prime to a. Note that if a is prime, there exists an integer $b \in A$ that is not a multiple of a, and hence, b is relatively prime to a. Further, if a is not prime and $a = \prod_{i=1}^{k} p_i^{\alpha_i}$ is the prime factorization of a, one can find $b_i \in A$ such that p_i does not divide b_i. Construct $b = \sum_{i=1}^{k} b_i \left(\prod_{j \neq i} p_j \right)$, show that $b \in A$ and b is relatively prime to a. Now, Bezout's Identity tells that there are positive integers x and y with $|ax - by| = 1$, which subsequently implies that there are two integers m_1 and m_2 such that $0 < m_2 - m_1 < n_2 - n_1$. This also proves the second part of part (a) directly. For part (b), let $n = n_0^2 + k = n_0^2 + qn_0 + r$, where $0 \leqslant r < n_0$. Rewrite it as $n = n_0(n_0 + q - r) + (n_0 + 1)r$ to conclude that n must belong to A.

2
Combinatorics

"Life is full of permutations and combinations. Sometimes the order you do things matters, sometimes it doesn't, but in order to find the solution in life, you must work through each possibility presented to find your opportunity."

–Gregory Willis

Combinatorics is formally the mathematical area concerned with counting, and certain properties of finite structures. The scope of combinatorics, however, is not limited to this. It is, in fact, closely related to many other areas of mathematics and has applications in diverse disciplines such as cryptography, logic, statistical physics, evolutionary biology and computer science. Naturally, it is crucial to have a good sense of the building blocks of combinatorial studies, and to understand their usefulness in solving problems of different flavours.

KEY RESULTS

Throughout this chapter, the following notations are used:
$\mathbb{N}$ = the set of natural numbers $\qquad$ $\mathbb{Z}$ = the set of integers
$\mathbb{R}$ = the set of real numbers $\qquad$ $\mathbb{Q}$ = the set of rational numbers
$\mathbb{C}$ = the set of complex numbers

Let us start with two main counting principles of combinatorics. These are the key results to tackle different problems in this chapter.

Theorem 2.1 (Basic Counting Principle): We say a finite set S is partitioned into parts $S_1, \ldots, S_k$ if the parts are disjoint and their union is S. In that case, the addition principle says that

$$|S| = \sum_{i=1}^{k} |S_k|$$

On the other hand, if a finite set S is the product of sets $S_1,\ldots,S_k$, then the multiplication principle implies

$$|S| = \prod_{i=1}^{k} |S_k|$$

Applications of the above principles abound. For example, suppose we want to find out the total number of 5-letter words. We can use either of the above counting principles to solve this problem. Let S denotes the set of all 5-letter words. If W_j (for $j = 1,2,\ldots,26$) denotes the set of all 5-letter words starting with A, B, ..., Z, then the addition principle suggests that $|S| = |W_1| + |W_2| + \ldots + |W_{26}|$. We can also consider S_i (for $i = 1,2,\ldots,5$) as the set of all possible letters in the ith position, in which case, $S = S_1 \times \ldots \times S_5$. The multiplication principle then implies that $|S| = |S_1| \times |S_2| \times \ldots \times |S_5|$. Either way, we can get a total of 26^5 5-letter words.

A generalization of the addition principle is as follows.

Theorem 2.2 (Principle of Inclusion-Exclusion): This is a counting technique that generalizes the familiar method of obtaining the total number of elements in the union of two finite sets; namely, the result $|A \cup B| = |A| + |B| - |A \cap B|$. In particular, for n finite sets $A_1, A_2, \ldots, A_n$, the principle says that

$$\left|\bigcup_{i=1}^{n} A_i\right| = \sum_{i=1}^{n} |A_i| - \sum_{1 \leq i_1 < i_2 \leq n} \left|\bigcap_{j=1}^{2} A_{i_j}\right| + \sum_{1 \leq i_1 < i_2 < i_3 \leq n} \left|\bigcap_{j=1}^{3} A_{i_j}\right| + \ldots + (-1)^n \left|\bigcap_{j=1}^{n} A_j\right|$$

> **Useful Tip:** The principle of inclusion-exclusion is one of the most popular techniques used for solving combinatorial counting problems. It is also crucial in the study of statistics and probability, which will be discussed in detail in Chapter 7.

Theorem 2.3 (Bijection Principle): For two finite sets S and T, $|S| = |T|$ if and only if there is a bijection between S and T.

Theorem 2.4 (Permutation): A standard permutation is an ordered arrangement of all the elements in a set S. If $|S| = n$, then the number of possible permutations is $n! = 1 \times 2 \times \ldots \times n$. A k-permutation is an ordered arrangement of k distinct elements of S, and the number of possible k-permutations is given by

$$P(n,k) = \frac{n!}{(n-k)!}$$

Theorem 2.5 (Circular Permutation): A circular k-permutation for a set S with $|S| = n$ is an ordered arrangement of k elements of S, where only the relative ordering, and not the absolute ordering, is important. Thus, in a circular permutation, there is no specific starting or ending position. The number of possible circular k-permutations of S is given by

$$P_c(n,k) = \frac{n!}{k(n-k)!}$$

Theorem 2.6 (Combination): A k-combination of a set S with $|S| = n$ is a selection of k distinct elements of S, and the number of possible combinations is given by

$$C(n,k) = \binom{n}{k} = \frac{n!}{k!(n-k)!}$$

It is easy to note that $\binom{n}{k} = \binom{n}{n-k}$. $\binom{n}{k}$ is known as the binomial coefficient, and it is connected to the following popular algebraic identity.

Theorem 2.7 (Binomial Theorem): If x, y are two real numbers and if n is a non-negative integer, then

$$(x+y)^n = \sum_{k=0}^{n} \binom{n}{k} x^{n-k} y^k$$

> **Useful Tip:** Special cases of the Binomial Theorem provide interesting identities regarding the binomial coefficients, some of which are discussed below. Similar tricks can be useful in solving various problems related to binomial coefficients.

Lemma 2.1 (Pascal's Identity): If k, n are integers satisfying $n > 0$, $1 \leqslant k \leqslant n$, then

$$\binom{n}{k} = \binom{n-1}{k} + \binom{n-1}{k-1}$$

Theorem 2.8 (Other Identities in Binomial Coefficients): Let $n \in \mathbb{N}$ and k be an integer such that $0 \leqslant k \leqslant n$. Define $\binom{a}{b} = 0$ for all $a < b$.

(a) $\sum_{k=0}^{n} \binom{n}{k} = 2^n$. It can be proved using $x = y = 1$ in the Binomial Theorem.

(b) $\sum_{k=0}^{n} \binom{n}{k}(-1)^k = 0$. In other words, the sum of the binomial coefficients for even k is the same as the sum of the binomial coefficients for odd k. It can be proved using $x = 1, y = -1$ in the Binomial Theorem.

(c) For any integer $r \leqslant n$, $\sum_{k=0}^{n} \binom{k}{r} = \binom{n+1}{r+1}$. It can be proved using the principle of mathematical induction.

(d) For any integer $r \leqslant n$, $\sum_{k=0}^{n} \binom{r+k}{k} = \binom{n+r+1}{n}$. This result can be proved using the above identities.

(e) For $n, m, r \in \mathbb{N}$, $\sum_{j=0}^{n} \binom{n}{j}\binom{m}{r-j} = \binom{n+m}{r}$. This result can be proved using the Binomial Theorem, as one can show that the term on the left-hand side of the identity is the coefficient of x^r in the expansion of $(1+x)^n(1+x)^m$. This is known as Vandermonde's convolution.

Proposition 2.1: The total number of permutations of a set of m identical objects and another set of n identical objects taken together is $\binom{m+n}{m}$.

Proposition 2.2: There are $\binom{n+r-1}{n}$ distinct non-negative integral solutions to the equation $a_1 + a_2 + \ldots + a_r = n$.

The above result can be discussed using the aforementioned bijection principle. Observe that the number of solutions to the equation is the same as the number of ways to distribute n balls in r boxes, where one or more boxes can remain empty. Then, the above result can be argued by considering an arrangement of n balls and $r-1$ sticks, where the number of balls between the ith and $(i+1)$th sticks indicates how many balls are in the $(i+1)$th box (number of balls to the left of the first stick corresponds to the first box and the number of balls to the right of the last stick corresponds to the last box). The result immediately follows using Proposition 2.1. It also leads to another useful result, which is as follows.

Proposition 2.3: There are $\binom{n-1}{r-1}$ distinct positive integral solutions to the equation $a_1 + a_2 + \ldots + a_r = n$.

> **Useful Tip:** The above propositions are instrumental in various challenging problems in combinatorics. A good problem-solving strategy can be to find a bijection between the given problem and one of the above three propositions. We shall see a few such examples below.

Theorem 2.9 (The Pigeonhole Principle): If $n+1$ or more pigeons are placed in n holes, then one hole must contain two or more pigeons.

This is also known as Dirichlet's box principle, Dirichlet principle or box principle. Although this theorem seems obvious, many challenging combinatorial problems can be solved using this. Often, a clever choice of holes is necessary. On a related note, the extended version of the Pigeonhole Principle states that if k objects are placed in n boxes, then at least one box must hold at least $\lceil k/n \rceil$ objects.

Solved Examples

1. Let $S = \{1, 2, \ldots, n\}$, $(n \geq 7)$. In how many ways can four distinct integers be chosen from S such that no two are consecutive?

Solution: Let the four integers be x_1, x_2, x_3, x_4. Since no two of these are consecutive, $x_1, x_2 - 1, x_3 - 2, x_4 - 3$ are distinct integers between 1 and $n - 3$, both inclusive. Further, for any four distinct integers from $1, 2, \ldots, n-3$, if we add $0, 1, 2, 3$, respectively, we obtain four distinct integers, no two of which are consecutive. Hence, to choose four distinct integers from $\{1, 2, \ldots, n\}$ such that no two are consecutive is equivalent to choosing four distinct integers from $\{1, 2, \ldots, n-3\}$. This gives us the total number of possible choices as $\binom{n-3}{4}$.

> **Useful Tip:** This is a good example of an application of the bijection principle. A similar strategy can be adopted in other problems as well.

2. Using only the letters A, B and C, how many six-letter words can be formed such that each letter appears at least once in the word?

Solution: The principle of inclusion-exclusion can be used for this problem. First of all, the total number of words that can be formed using the three letters is 3^6.

Use S_A, S_B, S_C to denote the set of 6-letter words that do not contain A, B and C, respectively. So, the number of words that do not contain at least one of the three letters is $|S_A \cup S_B \cup S_C| = (|S_A| + |S_B| + |S_C|) - (|S_A \cap S_B| + |S_B \cap S_C| + |S_C \cap S_A|) + |S_A \cap S_B \cap S_C|$. Since $|S_A| = 2^6$ and $|S_B \cap S_C| = 1^6$ (similarly for other cases), one can compute that the number of words for which each letter appears at least once is $3^6 - 189 = 540$.

3. Find the number of positive integers with at most 8 digits such that the sum of digits equals 7.

Solution: We are considering only natural numbers with at most 8 digits. Let us denote these digits as $a_1, a_2, \ldots, a_8$. Remember that these digits can be 0. Now, the number of natural numbers whose sum of digits equals 7 is the number of non-negative integral solutions of the equation $a_1 + a_2 + \ldots + a_8 = 7$, and that is equal to $\binom{8+7-1}{7} = \binom{14}{7}$.

> **Useful Tip:** This is an example of finding a bijection between the given problem and Proposition 2.2. The reader is advised to avoid the common mistake of confusing Proposition 2.2 and Proposition 2.3. The following problem, for instance, shows an application of both the propositions.

4. Find the number of non-negative integer solutions of the equation $\sum_{i=1}^{k} n_i = 100$. How many positive integer solutions are there for the inequality $\sum_{i=1}^{4} n_i < 100$?

Solution: We know that the number of non-negative integral solutions of the equation $a_1 + a_2 + \ldots + a_r = n$ is $\binom{n+r-1}{n}$. Using this formula, the number of possible k-tuples that satisfy the first equation is $\binom{k+99}{100}$.

For the second part, since $\sum_{i=1}^{4} n_i < 100$, we can introduce a new variable n_5 such that $\sum_{i=1}^{5} n_i = 100$. Note that n_5 must be a positive integer as well. Here, we use the result that the number of distinct positive integer solutions to the equation $a_1 + a_2 + \ldots + a_r = n$ is $\binom{n-1}{r-1}$. Thus, the number of possible solutions to the given inequality is $\binom{99}{4}$.

5. Let $S = \{2, 3, \ldots, 9\}$ and let $\{A_1, A_2, A_3, A_4\}$ denote a partition of S, with $|A_i| = 2$ for all i. In how many ways can this partition be formed such that the greatest common divisor of the two integers in A_i is not equal to 2 for all i?

Solution: First note that there are only four integers in the set that are divisible by 2 and all but one pair from them (namely, 4 and 8) has 2 as their greatest common divisor. So, we consider two separate cases to solve this problem.

Case 1: $(4, 8)$ is one of the four pairs. Then, we must have 2 and 6 in two different pairs and we can choose the other element of these pairs in $4 \times 3 = 12$ ways. It automatically gives us the fourth pair. And so, in this case, the total number of possible ways of dividing the set into 4 pairs is 12.

Case 2: Here we consider that no two even numbers are in the same pair. So, every even number is paired with an odd number and that essentially means we have to consider permutations of the odd numbers. For example, if we take the permutation $\{9, 3, 7, 5\}$, we get the pairings as $\{(2, 9), (4, 3), (6, 7), (8, 5)\}$. Clearly, the total number of possible pairings in this case is $4! = 24$.

Hence, in total, there are $12 + 24 = 36$ ways in which we can partition the set while satisfying the given conditions.

6. Let $f: S \to S$ be a function on $S = \{1, 2, 3, \ldots, n\}$. We call a set $D \subset S$ invariant if $x \in D$ implies $f(x) \in D$. Let $\deg(f)$ be the number of invariant subsets of S for f. By default, the empty set and the complete set S are considered to be invariant for f. Show that for every $k \in \mathbb{N}, 1 \leqslant k \leqslant n$, one can find a function $f: S \to S$ satisfying $\deg(f) = 2^k$.

Solution: First, we prove the result for $k = 1$. Let f be the cycle permutation, that is, take $f(1) = 2, f(2) = 3, \ldots, f(n-1) = n, f(n) = 1$. It is clear that the only invariant subsets are the empty set and S. That clearly satisfies $\deg(f) = 2$.

Now, we can use a similar idea for any k. Take $f(1) = 1, f(2) = 2, \ldots, f(k-1) = k-1$ and let f be a cyclic permutation on the set $\{k+1, k+2, k+3, \ldots, n\}$.

Then, for this f, $\{1\}, \{2\}, \{3\}, \ldots, \{k-1\}, \{k, k+1, k+2, \ldots, n\}$ are invariant subsets. Also, any invariant subset of S must be a union of one or more subsets from them. As there are k such elements, the total number of invariant subsets of f is precisely the set of subsets of these k elements, which implies $\deg(f) = 2^k$.

7. Consider a tournament of n players. Suppose that each of the players plays all the others exactly once in a round-robin league system, and each game results in a win for one of the players. At the end of the tournament, the players are asked to write down the names of those whom they defeated (say, the set S), and also of those who the players in set S defeated. Prove that there is at least one person who has written down the names of all the other $n-1$ players.

Solution: We intend to use mathematical induction to approach this problem. First, if there are only two players in the tournament, then clearly, one must beat the other and write his name.

For the induction hypothesis, assume that there is someone (call him A) among a tournament of k players who writes the names of all the other $k-1$ players. Now let a new guy, B, join the tournament to form a group of $k+1$. If we can show that A's existence implies that someone among the $k+1$ writes the names of all the other players, the result follows.

Clearly, if A defeats B, we know that A writes the names of all the other players. Also, if anyone who was defeated by A defeats B, the list of A contains B's name.

Finally, if none of the above happens, it would imply that B has defeated A and everyone else, and in that case, B's list has everyone's names. This completes the proof.

8. Assume that in a club, each member is on two committees and any two committees have exactly one member in common. If there are exactly five committees, how many members does the club have?

Solution: Suppose the club has n members. If we list the names of all the members in all five committees, we can say that the name of each member will occur twice (since each member is on exactly two committees) and so, there will be $2n$ names.

However, each member of a committee is in one of the other committees too and it is different for different members of the same committee. To understand it better, suppose $C_1,\ldots,C_5$ are the committees. Now, there is one member of C_1 who is in C_2, there is another one who is in C_3, and so on (these are different people since everyone can be on exactly two committees). Clearly, there have to be 4 members in each committee.

So, in the list mentioned above, there must be $5 \times 4 = 20$ names, and thus, we get $2n = 20$. Hence, the club has 10 members. Numbering the persons as $1,2,\ldots,10$, we can show the committees as follows:

$$C_1 : 1,2,3,4, \; C_2 : 1,5,6,7, \; C_3 : 2,5,8,9, \; C_4 : 3,6,8,10, \; C_5 : 4,7,9,10.$$

9. Suppose that there are 1000 wizards $W_1, W_2, \ldots, W_{1000}$ and 1000 potions $P_1, P_2, \ldots, P_{1000}$. Initially all the potions are poisonous, but every wizard has the ability to turn a poisonous potion to a non-poisonous one (and the other way round as well). The wizards now start to play a game in the following way. In the first turn, the wizard W_1 makes all the potions non-poisonous. Then, W_2 changes $P_2, P_4, \ldots, P_{1000}$ back to poisonous, but leaves the odd-numbered potions as they are. Next, W_3 changes the state of every third potion, that is, $P_3, P_6, \ldots, P_{999}$. Continuing in this way, in the mth turn, W_m changes the state of the potions $P_m, P_{2m}, \ldots$ while leaving the others untouched, and this goes on up to $m = 1000$. At the end, how many potions are safe to drink?

Solution: To start with, we can note that the state of the ith potion is changed by W_j if and only if j is a divisor of i. Thus, the state of P_i changes d_i number of times, where d_i is the number of divisors of i. Since initially all the potions are poisonous, at the end, P_i is safe to drink if and only if the state has been changed an odd number of times, that is, if and only if d_i is odd.

Consider the prime factorization of a natural number n as follows:

$$n = p_1^{\alpha_1} p_2^{\alpha_2} \cdots p_k^{\alpha_k}$$

Then, any factor of n is of the form $p_1^{\beta_1} p_2^{\beta_2} \cdots p_k^{\beta_k}$, where β_i is an integer from 0 to α_i, and so, each β_i can be chosen in $(1+\alpha_i)$ ways. Hence, the number of divisors of n is $(1+\alpha_1)(1+\alpha_2)\ldots(1+\alpha_k)$. Clearly, the number of divisors of n is odd if and only if each α_i is even. It further implies that a natural number has an odd number of divisors if and only if it is a perfect square.

Combining the above arguments, we can say that P_i is safe to drink if and only if i is a perfect square and, since $31^2 < 1000 < 32^2$, we can say that the required answer is 31.

> **Useful Tip:** This problem shows an interesting case of an amalgamation between the concepts of number theory and combinatorics. Similar methods can be followed in other problems as well, one of which is the following.

10. Consider a set $S \subset \mathbb{N}$, with $|S| = 100$. Show that there exists $B \subset S$ such that the sum of elements in B is divisible by 100.

Solution: Recall that in modulo 100, there are exactly 100 residue classes corresponding to the remainders $0, 1, \ldots, 99$, where a residue class of r modulo 100 is defined as the complete set of integers that are $r \pmod{100}$.

Let us denote the given 100 numbers as $x_1, \ldots, x_{100}$. We consider the 100 subsets $\{x_1\}$, $\{x_1, x_2\}, \ldots, \{x_1, \ldots, x_{100}\}$. If the sum of any of these subsets is divisible by 100, we get the required result. If that is not true, then there are 100 sums, and there are 99 possible residue classes modulo 100 (excluding 0). Therefore, by the Pigeonhole Principle, two of these sums belong to the same residue class. Let them be $\{x_1,\ldots,x_i\}$ and $\{x_1,\ldots,x_j\}$ (with $i < j$). Then, it is easy to argue that $x_{i+1} + \cdots + x_j \equiv 0 \pmod{100}$, and that completes the proof.

> **Useful Tip:** A generalized version of the above problem is that for integers $a_1,\ldots,a_n$, there exist integers k and r such that $a_k + a_{k+1} + \ldots + a_{k+r}$ is divisible by n.

11. Consider a group of five people where any two are defined to be either friends or enemies. It is known that no three of them are friends to each other and no three of them are enemies of each other as well. Show that every person in the group has exactly two friends.

Solution: Let us denote the persons as A, B, C, D, E. Now, suppose A has at least three friends (without loss of generality, let us assume they are B, C, D). Then, if any two of B, C, D are friends with each other, we get three persons who are friends of each other, which is not possible. However, it would mean that B, C, D are enemies of each other and that is, again, not possible. Thus, A cannot have at least three friends. By the same logic, no one can have at least three friends.

We can use similar arguments as above to show that no one can have at least three enemies either. And that leaves us with the only possibility, which is that every person in the group has exactly two friends.

> **Useful Tip:** Note that this is another example of the proof of contradiction, which we learnt in the previous chapter.

12. Let us assign the numbers $1, 2, \ldots, 11$ to eleven people in a group. In how many ways can the entire group be seated on eleven chairs arranged around a circular table such that the number of any two adjacent persons differs by at most two?

Solution: Since it is a circular arrangement, we can start from anywhere. Suppose 1 sits on one of the eleven chairs. Given the condition, only 2 and 3 can sit on the chairs beside 1. Let us assume that 2 sits on the left of 1 and 3 sits on the right of 1.

Note that the above arrangement means that 4 must sit on the other side of 2 and 5 on the other side of 3, and we can continue like this to eventually get a unique possible arrangement for the players, once we fix the positions of 1, 2 and 3.

Thus, everything depends on how the first three are seated. Now, 1 can take any position as it is a circular arrangement, and after 1 is seated, 2 and 3 can take their positions in two different ways. Hence, the possible number of arrangements is 2.

13. A 2×1 rectangle is commonly known as a domino. Find out the values of $m, n \in \mathbb{N}$ for which we can cover an $m \times n$ rectangle with non-overlapping dominoes.

Solution: We can visualize an $m \times n$ rectangle as a chessboard with mn cells inside it. Let us colour them using two colours, black and white, alternately, just like in a chessboard. Note that if we place a domino on the chessboard, it always covers one white and one black square, irrespective of whether it is placed horizontally or vertically. Thus, if we are using k dominoes to cover the chessboard, in total, we can cover k white and k black squares ($2k$ squares in total). So, the chessboard must have an even number of squares, meaning that either m or n must be even.

Without loss of generality, let m be even (say, $2r$). That means the chessboard has $2r$ rows and n columns. Note that each column can now be completely covered using r dominoes. Thus, whatever n might be, we will always be able to cover the whole rectangle using non-overlapping dominoes. A similar situation will occur if n is even.

Hence, we can cover the rectangle with non-overlapping dominoes if and only if at least one of m and n is even.

14. Consider a set of n numbers $a_1, a_2, \ldots, a_n$ such that each a_i is either 1 or -1. If
$$a_1 a_2 a_3 a_4 + a_2 a_3 a_4 a_5 + \ldots + a_n a_1 a_2 a_3 = 0,$$
show that 4 divides n.

Solution: Let us denote the sum as S. Suppose that we decide to change a_i to $-a_i$. A consequence is that four terms in the sum change sign, and subsequently, we can say that S remains the same in congruent modulo 4, that is, the term $S \pmod{4}$ remains invariant under the operation we consider.

Now, let us change each negative a_i to $-a_i$, thereby making it 1. We know that every time we perform this operation, the sum remains the same in $\pmod 4$. Also, after a number of such operations, all numbers in the sequence become 1, and thus, the new sum is $S = n$. However, it should remain the same in $\pmod 4$. Since originally the sum is 0, we get $4 \mid n$.

> **Useful Tip:** You might remember that the above problem was solved in the previous chapter using number theoretic techniques. Here, we solve it by finding a property that remains the same after every iteration. In combinatorics, this is commonly known as the invariance principle and it is immensely useful.

15. Let $S = \{k : k \in \mathbb{N}, 1000 \leqslant k \leqslant 99999\}$. $x, y \in S$ are said to be in the same equivalence class if the digits appearing in x and y are the same. How many equivalence classes can be formed from S?

Solution: S contains only four- and five-digit natural numbers. So, the number of distinct digits in an element from S is at least 1 and at most 5. Now, we can choose r distinct digits in $\binom{10}{r}$ ways and all the numbers formed by those r digits are in the same equivalence class. However, when we choose 1 digit from the ten available digits, there is a case where only 0 is selected and that choice does not give us an equivalence class. Thus, the total number of possible equivalence classes is

$$\sum_{i=1}^{5} \binom{10}{i} - 1 = \frac{1}{2} \sum_{i=0}^{10} \binom{10}{i} - 2\binom{10}{0} - 1 + \frac{1}{2}\binom{10}{5} = 2^{10} - 3 + \frac{1}{2} \times \frac{10!}{(5!)^2} = 1137$$

16. Let $e_1, e_2, \ldots, e_k \in \mathbb{N} + \{0\}$. Let A_k denote the set of all k-tuples of integers $(f_1, f_2, \ldots, f_k)$ such that $0 \leq f_i \leq e_i$ for all i and $\sum_{i=1}^{k} f_i$ is even. Similarly, B_k denotes the same where $\sum_{i=1}^{k} f_i$ is odd. Prove that $|A_k| = |B_k|$ or $|A_k| = |B_k| + 1$.

Solution: For $k = 1$, it is quite easy to observe since each integer is either even or odd and depending on whether e_k is odd or even, we will get $|A_k| - |B_k|$ to be 0 or 1, respectively.

We can prove it for any natural number k using a similar concept, by ordering all possible k-tuples according to their components. Let us call a k-tuple of even order if the sum of the components is even, that is, if it belongs to A_k, and of odd order otherwise.

Here is the ordering scheme (similar to the dictionary scheme): If $(f_1, f_2, \ldots, f_k)$ and $(g_1, g_2, \ldots, g_k)$ are two k-tuples satisfying $0 \leq f_i, g_i \leq e_i$ for all i, then $(f_1, f_2, \ldots, f_k) < (g_1, g_2, \ldots, g_k)$ if and only if there exists $j \geq 0$ satisfying $f_1 = g_1, f_2 = g_2, \ldots, f_j = g_j, f_k < g_k$ for all $k > j$. For example, the first three terms of this ordering are $(0, 0, \ldots, 0, 0), (0, 0, \ldots, 0, 1), (0, 0, \ldots, 0, 2)$ while the last term is $(e_1, e_2, \ldots, e_k)$.

Now, observe that in this list, the first entry, that is, $(0, 0, \ldots, 0, 0)$, is of even order, the second one is of odd order, the third is of even order, and so on. Clearly, those k-tuples that are in odd numbered positions in the list belong to A_k while the others are in B_k. Hence, the cardinality of the two sets is equal if there are even number of k-tuples in the list. However, that is possible if at least one of the e_ks is odd, as the total number of possible k-tuples is $(e_1 + 1)(e_2 + 1) \ldots (e_k + 1)$. Otherwise, the number of even ordered tuples is 1 more than the number of odd ordered tuples. Hence, $|A_k| - |B_k| = 0$ or 1 (it is 1 only when all e_ks are even).

17. Let us use F to denote the set of all functions

$$f : \{1, 2, \ldots, n\} \to \{1, 2, \ldots, k\} \quad (n \geq 3, k \geq 2)$$

such that $f(i) \neq f(i+1)$ for all $i \in \{1, 2, \ldots, n-1\}$.

(a) Prove that $|F| = k(k-1)^{n-1}$.

(b) Let $s(n,k)$ be the number of functions in F such that $f(n) \neq f(1)$. For $n \geq 4$, prove that
$$s(n,k) = k(k-1)^{n-1} - s(n-1,k).$$

(c) Using the previous part, prove that for $n \geq 4$,
$$s(n,k) = (k-1)^n + (-1)^n(k-1).$$

Solution:

(a) There are k choices to assign to $f(1)$. Next, for each of $2, 3, \ldots, n$, we have $(k-1)$ choices since $f(j)$ cannot be equal to $f(j-1)$. Hence, in total, there are $k(k-1)^{n-1}$ choices and the proof is complete.

(b) Let us use $D_{n,k}$ to denote the set of functions in F for which $f(n) = f(1)$. Then, $s(n,k) = k(k-1)^{n-1} - |D_{n,k}|$. Now, consider a function f in $D_{n,k}$. We have $f(n) \neq f(n-1)$ and $f(n) = f(1)$ and so, $f(n-1) \neq f(1)$. Thus, we can say that each function from $D_{n,k}$ satisfies the condition $f(n-1) \neq f(1)$, and hence, $|D_{n,k}| = s(n-1,k)$, giving us the required result.

(c) Using the above recursion relation, one can show that
$$s(n,k) = k(k-1)^{n-1} - k(k-1)^{n-2} + s(n-2,k)$$

Proceeding this way and using the fact that $c(1,k) = 0$, it can be further generalized to
$$s(n,k) = \sum_{r=1}^{n-1} (-1)^{r+1} k(k-1)^{n-r}$$

The above is clearly a geometric progression with common ratio $-1/(k-1)$ and first term $k(k-1)^{n-1}$. Hence, we get that
$$s(n,k) = k(k-1)^{n-1} \times \frac{1 + (-1/(k-1))^{n-1}}{1 + 1/(k-1)} = (k-1)^n + (-1)^n(k-1)$$

Useful Tip: In many mathematical areas, using a recursion relation is often useful to arrive at the answer. This is one such example. You can always try to identify such recursion relations while solving a problem. For instance, consider the next one.

18. For a triangle *ABC*, take n distinct points on *AB* that are different from the vertices, and connect all of them by straight lines to the vertex *C*. Similarly, take n points on *AC* and connect them to *B*. Find the number of regions the triangle *ABC* has been partitioned into by these lines.

Let us continue along the same line and take n points on *BC* and join them with *A*. If we assume that no three straight lines meet at a point other than the vertices, find the number of regions the triangle *ABC* has been partitioned into now.

Solution: We proceed using the concept of recursion. Suppose, with n points on *AB* and n points on *AC*, the triangle is partitioned into p_n number of regions. Now we aim to find out what would have happened if we had chosen $(n+1)$ points instead. So, we take one more point on each of these two sides and join them to the opposite vertices.

When we take the $(n+1)$th point on *AB* and join it to *C*, the line intersects all the n lines emerging from *B* (formed by joining the n points on *AC* to the vertex *B*), and thus, it creates $(n+1)$ new regions.

Now, if we take a new point on *AC* and join it to *B*, it intersects all the $(n+1)$ lines emerging from *C*, and so, using similar arguments as before, we can say that $(n+2)$ new regions are created. Thus, because of introducing the $(n+1)$th point on both *AB* and *AC*, the number of regions has increased by $(2n+3)$, and so, we can say that

$$p_{n+1} = p_n + (2n+3)$$

Clearly, using this recursion relation and the fact that $p_0 = 1$, one can get

$$p_n = 1 + 3 + 5 + \ldots + (2n-1) + (2n+1) = (n+1)^2$$

Hence, the triangle is partitioned into $(n+1)^2$ regions.

For the second part, consider that we already have n points on *AB* and n points on *AC* and lines are drawn from them as mentioned. So, from the previous part, we know that $(n+1)^2$ regions are created.

Now, let us take a single point on *BC* and join it to *A*. Since we are assuming that no three straight lines meet at a point other than the vertices, we can say that this new line intersects the existing $2n$ lines at distinct points, and hence, $(2n+1)$ new regions are created. And with every new point on *BC*, the same thing occurs, thereby implying that if we take further n points on *BC* and join them with *A*, in total, we get $n(2n+1)$ new regions.

Thus, the total number of regions in this case is $(n+1)^2 + n(2n+1) = 3n^2 + 3n + 1$.

19. Consider five distinct boxes labeled U, V, W, X, Y and suppose that 10 mangoes are to be placed in these boxes such that a box may contain any number of mangoes, including 0 and 10. Find the number of ways to distribute the mangoes so that exactly two of the boxes contain exactly two mangoes each.

Solution: The mangoes should be considered to be identical. We can choose the two boxes with two mangoes each in $\binom{5}{2} = 10$ ways. Now, once these two boxes are chosen, there are 6 mangoes to be placed in 3 boxes such that each box can have any number of mangoes. This is equivalent to the number of non-negative integer solutions of the equation

$$x_1 + x_2 + x_3 = 6$$

We can obtain the required number of solutions to the above equation as $\binom{6+3-1}{6} = \binom{8}{6} = 28$.

Combining the above, it is easy to infer that the total number of ways to distribute the mangoes according to the given rule is $10 \times 28 = 280$.

20. If we arrange all the permutations of the letters a, b, c, d, e in their alphabetical order (dictionary scheme), what is the position of the arrangement *decab*?

Solution: In order to obtain the required position, we need to cover all the arrangements starting with a, b and c. For each of these cases, after fixing the first letter, there are $4! = 24$ possible combinations, and so, in total, there are $3 \times 24 = 72$ arrangements starting with a, b, c.

Next, we have arrangements starting with da, db and dc. As before, there are $3 \times 3! = 18$ arrangements. Now, we have reached those arrangements that start with de. If we arrange the other three letters according to the dictionary, we get abc, acb, bac, bca, cab and this is what we are looking for. Hence, *decab* is in the $(72 + 18 + 5) = 95$th position in this dictionary.

> **Useful Tip:** These problems are very common in all entrance tests as well as in the board examinations.

21. In how many ways can you choose a set of distinct positive integers, all $\leqslant 50$, such that their sum is odd?

Solution: There are 25 even numbers and 25 odd numbers available to us. In order to obtain an odd sum, we need to take an odd number of odd numbers and any number of even numbers. Now, we can select r odd numbers in $\binom{25}{r}$ ways. Since $\binom{25}{r} = \binom{25}{25-r}$, the sum of $\binom{25}{r}$ with odd r is the same as the sum of $\binom{25}{r}$ with even r. Thus, the total number of possible ways of selecting an odd number of odd numbers is

Combinatorics

$$\binom{25}{1}+\binom{25}{3}+\ldots+\binom{25}{25}=\frac{1}{2}\sum_{i=0}^{25}\binom{25}{i}=\frac{1}{2}\times 2^{25}=2^{24}$$

On the other hand, since each even number can be included or not included, there are a total of 2^{25} choices. Hence, the total number of ways of choosing a set of positive integers such that the sum is odd is $2^{24}\times 2^{25}=2^{49}$.

22. Consider a set $\mathcal{P}=\{A_1,A_2,\ldots,A_k\}$ such that $A_1,A_2,\ldots,A_k$ are disjoint and non-empty subsets of a set A. If the union of $A_1,A_2,\ldots,A_k$ is A, $\mathcal{P}$ is called a partition of A into k classes. Let S_k^n denote the number of possibles partitions of a set with n elements into k classes.

(a) What is the value of S_2^n?

(b) Prove the recursive relation $S_k^{n+1}=S_{k-1}^n+kS_k^n$.

Solution:

(a) For S_2^n, we need to find out the number of ways to partition a set of n elements into two disjoint, non-empty subsets. Each element can be in either of the two subsets, and so, the possible choices for placing the elements in two different subsets is 2^n. However, this is for ordered pairs and since partition means the subsets are unordered, we have actually counted every possible partition twice in the above calculation. Thus, S_2^n is equal to $2^n/2=2^{n-1}$.

(b) Suppose we have a set with $n+1$ elements, numbered as $a_1,a_2,\ldots,a_{n+1}$. There are two possible cases.

First, a_{n+1} can form a singleton, implying that one of the classes is $\{a_{n+1}\}$, and therefore, we need to partition the other n elements in $k-1$ subsets, which can be done is S_{k-1}^n ways. Second, suppose a_{n+1} is included with some other element(s). Now, consider a partition of n elements into k subsets, which can be done in S_k^n ways. a_{n+1} can be included in any of the k existing subsets, and so, the total number of possible partitions in this case is kS_k^n.

Since partitioning $n+1$ elements into k classes is essentially the combination of the above two cases, the required result follows automatically.

23. How many $n\times n$ matrices are there such that all elements are either 1 or -1 and where the product of the entries in each row and each column equals -1?

Solution: Consider the first $(n-1)\times(n-1)$ submatrix. The total number of possible ways of filling it randomly with ± 1 is $2^{(n-1)^2}$, since for each position, we have two choices.

Now, consider the product of the entries in the first $(n-1)$ positions in the first column. If that product is 1, the nth position must be -1, and vice versa. So, the choice is unique. Similarly, for the nth entry of the first $(n-1)$ columns. Further, if we now look at the first row, using exactly the same arguments as above, we can say that we have a unique choice for the nth cell of that row, and the argument follows for all of the first $(n-1)$ rows as well.

Thus, we are left with only the (n,n)th element. We only have to make sure that there is exactly one choice for the last cell, whether we look at it row-wise or column-wise. Without loss of generality, suppose n is even and that the first $(n-1) \times (n-1)$ submatrix has an odd number of -1s in total. Then, there is an even number of -1s in the first $(n-1)$ cells of the nth row, since the product of all the elements in the $n \times (n-1)$ submatrix must be -1. And similarly, there is an even number of -1s in the first $(n-1)$ cells of the nth column as well. Hence, the choice for the (n,n)th cell is also unique, thereby implying that the total number of ways in which the required condition is satisfied is $2^{(n-1)^2}$.

24. Let $a, b \in \mathbb{N}$ and consider an $a \times b$ rectangle with ab unit squares. If you draw a diagonal of this $a \times b$ rectangle, how many of those unit squares contain a segment of positive length of this diagonal?

> **Useful Tip:** In this kind of exercise, it is often helpful to draw the structure first. For example, an illustration of this problem, for $a = 12, b = 8$, is given below.

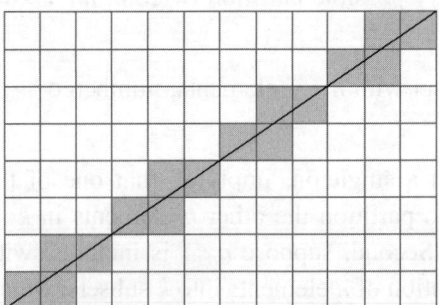

Solution: We can think of the diagonal as the path of a point that travels from one end to the opposite end of a rectangle in a straight line. Clearly, in order to reach the opposite end, the point must pass through a horizontal squares and b vertical squares, and so, the diagonal should pass through $a+b$ squares in total. However, whenever the diagonal passes through a vertex of the smallest squares, a vertical square can be considered the same as a horizontal square and the count is one less in those cases.

Now, let us embed the rectangle in an xy-plane as follows. If we draw the rectangle with one vertex at the origin and two sides along the two axes, then the diagonal is the line joining $(0,0)$ and (a,b), and hence, the equation of the diagonal is $ay - bx = 0$.

Combinatorics 2.17

On the other hand, after dividing the rectangle into unit squares, the vertices of each unit square have integer coordinates, and so, the diagonal passes through a vertex of a unit square if and only if there are positive integers $h \leqslant a, k \leqslant b$ satisfying $hb = ka$.

Let us assume that the gcd of a and b is d, that is, $a = dp, b = dq$, where p, q are relatively prime. Also, without loss of generality, assume that $p \geqslant q$. Note that $hq = kp$, that is, $h/k = p/q$. Since p, q are relatively primes, the only possible choices for (h, k) are $(p, q), (2p, 2q), \ldots, (dp, dq)$. Thus, the diagonal passes through exactly d of the grid points, and therefore, the total number of unit squares that would contain a segment of positive length of this diagonal is $a + b - (a, b)$.

25. Consider a round-robin league tournament among six teams A, B, C, D, E, F, where the teams play each other exactly once, and each game ends in a win for one of the teams. Each win is worth two points and a loss does not get any point. Based on the following information, find the individual scores of all six teams at the end of the tournament:

   (i) A, B and D got more points than the other three teams.

   (ii) E defeated F.

   (iii) D, E and F won their games against A, B and C, respectively.

   (iv) The last three matches in the league were played between A and D, between B and E, and between C and F. Before these games were played, A had 6 points, B had 8 points and C had 4 points.

Solution: From condition (iv), we can say that B won against A, C, D, F. Now, since A had 6 points before playing against D and since A lost against B, it is clear that A defeated C, E, F. Using similar logic, we can also say that C won against D and E.

Combining the above with the information given in (ii) and (iii), we can write down the following, which shows the winners of all the matches except the ones between (D, E) and (D, F).

	A	B	C	D	E	F
A		B	A	D	A	A
B	B		B	B	E	B
C	A	B		C	C	F
D	D	B	C		?	?
E	A	E	C	?		E
F	A	B	F	?	E	

From the above, we can say that A, B, C eventually got 6, 8 and 4 points, respectively. D got at least 2 points, E got at least 4 points and F got at least 2 points.

Now, since D is one among the top three, E and F must have lost against D. Thus, D finished with 6 points, and consequently, the final scores of the six teams are $6, 8, 4, 6, 4, 2$, respectively.

26. For $N = \{x_1, x_2, \ldots, x_n\}$, let $C = \{S : S \subseteq N\}$ be the power set of N. Consider a function $f : C \to \{0, 1\}$. Let us call an element of C a winning or a losing coalition depending on whether $f(s) = 1$ or $f(s) = 0$, respectively. Further, f is called a voting game if the following conditions hold:

   (a) The original set N is a winning coalition.

   (b) The empty set is a losing coalition.

   (c) Two winning coalitions must have a common element.

   (d) Any superset of a winning coalition is also a winning coalition.

Prove that the maximum number of winning coalitions of a voting game is 2^{n-1}, and find a voting game for which this value is attained.

Solution: For convenience, we call every subset of N as a coalition. Clearly, for any coalition S, S^c is also a coalition. Since $S \cap S^c = \phi$, because of property (c), we can say that both S and S^c cannot be winning coalitions. Thus, for every such pair, at most one is a winning coalition. This means that at most half of all the coalitions can be winning coalitions.

Since the total number of coalitions (the total number of possible subsets of N) is 2^n, we get the maximum number of winning coalitions of a voting game as 2^{n-1}. Now, the required result is proved if we can find a voting game for which the number of winning coalitions is exactly 2^{n-1}.

Define f in the following way:

$$f(S) = \begin{cases} 1 & \text{if } 1 \in S, \\ 0 & \text{if } 1 \notin S. \end{cases}$$

We can see that properties (a) and (b) automatically hold. Next, if both S and S' are winning coalitions, they have 1 as a common element. Further, if S is a winning coalition and if $S \subseteq S'$, then 1 must be in both the subsets, and therefore, S' is also a winning coalition. So, all the properties are satisfied and we can say that the above f is a voting game. Since 1 is included in exactly 2^{n-1} subsets of N, we get the number of winning coalitions in this case as 2^{n-1} and that completes the proof.

Combinatorics

27. Let us colour each of the vertices of a regular polygon with nine equal sides using black or white.

   (a) Prove that there must be two adjacent vertices with the same colour.

   (b) Prove that using the vertices of the polygon, one can form a monochromatic isosceles triangle.

Solution: Name the vertices $A_1, A_2, ..., A_9$ in cyclic order.

(a) Assume that no two adjacent vertices are of the same colour. Without loss of generality, let A_1 be white. Then, A_2 is black, A_3 is white, and so on, until we get A_9 as white. This is, however, a contradiction to our assumption. Hence, there must be two adjacent vertices of the same colour.

(b) From (a), we know that there are two adjacent vertices with the same colour. Without loss of generality, let us assume that A_1, A_2 are both black. If A_3 or A_9 are black, we have a monochromatic isosceles triangle. Otherwise, assume that both A_3 and A_9 are white. Then, $A_1 A_6 A_2$ forms a black isosceles triangle if A_6 is black or $A_3 A_6 A_9$ forms a white isosceles triangle if A_6 is white. This completes the proof.

> **Useful Tip:** Colouring is an effective method of proving combinatorial results. You will come across more colouring-oriented problems in the Exercises section below.

28. In chess, the bishops are allowed to attack diagonally, that is, only on the lines parallel to the two main diagonals. Prove that the maximum number of non-attacking bishops you can place on an $n \times n$ chessboard is $2n - 2$.

Solution: This problem can be solved using a particular colouring scheme. First, we show that if we place $(2n - 1)$ bishops, there are at least two who attack each other, and then we show that it is possible to place $(2n - 2)$ non-attacking bishops on an $n \times n$ chessboard.

For the first part, we use $(2n - 2)$ colours for an $n \times n$ chessboard. Let us colour one diagonal, from $(1, 1)$ to (n, n), using colour 1. The next diagonal, from $(1, 2)$ to $(n - 1, n)$, will be coloured using colour 2. The third diagonal, from $(1, 3)$ to $(n - 2, n)$, will be coloured using colour 3, and so on. It is easy to note that there are $(2n - 3)$ diagonals except for the two cells which are at the opposite ends of the other diagonal, that is, the cells at the $(1, n)$ and $(n, 1)$ positions. So, we have used $(2n - 3)$ colours for all the cells other than those two cells and that pair of diagonally opposite boxes will be coloured using the $(2n - 2)$th colour.

We illustrate the above colouring scheme for $n = 4$ in the figure below.

1	2	3	4
5	1	2	3
6	5	1	2
4	6	5	1

Clearly, if we want to place $(2n-1)$ bishops on the chessboard, using the Pigeonhole Principle, we can say that at least two of them fall on two boxes of the same colour. However, any colour covers boxes in the same diagonal, meaning that those two bishops attack each other. Thus, one cannot place $(2n-1)$ non-attacking bishops on an $n \times n$ chessboard.

The second part is very easy to observe. Note that if we place n bishops on the leftmost column and $(n-2)$ bishops on all but the end-cells on the rightmost column, none of them fall on the same diagonal. Thus, these bishops are not attacking each other, implying that $(2n-2)$ non-attacking bishops can be placed on the chessboard.

Hence, the maximum number of non-attacking bishops on an $n \times n$ chessboard is $(2n-2)$.

29. The figure below displays a $3^2 \times 3^2$ grid divided into 3^2 subgrids, each of size 3×3.

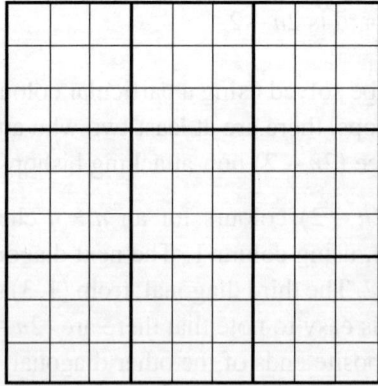

Along a similar line, consider an $n^2 \times n^2$ grid divided into n^2 subgrids, each of size $n \times n$. In how many ways can you select n^2 cells from this grid such that there is exactly one cell from each row, each column and each subgrid?

Combinatorics

Solution: We can begin by selecting one cell at a time, keeping the constraints in mind. In the first step, there are n^2 ways to choose the cell from the first column. Then, we cannot choose any cell from the same subgrid, and so, there are $n^2 - n = n(n-1)$ ways to choose a cell from the second column. Similarly, there are $n(n-2)$ ways to choose a cell from the third column, and so on, until n ways to choose a cell from the nth column.

Thus, we can choose n cells from the first n columns (one from each) in $n^2(n(n-1))(n(n-2))\ldots(n)$ ways. Observe that

$$n^2(n(n-1))(n(n-2))\ldots(n) = n^n(n!)$$

Next, we proceed in the same way as above. For the $(n+1)$th column, note that we are in a new grid, and so, there are $n^2 - n = (n-1)n$ ways to choose a cell from it (since we cannot select the cell from any of the n rows already selected).

For the next column, note that the cell cannot be in the same subgrid as the previous one, and the cell cannot be in the same row as any of the $(n-1)$ cells in the first n columns that are not in the subgrid with the same row as the subgrid of the $(n+1)$th cell. So, there will be $(n-1)(n-1)$ ways to choose a cell from the $(n+2)$th column. We can proceed likewise until $(n-1)$ ways to choose the cell in $(2n)$th column.

So, for columns $(n+1)$th to $(2n)$th, the number of ways of selecting n cells is

$$((n-1)n)((n-1)(n-1))((n-1)(n-2))\ldots(n-1) = (n-1)^n(n!)$$

Clearly, we can continue this way and eventually, we get the total number of possible ways of selecting n^2 cells from the grid such that there is exactly one cell from each subgrid, one from each row and one from each column as

$$\{n^n(n!)\}\{(n-1)^n(n!)\}\ldots\{1^n(n!)\} = \{n(n-1)\ldots 1\}^n(n!)^n = (n!)^{2n}$$

30. Let $n \in \mathbb{N}, n > 1$. Prove that

$$2^n < \binom{2n}{n} < \frac{2^n}{\prod_{i=0}^{n-1}(1-i/n)}.$$

Solution: First, observe that the denominator in the third term in the above inequality can be simplified to be $\prod_{i=0}^{n-1}(1-i/n) = n!/n^n$. Thus, the inequality we need to prove can be re-written as

$$2^n n! < \frac{(2n)!}{n!} < (2n)^n$$

We shall follow combinatorial arguments in the proof. Suppose we have n boys $(B_1, B_2, \ldots, B_n)$ and n girls $(G_1, G_2, \ldots, G_n)$. We describe three scenarios below by which we need to select n persons and consider all possible permutations of them. Note that we design these scenarios in such a way that they correspond to the above three terms.

(a) Let us pair the boys and the girls as $(B_1, G_1), (B_2, G_2), \ldots, (B_n, G_n)$ and we fix the criteria that from each pair, only one can be selected. Then, it is obvious that the total number of ways by which we can get n persons from these n pairs is 2^n. We can then arrange them in $n!$ ways, thereby giving us the total number of possibilities of these arrangements as $2^n \times n!$.

(b) Here, we simply consider that anyone can be selected but no one can be chosen more than once. Then, the number of possible ways in which we can pick n persons is $\binom{2n}{n}$ and, as before, we can arrange them in $n!$ ways. Hence, we get the second term.

(c) Finally, we relax our condition and consider that each person can be selected more than once. Then, the first position of the arrangement can be filled in $2n$ ways, the second position can be filled in $2n$ ways, and so on. Since for each position, we have $2n$ options, we can say that the total number of possible arrangements is $(2n)^n$.

The key observation here is that we restrict ourselves in the first case by deciding that only one person can be selected from each pair. Then, we consider the usual case where each one can be selected but one can be selected only once, and finally, we allow everyone to be selected more than once. Since we keep on relaxing the condition, it is evident that the number of possibilities for one case is more than the previous cases, and hence, we get the required result as

$$2^n \times n! < \binom{2n}{n} \times n! < (2n)^n$$

> **Useful Tip:** This problem has been solved using combinatorial arguments. This is a valuable trick to prove algebraic relationships that involve expressions commonly found in combinatorics, such as binomial coefficients or factorials.

Multiple Choice Questions

1. The word COMBINATORICS consists of 13 letters. The number of distinct ways to rearrange these letters is

(a) 13!   (b) 13!/2   (c) 13!/4   (d) 13!/8

Solution: (d)

Among the 13 letters, three (C, O and I) are repeated twice. Thus, the total number of distinct ways to rearrange the letters is $13!/(2!)^3$, which leads to the answer (d).

Combinatorics

2. For a group of 8 boys and 7 girls, how many ways are there to arrange them in a line such that all boys stand contiguously and all girls stand contiguously; that is, no girl is present between any two boys and no boy is present between any two girls?

(a) $16 \times (7!)^2$ (b) $(8!)(7!)$ (c) $15!/8!$ (d) $(8!)(7!)/2$

Solution: (a)

It is clear that the boys must stand together in a block (which can be arranged in 8! ways) and the girls must stand together in another block (which can be arranged in 7! ways). Since these two blocks can also be interchanged between themselves, the total number of possible arrangements is $2 \times (8!)(7!)$, which is equal to $16 \times (7!)^2$.

3. The coefficients of three consecutive terms in the expansion of $(1+x)^n$ are 165, 330 and 462. What is the value of n?

(a) 10   (b) 11   (c) 12   (d) 13

Solution: (b)

The given information can be presented as

$$\binom{n}{k} = 165, \quad \binom{n}{k+1} = 330, \quad \binom{n}{k+2} = 462$$

From the first two equations

$$\binom{n}{k+1} \Big/ \binom{n}{k} = 2 \implies \frac{n-k}{k+1} = 2 \implies n = 3k+2$$

Similarly, from the last two equations, we get

$$\binom{n}{k+2} \Big/ \binom{n}{k+1} = \frac{14}{10} \implies \frac{n-k-1}{k+2} = \frac{7}{5} \implies 5n = 12k+19$$

Solving the above two equations, it is easy to argue that $n = 11$.

4. There are 14 intermediate stations between stations A and B. If a train is to be arranged from A to B, such that it stops at exactly 5 stations (including A and B), no two of which are consecutive, in how many ways can the route be designed?

(a) $\binom{14}{3}$ (b) $\binom{14}{3} - \binom{14}{2} + \binom{14}{1}$ (c) $\binom{12}{7}$ (d) $\binom{10}{3}$

Solution: (d)

Let us number the stations as $1, 2, \ldots, 16$, where 1 and 16 indicate A and B, respectively. Let the number of the stations be $1 = x_1 < x_2 < x_3 < x_4 < x_5 = 16$. Then, the given restrictions suggest that

$$y_1 = x_2 - x_1 > 1, y_2 = x_3 - x_2 > 1, y_3 = x_4 - x_3 > 1, y_4 = x_5 - x_4 > 1$$

Further, we know that $y_1 + y_2 + y_3 + y_4 = 15$. Clearly, the required answer is the same as the number of non-negative integer solutions to the equation $z_1 + z_2 + z_3 + z_4 = 7$. It is equal to $\binom{10}{7}$, that is, option (d).

5. The number of ways in which three balls numbered 1, 2, 3 can be placed in three boxes labelled A, B, C, such that at most one box is empty is

(a) 6   (b) 18   (c) 24   (d) 42

Solution: (c)

We can consider two cases. First, if no box is left empty, then the total number of ways is obviously $3! = 6$. Second, if exactly one box is empty, then it can be chosen in three ways. For each such choice, the remaining two balls can be put into the other two boxes in $2\binom{3}{2} = 6$ ways. Thus, the required answer is $6 + 3 \times 6 = 24$.

6. If the constant term in the expansion of $(\sqrt{x} - k/x^2)^{10}$ is 405, then k is

(a) $\pm 3^{1/4}$ (b) ± 2 (c) $\pm 4^{1/3}$ (d) ± 3

Solution: (d)

The $(r+1)$th term in the expansion of $(\sqrt{x} - k/x^2)^{10}$ is of the form

$$\binom{10}{r}(\sqrt{x})^r \left(-\frac{k}{x^2}\right)^{10-r} = \binom{10}{r}(-k)^{10-r} x^{r/2 - 20 + 2r},$$

which implies that the constant term is obtained for $5r/2 = 20$, that is, for $r = 8$. Thus

$$\binom{10}{8}(-k)^{10-8} = 405 \implies \left(\frac{10 \times 9}{2}\right) k^2 = 405 \implies k = \pm 3$$

7. The expression

$$1 + \frac{1}{2}\binom{n}{1} + \frac{1}{3}\binom{n}{2} + \ldots + \frac{1}{n}\binom{n}{n-1}$$

is equal to

Combinatorics

(a) $\dfrac{2^{n+1}-1}{n+1}$ (b) $\dfrac{2(2^n-1)}{n+1}$ (c) $\dfrac{2(2^{n+1}-1)}{n+1}$ (d) $\dfrac{2^n-1}{n}$

Solution: (b)

We can write the rth term of the given expression as

$$\frac{1}{r}\binom{n}{r-1} = \frac{n!}{r \times (r-1)!(n-r+1)!} = \left(\frac{1}{n+1}\right)\frac{(n+1)!}{r!(n-r+1)!} = \frac{1}{n+1}\binom{n+1}{r}$$

Since

$$\sum_{r=1}^{n}\binom{n+1}{r} = 2^{n+1} - \binom{n+1}{0} - \binom{n+1}{n+1},$$

we obtain the answer as (b).

8. Let n be an odd integer. In some field, n gunmen are placed so that all pairwise distances between them are different. At a signal, every gunman takes out his gun and shoots the person closest to him. Then,

(a) all the gunmen must be shot;
(b) at least one gunman must survive;
(c) at least two gunmen must survive;
(d) none of the above statements hold.

Solution: (b)

For $n = 1$, we know that one gunman survives. Then, we can use inductive arguments. It is easy to see that the two gunmen closest to each other would shoot each other. If any of them is shot by at least one other person, then by the pigeonhole principle, (b) holds. Assume that it is not true. Then, we can remove these two gunmen from the group and proceed in a similar way. In the worst possible scenario, it will lead to only one gunman remaining in the field who must survive.

Note that if n is even, then the gunmen can be placed in a pairwise manner so that each pair only shoots each other.

9. In how many ways can three distinct numbers be chosen from the set $\{1, 2, \ldots, 2022\}$ such that the numbers are in an arithmetic progression?

(a) $2\binom{1011}{2}$ (b) $2\binom{2022}{3}$ (c) $\binom{1011}{3}$ (d) $\binom{2022}{2}$

Solution: (a)

If the three numbers chosen are written as $x-d, x, x+d$, then we can see that it is equivalent to choosing two numbers $x-d$ and $x+d$ such that both have the same parity (that is, both even or both odd). Since there are exactly 1011 odd numbers and 1011 even numbers, the total number of possible ways to satisfy the given condition is $2\binom{1011}{2}$.

10. A box contains 100 red cards numbered $1, 2, \ldots, 100$ and 100 black cards numbered $1, 2, \ldots, 100$. In how many ways can we choose 100 cards from the box such that there are exactly 10 *matches*, where a *match* means a red card and a black card with the same number?

(a) $\binom{100}{10}\binom{90}{80}$ (b) $\binom{100}{10} 2^{90}$ (c) $\binom{100}{10}\binom{90}{80} 2^{80}$ (d) $\binom{100}{10} 2^{80}$

Solution: (c)

Since 100 cards are chosen in total with exactly 10 matches, we can argue that there are exactly 10 numbers, each with two cards from the two colours; and 80 other numbers, each with one card from either red or black. Thus, the required answer is

$$\binom{100}{10}\binom{90}{80} 2^{80}$$

Exercises

1. How many positive integers ≤ 6300 are there that are not divisible by 3, 5 or 7?

2. Consider the set $S = \{(i,j) : i, j \in \mathbb{Z}, 0 \leq i, j \leq 24\}$. How many squares with sides parallel to the axes in the regular xy-plane can be formed such that the vertices are elements of S?

3. In a class of 100 students, let A_i denote the number of friends of the ith student and let C_i denote the number of students with more than i friends. Prove the following identity:
$$\sum_{i=1}^{100} A_i = \sum_{i=0}^{99} C_i.$$

4. In how many ways can 7 different gifts be presented to 3 children so that each child receives at least one gift?

5. Consider two sets A and B. We call f a function from A into B if for every $x \in A$, there is a unique $y \in B$ such $f(x) = y$. Further, f from A into B is called an onto function if for every $y \in B$, there exists $x \in A$, such that $f(x) = y$. Find the number of onto functions from $A = \{1, 2, \ldots, n\}$ into $B = \{1, 2, 3\}$.

6. Let A and B be subsets of the xy-plane. We call them equivalent if there is a function $f : A \to B$ that is both one-to-one and onto.

   (a) Prove that any two line segments are equivalent.

   (b) Prove that any two circles are equivalent as well.

7. In how many ways can you select three numbers from $\{1, 2, \cdots, 4n\}$, such that the sum of the numbers is divisible by 4?

8. Consider a round-robin tournament among k teams, where each team plays against all the other teams exactly once and no game ends in a draw. Let the number of wins and losses for the ith team be w_i and l_i, respectively. Prove that
$$\sum_{i=1}^{k} l_i^2 = \sum_{i=1}^{k} w_i^2.$$

9. How many rational numbers m/n are there such that $\gcd(m,n) = 1$, $m < n$ and $mn = 25!$?

10. Let $S = \{1, 2, \ldots, n\}$ and let $\{A, B\}$ be subsets of S. How many unordered pairs of $\{A, B\}$ are there such that A and B are disjoint?

11. An ant starts moving on the integer coordinates of the xy-plane in such a way that each move is a diagonal step, that is, a step consists of one unit to the right or left followed by one unit either up or down.

(a) Describe the points (p,q) the ant can reach from the origin.

(b) Find the minimum number of moves the ant needs to reach a point (p,q).

12. In how many ways can you colour the faces of a cube using six different colours?

13. (a) In how many ways can you distribute m identical objects in k boxes marked $1, 2, \ldots, k$, so that no box goes empty?

    (b) Consider an arrangement of m identical H and n identical T. We call an uninterrupted sequence of one kind of symbol a 'run'. For instance, the arrangement $HHTTHTH$ has an H-run of length 2, followed by a T-run of length 2, followed by three runs of length 1 of H, T, H, respectively. Using the previous part or otherwise, find the number of arrangements of m identical H and n identical T, such that there are exactly k number of H-runs.

14. Consider the following phenomena. Assume that at time 0, a particle is at 0 on the real line. At time 1, it breaks into two particles and instantaneously after division, one particle moves 1 unit to the left and the other moves 1 unit to the right. Similarly, at every time-step, each of the existing particles divides into two, and one of the two new particles moves 1 unit to the left and the other moves 1 unit to the right. Also assume that when two particles meet, they destroy each other, leaving nothing behind. Find the remaining number of particles if the phenomena continues for $2^{11} + 1$ time-steps.

15. Fill the squares of an 8×8 chessboard with the numbers 1 to 64 in the following way: numbers 1 to 8 are written on the topmost row from left to right, 9 to 16 are written on the second row from left to right, ..., 57 to 64 are written on the bottom row from left to right. If you are asked to add up the numbers from 8 squares such that there is exactly one from each row and exactly one from each column, prove that you will always get the sum 260.

16. Let $a_1, a_2, \ldots, a_7 \in \mathbb{R}$, not necessarily distinct, such that $1 < a_i < 13$ for all i. Prove that it is always possible to choose three of them such that they are the lengths of the sides of a triangle.

17. For the set $N = \{1, 2, \ldots, n\}$, consider all r-element subsets of N, for $1 \leq r \leq n$. If $F(n, r)$ denotes the arithmetic mean of the smallest elements of these subsets, show that
$$F(n,r) = \frac{n+1}{r+1}.$$

18. Suppose there are 100 people and exactly 100 seats numbered from 1 to 100. The people are seated in the following way. The first person can choose any seat. The nth person, for $n = 2, 3, \ldots, 100$, must sit on the seat numbered n if it is unoccupied;

otherwise he can take any of the unoccupied seats. If it is found that the 100th person occupies seat number 100, in how many ways can the previous 99 seats be filled up?

19. Suppose that every point in the *xy*-plane is coloured either red or blue.

   (a) If there is no monochromatic equilateral triangle in the plane, prove that there exist three points A, B, C of the same colour such that B is the midpoint of AC.

   (b) Using the above or otherwise, prove that there must be a monochromatic equilateral triangle.

20. Consider a circular arrangement of n chairs ($n > 1$). A child decides to play around the chairs in the following way. He always moves clockwise. From the staring point, he skips 1 chair and goes to the next. Then he skips 2 chairs at once and goes to the next one. Similarly, in the third turn, he skips 3 chairs, in the forth, he skips 4 chairs, and so on. In this manner, the child keeps moving round and round the circle of chairs. If you know that the child reaches each chair at least once, prove that n must be even.

Hints

1. If A_r denotes the set of positive integers that are less than or equal to 6300 and are divisible by r, then note that $6300 - |A_3 \cup A_5 \cup A_7|$ is the required answer. Use the principle of inclusion-exclusion to find out this number.

2. Note that all squares are from a big 24×24 square. Call it D. Now, show that the number of $k \times k$ squares inside D, for $1 \leq k \leq 24$, is $(25-k)^2$. Then, the required answer is $\sum_{k=1}^{24}(25-k)^2$.

3. Without loss of generality, consider the first student and suppose $A_1 = k$. Then, that student has more than r friends for $r = 0, 1, \ldots, k-1$, and is therefore counted in each of C_0, C_1, C_2. The required result can be proved using a similar idea for all the students.

4. Each gift can be given to one of the three children, and hence, the total possible number of ways of giving these gifts to 3 children is 3^7. Next, let A_k be the set of arrangements where the kth child does not get any gift. Then, the number of arrangements in which at least one child does not get a gift is $\left|\cup_{i=1}^{3} A_i\right|$. One can use the principle of inclusion-exclusion to find the required answer from there.

5. Consider $B_S = \{1,2,3\} \setminus S$, for $S \subset B$. Then, the number of into functions from A into B_S is $(3-|S|)^n$, since every element in A can be mapped to any of the $(3-|S|)$ possible elements in B_S. Use this result and the principle of inclusion-exclusion to arrive at the answer $3(3^{n-1} - 2^n + 1)$.

6. For the first part, define a function f that maps a point A on the first line segment to a point B on the second line segment such that both points divide the corresponding line segments in the same ratio. Show that this function is a bijection. For the second part, first show that translating a circle to another location is a bijection. Then, consider two concentric circles and draw a common radius for them to argue that there exists a bijection between two concentric circles. Now, combine these two results to prove the required equivalence.

7. Consider a partition of the set $\{1, 2, \cdots, 4n\}$ into four residue classes, based on congruent modulo 4. Then, one can argue the cases in which the sum of the three selected numbers is divisible by 4. Calculating the corresponding number of possible ways leads to the final answer $\binom{n}{3} + 3\binom{n}{1}\binom{n}{2} + n^3$.

8. Since no game ends in a draw, $l_i + w_i$ must be equal to $k - 1$ for every $i = 1, 2, \ldots, k$, thereby implying that $l_i^2 - w_i^2 = (k-1)(l_i - w_i)$. Now, $\sum_{i=1}^{k} l_i$ denotes the total number of losses by all the teams. Hence, it is equal to the total number of games played. The same thing holds for $\sum_{i=1}^{k} w_i$. These results together imply that $\sum_{i=1}^{k} l_i^2 = \sum_{i=1}^{k} w_i^2$.

9. Write the prime factorization of $mn = 25!$. Since m, n are relatively prime, they cannot have any common prime factor. Use that to compute the number of ways in which the prime divisors (along with the corresponding exponents) of mn can be distributed between m and n so that $m < n$.

10. Each element of S can be in A or in B or in neither. Also, $\{A, B\}$ and $\{B, A\}$ are the same unordered pairs. Thus, the total number of disjoint unordered pairs, keeping $\{\phi, \phi\}$ in mind, is $(3^n + 1)/2$.

11. Four types of moves are allowed: (1) Up and right, (2) Up and left, (3) Down and right, (4) Down and left. Suppose one takes a, b, c and d steps of these four types, respectively, to reach (p, q) from $(0, 0)$. Then, $p = a - b + c - d, q = a + b - c - d$, implying that p and q must be of the same parity. That it is a sufficient condition can be proved by showing that integers a, b, c, d exist, which satisfy the conditions $p = a - b + c - d, q = a + b - c - d$. For the second part, we need to minimize $a + b + c + d$, subject to the restrictions $a - d = (p+q)/2, b - c = (q-p)/2$. One can then argue that the minimum number of steps needed to reach (p, q) from the origin is $(|p+q| + |p-q|)/2$.

12. While colouring the six sides one by one, at first, we can colour any side with the first colour. Next, consider two different cases. First, suppose we use colour 2 on a side adjacent to colour 1. One can argue that number of possible colourings in this case is 4!. Second, if we use colour 2 on the opposite side of colour 1, then four colours need to be arranged in a circular fashion, and that can be done in 3! ways. Hence, in

total there are 30 possible ways.

13. The first part is a straightforward application of Proposition 2.3. For the second part, note that there are k number of H-runs (length of each run is positive) and $(k+1)$ number of T-runs (lengths of the first and last runs are non-negative, length of every other run is positive). This leads to two equations. First, $t_1 + t_2 + \ldots + t_{k+1} = n$, where $t_1 \geqslant 0, t_2, t_3, \ldots, t_k \geqslant 1, t_{k+1} \geqslant 0$. Second, $h_1 + \ldots + h_k = m$, where each h_i is a positive integer. We can now apply the result from the first part to find out the possible arrangements of such runs.

14. Let us code the existence of particles along the real line in a sequence with 1 denoting the presence of a particle, 0 denoting the absence, and origin being in the middle. Then, observe how the sequence of 1 and 0 evolves in time. Using the principles of mathematical induction, one can prove that at $n = 2^k$, there are only two 1s $2^{k+1} - 1$ distance apart. Clearly, it is easy to see that there will be 4 particles after time $2^{11} + 1$.

15. Note that the number in the (i, j)th square is $8(i-1) + j$ for $i = 1, 2, \ldots, 8; j = 1, 2, \ldots, 8$. Since we choose 8 squares such that there is exactly one from each row and exactly one from each column, we choose the numbers $8(i-1) + j$ for all possible values of i and j in some order.

16. Assume that c and d are the two smallest elements among $a_1, a_2, \ldots, a_7$. If the numbers do not have the triangle property, then the largest must be at least $5c + 8d$. However, that leads to a contradiction since all numbers are less than 13.

17. The sum of the smallest elements of the r-element subsets of the given n-element set is $\binom{n}{r} F(n, r)$. We have to prove that $F(n, r) = (n+1)/(r+1)$, which is equivalent to saying that the sum of the smallest elements of the r-element subsets of the n-element set is $\binom{n+1}{r+1}$. Keeping that in mind, define a mapping from $\{0, 1, 2, 3, \ldots, n\}$ to $\{1, 2, \ldots, n\}$ as follows. Consider an $(r+1)$-element subset of $\{0, 1, 2, 3, \ldots, n\}$, and map it to the r-element subset of $\{1, 2, \ldots, n\}$ by removing the smallest number from it. One can prove that this mapping is onto. Then, find the pre-images of a subset of $\{0, 1, 2, 3, \ldots, n\}$ under this mapping and use that to argue why $F(n, r) = (n+1)/(r+1)$.

18. If the first person sits on the seat numbered 1, everyone sits at their intended place and that is one possible arrangement. Next, if the first person sits at $k_1 \neq 1$, one can find a sequence $2 \leqslant k_1 < k_2 < \ldots k_r \leqslant 99$, which corresponds to one possible seating arrangement. Thus, the total number of seating arrangements where the first person does not sit on the first seat is equal to the number of subsets of the set $\{2, 3, \ldots, 99\}$, which is equal to 2^{98}. Thus, the required answer is $2^{98} + 1$.

19. Consider an equilateral triangle PQR. Without loss of generality, assume that P and Q are blue. Now, reflect R on PQ and name this point T. By construction, PQT is also an equilateral triangle. If there is no monochromatic equilateral triangle, then both R and T must be red. Now, consider the midpoint of PQ and argue why there must exist three points A, B and C of the same colour such that B is the midpoint of AC. For the second part, suppose there is no equilateral triangle with all vertices of the same colour. Then, there are A, B, C of the same colour such that B is the midpoint of AC. Now, construct an equilateral triangle ACD. Let the midpoints of AD and CD be E and F, respectively. Then, AEB, BCF and DEF are all equilateral. Use this to prove that there must exist an equilateral triangle with all the vertices of the same colour.

20. Suppose n is odd. Following the way the child moves, it can be shown that at the rth step, the child is at the chair numbered $(1+2+\ldots+r) \pmod{n}$. Consider remainders 0 and n to be equivalent. Consequently, at the $(n-1)$th step, since n is odd, the child must be in the nth chair. Continuing, in the next step, he comes back to the same chair, and thereafter, he retraces his path. Thus, the child's path consists of the chairs he has been at in the first $(n-1)$ steps. Applying the Pigeonhole Principle, one can easily argue that it is impossible to reach each chair at least once.

3
Algebra

"Algebra is the metaphysics of arithmetic."

–John Ray

This chapter is dedicated to some crucial concepts that are instrumental in any field of mathematics. Algebra is the unifying thread that ties almost all of mathematics together. One can define algebra as the study of mathematical symbols and the rules for manipulating these symbols. It is one of the most general sections of mathematics and includes a plethora of topics that are essential for any study of mathematics, science, engineering, economics or medicine.

Our discussions and the problems in this chapter will be limited to elementary algebra and linear algebra, while advanced topics like abstract or modern algebra may be of interest to students pursuing mathematics at a higher level.

KEY RESULTS

Throughout this chapter, the following notations are used:
$\mathbb{N}$ = the set of natural numbers $\qquad$ $\mathbb{Z}$ = the set of integers
$\mathbb{R}$ = the set of real numbers $\qquad$ $\mathbb{Q}$ = the set of rational numbers
$\mathbb{C}$ = the set of complex numbers

Definition 3.1 (Complex Number): A complex number is an expression of the form $z = a + \iota b$, where a, b are real numbers and $\iota = \sqrt{-1}$. The real number $\sqrt{a^2 + b^2}$ is known as the modulus of the complex number while a value of $\theta \in (-\pi, \pi]$ that satisfies $\tan \theta = b/a$ is known as the amplitude or argument of z. The modulus and argument are commonly denoted as $|z|$ and $arg(z)$, respectively.

Complex numbers can be geometrically treated and interpreted as well. In the xy-plane, $z = a + \iota b$ can be represented by the point (a, b). In that case, $|z|$ is the distance from the origin, and the amplitude is the angle the point makes at the origin along the positive x-axis. These concepts and related problems will be discussed at length in Chapter 6. Here, two particularly important definitions and results are mentioned below.

Definition 3.2 (Conjugacy): The conjugate of a complex number $z = a + \iota b$ is given by $\bar{z} = a - \iota b$.

It is evident that the conjugate of a complex number is obtained by reflecting it around the x-axis. One can also argue that the modulus of z is equal to that of $\bar{z}$, whereas the arguments are equal in magnitude but opposite in sign.

> **Useful Tip:** One of the most crucial identities to remember in the context of complex numbers is that $|z|^2 = z\bar{z}$.

Definition 3.3 (Polar Form): Any complex number can be written as $z = r(\cos\theta + \iota\sin\theta)$, where r is the modulus and θ is the amplitude. Conventionally, $\cos\theta + \iota\sin\theta$ is denoted as $e^{\iota\theta}$.

Theorem 3.1 (De Moivre's Theorem): For any integer n,

$$(\cos\theta + \iota\sin\theta)^n = \cos(n\theta) + \iota\sin(n\theta)$$

> **Useful Tip:** The proof of the above theorem can be obtained using the principles of mathematical induction, and it is left to the reader as an exercise. Remember that, geometrically, any complex number of the form $e^{\iota\phi}$ represents a point on the unit circle centred at the origin.

Definition 3.4 (Polynomial): A polynomial is a function in one (or more) variable(s) that consists of a sum of variables raised to non-negative, integral powers and multiplied by real (or complex) coefficients. In general, for $x \in \mathbb{C}$, a polynomial of degree k is of the form $P(x) = a_k x^k + a_{k-1} x^{k-1} + \ldots + a_1 x + a_0$, where $a_i \in \mathbb{R}$ (or $\mathbb{C}$) and $a_k \neq 0$. If $a_k = 1$, it is known as a monic polynomial.

Definition 3.5 (Root of a Polynomial): For a polynomial $P(x)$, if x satisfies $P(x) = 0$, it is called a root. A polynomial of degree k has exactly k number of roots, real or complex.

Theorem 3.2 (Division Algorithm for Polynomials): Let $P(x)$ be a n-degree polynomial and $G(x)$ be a k-degree polynomial (typically, $k \leq n$), both with coefficients in $\mathbb{R}$ (true for $\mathbb{Q}$ or $\mathbb{C}$ as well). Then, there exist unique polynomials $Q(x)$ and $R(x)$, both with coefficients in $\mathbb{R}$, such that the degree of $R(x)$ is strictly less than k, and

$$P(x) = Q(x)G(x) + R(x)$$

The above theorem is in the same spirit as the Division Algorithm studied in Chapter 1. In particular, $Q(x)$ and $R(x)$ are known as the quotient polynomial and the remainder polynomial, respectively. Further, if $R(x)$ is identically equal to 0, then $G(x)$ is called a factor of $P(x)$. The following results flow from the Division Algorithm.

Theorem 3.3 (Remainder Theorem): If $P(x)$ is a polynomial with real coefficients, then $P(a)$ is the remainder when $P(x)$ is divided by $(x-a)$.

Theorem 3.4 (Fundamental Theorem of Algebra): Let $P(x)$ be a polynomial of degree k, with leading coefficient a_k. If $x_1, x_2, \ldots, x_k$ are the roots (not necessarily distinct) of the polynomial, then

$$P(x) = a_k(x-x_1)(x-x_2)\ldots(x-x_k)$$

The above theorem implies the following important results for $P(x) = a_k x^k + a_{k-1} x^{k-1} + \ldots + a_1 x + a_0$.

- The sum of the roots is $-a_{k-1}/a_k$.
- The product of the roots is $(-1)^k a_0/a_k$.
- In general, if we consider all the terms of the form $x_1 \ldots x_r$ (product of r number of roots), where x_is are the roots of the polynomial, then the sum of these terms is given by $(-1)^r a_{k-r}/a_k$.
- If there is a rational root p/q with $(p,q) = 1$, then p is a divisor of a_0 and q is a divisor of a_k. This is also known as the *rational root theorem*.
- If the coefficients $a_0, a_1, \ldots, a_k$ are real, then the complex roots would always occur in conjugate pairs; that is, $(a+\imath b)$ would be a root of $P(x)$ if and only if $(a-\imath b)$ is a root as well.

A 2-degree polynomial is commonly known as a quadratic equation. The two roots of the quadratic equation can be obtained by using the following result.

Theorem 3.5 (Sridhar Acharya's Formula): For a quadratic equation of the form $ax^2 + bx + c = 0$, the two solutions are given by

$$x = \frac{-b \pm \sqrt{b^2 - 4ac}}{2a}$$

A few properties of the roots of a quadratic equation $ax^2 + bx + c = 0$ are as follows.

- The sum of the roots is $-b/a$.
- The product of the roots is c/a.
- If the coefficients are real numbers, then the equation has real roots if and only if $b^2 - 4ac \geqslant 0$. This is known as the discriminant of the equation.

Theorem 3.6 (Cube Roots of Unity): The polynomial $x^3 = 1$ has three solutions, and these solutions are known as the cube roots of unity. Following the results mentioned above, one can show that the solutions are 1 and $(-1 \pm \iota\sqrt{3})/2$. Another common way to write this is to use the symbols $1, \omega, \omega^2$, where ω denotes any of the complex roots of the equation.

> **Useful Tip:** Note that ω can be written in the form of $e^{\iota\theta}$, which allows efficient calculation by virtue of De Moivre's Theorem. The reader is further encouraged to read about the nth roots of unity, a generalization of the above result, and make the connection to the polar forms of complex numbers.

We now turn our attention to various inequalities that are essential in algebraic problems. Basic notions of inequalities are assumed to be known to the reader and are omitted here.

Theorem 3.7 (Triangle Inequality): For any two numbers x, y, real or complex,

$$|x| - |y| \leqslant |x+y| \leqslant |x| + |y|$$

Definition 3.6 (Progression): In mathematics, a progression is a sequence that advances in a logical and predictable pattern. Three types of progression are popular in this level. The sequence $(x_n), n \in \mathbb{N}$, is said to be in arithmetic progression if $x_{n+1} - x_n$ is constant for all n. It is in geometric progression if x_{n+1}/x_n (with $x_n \neq 0$) is constant for all n. Finally, the sequence $(x_n), n \in \mathbb{N}$, is in harmonic progression if $(1/x_n), n \in \mathbb{N}$, is in an arithmetic progression.

Theorem 3.8 (AM-GM-HM Inequality): In connection to the progressions mentioned above, for n real numbers $x_1, x_2, \ldots, x_n$, the arithmetic mean (AM), geometric mean (GM) and harmonic mean (HM) are defined as

$$\text{AM} = \frac{1}{n}\sum_{i=1}^{n} x_i, \quad \text{GM} = \left(\prod_{i=1}^{n} x_i\right)^{1/n}, \quad \text{HM} = \left(\frac{1}{n}\sum_{i=1}^{n} \frac{1}{x_i}\right)^{-1}$$

It can be shown that for any set of positive real numbers, if all of the above means are defined, then $\text{AM} \geqslant \text{GM} \geqslant \text{HM}$. Equality holds if and only if all the numbers are equal.

Theorem 3.9 (Cauchy–Schwarz Inequality): Consider two sets of real numbers (a_i) and (b_i), $1 \leqslant i \leqslant n$. Then,

$$\left(\sum_{i=1}^{n} a_i^2\right)\left(\sum_{i=1}^{n} b_i^2\right) \geqslant \left(\sum_{i=1}^{n} a_i b_i\right)^2,$$

where equality holds if a_i/b_i is constant for all i.

Algebra

Theorem 3.10 (Chebycheff's Inequality): Consider two sets of non-negative real numbers (a_i) and (b_i), $1 \leqslant i \leqslant n$ such that $a_1 \geqslant \ldots \geqslant a_n$ and $b_1 \geqslant \ldots \geqslant b_n$. Then,

$$\left(\frac{a_1+\ldots+a_n}{n}\right)\left(\frac{b_1+\ldots+b_n}{n}\right) \leqslant \left(\frac{a_1 b_1+\ldots+a_n b_n}{n}\right),$$

where equality holds if and only if either all a_is are equal or all b_is are equal.

> **Useful Tip:** One can consider r number of non-decreasing sequences of non-negative real numbers ($r \geqslant 3$) and apply Chebycheff's inequality multiple times to obtain a generalized version.

A few interesting results can be derived from the above inequalities. For example, the root mean square (RMS) of a_is, which is defined as

$$\text{RMS} = \sqrt{\frac{a_1^2+\ldots+a_n^2}{n}},$$

can be shown to be always greater than or equal to the AM. One may prove this by Chebycheff's inequality or by the Cauchy–Schwarz inequality.

Theorem 3.11 (Rearrangement Inequality): Consider two sets of real numbers (a_i) and (b_i), $1 \leqslant i \leqslant n$ such that $a_1 \leqslant \ldots \leqslant a_n$ and $b_1 \leqslant \ldots \leqslant b_n$. Let $a'_1, \ldots, a'_n$ be a permutation of the a_is. Then,

$$a_1 b_n + a_2 b_{n-1} + \ldots + a_n b_1 \leqslant a'_1 b_1 + a'_2 b_2 + \ldots a'_n b_n,$$
$$a_1 b_1 + a_2 b_2 + \ldots + a_n b_n \geqslant a'_1 b_1 + a'_2 b_2 + \ldots a'_n b_n$$

In other words, the sum $\sum a_i b_i$ is maximum when the sequences are similarly ordered and it is minimum when they are oppositely ordered.

Solved Examples

1. A container has x gallons of milk and another has y gallons of water. From each container, z gallons are taken out and transferred to the other. Next, z gallons are again taken out from the resulting mixture in each container, and transferred to the other. Following the second transfer, if the quantity of milk in each container remains the same as it was after the first transfer, show that $z(x+y) = xy$.

Solution: After the first transfer, the first container contains a mixture of $(x-z)$ gallons of milk and z gallons of water and the second container contains a mixture of z gallons of milk and $(y-z)$ gallons of water.

Now, z gallons are taken from the mixture in the first container. Since the ratio of milk to water is $(x-z):z$, the volume of milk taken out is $\frac{z(x-z)}{x}$. Similarly, when z gallons are taken from the mixture in the second container (where the ratio of milk to water is $z:(y-z)$), the milk taken out is $\frac{z^2}{y}$.

So, after the second transfer, the milk content in the first container is $x - \frac{z(x-z)}{x} + \frac{z^2}{y}$ and the same in the second container is $z - \frac{z^2}{y} + \frac{z(x-z)}{x}$.

According to the condition provided, the amount of milk remains the same as it was after the first transfer. Hence,

$$\frac{z(x-z)}{x} = \frac{z^2}{y} \implies \frac{(x-z)}{x} = \frac{z}{y}$$

The above can then be easily simplified to obtain $z(x+y) = xy$.

2. Suppose,

$$x_n = \frac{1}{2} \cdot \frac{3}{4} \cdot \frac{5}{6} \cdots \frac{2n-1}{2n}$$

Prove that

$$x_n \leqslant \frac{1}{\sqrt{3n+1}}, \quad \text{for all} \quad n = 1, 2, 3, \ldots$$

Solution: We can use the principles of mathematical induction to arrive at the result. First of all, for $n = 1$,

$$x_1 = \frac{1}{2} \leqslant \frac{1}{\sqrt{3+1}} = \frac{1}{\sqrt{3n+1}}$$

Let us assume that the result is true for all $n \leqslant k$. We have to prove the result for $n = k+1$, that is, we have to show that

$$x_{k+1} = x_k \cdot \frac{2k+1}{2k+2} \leqslant \frac{1}{\sqrt{3k+1}} \cdot \frac{2k+1}{2k+2}$$

So, it is enough to prove that the above quantity is less than $1/\sqrt{3(k+1)+1}$. Since k is a positive integer, it will be true if and only if

$$\frac{2k+1}{2k+2} \leqslant \frac{3k+1}{\sqrt{3k+4}},$$

which is equivalent to $(2k+1)^2(3k+4) \leqslant 4(k+1)^2(3k+1)$. One can simplify the above inequality to say that the required result is true if and only if

$$12k^3 + 28k^2 + 19k + 4 \leqslant 12k^3 + 28k^2 + 20k + 4,$$

Algebra

which is trivially true since k is a positive integer. Thus, using mathematical induction, we can say that the result is true for all $n = 1, 2, 3, \ldots$.

> **Useful Tip:** Though this is an inequality exercise, note that the required result is an expression in $n \in \mathbb{N}$. In such problems, often the easiest trick is to apply the principles of mathematical induction.

3. (a) Find m such that the polynomial
$$x^4 - (3m+2)x^2 + m^2 = 0$$
has four real roots which are in arithmetic progression.

   (b) Let $a, b \in \mathbb{R}$. If the absolute values of the roots of the equation
$$x^2 - ax - b = 0$$
are less than one, show that $|b| < 1$, $a + b < 1$ and $b - a < 1$.

Solution:

(a) Suppose the roots are $a - 3d, a - d, a + d, a + 3d$ for some a and d (since they are in arithmetic progression, we can write them in this form). From the equation, we can see that the sum of the roots is 0, as the coefficient of x^3 is 0. Thus, $a = 0$ (sum of the roots is $4a$). Next, the product of the roots is $(-3d)(-d)(d)(3d) = 9d^4$ and we obtain $m^2 = 9d^4$. Further, if we consider the sum of the roots taken two at a time, we get
$$-(3m+2) = (-3d)(-d) + (-3d)(d) + (-3d)(3d) + (-d)(d) + (-d)(3d) + (d)(3d),$$
which gives us the equality $3m + 2 = 10d^2$. Thus, $m^2/9 = (3m+2)^2/100$, leading to the equation
$$100m^2 = 9(9m^2 + 12m + 4) \implies 19m^2 - 108m - 36 = 0$$
A direct application of Sridhar Acharya's formula then gives us the solutions $m = 6, -6/19$.

(b) Suppose the roots are α, β. Then, $|\alpha|, |\beta| < 1$, that is, $-1 < \alpha, \beta < 1$. Now, using the properties of quadratic equations, $\alpha + \beta = a$, $\alpha\beta = -b$. Since both the roots have absolute values less than 1, their product will also have an absolute value less than 1, and thus, $|b| < 1$.

Next, note that $1 - a - b = 1 - \alpha - \beta + \alpha\beta = (1-\alpha)(1-\beta)$. Because of the assumption, both these factors are positive, and hence, the product is positive as well, giving us $a + b < 1$.

Finally, for the last part, similar to the above, we write $1 + a - b = 1 + \alpha + \beta + \alpha\beta = (1+\alpha)(1+\beta)$. Once again, this product is positive since both roots are greater than -1 and we get $b - a < 1$.

4. A line of students is 5 metres long. As the students start walking, Jon who is at the end of the file steps out and starts marching forward at a higher speed. After reaching the head of the column, he immediately turns around and marches back at the same speed. As soon as he reaches the end of the file, everyone stops walking, and it is found that the line has moved by exactly 5 metres. What distance has Jon travelled?

Solution: Let us suppose that Jon moves with velocity v units (metres per second, say) and the line moves with velocity u units. Now, when Jon marches forward, the relative speed with respect to the others is $(v - u)$ units and he has travelled 5 metres with respect to the main line. So, the time taken to reach the beginning of the line is $5/(v - u)$ seconds.

Similarly, when Jon marches back, the relative velocity with respect to the main line is $(v + u)$ units as they are moving in opposite directions. Thus, the time taken by him to reach the end of the line is $5/(v+u)$ seconds.

In this total time, the main line moves 5 metres, and hence, the total time is $5/u$ seconds. One can then obtain the equality

$$\frac{5}{(v-u)} + \frac{5}{(v+u)} = \frac{5}{u}$$

Simplifying the above equation, we arrive at

$$\left(\frac{v}{u}\right)^2 - 2\left(\frac{v}{u}\right) - 1 = 0 \implies \frac{v}{u} = (1+\sqrt{2}),$$

taking the positive root of the quadratic equation. Hence, if with velocity u, the line has covered 5 metres, then with velocity v in the same time, Jon has covered $5(1+\sqrt{2})$ metres.

5. Show that

$$\binom{n}{0} + \binom{n}{3} + \binom{n}{6} + \ldots + \binom{n}{3k} \leq \frac{1}{3}(2^n + 2),$$

where n is a positive integer and k is the largest integer such that $3k \leq n$.

Solution: We use Binomial Theorem to prove the result. In the binomial expansion of $(1+x)^n$, using $1, \omega$ and ω^2 in place of x (where ω is an imaginary cube root of unity), we get

$$(1+1)^n = \binom{n}{0} + \binom{n}{1} + \binom{n}{2} + \binom{n}{3} + \binom{n}{4} + \ldots + \binom{n}{n},$$

Algebra

$$(1+\omega)^n = \binom{n}{0} + \binom{n}{1}\omega + \binom{n}{2}\omega^2 + \binom{n}{3}\omega^3 + \binom{n}{4}\omega^4 + \ldots + \binom{n}{n}\omega^n,$$

$$(1+\omega^2)^n = \binom{n}{0} + \binom{n}{1}\omega^2 + \binom{n}{2}\omega^4 + \binom{n}{3}\omega^6 + \binom{n}{4}\omega^8 + \ldots + \binom{n}{n}\omega^{2n}$$

Now, recall that if ω is an imaginary cube root of unity, then $\omega^3 = 1$ and $1 + \omega + \omega^2 = 0$. Adding the above three equations and using these two relations, one can write

$$2^n + (-\omega^2)^n + (-\omega)^n = 3\left[\binom{n}{0} + \binom{n}{3} + \binom{n}{6} + \ldots + \binom{n}{3k}\right],$$

where k is the largest integer for which $3k \leq n$. Now, for any n not divisible by 3, $(-\omega^2)^n + (-\omega)^n = (-1)^n(\omega + \omega^2) = (-1)^{n+1}$, and if n is divisible by 3, $(-\omega^2)^n + (-\omega)^n = 2$. So, for any n, we can say that $(-\omega^2)^n + (-\omega)^n \leq 2$. Hence, combining all these, we get our required result

$$\binom{n}{0} + \binom{n}{3} + \binom{n}{6} + \ldots + \binom{n}{3k} \leq \frac{1}{3}(2^n + 2)$$

> **Useful Tip:** Applying the concepts of complex numbers, especially the cube roots of unity, is a trick to remember for problems related to binomial expansions. See the following problem for another such example.

6. Calculate the value of

$$\sum_{k=0}^{3n-1} (-1)^k \binom{6n}{2k+1} 3^k.$$

Solution: Note that the given expression (hereafter denoted as S_n) can be written as

$$S_n = \sum_{k=0}^{3n-1} \binom{6n}{2k+1} (\iota\sqrt{3})^{2k} = \frac{1}{\iota\sqrt{3}} \sum_{k=0}^{3n-1} \binom{6n}{2k+1} (\iota\sqrt{3})^{2k+1}$$

Recall the binomial expansion of $(1+x)^m$, and note that the above summation is essentially the sum of the odd terms for the binomial expansion of $(1+\iota\sqrt{3})^{6n}$. Further, observe that the even terms in the same expansion are real numbers while the odd terms are imaginary numbers. Let $\text{Im}(z)$ and $\text{Re}(z)$ be used to denote the imaginary and real parts of a complex number z. Then,

$$S_n = \frac{1}{\iota\sqrt{3}} \text{Im}\left[(1+\iota\sqrt{3})^{6n}\right] = \frac{2^{6n}}{\iota\sqrt{3}} \text{Im}\left[\left(\cos\frac{\pi}{3} + \iota\sin\frac{\pi}{3}\right)^{6n}\right]$$

Finally, an application of De Moivre's Theorem implies that the imaginary term of the expression inside the bracket is $\sin 2n\pi$, which is equal to 0 for all positive integers n. Hence, $S_n = 0$.

7. Prove the following identity, for $n \in \mathbb{N}$,

$$\frac{3}{1.2.4} + \frac{4}{2.3.5} + \ldots + \frac{n+2}{n(n+1)(n+3)} = \frac{1}{6}\left[\frac{29}{6} - \frac{4}{n+1} - \frac{1}{n+2} - \frac{1}{n+3}\right].$$

Solution: We express the rth term in the left-hand side of the given equation as the sum of three simpler terms. Let us assume that the rth term can be written as

$$\frac{r+2}{r(r+1)(r+3)} = \frac{A}{r} + \frac{B}{r+1} + \frac{C}{r+3}$$

The above implies that $A(r+1)(r+3) + Br(r+3) + Cr(r+1) = r+2$. Comparing the coefficients, we obtain the system of equations:

$$A + B + C = 0, \quad 4A + 3B + C = 1, \quad 3A = 2$$

Thus, $A = 2/3$, giving us $B + C = -2/3$ and $3B + C = -5/3$. We solve these equations to get $A = 2/3, B = -1/2, C = -1/6$. Then, the sum in the left-hand side (LHS) of the equation can be written and simplified as follows:

$$\begin{aligned}
\text{LHS} &= \sum_{r=1}^{n}\left[\frac{2/3}{r} - \frac{1/2}{r+1} - \frac{1/6}{r+3}\right] \\
&= \frac{2}{3}\sum_{r=1}^{n}\frac{1}{r} - \frac{1}{2}\sum_{r=2}^{n+1}\frac{1}{r} - \frac{1}{6}\sum_{r=4}^{n+3}\frac{1}{r} \\
&= \frac{2}{3}\sum_{r=1}^{3}\frac{1}{r} - \frac{1}{2}\left(\frac{1}{2} + \frac{1}{3} + \frac{1}{n+1}\right) - \frac{1}{6}\sum_{r=n+1}^{n+3}\frac{1}{r} + \sum_{r=4}^{n}\left(\frac{2}{3} - \frac{1}{2} - \frac{1}{6}\right)\frac{1}{r} \\
&= \frac{2}{3} \times \frac{11}{6} - \frac{1}{2}\left(\frac{5}{6} + \frac{1}{n+1}\right) - \frac{1}{6}\left(\frac{1}{n+1} + \frac{1}{n+2} + \frac{1}{n+3}\right) \\
&= \frac{1}{6}\left(\frac{22}{3} - \frac{5}{2}\right) - \frac{1}{6}\left(\frac{4}{n+1} + \frac{1}{n+2} + \frac{1}{n+3}\right) \\
&= \frac{1}{6}\left[\frac{29}{6} - \frac{4}{n+1} - \frac{1}{n+2} - \frac{1}{n+3}\right]
\end{aligned}$$

> **Useful Tip:** A direct algebraic proof is shown here. However, since the given equation involves only natural numbers, one can guess that mathematical induction is also a valid and convenient procedure to adopt.

8. Let $f(x)$ and $g(x)$ be two quadratic expressions with rational coefficients. If $f(x)$ and $g(x)$ have a common irrational root, prove that $g(x) = rf(x)$ for some rational number r.

Algebra

Solution: Let $f(x) = a_1 x^2 + b_1 x + c_1$ and $g(x) = a_2 x^2 + b_2 x + c_2$, where all coefficients are rational. The roots of $f(x)$ are $(-b_1 \pm \sqrt{b_1^2 - 4a_1 c_1})/2a_1$ and similarly one can find the same for $g(x)$.

Since the two polynomials have a common irrational root, $b_1/a_1 = b_2/a_2$ and

$$\frac{\sqrt{b_1^2 - 4a_1 c_1}}{a_1} = \frac{\sqrt{b_2^2 - 4a_2 c_2}}{a_2} \implies \sqrt{\frac{b_1^2}{a_1^2} - \frac{4c_1}{a_1}} = \sqrt{\frac{b_2^2}{a_2^2} - \frac{4c_2}{a_2}},$$

which further implies that $c_1/a_1 = c_2/a_2$. So,

$$f(x) = a_1\left(x^2 + \frac{b_1}{a_1}x + \frac{c_1}{a_1}\right) = a_1\left(x^2 + \frac{b_2}{a_2}x + \frac{c_2}{a_2}\right) = \frac{a_1}{a_2}(a_2 x^2 + b_2 x + c_2) = \frac{a_1}{a_2}g(x)$$

Since a_1, a_2 are rational numbers, their ratio is rational too, and hence, we get $f(x) = rg(x)$ for some rational number r.

9. Let c be a real number between 0 and 1. Show that the values taken by the function

$$f(x) = \frac{x^2 + 2x + c}{x^2 + 4x + 3c}, \text{ for } x \in \mathbb{R},$$

range over all real numbers.

Solution: Letting $y = f(x)$, the equation can be rewritten as $x^2 + 2x + c = x^2 y + 4xy + 3cy$, that is, $(1-y)x^2 + (2-4y)x + (c-3cy) = 0$. Since x is a real number, the discriminant of the equation (D, say) must be non-negative. Note that $D = (2-4y)^2 - 4(1-y)(c-3cy)$, which can be further simplified to

$$D = 4(1 - 4y + 4y^2 - c + 4cy - 3cy^2) = 4[(4-3c)y^2 + (4c-4)y + (1-c)]$$

Since $D \geqslant 0$, we can say that the above quadratic expression in y is always on or above the x-axis. This would happen only if the leading coefficient is positive and if the equation has imaginary or equal roots. Thus, the required conditions are $4 - 3c > 0$ (which is true since $c < 1$) and $(4c-4)^2 - 4(4-3c)(1-c) \leqslant 0$. The last expression can be simplified to the following:

$$(4c-4)^2 - 4(4-3c)(1-c) = 16c^2 - 32c + 16 - 16 + 28c - 12c^2 = 4c^2 - 4c$$

Since $0 < c < 1$, it is straightforward to see that the above expression is negative, and hence, we get that for all real values of y, $D \geqslant 0$. Thus, y ranges over all real numbers and the proof is complete.

10. Find the set of real numbers x for which $2\log_{2x+3} x < 1$.

Solution: First, $2\log_{2x+3} x < 1$ is defined when $x > 0, 2x+3 > 0, 2x+3 \neq 1$. Now, $x > 0$ already implies the other two conditions and also that the base is greater than 3. Hence, x should satisfy $x < (2x+3)^{1/2}$, which gives us the quadratic equation $x^2 - 2x - 3 < 0$. This is equivalent to $(x+1)(x-3) < 0$. Since x is positive, we must have $x - 3 < 0$ and that gives us the require answer: the set of real numbers x that satisfy $2\log_{2x+3} x < 1$ is $(0,3)$.

11. Solve the equation
$$6x^2 - 25x + 12 + \frac{25}{x} + \frac{6}{x^2} = 0.$$

Solution: The equation can be simplified to $6x^4 - 25x^3 + 12x^2 + 25x + 6 = 0$ for $x \neq 0$ and, by trying a few small values, it can be seen that 2 is a solution for this equation. We can then aim to rewrite the polynomial using a factor of $(x-2)$ in the following way:

$$6x^4 - 25x^3 + 12x^2 + 25x + 6$$
$$= 6x^4 - 12x^3 - 13x^3 + 26x^2 - 14x^2 + 28x - 3x + 6$$
$$= (x-2)(6x^3 - 13x^2 - 14x - 3)$$

Further, it can be observed that 3 is a solution to the above 3-degree polynomial and following the same idea as above, we write

$$6x^3 - 13x^2 - 14x - 3 = 6x^3 - 18x^2 + 5x^2 - 15x + x - 3 = (x-3)(6x^2 + 5x + 1)$$

Thus, two roots are 2 and 3. To obtain the other two roots, we can use Sridhar Acharya's Formula and obtain the solutions $x = (-5 \pm 1)/12$. Hence, the four solutions to the given equation are
$$x = 2, 3, -\frac{1}{3}, -\frac{1}{2}$$

> **Useful Tip:** One can see that trial and error with small integer values can lead to the solutions. A smarter way to solve this problem is to identify that the given equation can be written as a quadratic function of $(x - 1/x)$ in the following way:
> $$6\left(x - \frac{1}{x}\right)^2 - 25\left(x - \frac{1}{x}\right) + 24 = 0$$
> Try solving for x from the above.

12. Let $a \in \mathbb{R}$. Consider the following system of equations in x and y:
$$x + y + axy = a,$$
$$x - 2y - xy^2 = 0.$$

Algebra

Prove that these equations have real solutions in x and y.

Solution: From the two equations, expressing x in terms of y and a, we get

$$x = \frac{a-y}{1+ay}, \quad x = \frac{2y}{1-y^2}$$

Equating the two expressions, one can write the following:

$$(a-y)(1-y^2) = 2y(1+ay) \implies y^3 - ay^2 - y + a = 2y + 2ay^2$$
$$\implies y^3 - 3ay^2 - 3y + a = 0$$

Since the above is a cubic equation in y, it must have a real root. Subsequently, the solution of x is real if y is not equal to ± 1 or $-1/a$. We can check these cases separately.

If $y = \pm 1$, from the second equation in the system, we get $x \pm 2 - x = 0$, which is absurd. On the other hand, for $y = -1/a$, the first equation gives us $x - 1/a - x = a$, implying that $a^2 + 1 = 0$, which violates the assumption about a. Hence, we can always obtain real x and y that satisfy the given equations.

13. Let α, β, γ be the roots of the equation $x^3 + px^2 + qx + r = 0$. Find a cubic equation whose roots are $\alpha - \frac{1}{\beta\gamma}, \beta - \frac{1}{\alpha\gamma}$ and $\gamma - \frac{1}{\alpha\beta}$.

Solution: Based on the relationship between the roots and the coefficients, we can start with the following equations:

$$\alpha + \beta + \gamma = -p,$$
$$\alpha\beta + \beta\gamma + \alpha\gamma = q,$$
$$\alpha\beta\gamma = -r$$

Let us denote $\alpha - \frac{1}{\beta\gamma}, \beta - \frac{1}{\alpha\gamma}$ and $\gamma - \frac{1}{\alpha\beta}$ by u_1, u_2, u_3. It is straightforward to see that they are the roots of the equation $x^3 - (u_1 + u_2 + u_3)x^2 + (u_1u_2 + u_2u_3 + u_1u_3)x - (u_1u_2u_3) = 0$. Below, we find out the values of these quantities.

First

$$u_1 + u_2 + u_3 = (\alpha + \beta + \gamma) - \frac{1}{\alpha\beta\gamma}(\alpha + \beta + \gamma) = -p(1 + 1/r)$$

Next, note that

$$u_1 u_2 = \left(\alpha - \frac{1}{\beta\gamma}\right)\left(\beta - \frac{1}{\alpha\gamma}\right) = \alpha\beta - \frac{2}{\gamma} - \frac{1}{r\gamma} = \alpha\beta - \frac{1}{\gamma}(2 + 1/r)$$

We can find u_2u_3, u_1u_3 in a similar manner. Then

$$\begin{aligned}
u_1u_2 + u_2u_3 + u_1u_3 &= (\alpha\beta + \beta\gamma + \alpha\gamma) - (2+1/r)\left(\frac{1}{\alpha} + \frac{1}{\beta} + \frac{1}{\gamma}\right) \\
&= q - \frac{1}{\alpha\beta\gamma}(2+1/r)(\alpha\beta + \beta\gamma + \alpha\gamma) \\
&= q + \frac{1}{r}(2+1/r)q \\
&= q\left(1 + \frac{2}{r} + \frac{1}{r^2}\right) \\
&= q(1+1/r)^2
\end{aligned}$$

Finally

$$\begin{aligned}
u_1u_2u_3 &= \left(\alpha\beta - \frac{1}{\gamma}(2+1/r)\right)\left(\gamma - \frac{1}{\alpha\beta}\right) \\
&= \alpha\beta\gamma - (2+1/r) - 1 + \frac{1}{\alpha\beta\gamma}(2+1/r) \\
&= (-r) - 2 - \frac{1}{r} - 1 - \frac{1}{r}(2+1/r) \\
&= -r - 3 - \frac{3}{r} - \frac{1}{r^2} \\
&= -r(1+1/r)^3
\end{aligned}$$

Hence, the required equation is

$$x^3 + p(1+1/r)x^2 + q(1+1/r)^2 x + r(1+1/r)^3 = 0$$

> **Useful Tip:** Problems involving the relationship between roots and coefficients of a polynomial are extremely common in various entrance tests.

14. If all the roots of the polynomial $x^4 - 4x^3 + ax^2 + bx + 1$ are positive real numbers, prove that the roots must be equal.

Solution: If the roots are denoted by α_i (for $i = 1, 2, 3, 4$), using the relationship between roots and coefficients, we can write

$$\sum_{i=1}^{4} \alpha_i = 4, \quad \prod_{i=1}^{4} \alpha_i = 1$$

Algebra

Since these are positive real numbers, we apply the AM-GM inequality and get

$$\frac{1}{4}\sum_{i=1}^{4}\alpha_i \geq \left(\prod_{i=1}^{4}\alpha_i\right)^{1/4}$$

However, from the above relationship, we can see that the two sides are actually equal (both are equal to 1) and that can happen only when all the quantities are equal. Hence, all the roots of the polynomial must be equal.

15. Let $f(x)$ be a polynomial with integer coefficients. Suppose that there exist distinct integers a_1, a_2, a_3, a_4 such that $f(a_1) = f(a_2) = f(a_3) = f(a_4) = 3$. Show that there does not exist any integer b with $f(b) = 14$.

Solution: Suppose there exists an integer b such that $f(b) = 14$. Now, a_1, a_2, a_3, a_4 all are roots of the equation $f(x) - 3 = 0$. Since $f(x)$ is a polynomial with integer coefficients,

$$f(x) - 3 = (x - a_1)(x - a_2)(x - a_3)(x - a_4)g(x),$$

where g is another polynomial with integer coefficients.

Substituting $x = b$ in the above, $11 = (b - a_1)(b - a_2)(b - a_3)(b - a_4)g(b)$, where $(b - a_1), (b - a_2), (b - a_3), (b - a_4)$ are all distinct integers. However, 11 can be expressed as the product of at most three distinct integers, $1, -1$ and -11. So, we arrive at a contradiction, and hence, there does not exist any integer b such that $f(b) = 14$.

> **Useful Tip:** Different versions of this problem have appeared multiple times in mathematical olympiads and the ISI and CMI entrance tests. For example, in B. Math Admission Test 2008, the following problem appeared: *If a polynomial P with integer coefficients has three distinct integer zeros, then show that $P(n) \neq 1$ for any integer n.*

16. We have a three-digit positive number. It is known that the sum of the rightmost two digits is 4 times the digit in the hundreds place. The sum of the squares of the digits is known to be 146. Further, if we reverse the order of the digits, the new number is 297 more than the original. What is the number?

Solution: Suppose the three digits, from left to right, are x, y, z, respectively. So, the number is $100x + 10y + z$. Now, from the given conditions, we obtain the following system of equations:

$$x^2 + y^2 + z^2 = 146, \quad y + z = 4x, \quad (100z + 10y + x) - (100x + 10y + z) = 297$$

The last equation implies $99(z-x) = 297$, and so, $z = x+3$. Then, from the second equation, $y = 3x - 3$. Using these in the first equation, we get

$$x^2 + 9(x-1)^2 + (x+3)^2 = 146$$

Simplifying the above equation gives the quadratic equation $11x^2 - 12x - 128 = 0$. Applying Sridhar Acharya's Formula after that, it is easy to find out that the two solutions are 4 and $-32/11$. Since x is a digit, the only possible solution is $x = 4$, and then, $y = 3x - 3 = 9$, $z = x + 3 = 7$. Hence, the original number is 497.

17. For which real values of m can $y = \frac{x^2 - x}{1 - mx}$ take all real values?

Solution: The given equation can be rewritten as

$$y(1 - mx) = x^2 - x \implies x^2 + (my - 1)x - y = 0$$

Since x is a real number, the discriminant of the above equation must be non-negative. Thus, $(my - 1)^2 + 4y \geq 0$, which implies $m^2 y^2 + (4 - 2m)y + 1 \geq 0$. Thus, if y can take all real values, the above quadratic equation in y must always be true. That would happen only if the discriminant is ≤ 0 and if the leading coefficient is positive. The latter holds whenever $m \neq 0$. Now, the discriminant is $(4 - 2m)^2 - 4m^2 = 16 - 16m$, which is ≤ 0 if and only if $m \geq 1$. Hence, the set of all values of m for which y can take all real values is $[1, \infty)$.

18. If $n \in \mathbb{N}$, for $x > 0$, show that $\frac{x^n - 1}{x - 1} \geq nx^{\frac{n-1}{2}}$.

Solution: It is easy to note that the left-hand side of the inequality can be written as $1 + x + x^2 + \ldots + x^{n-1}$. For $x > 0$, all these terms are positive and we can use the AM-GM inequality, which implies the following:

$$\frac{1}{n}\sum_{i=1}^{n} x^{i-1} \geq \left(\prod_{i=1}^{n} x^{i-1}\right)^{1/n} \implies \frac{x^n - 1}{x - 1} \geq n\left(x^{1+2+\ldots+(n-1)}\right)^{1/n}$$

Since $1 + 2 + \ldots + (n-1) = n(n-1)/2$, straightforward algebraic manipulation implies that the right-hand side of the above inequality is equal to $nx^{\frac{n-1}{2}}$, and that completes the proof.

19. For $x, y, z \in \mathbb{R}$, prove the following inequality:

$$|x| + |y| + |z| \leq |x + y - z| + |y + z - x| + |z + x - y|.$$

Algebra

Solution: For any two real numbers a, b, the triangle inequality says that $|a|+|b| \geq |a+b|$. So, if we use the triangle inequality for $x+y-z, y+z-x, z+x-y$, taken two at a time, we get the following:

$$|x+y-z|+|y+z-x| \geq |x+y-z+y+z-x| = 2|y|,$$
$$|y+z-x|+|z+x-y| \geq |y+z-x+z+x-y| = 2|z|,$$
$$|x+y-z|+|z+x-y| \geq |x+y-z+z+x-y| = 2|x|$$

Adding the above three inequalities, we get

$$2(|x+y-z|+|y+z-x|+|z+x-y|) \geq 2(|x|+|y|+|z|),$$

which is equivalent to the result we need to prove.

20. Consider two real numbers a and b satisfying $a > 0, b > 0, a+b = 1$. Show that

$$\left(a+\frac{1}{a}\right)^2 + \left(b+\frac{1}{b}\right)^2 \geq \frac{25}{2}.$$

Solution: The expression on the left-hand side of the inequality can be simplified as

$$\left(a+\frac{1}{a}\right)^2 + \left(b+\frac{1}{b}\right)^2 = a^2 + b^2 + \frac{1}{a^2} + \frac{1}{b^2} + 4$$

At first, using the Cauchy–Schwarz inequality for a, b and $1, 1$,

$$(a^2+b^2)(1^2+1^2) \geq (a+b)^2 \implies a^2+b^2 \geq \frac{(a+b)^2}{2} = \frac{1}{2}$$

Next, using the Cauchy–Schwarz inequality for $1/a, 1/b$ and $1, 1$,

$$\frac{1}{a^2} + \frac{1}{b^2} \geq \frac{1}{2}\left(\frac{1}{a}+\frac{1}{b}\right)^2 = 2\left(\frac{1/a+1/b}{2}\right)^2$$

Let us use the AM-HM inequality for the expression on the right-hand side of the above. That gives us

$$2\left(\frac{1/a+1/b}{2}\right)^2 \geq 2\left(\frac{2}{a+b}\right)^2 = \frac{8}{(a+b)^2} = 8$$

Combining all of the above, we get the required result as

$$a^2+b^2+\frac{1}{a^2}+\frac{1}{b^2}+4 \geq \frac{1}{2}+8+4 = \frac{25}{2}$$

21. Let a, b, c, d be positive real numbers such that $abcd = 1$. Prove that

$$(1+a)(1+b)(1+c)(1+d) \geqslant 16$$

Solution: Since a is positive, applying the AM-GM inequality to 1 and a, one can get $1 + a \geqslant 2\sqrt{a}$. Similarly, for b, c, d

$$1 + b \geqslant 2\sqrt{b}, \quad 1 + c \geqslant 2\sqrt{c}, \quad 1 + d \geqslant 2\sqrt{d}$$

Multiplying all the inequalities and using $abcd = 1$, we finally obtain

$$(1+a)(1+b)(1+c)(1+d) \geqslant 16\sqrt{abcd} = 16,$$

and the proof is complete.

22. Prove that there is exactly one real value of x that satisfies the equation

$$2\cos^2(x^3 + x) = 2^x + 2^{-x}.$$

Solution: First, note that the right-hand side of the above equation is of the form $a + 1/a$, where $a = 2^x > 0$. Using the AM-GM inequality for a and $1/a$, we get

$$\frac{a + 1/a}{2} \geqslant \left(a \times \frac{1}{a}\right)^{1/2} \implies a + \frac{1}{a} \geqslant 2,$$

where equality holds when $a = 1/a = 1$. Thus, the minimum value of the right-hand side is 2 and the minimum is attained when $2^x = 1$, that is, when $x = 0$.

However, $\cos^2 y \leqslant 1$ for any y. Thus, $2\cos^2(x^3 + x) \leqslant 2$, implying that the only possibility is

$$2\cos^2(x^3 + x) = 2^x + 2^{-x} = 2$$

Hence, the only possible solution is $x = 0$.

23. Find real solutions to the following set of equations:

$$\begin{aligned}
3a &= (b+c+d)^3, \\
3b &= (c+d+e)^3, \\
3c &= (d+e+a)^3, \\
3d &= (e+a+b)^3, \\
3e &= (a+b+c)^3.
\end{aligned}$$

Solution: Suppose $a \geqslant b$. Then, $(b+c+d) \geqslant (c+d+e)$, since the function $f(x) = x^3$ is monotonically increasing for all real x. Thus, we have $a \geqslant b \geqslant e$.

Algebra

Now, using $a \geqslant e$, we again get $(b+c+d) \geqslant (a+b+c)$, implying $d \geqslant a$, and thereby $d \geqslant a \geqslant b \geqslant e$.

Since $d \geqslant e$, $(e+a+b) \geqslant (a+b+c)$, giving us $e \geqslant c$. Hence, we get the order of the numbers as $d \geqslant a \geqslant b \geqslant e \geqslant c$. However, because of this ordering, $(d+e+a) \geqslant (e+a+b)$, and so, $c \geqslant d$. Clearly, all of the numbers must be equal.

Starting from $a \leqslant b$, we can reach the same conclusion, in exactly the same fashion as above. Thus, we must have $a = b = c = d = e$, and then, each number is a solution of the equation $3x = (3x)^3$ i.e. $9x^3 - x = 0$, which implies

$$x = 0, \pm \frac{1}{3}$$

Hence, the possible solutions are $a = b = c = d = e = 0$ or $1/3$ or $-1/3$.

24. Consider the equation $P(z) = az^2 + bz + c$, where $a, b, c \in \mathbb{C}$.

   (a) If $P(z)$ is real for all $z \in \mathbb{R}$, prove that a, b, c are real numbers.

   (b) Further, assume that $P(z)$ is not real whenever z is not real. Then prove that $a = 0$.

Solution:

   (a) For $z = 0, 1, -1$, we get $P(0) = c, P(1) = a+b+c, P(-1) = a-b+c$. From the given assumption, these must be real numbers, which implies that c is real. Also, $2a + 2c = P(1) + P(-1)$ is real and so is a. Finally, since a, c and $a+b+c$ are real, we can argue that b is real. Hence, all three coefficients are real numbers.

   (b) Let us assume that $a \neq 0$. For $z = x + iy$

   $$P(z) = a(x+iy)^2 + b(x+iy) + c = a(x^2 - y^2) + bx + c + i(2axy + by)$$

   For $y \neq 0$, that is, when z is not real, $P(z)$ is not real, implying that $2axy + by \neq 0$, which further implies that $2ax + b \neq 0$ for all x. However, if we take $x = -b/2a$ (this is real and defined since a is non-zero), we get $2ax + b = 0$.

   Thus, $P(z)$ is a real number if we take a complex number z (with a non-zero imaginary quantity) which has a real part $-b/2a$, and that is a contradiction. So, our assumption that a is non-zero cannot be true and that completes the proof.

25. Consider a sequence $\{x_n\}$ that satisfies $x_1 = 2, x_2 = 1$ and $2x_n - 3x_{n-1} + x_{n-2} = 0$ for $n > 2$. Find an algebraic expression for x_n.

Solution: Suppose $f(t) = \sum_{n=1}^{\infty} x_n t^n$, where t is a real number with $|t| < 1$. Now, for all $n > 2$, $2x_n = 3x_{n-1} - x_{n-2}$. Multiplying both sides of this equation by t^n and adding for all

$n \geqslant 3$, we get

$$2\sum_{n=3}^{\infty} x_n t^n = 3\sum_{n=3}^{\infty} x_{n-1} t^n - \sum_{n=3}^{\infty} x_{n-2} t^n = 3t \sum_{n=2}^{\infty} x_n t^n - t^2 \sum_{n=1}^{\infty} x_n t^n$$

The term on the left-hand side is equal to $2f(t) - 2x_1 t - 2x_2 t^2 = 2f(t) - 4t - 2t^2$. Similarly, the term on the right-hand side of the above equation is equal to $3t[f(t) - x_1 t] - t^2 f(t) = f(t)(3t - t^2) - 6t^2$. Equating the two sides, we get $f(t)(t^2 - 3t + 2) = 4t - 4t^2$. Since $t^2 - 3t + 2 = (t-1)(t-2)$, it further implies that $f(t) = \frac{2t}{1-t/2}$. Now, using the infinite geometric series expansion, we can say that

$$\frac{1}{1-t/2} = \sum_{n=0}^{\infty} \left(\frac{t}{2}\right)^n \implies f(t) = 2\sum_{n=0}^{\infty} \frac{t^{n+1}}{2^n} = \sum_{n=1}^{\infty} 2^{2-n} t^n$$

Since $f(t)$ is equal to $\sum_{n=1}^{\infty} x_n t^n$ for all $|t| < 1$, coefficients of both series expansions must be equal, and hence, $x_n = 2^{2-n}$.

> **Useful Tip:** The above technique utilizes the concept of generating functions, which is a standard way of encoding an infinite sequence $\{x_n\}$ by treating them as the coefficients of an infinite series.

26. Can there be a non-constant polynomial $P(x)$ with integer coefficients such that $P(n)$ is a prime number for all $n \in \mathbb{N}$?

Solution: Suppose there is a non-constant polynomial $P(x)$ such that $P(n)$ is prime for all $n \in \mathbb{N}$. Let us assume that the polynomial is written as

$$P(x) = a_0 + a_1 x + a_2 x^2 + \ldots + a_m x^m$$

Now, $P(1) = a_0 + a_1 + \ldots + a_m$ must be prime. Let us call it p. We know that for any x and y, $(x-y)$ divides $P(x) - P(y)$. Thus, for any natural number r, if we take $x = rp + 1$ and $y = 1$, we get that rp divides $P(rp+1) - P(1)$. However, $P(1)$ is p which is prime, implying that p divides $P(rp+1)$ for all $r \in \mathbb{N}$.

Our assumption says that $P(n)$ is prime for all positive integer n, and from the above, we can now say that

$$P(1) = P(p+1) = P(2p+1) = \ldots = P(kp+1) = \ldots == p, \ \forall\, k \in \mathbb{N}.$$

Thus, if we consider the equation $P(x) - p = 0$, all numbers of the form $(rp+1)$ (for $r = 0, 1, 2, \ldots$) will be roots of this equation. However, since $P(x)$ is only a polynomial with

Algebra

degree m, the above equation can have at most m roots, and we arrive at a contradiction, unless $P(x)$ is a constant polynomial.

Hence, no non-constant polynomial with integer coefficients exists such that $P(n)$ is prime for all $n \in \mathbb{N}$.

27. Find all the solutions to $x^4 + x^3 + 2x^2 + x + 1 = 0$.

Solution: The given equation can be factorized in the following way:
$$x^2(x^2 + x + 1) + x^2 + x + 1 = 0 \implies (x^2 + 1)(x^2 + x + 1) = 0$$

Thus, there are two possibilities. First, $x^2 + 1 = 0$, which occurs if $x = \pm \iota$. Second, the above is also satisfied if $x^2 + x + 1 = 0$. Applying Sridhar Acharya's Formula to this quadratic equation, one can obtain the set of solutions to the given equation as
$$x \in \left\{ \pm \iota, -\frac{1}{2} \pm \iota \sqrt{\frac{3}{2}} \right\}.$$

28. Consider the infinite sequence $1, 1/2, 1/4, 1/8, \ldots$. Is it possible to find a sub-sequence of this such that the sub-sequence forms an infinite geometric series with the sum of $1/5$?

Solution: We note that the given sequence is an infinite geometric progression with the nth term as $1/2^{n-1}$. Suppose that a sub-sequence $\{y_m\}$ can be formed such that
$$y_m = \left(\frac{1}{2^k}\right)\left(\frac{1}{2^r}\right)^{m-1}, \quad \sum_{m=1}^{\infty} y_m = \frac{1}{5}$$

Using the properties of infinite geometric progression, the above implies that
$$\frac{2^{-k}}{1 - 2^{-r}} = \frac{1}{5} \implies 2^k - 2^{k-r} = 5$$

Since both k and r are non-negative integers, we can argue that $k < r$, that is, $k - r < 0$ is not possible. Similarly, for $k > r$, the left-hand side is even while the right-hand side is odd. Thus, the only possibility is $k = r$, which leads to the equation $2^k = 6$, which does not have any solution in positive integers. Hence, it is impossible to find a sub-sequence of this sequence such that the sub-sequence forms an infinite geometric series with the sum of $1/5$.

> **Useful Tip:** Redo the above problem to show that it is possible to find a sub-sequence that forms an infinite geometric series with the sum of $1/7$.

29. Find all the complex numbers z that satisfy the equation
$$|z - |z+1|| = |z + |z-1||.$$

Solution: A complex number z would satisfy the given equation if and only if
$$|z - |z+1||^2 = |z + |z-1||^2$$

We use the identity $|u|^2 = u\bar{u}$ to write the above as
$$(z - |z+1|)(\bar{z} - |z+1|) = (z + |z-1|)(\bar{z} + |z-1|),$$

which is equivalent to
$$|z+1|^2 - |z-1|^2 = (z+\bar{z})(|z+1| + |z-1|)$$

Again, use the above identity to write $|z+1|^2 - |z-1|^2 = (z+1)(\bar{z}+1) - (z-1)(\bar{z}-1)$, which simplifies to $2(z+\bar{z})$. Thus, we arrive at the equation
$$(z+\bar{z})\{|z+1| + |z-1| - 2\} = 0,$$

implying that either $z + \bar{z} = 0$ or $|z+1| + |z-1| = 2$. The first condition holds if z is a purely imaginary number of the form ιy, $y \in \mathbb{R}$. For the second condition, note that the triangle inequality suggests $|z+1| + |z-1| \geqslant 2$, and hence, the only possibility is to have $z + 1 = x(1-z)$ for some real number $x \geqslant 0$. It subsequently implies that $z = (x-1)/(x+1)$, that is, z can be any real number between -1 and 1.

Combining the above, we arrive at the set of solutions
$$z \in \{\iota y : y \in \mathbb{R}\} \cup \{r : r \in \mathbb{R}, -1 \leqslant r \leqslant 1\}$$

30. Let $z_1, z_2, \ldots, z_n$ be distinct complex numbers, all with absolute value equal to R. Prove that
$$\sum_{1 \leqslant i < j \leqslant n} |z_i + z_j|^2 \geqslant n(n-2)R^2.$$

Solution: We can write $|z_i + z_j|^2 = (z_i + z_j)(\bar{z}_i + \bar{z}_j)$, which is equal to $2R^2 + \bar{z}_i z_j + z_i \bar{z}_j$. Thus
$$\sum_{1 \leqslant i < j \leqslant n} |z_i + z_j|^2 = 2R^2 \binom{n}{2} + \sum_{i \neq j} \bar{z}_i z_j$$

The second term can be further simplified to
$$\sum_{i=1}^{n} \sum_{j=1}^{n} \bar{z}_i z_j - \sum_{i=1}^{n} |z_i|^2 = \left(\sum_{i=1}^{n} z_i\right)\left(\sum_{i=1}^{n} \bar{z}_i\right) - nR^2 = \left|\sum_{i=1}^{n} z_i\right|^2 - nR^2$$

Algebra

Thus, the above quantity is at least $(-nR^2)$. Using it in the previous expression

$$\sum_{1 \leq i < j \leq n} |z_i + z_j|^2 \geq 2R^2 \binom{n}{2} - nR^2 = n(n-2)R^2,$$

and that completes the proof.

> **Useful Tip:** Recall that complex numbers are closely connected with the concepts of geometry. For example, in the above problem, one can consider a polygon $A_1 \ldots A_n$, where each A_i denotes the point with coordinates equal to z_i. Then, it is a cyclic polygon with circumradius R. Now, $|z_i + z_j|/2$ would indicate the midpoint of every side, and thus, one can translate the given algebraic problem to the geometric identity
>
> $$\sum_{1 \leq i < j \leq n} M_{ij}^2 \geq n(n-2)R^2,$$
>
> where M_{ij} is the midpoint of $A_i A_j$.
> One can now solve this problem geometrically as well. It is left as an exercise to the reader. We shall see some more examples in Chapters 6 and 8.

Multiple Choice Questions

1. If positive real numbers $a_1, a_2, \ldots, a_{2022}$ are chosen in such a way that the product $a_1 a_2 \ldots a_{2022} = 1$, which of the following is true about their sum $S = a_1 + a_2 + \ldots + a_{2022}$?
(a) S can be any positive number
(b) S must be less than 2022
(c) $S \geq 2022$, but it is bounded above
(d) $S \geq 2022$, and it is unbounded above

Solution: (d)

Since the numbers are positive real and the product is given, we can apply the AM-GM inequality to argue that

$$\frac{S}{2022} \geq (a_1 a_2 \ldots a_{2022})^{1/2022} = 1$$

Hence, the lower bound of S is 2022, but it is unbounded above.

2. What is the remainder when $f(x) = 7x^{32} + 5x^{22} + 3x^{12} + x^2$ is divided by $x^2 + 1$?
(a) A positive constant
(b) A negative constant
(c) A linear function with leading coefficient positive
(d) A linear function with leading coefficient negative

Solution: (a)

The remainder is the same as the expression $f(u)$ if u is chosen such that $u^2+1=0$. Since all the terms in the polynomial $f(x)$ have even powers of x, we can easily find that $f(u) = 7(-1)^{16} + 5(-1)^{11} + 3(-1)^6 + (-1) = 4$. Thus, the remainder is a positive constant.

3. The number of θ with $0 \leqslant \theta < 2\pi$ such that $4\sin(3\theta+2) = 1$ is

(a) 2   (b) 3   (c) 6   (d) None of these

Solution: (c)

For $\phi \in [0, 2\pi)$, the equation $\sin\phi = 1/4$ has exactly two solutions. In other words, for one full period, the equation $4\sin\phi = 1$ would lead to two solutions in ϕ. In this problem, given the range of θ, we can say that the equation covers three complete periods, and hence, the number of solutions in θ is 6.

4. A polynomial $f(x)$ with real coefficients leaves the remainder 15 when divided by $x-3$ and the remainder $2x+1$ when divided by $(x-1)^2$. What is the remainder if $f(x)$ is divided by $(x-3)(x-1)^2$?

(a) $2x^2 - 2x + 3$ (b) $6x - 3$ (c) $x^2 + 2x$ (d) $30x + 15$

Solution: (a)

Using the remainder theorem for polynomials, there exist some polynomials $q_1(x)$ and $q_2(x)$ such that
$$f(x) = q_1(x)(x-3) + 15, \quad f(x) = q_2(x)(x-1)^2 + 2x + 1$$
Let us write $q_2(x)$ as $q_3(x)(x-3) + c$. Then
$$f(x) = q_3(x)(x-3)(x-1)^2 + c(x-1)^2 + (2x+1)$$
Using $f(3) = 15$ in the above equation, we get
$$c(3-1)^2 + (2 \times 3 + 1) = 15 \implies c = 2$$
Hence, the required answer is $2(x-1)^2 + 2x + 1 = 2x^2 - 2x + 3$.

5. Consider real numbers a, b, c such that $ac \neq 0$. Define two polynomials $P(x) = ax^2 + bx + c$, $Q(x) = -ax^2 + bx + c$. How many roots of the polynomial $P(x)Q(x)$ are real?

(a) None   (b) At least two   (c) Exactly two   (d) All

Solution: (b)

The discriminants of the two quadratic equations are $b^2 - 4ac$ and $b^2 + 4ac$. Clearly both cannot be negative, although one of them can be negative, depending on the values of a, b, c. Hence, at least one of the quadratic equations must have two real roots.

6. For how many real values of p do the equations $x^2 + px + 1 = 0$ and $x^2 + x + p = 0$ have exactly one common root?

(a) 0 (b) 1 (c) 2 (d) 3

Solution: (b)

If α is a common root to the two equations $x^2 + px + 1 = 0$ and $x^2 + x + p = 0$, then one can infer that $(\alpha - 1)(p - 1) = 0$. If $p = 1$, then the given equations turn out to be exactly the same, and thus, they have two common roots. Therefore, $\alpha = 1$, which indicates that $p = -2$.

7. The system of inequalities

$$a - b^2 \geqslant \frac{1}{4}, \ b - c^2 \geqslant \frac{1}{4}, \ c - d^2 \geqslant \frac{1}{4}, \ d - a^2 \geqslant \frac{1}{4}$$

has

(a) no real solution;
(b) exactly one real solution;
(c) exactly two real solutions;
(d) infinitely many real solutions.

Solution: (b)

Adding all the inequalities and taking them to one side of the sign, we get

$$(a^2 + b^2 + c^2 + d^2) - (a + b + c + d) + 1 \leqslant 0,$$

which implies that

$$\left(a - \frac{1}{2}\right)^2 + \left(b - \frac{1}{2}\right)^2 + \left(c - \frac{1}{2}\right)^2 + \left(d - \frac{1}{2}\right)^2 \leqslant 0$$

Clearly, if a, b, c, d are real numbers, then each of the above square terms must be 0, and hence, the only solution is $a = b = c = d = 1/2$.

8. If $\log_{12} 18 = a$, then $\log_{24} 16$ is

(a) $\dfrac{8 - 4a}{5 - a}$ (b) $\dfrac{1}{3 + a}$ (c) $\dfrac{4a - 1}{2 + 3a}$ (d) $\dfrac{8 - 4a}{5 + a}$

Solution: (a)

Taking all logarithms in base e, we get
$$\log_{24} 16 = \frac{\log 16}{\log 24} = \frac{4\log 2}{3\log 2 + \log 3} = \frac{4}{3 + \log 3/\log 2} = \frac{4}{3+x},$$

if we use x to denote $\log 3/\log 2$. On the other hand, we have
$$\frac{\log 18}{\log 12} = a \implies \frac{2\log 3 + \log 2}{2\log 2 + \log 3} = a \implies \frac{2x+1}{2+x} = a$$

Solving the above leads to the equation $(2-a)x = 2a-1$, that is,
$$x = \frac{2a-1}{2-a} \implies 3+x = \frac{5-a}{2-a} \implies \frac{4}{3+x} = \frac{8-4a}{5-a}$$

9. Let $1, \omega, \omega^2$ be the cube roots of unity. Then, the least possible degree of a polynomial with real coefficients having $2\omega, 2+3\omega, 2+3\omega^2$ and $2-\omega-\omega^2$ as roots is

(a) 4   (b) 5   (c) 6   (d) 8

Solution: (b)

We know that ω and ω^2 are complex conjugates of each other. Also, $\omega + \omega^2 = -1$, implying that the quantity $2 - \omega - \omega^2$ is equal to 3. Thus, among the four roots, one is a real number, two are complex conjugates. Clearly, if a polynomial with real coefficients has these quantities as roots, then $2\omega^2$ must be a root as well. Hence, the least possible degree of such a polynomial is 5.

10. Let x_1, x_2 be the roots of $x^2 - 3x + a = 0$, and let x_3, x_4 be the roots of $x^2 - 12x + b = 0$. If x_1, x_2, x_3, x_4 form an increasing geometric progression, then ab is

(a) 5184   (b) 64   (c) -5184 (d) -64

Solution: (b)

From the given conditions, we can write
$$x_1 + x_2 = 3, \; x_1 x_2 = a, \; x_3 + x_4 = 12, \; x_3 x_4 = b$$

Let us assume that x_1, x_2, x_3, x_4 form a geometric progression with common ratio $r > 1$. Then, the above equations yield
$$x_1(1+r) = 3, \; x_1^2 r = a, \; x_1 r^2(1+r) = 12, \; x_1^2 r^5 = b$$

Clearly, $r^2 = 4$, that is, $r = 2$, which further implies that $x_1 = 1$. Hence, $ab = x_1^4 r^6 = 2^6 = 64$.

Algebra

Exercises

1. Let $a, b, c \in \mathbb{R}$, all greater than 1. What is the minimum possible value of $\log_a bc + \log_b ca + \log_c ab$.

2. Let $z \in \mathbb{C}$ such that z, z^2, z^3 are collinear in the complex plane. Prove that $z \in \mathbb{R}$.

3. (i) Consider the following identity
$$\frac{n!}{x(x+1)(x+2)\ldots(x+n)} = \sum_{k=0}^{n} \frac{A_k}{x+k}.$$
Show that $A_k = (-1)^k \binom{n}{k}$.

    (ii) Prove the following identity:
$$\binom{n}{0}\frac{1}{1\cdot 2} - \binom{n}{1}\frac{1}{2\cdot 3} + \binom{n}{2}\frac{1}{3\cdot 4} + \ldots + (-1)^n \binom{n}{n}\frac{1}{(n+1)(n+2)} = \frac{1}{n+2}.$$

4. Let $u_n = (3+\sqrt{5})^n + (3-\sqrt{5})^n$ for any positive integer n.

    (i) Prove that for each n, u_n must be an integer.

    (ii) Prove that $u_{n+1} = 6u_n - 4u_{n-1}$ for all $n \geq 2$.

    (iii) Use the above result to show that u_n is divisible by 2^n.

5. Prove that for a positive integer n greater than 2, $(n!)^2 > n^n$.

6. If the three equations $ax^2 - 2bx + c = 0$, $bx^2 - 2cx + a = 0$ and $cx^2 - 2ax + b = 0$ have only positive roots, prove that $a = b = c$.

7. Let $G, H \in \mathbb{C}$. If the equation $x^3 + Gx + H = 0$ has a pair of complex conjugate roots, show that both G and H are real.

8. Let a, b, c be positive real numbers. Prove that
$$\frac{b^2+c^2}{b+c} + \frac{c^2+a^2}{c+a} + \frac{a^2+b^2}{a+b} \geq a+b+c.$$

9. Suppose that $\theta_1, \theta_2, \ldots, \theta_{10}$ are some values from the closed interval $[0, \pi]$. Prove the following:
$$F = (1+\sin^2\theta_1)(1+\cos^2\theta_1)(1+\sin^2\theta_2)(1+\cos^2\theta_2)\ldots$$
$$\ldots(1+\sin^2\theta_{10})(1+\cos^2\theta_{10}) \leq \left(\frac{9}{4}\right)^{10}.$$

Further, find out the maximum value attainable by F. At what values of $\theta_1, \theta_2, \ldots, \theta_{10}$ is that maximum value attained?

10. Let $z_1, z_2 \in \mathbb{C}$. The pair (z_1, z_2) is said to have property $\mathcal{P}$ if for every $z \in \mathbb{C}$, there exist $r, s \in \mathbb{R}$ such that $z = rz_1 + sz_2$. Prove that a pair z_1, z_2 has property $\mathcal{P}$ if and only if $z_1, z_2, 0$ are not on the same line on the complex plane.

11. If $\frac{\sin^4 x}{a} + \frac{\cos^4 x}{b} = \frac{1}{a+b}$, prove that $\frac{\sin^6 x}{a^2} + \frac{\cos^6 x}{b^2} = \frac{1}{(a+b)^2}$.

12. Let $P_1, P_2, \ldots, P_n$ be different polynomials in x. If the polynomials all have integer coefficients such that $P_1 = P_1^2 + P_2^2 + \ldots + P_n^2$ and if P_1 is not the zero polynomial, then show that $P_1 = 1$ and $P_2 = P_3 = \ldots = P_n = 0$.

13. Find all the solutions to the system of equations

$$\sin x + \sin y = \sin(x+y), \quad |x| + |y| = 1.$$

14. Let $P(x) = x^4 + ax^3 + bx^2 + cx + d$ be a polynomial with $a, b, c, d \in \mathbb{Z}$. If the sums of the pairs of roots of $P(x)$ are given by 1, 2, 5, 6, 9 and 10, what is the value of $P(1)$?

15. Consider a polynomial $P(x) = a_n x^n + a_{n-1} x^{n-1} + a_{n-2} x^{n-2} + \ldots + a_1 x + a_0$ such that $a_i \in \mathbb{Z}$ for all i. If $P(0)$ and $P(1)$ are odd integers, prove that $P(x)$ does not have any integer root.

16. Let $k \in \mathbb{N}$. Prove that

$$2\left(\sqrt{k+1} - \sqrt{k}\right) < \frac{1}{\sqrt{k}} < 2\left(\sqrt{k} - \sqrt{k-1}\right).$$

Using the above or otherwise, calculate the integral part of $\frac{1}{\sqrt{2}} + \frac{1}{\sqrt{3}} + \ldots + \frac{1}{\sqrt{10000}}$.

17. Consider the recursive relations $a_1 = 1$, $a_n = n(a_{n-1} + 1)$ for $n \geq 2$. If

$$P_n = \left(1 + \frac{1}{a_1}\right) \ldots \left(1 + \frac{1}{a_n}\right),$$

find the limiting value of P_n as $n \to \infty$.

18. Let $P(x)$ be a monic polynomial of degree n such that

$$P(k) = \frac{k}{k+1}, \quad \text{for } k = 0, 1, \ldots, n.$$

What is the value of $P(n+1)$?

19. Find the values of $\alpha \in [0, \pi]$ for which

$$\sum_{k=0}^{n} \binom{n}{k} \cos(k\alpha) = 0.$$

Algebra

20. Let $z_1, z_2, \ldots, z_n$ be distinct complex numbers, all with absolute value equal to R. Prove that
$$\sum_{1 \leq i < j \leq n} \left| \frac{z_i + z_j}{z_i - z_j} \right|^2 \geq \frac{(n-1)(n-2)}{2}.$$

Hints

1. The given term (call it S) can be rewritten as
$$S = \log_a b + \log_b a + \log_b c + \log_c b + \log_c a + \log_a c$$
If we take $\log_a b = x$, then applying the AM-GM inequality, $\log_a b + \log_b a = x + \frac{1}{x} \geq 2$. In a similar way, one can extend this to show that $S \geq 6$ and $S = 6$ when $a = b = c$.

2. Suppose that the modulus and amplitude of z are r and θ, respectively. So, $z = re^{i\theta}$. Consequently, $z^2 = r^2 e^{2i\theta}$ and $z^3 = r^3 e^{3i\theta}$. Since z, z^2, z^3 are collinear in the complex plane, we can say that the lines that make angles $\theta, 2\theta$ and 3θ with the x-axis should be along the same line. That is possible only if $\theta = n\pi$ for some integer n, which implies that $z \in \mathbb{R}$.

3. We can use the identity $\sum_{k=0}^{n}(-1)^k \binom{n}{k} = 0$ for proving both results. For the first part, principles of mathematical induction can be used to prove the result. For the second part, note that the rth term in the equation can be written as
$$(-1)^{r-1} \binom{n}{r-1} \frac{1}{r(r+1)} = (-1)^{r-1} \binom{n}{r-1} \left(\frac{1}{r} - \frac{1}{r+1} \right)$$
Using this expression, one can simplify the equation on the left-hand side, and subsequently use the results related to binomial coefficients to arrive at the required result.

4. Use binomial expansion to show that
$$(3+\sqrt{5})^n + (3-\sqrt{5})^n = 2 \sum_{r \text{ is even}} \binom{n}{r} 3^{n-r} 5^{r/2}$$
Then use the above expression to argue why u_n is an integer. The second part is a straightforward algebraic manipulation of the given expression. For the third part, use the result from part (ii) and apply the principles of mathematical induction.

5. The principle of mathematical induction can be used to show the required result. Using the induction hypothesis, one can argue that it is enough to prove the inequality $k+1 > (1+1/k)^k$, which can be proved using binomial expansion.

6. Using Sridhar Acharya's Formula, one can show that the three equations have positive roots if $b^2 \geq ac > 0$, $c^2 \geq ab > 0$ and $a^2 \geq bc > 0$. Since all of them need to be true simultaneously, it is easy to argue that $a^2 = b^2 = c^2$, which gives the required result.

7. It is a cubic polynomial, and so, it has three roots. As two of them are complex conjugate, there is a real root. Let these roots be of the form $a \pm \imath b, c$, where $a, b, c \in \mathbb{R}$. One can then use the relationship between roots and coefficients to argue why G and H must be real.

8. Applying the Cauchy–Schwarz inequality for b, c and $1, 1$, one can show that
$$\frac{b^2 + c^2}{b+c} \geq \frac{b+c}{2}$$
Similar results can be obtained for the other two terms on the left-hand side of the inequality. Adding the three inequalities will give us the required result.

9. Consider the quantities $(1 + \sin^2 \theta_1), (1 + \cos^2 \theta_1), (1 + \sin^2 \theta_2), (1 + \cos^2 \theta_2), \ldots, (1 + \sin^2 \theta_{10}), (1 + \cos^2 \theta_{10})$, and apply the AM-GM inequality. It is easy to see that the AM of the quantities is $3/2$ since $(1 + \sin^2 \theta_i) + (1 + \cos^2 \theta_i) = 3$ for all i. Then, the inequality directly implies the result. F takes the value $(9/4)^{10}$ when all of the above quantities are equal. That happens if and only if $\sin^2 \theta_i = \cos^2 \theta_i = 1/2$ for all i, which subsequently implies that $\theta_i \in \{\pi/4, 3\pi/4\}$ for $i = 1, 2, \ldots, 10$.

10. Suppose $z_1 = x_1 + \imath y_1$ and $z_2 = x_2 + \imath y_2$; let $z = x + \imath y$. Then, z can be expressed as $rz_1 + sz_2$ if the following system of equations admits real solutions in (r, s):
$$\begin{bmatrix} x_1 & x_2 \\ y_1 & y_2 \end{bmatrix} \begin{pmatrix} r \\ s \end{pmatrix} = \begin{pmatrix} x \\ y \end{pmatrix}$$
If $z_1, z_2, 0$ are not collinear, one can show that the determinant of the above matrix $x_1 y_2 - y_1 x_2 \neq 0$, which implies that the above system of equations has real solutions in (r, s). This proves the necessary condition. To prove the sufficient condition, assume that z_1, z_2 are collinear. Then, $z_1 = cz_2$ for some $c \in \mathbb{R}$. Now, z can be written as $rz_1 + sz_2$ only if $z = (rc + s)z_2$, which implies that z must be a real multiple of z_2. Hence, (z_1, z_2) cannot satisfy property $\mathcal{P}$.

11. Writing $\sin^2 x = 1 - \cos^2 x$, the given equation can be simplified to obtain the equation $(\cos^2 x - b/(a+b))^2 = 0$. Thus, $\cos^2 x = b/(a+b)$, which implies that $\sin^2 x = a/(a+b)$. Substituting these values, one can prove the required result.

12. Define a new polynomial f in the following way:
$$f(x) = P_1(x)\{P_1(x) - 1\} + P_2^2(x) + P_3^2(x) + \ldots + P_n^2(x)$$
Clearly, $f(x)$ is a polynomial with integer coefficients and because of the given condition, $f(x) = 0$ for all x. However, for any non-constant polynomial g, $g(x)$ approaches ∞ or $-\infty$ for $x \to \infty$. Using this, it can be argued that if any P_i is non-constant, $f(x)$ approaches ∞ for large $x \in \mathbb{R}$, which is contradictory to the fact

Algebra 3.31

that $f(x) = 0$. Thus, each P_i must be a constant polynomial, and the constants must be integers. It is then straightforward to prove that the only such possibility is $P_1 = 1$ and $P_2 = P_3 = \ldots = P_n = 0$.

13. The first equation can be simplified to obtain

$$2\sin\left(\frac{x+y}{2}\right)\sin\left(\frac{x}{2}\right)\sin\left(\frac{y}{2}\right) = 0$$

Since the absolute values of both x and y must be less than 1 (because of the second equation), one can argue that either $x = 0$ or $y = 0$ or $x + y = 0$. If $x = 0$, $|y| = 1$ and if $y = 0$, $|x| = 1$. On the other hand, when $x + y = 0$, using the second equation, the possible cases are $x = 1/2, y = -1/2$ and $x = -1/2, y = 1/2$. It is easy to validate that all of these cases lead to possible solutions to the system of equations.

14. Suppose $\alpha \leqslant \beta \leqslant \gamma \leqslant \delta$ are the roots of the polynomial. Since each root can be paired up with three other roots, if we add all the sums of the pairs of the roots, we get each root three times. It can be used to show that $\alpha + \beta + \gamma + \delta = 11$. Now, using the order of the magnitude of the roots, one can write down the individual sums in one of the following two ways: (a) $\alpha + \beta = 1, \alpha + \gamma = 2, \alpha + \delta = 5, \beta + \gamma = 6, \beta + \delta = 9, \gamma + \delta = 10$; (b) $\alpha + \beta = 1, \alpha + \gamma = 2, \alpha + \delta = 6, \beta + \gamma = 5, \beta + \delta = 9, \gamma + \delta = 10$. The solutions obtained from case (a) contradict the assumption that the coefficients are integers. Then, solving the equations in case (b), one can get $\alpha = -1, \beta = 2, \gamma = 3, \delta = 7$, which leads to the polynomial $P(x) = (x+1)(x-2)(x-3)(x-7)$. It is now straightforward to find $P(1) = -24$.

15. Consider $P(m) = a_n m^n + a_{n-1} m^{n-1} + \ldots + a_1 m + a_0$ for some integer m. If m is even, $P(m) \equiv a_0 \pmod{2}$. However, $a_0 = P(0)$ and it is odd. Thus, $P(m)$ cannot be 0 for even m. For odd m, on the other hand, $a_i m^i \equiv a_i \pmod{2}$, and thus, $P(m) \equiv a_n + a_{n-1} + \ldots + a_0 \pmod{2}$. The term on the right-hand side of this equation is in fact equal to $P(1)$ and that is odd as well. It implies that $P(m) \neq 0$ for all odd m as well. The proof follows from this.

16. One can show that

$$2\left(\sqrt{k+1} - \sqrt{k}\right) = \frac{2}{\sqrt{k+1}+\sqrt{k}}, \quad 2\left(\sqrt{k} - \sqrt{k-1}\right) = \frac{2}{\sqrt{k}+\sqrt{k-1}}$$

From the above equation and using $\sqrt{k-1} < \sqrt{k} < \sqrt{k+1}$, the inequalities can be proved. For the second part, one can apply the above inequalities for $k = 2, 3, \ldots, 10000$. Then, adding all the inequalities, one can find out that the integral part of the given term is 197.

17. From the given recursion relations, substituting the expression for a_k repeatedly, it can be seen that
$$a_n = n! + \frac{n!}{1!} + \frac{n!}{2!} + \ldots + \frac{n!}{(n-1)!}$$
Further, using $a_n + 1 = a_{n+1}/(n+1)$, one can show that $P_n = (a_n+1)/n!$. Thus, the limit of P_n as $n \to \infty$ is the same as that of $a_n/n!$, which, from the above relationship, can be computed as e.

18. Consider a new polynomial Q such that $Q(x) = (x+1)P(x) - x$. Since $P(x)$ is a polynomial of degree n, Q is a polynomial of degree $n+1$. Further, using the fact $P(k) = k/(k+1)$ for $k = 0, 1, \ldots, n$, one can argue that the only possible roots of $Q(x)$ are $0, 1, \ldots, n$. Thus
$$Q(x) = a_n x(x-1)(x-2)\ldots(x-n),$$
where a_n is the leading coefficient of $P(x)$. It is then easy to show that
$$P(n+1) = \frac{(n+1)! + (n+1)}{n+2}$$

19. One can use the concepts of complex numbers to solve this problem. Let $z = \cos\alpha + \iota\sin\alpha$ and denote
$$C_n = \sum_{k=0}^{n} \binom{n}{k} \cos(k\alpha), \quad S_n = \sum_{k=0}^{n} \binom{n}{k} \sin(k\alpha)$$
Then, using De Moivre's Theorem, argue that $C_n + \iota S_n = (1+z)^n$. Next, express $(1+z)$ in terms of $\alpha/2$ to obtain that $C_n = 0$ implies
$$\left(2\cos\frac{\alpha}{2}\right)^n \left(\cos\frac{n\alpha}{2}\right) = 0$$
Evidently, the above holds if $\alpha = \pi$ or if α is of the form $(2m+1)\pi/n$, where m is a positive integer satisfying $2m+1 < n$.

20. We can use the concepts of a polygon and its circumcircle to address this problem. Let $A_1, \ldots, A_n$ denote the points that have coordinates $z_1, \ldots, z_n$. Denote the midpoint of the line segment $A_i A_j$ as M_{ij}, and observe that the coordinate of it is given by $(z_i + z_j)/2$. The polygon $A_1 \ldots A_n$ is inscribed in the circle centred at the origin (let it be denoted as O) and with radius R. Now, use the identity $4OM_{ij}^2 + A_i A_j^2 = 4R^2$ to write
$$\sum_{1 \leq i < j \leq n} \left|\frac{z_i + z_j}{z_i - z_j}\right|^2 = \sum_{1 \leq i < j \leq n} \frac{4OM_{ij}^2}{A_i A_j^2} = \sum_{1 \leq i < j \leq n} \frac{4R^2}{A_i A_j^2} - \binom{n}{2}$$
The required result would then follow by applying the AM-HM inequality for the first term on the right-hand side of the above equation.

4
Calculus

"Calculus is the most powerful weapon of thought yet devised by the wit of man."
–Wallace Smith

Historically, Sir Isaac Newton is known to have compiled the concepts of calculus into one mathematical science in the seventeenth century, while famous mathematician Gottfried Leibniz is credited with the majority of the notations we use today.

It is understood that the discovery of this branch of mathematics was inspired by two classical problems from geometry. The first is to find the slope of the tangent line to a curve at a point and the second is to find the area bounded by a curve.

We shall cover some problems related to the second topic in this chapter, while most of the problems related to the first topic will be discussed in Chapter 6. In addition, many interesting concepts related to functions, limits, differentiation, integration and other relevant problems will be covered in this chapter. Remember that the concepts of calculus are heavily used in various applications, such as to analyze instantaneous rates of change, volumes of irregular solids, and so on.

KEY RESULTS

Throughout this chapter, the following notations are used:	
$\mathbb{N}$ = the set of natural numbers	$\mathbb{R}-$ = the set of negative real numbers
$\mathbb{Z}$ = the set of integers	$\mathbb{Q}$ = the set of rational numbers
$\mathbb{R}$ = the set of real numbers	$\mathbb{C}$ = the set of complex numbers
$\mathbb{R}+$ = the set of positive real numbers	

We start with a formal definition of relations and functions, which serve as the key to understanding calculus.

Definition 4.1 (Relation and Function): Consider two sets A and B. A relation from A to B is defined by a set with elements that are ordered pairs from A and B, that is, a relation $\mathcal{R}$ can be written as $\mathcal{R} = \{(x,y) : x \in A, y \in B\}$. A relation is called one–one if for two elements $(x_1,y_1), (x_2,y_2) \in \mathcal{R}$, $x_1 = x_2$ implies $y_1 = y_2$ and vice versa. A relation is called many–one if there is at least one example of $(x_1,y_1), (x_2,y_2) \in \mathcal{R}$ such that $x_1 \neq x_2, y_1 = y_2$. One–many relations are defined similarly.

A function f from a set A to a set B (not necessarily distinct) is a relation $\mathcal{R}$ that is either one–one or many–one such that for every $x \in A$, there is $y \in B$ satisfying $(x,y) \in \mathcal{R}$. It is typically written as $f : A \to B$, where A and B are known as the domain and the codomain, respectively. For $(x,y) \in \mathcal{R}$, one would write $f(x) = y$. The range of a function is defined by the set of values in the codomain for which there is at least one $x \in A$ satisfying $f(x) = y$.

The following are some important characterizations of a function.

Definition 4.2 (Injective, Surjective and Bijective Functions): If a function is one–one, it is also called an injective function. If the range of a function is equal to the codomain, then it is called a surjective or onto function. A bijective function is one that is both injective and surjective. If $f : A \to B$ is a bijective function, one can find another function $g : B \to A$ such that $f(x) = y$ is equivalent to $g(y) = x$. This function g is known as the inverse of f, and it is typically denoted by f^{-1}. Thus, a bijective function is also called an invertible function.

Definition 4.3 (Even and Odd Functions): Consider a real-valued function f that is defined on a domain symmetric around 0. This function is called even if $f(-x) = f(x)$ for every x in its domain and it is called odd if $f(-x) = -f(x)$ for every x in its domain.

Definition 4.4 (Periodic Function): A real-valued function f is called periodic if for some constant $c > 0$, $f(x+c) = f(x)$ for every x in its domain.

> **Useful Tip:** A function can be represented by a graph on the xy-plane. It is often easier to understand the properties of a function by visualizing it using a graph. For instance, if a function f intersects with the x-axis at a point c, then $f(c) = 0$, that is, c is a root or zero of the function. Another example of such visualizations is to check that the graph of an even function is symmetric about the y-axis whereas an odd function is symmetric about the origin. Consider how a periodic function or an invertible function from $\mathbb{R}$ to $\mathbb{R}$ would appear in a graph.

Next, we discuss the limit of a function, which is one of the most important concepts in calculus. This is, in fact, what separates calculus from the other pre-calculus mathematical branches. We restrict ourselves to all real-valued functions, but in higher mathematics, these definitions can be generalized for other possible sets.

Calculus

Definition 4.5 (Limit of a Function): Let $f : S \to \mathbb{R}$ be a function such that $S \subset \mathbb{R}$. Then, for a real number L, we say that $\lim_{x \to c} f(x) = L$ if for every $\varepsilon > 0$, there exists a $\delta > 0$ such that $0 < |x - c| < \delta$ implies $|f(x) - L| < \varepsilon$.

The implication of the above is that if x is taken very close to the value c, then the value of $f(x)$ would be very close to the value of L. It is imperative to point out that the limit of a function at a point may not always exist. However, if it exists, it will always be unique. This is used to define the following.

Definition 4.6 (Continuity of a Function): Consider a real-valued function f. It is continuous at $x = c$, if $\lim_{x \to c} f(x)$ exists and if $\lim_{x \to c} f(x) = f(c)$.

Definition 4.7 (Differentiability of a Function): Consider a real-valued function f. It is differentiable at $x = c$, if it is continuous at $x = c$ and if $\lim_{h \to 0} \frac{f(c+h) - f(c)}{h}$ exists. The value of the limit is known as the derivative of the function and the following notations are used in this regard:

$$f'(c) = \left.\frac{df(x)}{dx}\right|_{x=c} = \lim_{h \to 0} \frac{f(c+h) - f(c)}{h}$$

> **Useful Tip:** For checking the continuity or differentiability of a function, often it is most useful to check the right-hand limit and the left-hand limit separately. Since the limit is unique, if it exists, these two values must be equal. Conventionally, right-hand and left-hand limits are denoted as $\lim_{x \to c+} f(x)$ and $\lim_{x \to c-} f(x)$.

Theorem 4.1 (L'Hospital's Rule): Let f and g be two differentiable functions in an open interval I, except possibly at a point $c \in I$. If $\lim_{x \to c} f(x)$ and $\lim_{x \to c} g(x)$ are both 0, ∞ or $-\infty$, and $g'(x) \neq 0$ for all $x \in I - \{c\}$, and $\lim_{x \to c} f'(x)/g'(x)$ exists, then

$$\lim_{x \to c} \frac{f(x)}{g(x)} = \lim_{x \to c} \frac{f'(x)}{g'(x)}$$

> **Useful Tip:** L'Hospital's Rule is one of the most used tricks to evaluate the limits of indeterminate forms.

Definition 4.8 (Critical Point): For a function $f(x)$, $x = c$ is a critical point if $f(c)$ exists and if either $f'(c) = 0$ or $f(x)$ is not differentiable at $x = c$.

Definition 4.9 (Maxima and Minima): A function $f(x)$ is said to have an absolute or global maxima at $x = c$ if and only if $f(x) \leq f(c)$ for every x in the domain of f. On the other hand, $f(x)$ is said to have a local maxima at $x = c$ if and only if there is some $\delta > 0$ such that $f(x) \leq f(c)$ for every $x \in (c - \delta, c + \delta)$. Global minima and local minima are defined similarly.

Maxima and minima are collectively known as the extrema of a function. The following theorems are critical in finding these values.

Theorem 4.2 (Extreme Value Theorem): Suppose that $f(x)$ is a continuous function with the domain $[a,b]$. Then, there are two numbers $c, d \in [a,b]$ such that $f(c)$ is a maxima and $f(d)$ is a minima for the function.

Theorem 4.3 (Fermat's Theorem): If the function $f(x)$ has a local extrema at $x = c$ and if $f(x)$ is differentiable at $x = c$, then $x = c$ is a critical point of $f(x)$, such that $f'(c) = 0$.

This theorem can be used to find out the maxima and minima of a function. The usual approach is to first find out a point at which the first order derivative is 0, and then to observe the behaviour of the second order derivative at that point. In case the second order derivative at that point is positive (or negative), it indicates a local minima (or a local maxima). However, one must remember that an extrema can occur at a point where the derivative does not exist. Simultaneously, there can be a critical point where the first order derivative is 0, but the function does not attain an extrema.

Definition 4.10 (Saddle Point and Inflection Point): For a function $f(x)$, the point c is called a saddle point if it is a critical point but not an extrema. An inflection point, meanwhile, is a point at which the sign of the curvature (that is, the concavity) for the function changes.

From this definition, one can observe that for a twice-differentiable real-valued function $f(x)$, $x = c$ is an inflection point if $f''(c) = 0$. Further note that it does not require $x = c$ to be a critical point. An example is $f(x) = x^3 + x$, for which $x = 0$ is an inflection point, but not a saddle point. An important corollary is that if $x = c$ is both a critical point and an inflection point, then it is a saddle point as well.

Theorem 4.4 (Rolle's Theorem): Let $f(x)$ be a real-valued function such that it is continuous on the closed interval $[a,b]$, differentiable on the open interval (a, b) and $f(a) = f(b)$. Then there is a real number $c \in (a,b)$ such that $f'(c) = 0$. In other words, $f(x)$ has a critical point in the open interval (a,b).

Rolle's Theorem is a special case of the following.

Theorem 4.5 (Mean Value Theorem): Let $f(x)$ be a real-valued function such that it is continuous on the closed interval $[a,b]$ and is differentiable on the open interval (a,b). Then, there is a real number $c \in (a,b)$ such that

$$f'(c) = \frac{f(b) - f(a)}{b - a}$$

We omit the formulae for the derivatives of various functions, as they are readily available in any textbook. We turn our attention to some important types of problems where differentiation serves as the key tool. One should note that the derivative can be interpreted

Calculus

as the rate of change of the function at the given point. Thus, it can be used to calculate relative rates, such as velocity, acceleration and instantaneous rate of change of a physical state. One may also need to apply the concepts of extrema to solve related problems. Pertinent to this, a common type of exercise in all examinations is to find the tangent line to a curve. This topic is deferred to Chapter 6 and will be discussed in the light of coordinate geometry.

Another related exercise is to draw a rough sketch of the graph of $y = f(x)$. In order to do this, one needs to find the domain of the function, assess continuity and differentiability, compute the limiting values at appropriate points, understand the nature of first and second order derivatives to subsequently determine the extremas, and find asymptotes, if any. We illustrate this using an example below, where we draw a rough sketch of the function

$$f(x) = \frac{5 - 3x^2}{1 - x^2}$$

One should start with the domain of the function. It is clear that $f(x)$ is not defined for $x = \pm 1$, and thus, the domain is $\mathbb{R} - \{-1, 1\}$. Next, observe that the function is even and that it has two real roots: $x = \pm\sqrt{5/3}$. On the other hand, the y-intercept is 5. Further, since the function is even, it is enough to understand the behaviour of the function for $x \geq 0$. We can then take the mirror image of the graph about the y-axis to draw the graph for all x.

Now, we can write the function as $f(x) = 3 + 2/(1 - x^2)$. It is a straightforward exercise to show that $f(x)$ is neither continuous nor differentiable at $x = \pm 1$. In fact, as x approaches 1 from the left-hand side, the function approaches ∞ whereas $f(x) \to -\infty$ as $x \to 1+$, and so, there is an asymptote at $x = 1$. Also, as $x \to \infty$, $y \to 3$. Next, taking the first order derivative for all $x \geq 0$ ($x \neq 1$), we get

$$f'(x) = \frac{4x}{(1-x^2)^2} \geq 0$$

So, the function is increasing for all positive x. Taking another derivative

$$f''(x) = \frac{4(1-x^2)^2 + (4x)(4x)(1-x^2)}{(1-x^2)^4} = \frac{4(1-x^2) + 16x^2}{(1-x^2)^3} = \frac{4(3x^2+1)}{(1-x^2)^3}$$

Thus, the second order derivative is positive if $x^2 < 1$ and is negative otherwise. It implies that the function does not have any extrema, is convex for all $x < 1$ and is concave for all $x > 1$. Combining all of the above information, we can draw the graph as follows.

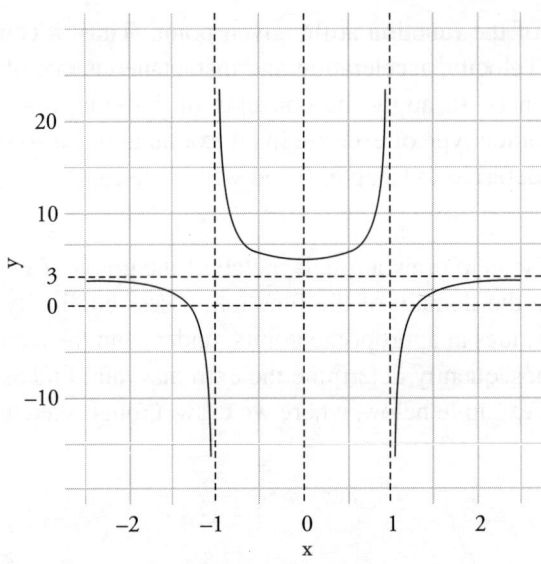

The last crucial topic of this chapter is the concept of integration, and we start with the formal definition of antiderivative.

Definition 4.11 (Antiderivative): If $f(x)$ is the derivative of another function $F(x)$, then F is called the antiderivative of f. Note that if $F(x)$ is an antiderivate of $f(x)$, then so is $F(x)+c$ for some real constant c. It is also written in the indefinite integral form as $\int f(x)\,dx = F(x)+c$.

As mentioned earlier, the formulae for various indefinite integrals can be found in any textbook and are omitted here. We focus on definite integrals and some important problem-solving techniques.

Definition 4.12 (Riemann Sum): Consider a function $f(x)$ defined on a closed interval $[a,b]$. Suppose that the interval $[a,b]$ is partitioned into n sub-intervals of the form $[x_{i-1},x_i]$ ($1 \leqslant i \leqslant n$), each of width Δx. Further, for each i, let x_i^* be any point in $[x_{i-1},x_i]$. Then, a Riemann sum for $f(x)$ is defined as

$$\sum_{i=1}^{n} f(x_i^*)\Delta x$$

Definition 4.13 (Definite Integral): For a function $f(x)$ defined on a closed interval $[a,b]$, the definite integral is defined as a limiting form of a Riemann sum (provided the limit exists), where the width of each sub-interval approaches zero. Formally, one can write

$$\int_a^b f(x)\,dx = \lim_{n\to\infty} \frac{1}{n} \sum_{i=1}^{n} f\left(a + \frac{(b-a)i}{n}\right) = \lim_{n\to\infty} \frac{1}{n} \sum_{j=0}^{n-1} f\left(a + \frac{(b-a)j}{n}\right)$$

Calculus

A function for which the above limit exists is called an integrable function. All continuous functions are known to be integrable. Remember that the definite integral represents the area under the curve $y = f(x)$ in the interval $[a, b]$, and that is a crucial topic for most examinations.

> **Useful Tip:** Calculating the definite integral following known formulae may lead to negative values, if the curve is below the x-axis. While computing the area under the curve for such functions, these negative values should be treated appropriately.

Theorem 4.6 (Comparison Theorem): If f and g are two integrable functions defined in $[a,b]$ and if $f(x) \geqslant g(x)$ for all $x \in [a,b]$, then

$$\int_a^b f(x)\,dx \geqslant \int_a^b g(x)\,dx$$

Theorem 4.7 (Fundamental Theorem of Calculus): If f is a continuous function defined in $[a,b]$ and if $F(x) = \int_a^x f(t)\,dt$, then $F'(x) = f(x)$ for all $x \in [a,b]$. On the other hand, if F is the antiderivate of f, then

$$\int_a^b f(x)\,dx = F(b) - F(a)$$

Theorem 4.8 (Mean Value Theorem for Integrals): If f is a continuous function defined in $[a,b]$, then there exists at least one point $c \in [a,b]$ such that

$$\int_a^b f(x)\,dx = f(c)(b-a)$$

Theorem 4.9 (Leibniz Integral Rule): The derivative of the definite integral of the function $f(x,t)$ in the interval $[a(x), b(x)]$ is given by the following formula:

$$\frac{d}{dx}\left(\int_{a(x)}^{b(x)} f(x,t)\,dt\right) = f(x,b(x))\frac{d}{dx}b(x) - f(x,a(x))\frac{d}{dx}a(x) + \int_{a(x)}^{b(x)} \frac{\partial}{\partial x} f(x,t)\,dt,$$

where the last term involves partial derivatives of $f(x,t)$ with respect to x.

> **Useful Tip:** The following two special forms of the Leibniz Rule are commonly used in practice:
> $$\frac{d}{dx}\left(\int_{a(x)}^{b(x)} f(t)\,dt\right) = f(b(x))\frac{d}{dx}b(x) - f(a(x))\frac{d}{dx}a(x),$$
> $$\frac{d}{dx}\left(\int_a^b f(x,t)\,dt\right) = \int_a^b \frac{\partial}{\partial x} f(x,t)\,dt$$

Solved Examples

1. Let $f(x)$ be a real-valued function for $x \in \mathbb{R}$ such that $2f(x) + 3f(-x) = 15 - 4x$. Find the value of $f(-1)$.

Solution: Using $-x$ in place of x in the given equation, we get $2f(-x) + 3f(x) = 15 + 4x$ for all x. One can solve the above two equations as follows:

$$5f(x) = 3\{2f(-x) + 3f(x)\} - 2\{2f(x) + 3f(-x)\} \implies 5f(x) = 20x + 15$$

Hence, the expression for the function is $f(x) = 4x + 3$. Clearly, $f(-1) = -1$.

> **Useful Tip:** A useful strategy to solve problems related to functions in calculus is to find the expressions for some special cases, such as $f(-x)$, $f(0)$, $f(1)$, etc. The following problem shows another application of this.

2. Show that there is a real root for the equation $\sqrt[3]{x} + \sqrt{x} = 1$.

Solution: Consider the function $f(x) = \sqrt[3]{x} + \sqrt{x} - 1$. Clearly, the domain of the function is $[0, \infty)$. Now, the function is a continuous function since both $\sqrt[3]{x}$ and $\sqrt{x}$ are continuous in the interval $[0, \infty)$.

Observe that $f(0) = -1$ and $f(1) = 1$. Thus, the function changes its sign from negative to positive, from 0 to 1. Since it is continuous, we can say that there is a real $x \in (0,1)$ for which $f(x) = 0$. Hence, there is at least one real value of x for which $\sqrt[3]{x} + \sqrt{x} = 1$.

3. If $f : \mathbb{R} \to \mathbb{R}$ is a function satisfying $|f(x) - f(y)| \leqslant 39|x - y|^2$ for all x, y, show that f is a constant function.

Solution: We start by checking the continuity and differentiability of the function. For any real number a, using the given condition, one can write $|f(x) - f(a)| \leqslant 39|x - a|^2$. Thus, for both $x \to a$ from the right and from the left, one can argue that $|f(x) - f(a)| \leqslant 0$, and therefore, $\lim_{x \to a} f(x) = f(a)$.

For checking differentiability, note that

$$\frac{|f(x) - f(a)|}{|x - a|} \leqslant 39|x - a|$$

Then, applying similar arguments as above, one can obtain

$$\lim_{x \to a} \frac{|f(x) - f(a)|}{|x - a|} = 0,$$

which indicates $f'(a) = 0$ for all $a \in \mathbb{R}$. Hence, f is a constant function.

Calculus

4. Consider the closed unit disc $D = \{(x,y) | x^2 + y^2 \leq 1\}$. At which point in this disc does the function $f(x,y) = x+y$ attain its maximum?

Solution: Let us assume that $x^2 + y^2 = r^2$, where $|r| \leq 1$. We can safely start with the assumption that in order to maximize $f(x,y) = x+y$, both x and y must be positive. Then

$$f(x,y) = x + \sqrt{r^2 - x^2}$$

Let us call it $g(x)$, and taking the derivative, we can get

$$g'(x) = 1 + \frac{(-2x)}{2\sqrt{r^2 - x^2}} = 1 - \frac{x}{\sqrt{r^2 - x^2}},$$

which further implies that

$$g''(x) = -\frac{1}{\sqrt{r^2 - x^2}} + \frac{x(-2x)}{2(r^2 - x^2)^{3/2}} = -\frac{r^2}{(r^2 - x^2)^{3/2}}$$

From the above, it is clear that $g''(x) < 0$ for any x and $g'(x) = 0$ when $x^2 = r^2 - x^2$, that is, when $x = r/\sqrt{2}$. Thus, at $x = r/\sqrt{2}$, we have a local maxima and that maximum value is

$$g\left(\frac{r}{\sqrt{2}}\right) = \frac{r}{\sqrt{2}} + \sqrt{r^2 - \frac{r^2}{2}} = r\sqrt{2}$$

Now, since the absolute value of r can be anything between 0 and 1, we can say that the function $f(x,y)$ attains its maximum for $r = 1$ and the corresponding maximum value is $\sqrt{2}$. Also, note that this solution is obtained for $x = 1/\sqrt{2}, y = 1/\sqrt{2}$.

5. Suppose that $a_0 = 0 < a_1 < a_2 < \ldots < a_k$ are all real numbers. Let $p(t)$ be a real-valued polynomial of degree k such that

$$\int_{a_j}^{a_{j+1}} p(t) dt = 0,$$

for all $0 \leq j \leq k-1$. Prove that $p(t)$ has exactly one root in the interval (a_j, a_{j+1}) for all $0 \leq j \leq k-1$.

Solution: Note that any polynomial is an integrable function. Let $f(t)$ be a real-valued polynomial of degree $k+1$ such that $f'(t) = p(t)$ for all $t \in \mathbb{R}$. Now, from the condition

$$\int_{a_j}^{a_{j+1}} p(t) dt = 0 \quad \text{for all } 0 \leq j \leq k-1,$$

we can say that $f(a_{j+1}) - f(a_j) = 0$ for all $0 \leq j \leq k-1$.

Next, using Rolle's Theorem, it is easy to observe that $f'(t) = 0$ must have a root between a_j and a_{j+1} for all $0 \leq j \leq n-1$. That means, the polynomial $p(t)$ has at least one root in every interval (a_j, a_{j+1}) for $0 \leq j \leq k-1$. However, since $a_0 = 0 < a_1 < a_2 < \ldots < a_k$, all these intervals are disjoint and there are n intervals in total, implying that $p(t)$ has at least n roots.

Since $p(t)$ is a polynomial of degree n, it can have at most n real roots, and hence, from the above discussion, it is straightforward to conclude that the polynomial $p(t)$ has exactly one root in the interval (a_j, a_{j+1}) for all $0 \leq j \leq k-1$.

6. Consider two twice-differentiable non-decreasing functions $f(x)$ and $g(x)$ satisfying $f''(x) = g(x)$, $g''(x) = f(x)$, and assume that $f(x)g(x)$ is a linear function. Prove that $f(x) = g(x) = 0$.

Solution: Since $f''(x) = g(x)$ and $g''(x) = f(x)$, it is enough to prove that the product $f(x)g(x)$ is 0. We know that it is a linear function, and so, the second order derivative must be 0. Observe that

$$\begin{aligned}
\frac{d^2}{dx^2} f(x)g(x) &= \frac{d}{dx} \left[f'(x)g(x) + f(x)g'(x) \right] \\
&= f''(x)g(x) + f'(x)g'(x) + f'(x)g'(x) + f(x)g''(x) \\
&= g(x)^2 + f(x)^2 + 2f'(x)g'(x)
\end{aligned}$$

Since f and g are real-valued functions, the first two terms of the above expression are non-negative. On the other hand, it is given that f, g are non-decreasing functions, implying that the first order derivatives of both are non-negative too. Thus, $f'(x)g'(x) \geq 0$ as well. Clearly, each term on the right-hand side of the equation must be identically equal to 0, thereby implying that $f(x) = g(x) = 0$.

7. Consider a continuous function $f : \mathbb{R} \to \mathbb{R}$. Suppose that for all $x \in R$ and for all $t > 0$

$$f(x) = \frac{1}{t} \int_0^t (f(x+y) - f(y)) \, dy.$$

Prove that $f(x) = cx$ for some real constant c.

Solution: Let us denote the function $\int_0^t f(r) \, dr$ by $g(t)$. Then, g is a continuously differentiable function such that $g'(t) = f(t)$. We use the given equation

$$f(x) = \frac{1}{t} \int_x^{t+x} f(r) \, dr - \frac{1}{t} \int_0^t f(y) \, dy,$$

which implies that $tf(x) = g(t+x) - g(x) - g(t)$. Now, taking the first order derivative with respect to t, we can write $f(x) = g'(t+x) - g'(t) = f(t+x) - f(t)$.

Clearly, the relation $f(t+x) = f(t) + f(x)$ holds for all $x \in \mathbb{R}$ and for all $t > 0$. Substituting $x = 0$, we get $f(0) = 0$. Let us write $f(1) = c$. We shall prove the required result in four steps as follows.

Step 1: (Proving for natural numbers) Suppose, for some natural number $k > 1$, $f(k) = ck$. Then, $f(k+1) = f(k) + f(1) = ck + c = c(k+1)$. Thus, using the principles of mathematical induction, we can say that for all natural numbers n, $f(n) = cn$.

Step 2: (Proving for positive rational numbers) First, note that $f(2x) = 2f(x)$ for $x > 0$. Next, assuming that $f(kx) = kf(x)$ for some $k \in \mathbb{N}$, we can show that $f((k+1)x) = (k+1)f(x)$, and thus, once again using the principles of mathematical induction, $f(mx) = mf(x)$ for all $m \in \mathbb{N}$ and for all $x > 0$.

Using the above, if r is a positive rational number, since we can write it as $r = p/q$ for $p, q \in \mathbb{N}$, we get $f(r) = pf(1/q)$. However, $f(1) = f(q/q) = qf(1/q)$, implying that $f(1/q) = c/q$. Combining these, we get $f(r) = pc/q = cr$, and thus, for any $r \in \mathbb{Q}^+$, $f(r) = cr$.

Step 3: (Proving for positive irrational numbers) We know that for every positive rational number, the relation $f(x) = cx$ holds. Now, consider an irrational number s. Since f is a continuous function, we can obtain a sequence of rational numbers $r_1, r_2, \ldots$ converging to s such that $|f(s) - f(r_n)|$ approaches 0 as n goes to ∞. In other words

$$\lim_{n \to \infty} f(r_n) = f(s) \implies \lim_{n \to \infty} cr_n = f(s)$$

However, $r_n \to s$ as $n \to \infty$, and hence, we get $f(s) = cs$. So, the result is true for positive irrational numbers too.

Step 4: (Proving for negative real numbers) We have already proved that $f(x) = cx$ for all positive real x. In order to prove the same for all negative numbers, we only have to note that $f(0) = f(x) + f(-x)$, and so, $f(-x) = -f(x) = -cx$.

Hence, for all $x \in \mathbb{R}$, there exists a constant c (the value of $f(1)$) such that $f(x) = cx$.

> **Useful Tip:** In Step 3 of the above solution, an attractive method using the concept of limits of a sequence is presented. This can be effective in similar calculus problems.

8. Let $f(x)$ be a real-valued continuous function satisfying $f(x) = \int_0^x f(t)\, dt$. Prove that $f(x) = 0$.

Solution: We start with the definition of the derivative of a function. Note that from the given equation

$$\frac{f(x+h) - f(x)}{h} = \frac{1}{h} \int_x^{x+h} f(t)\, dt$$

Taking $h \to 0$, we get that f is differentiable and $f'(x) = f(x)$ for all x.

Next, if $f(0) = 0$, let a be the minimum positive real number such that $f(a)$ is non-zero, that is, we assume $f(x) = 0$ for all non-negative $x < a$ and $f(a) \neq 0$. Also, if $f(0) \neq 0$, set $a = 0$, and without loss of generality, let us assume that $f(a) > 0$.

Since both $f'(x)$ and $f(x)$ are continuous functions, we can always find an interval (a,b) with $b < a+1$ such that $f'(x) > 0$ for all $x \in (a,b)$, and therefore, $f(x)$ is increasing in (a,b). Clearly

$$f(b) = \int_a^b f(x)\,dx \leqslant \int_a^b f(b)\,dx = (b-a)f(b) < f(b),$$

and we arrive at a contradiction. Thus, there can never exist a non-negative real number a such that $f(a) \neq 0$, which implies that $f(x) = 0$ for all $x \geqslant 0$. Using similar arguments, we can prove that $f(x) = 0$ for all $x \leqslant 0$. That proves the required result.

9. Let $a \in \mathbb{R}$ be a fixed constant satisfying $|a| < 1$. Prove that $4x^3 - 3x + a = 0$ has three distinct real roots, all of which are in the interval $(-1, 1)$.

Solution: Consider the cubic polynomial $y = 4x^3 - 3x + a$. Clearly, the domain is the set of all real numbers and there is either one or three real roots. Since the leading coefficient is positive, we can say that y approaches ∞ and $-\infty$ as x goes towards ∞ and $-\infty$, respectively. We also have $y = a$ when $x = 0$.

Taking the derivatives

$$y' = 3(4x^2 - 1) = 3(2x+1)(2x-1); \quad y'' = 24x$$

So, the first order derivative is zero at $x = \pm 1/2$. Since the second order derivative is positive for all positive x and negative for negative x, we know that there is a local maxima at $x = -1/2$ and a local minima at $x = 1/2$. Also, the function is increasing for $x \in (-\infty, -1/2] \cup [1/2, \infty)$ and is decreasing otherwise. On the other hand, the function is convex for $x > 0$ (since $y'' > 0$ in that case) and is concave for $x < 0$.

Hence, for some a, the curve of $y = 4x^3 - 3x + a$ looks like the figure on the next page (the left panel corresponds to an example of $a > 0$ and the right panel corresponds to an example of $a < 0$).

We next focus on the values of y at specific points of x. The graph helps us in this. First, at $x = -1/2$, $y = 1 + a$ and that is a positive quantity since $|a| < 1$. By similar logic, for $x = -1$, $y = a - 1 < 0$), and so, there is a real root between -1 and $-1/2$. Further, at $x = 1/2$, $y = a - 1 < 0$ and at $x = 1$, $y = a + 1 > 0$. Clearly, there exists a real root in $(-1/2, 1/2)$ and another real root in the interval $(1/2, 1)$. Hence, for $0 < |a| < 1$, the

Calculus

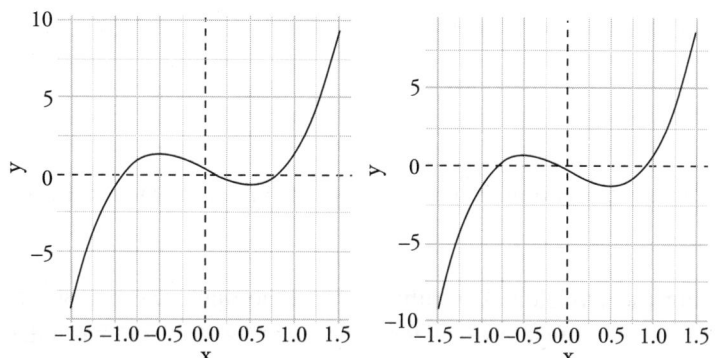

equation has three distinct real roots, all of which have their absolute values smaller than 1.

> **Useful Tip:** Here, the problem is solved using a graphical method, which is a useful technique for such exercises. Try to find a solution using the concept of polynomials.

10. For $t > 0$, let $f(t) = e^{-1/t}$, and for $n \in \mathbb{N}$, let P_n be the polynomial that satisfies $\frac{d^n}{dt^n} f(t) = P_n(\frac{1}{t})e^{-\frac{1}{t}}$ for all $t > 0$. Prove that for all $x > 0$

$$P_{n+1}(x) = x^2 \left(P_n(x) - \frac{d}{dx} P_n(x) \right).$$

Solution: We know that the derivative of $e^{-1/t}$ is $\frac{d}{dt} e^{-1/t} = e^{-1/t}/t^2$. Now, in order to prove the required recursion result, we take the $(n+1)$th derivative of $f(t)$. Using the given relationship

$$\frac{d^{n+1}}{dt^{n+1}} f(t) = \frac{d}{dt} \left[P_n\left(\frac{1}{t}\right) e^{-\frac{1}{t}} \right]$$

Clearly, the left-hand side is equal to $P_{n+1}(1/t)e^{-1/t}$, whereas the right-hand side is equal to

$$e^{-\frac{1}{t}} \frac{d}{dt} P_n\left(\frac{1}{t}\right) + P_n\left(\frac{1}{t}\right) \frac{d}{dt} e^{-\frac{1}{t}} = e^{-\frac{1}{t}} \frac{d}{dt} P_n\left(\frac{1}{t}\right) + P_n\left(\frac{1}{t}\right) \frac{e^{-\frac{1}{t}}}{t^2}$$

Next, canceling $e^{-1/t}$ from the two terms, we arrive at the equality

$$P_{n+1}\left(\frac{1}{t}\right) = \frac{d}{dt} P_n\left(\frac{1}{t}\right) + \frac{1}{t^2} P_n\left(\frac{1}{t}\right)$$

Let us now substitute $x = 1/t$. Since $dx/dt = -1/t^2 = -x^2$, we can rewrite the above equation to obtain the required result:

$$P_{n+1}(x) = -x^2 \frac{d}{dx} P_n(x) + x^2 P_n(x) = x^2 \left(P_n(x) - \frac{d}{dx} P_n(x) \right)$$

11. Let $p(x)$ be a polynomial of degree less than 100. If $(x^3 - x)$ does not divide $p(x)$ and if

$$\frac{d^{100}}{dx^{100}}\left(\frac{p(x)}{x^3 - x}\right) = \frac{f(x)}{g(x)},$$

for some non-constant polynomials $f(x)$ and $g(x)$, what is the smallest possible degree of $f(x)$?

Solution: Using the Division Algorithm for polynomials, we can write $p(x) = (x^3 - x)q(x) + r(x)$, where $q(x)$ must have a degree less than 97, and $r(x)$ has a degree of at most 2. Thus, the 100th derivative of $q(x)$ is 0, and we can write

$$\frac{f(x)}{g(x)} = \frac{d^{100}}{dx^{100}}\left(\frac{r(x)}{x^3 - x}\right).$$

If $(x^2 - 1)$ is a factor of $r(x)$, then there is some constant $r_0 \in \mathbb{R}$ such that

$$\frac{f(x)}{g(x)} = \frac{d^{100}}{dx^{100}}\left(\frac{r_0}{x}\right) = \frac{100! r_0}{x^{101}},$$

which further indicates that $f(x)$ is a constant polynomial – a contradiction. Thus, we can assume that $(x^2 - 1)$ does not divide $r(x)$ and that it can be written as $r(x) = a(x^2 - 1) + bx + c$. Since $(x^3 - x) = x(x-1)(x+1)$, it is further possible to find real constants A, B, C such that

$$\frac{r(x)}{x^3 - x} = \frac{A}{x} + \frac{B}{x-1} + \frac{C}{x+1} \implies \frac{f(x)}{g(x)} = \frac{100!A}{x^{101}} + \frac{100!B}{(x-1)^{101}} + \frac{100!C}{(x+1)^{101}}$$

Let us omit 100! from the above without loss of generality. Subsequently, simplifying the above, we get

$$f(x) = A(x^2 - 1)^{101} + B(x^2 + x)^{101} + C(x^2 - x)^{101}$$

Now, the coefficients of $x^{202}, x^{201}, x^{200}$ in the above expression are, respectively, equal to $A + B + C$, $101(B - C)$ and $\binom{101}{2}(B + C) - 101A$. Clearly, one can choose A, B, C in such a way that the first two coefficients are zero, but it is impossible to make all three of them zero. Hence, the least possible degree of $f(x)$ is 200.

12. Recall the definition of the greatest integer function $[x]$. Sketch on plain paper a graph of the function $f(x) = [x] - \sqrt{x - [x]}$ for $-5 \leq x \leq 5$. Further, prove that for any $y_0 \in \mathbb{R}$, there exists $x_0 \in \mathbb{R}$ satisfying $y_0 = f(x_0)$.

Solution: We know that the function $x - [x]$ represents the fractional part of the real number x and it is a periodic function with fundamental period 1. Thus, the second part of $f(x)$ is periodic. We can also say that $f(x)$ in $[k, k+1)$ (for $k \in \mathbb{Z}$) behaves in a similar manner as the function $g(x) = -\sqrt{x}$ in the interval $[0, 1)$. On the other hand, the first part of the given function is the integral part of x. Naturally, the value of $[x]$ remains the same (k) in the interval $[k, k+1)$.

Combining the above information, we know that in $[0, 1)$, $f(x)$ is the same as $g(x) = -\sqrt{x}$, and as it moves to $[1, 2)$, the nature of the function remains the same but is shifted one unit up. It continues similarly on both sides.

We now need to understand how $g(x)$ behaves within the interval $[0, 1)$. Taking the derivatives, we get
$$g'(x) = -\frac{1}{2\sqrt{x}}, \ g''(x) = \frac{1}{4x^{3/2}}$$

Clearly, $g'(x) < 0$ and $g''(x) > 0$ for all $x \in [0, 1)$. Thus, $g(x)$ decreases as a convex function from $g(0) = 0$ to $\lim_{x \to 1^-} g(x) = -1$. For $f(x)$, this pattern is repeated for any interval between two integers. We also note that $f(x)$ is discontinuous at all integer points.

We can now draw the required graph using the above information, as shown below.

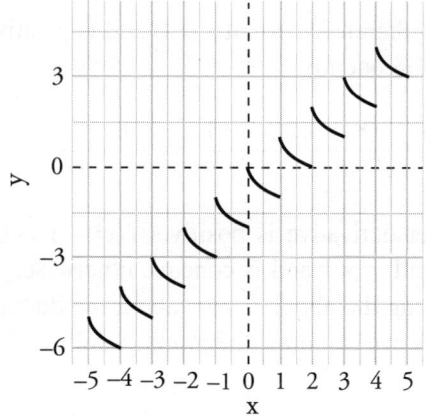

To prove the second part, we can easily deduce from the graph that the function ranges over the whole set of real numbers. To be more explicit, we can see that for y_0, we must have x_0 such that $[x_0] - \sqrt{x_0 - [x_0]} = y_0$ and that means $[x_0] = [y_0] + 1$. We can now solve the equation and obtain
$$x_0 = ([y_0] + 1 - y_0)^2 + [y_0] + 1,$$
which satisfies $f(x_0) = y_0$.

13. Draw a rough sketch of the following function:

$$f(x) = \frac{x-1}{x+1} + \frac{x+1}{x-1}.$$

Solution: The domain of the function is $\mathbb{R} - \{-1, 1\}$ and it can be simplified as

$$f(x) = \frac{(x-1)^2 + (x+1)^2}{x^2 - 1} = \frac{2(x^2+1)}{x^2-1} = 2 + \frac{4}{x^2-1}$$

Note that $f(x) = 0$ implies $x^2 + 1 = 0$, which is impossible for real x. So, the function has no real root. Also, the function is even, and so, it is sufficient to look at the function's behaviour for non-negative x. We can then take the mirror image with respect to the y-axis to draw the graph for all x.

Next, taking the limit of the function as $x \to 1$, we get $\lim_{x \to 1+} f(x) = \infty$, $\lim_{x \to 1-} f(x) = -\infty$, implying that at $x = 1$, there is an asymptote. Moreover, if $x \to \infty$, then $f(x) \to 2$. Now, taking the first order derivative of $f(x)$

$$f'(x) = -\frac{8x}{(x^2-1)^2}$$

The first order derivative is therefore zero at $x = 0$ and is positive for all $x > 0$. Thus, f is increasing for all $x \geqslant 0$. Subsequently

$$f''(x) = -\frac{8(x^2-1)^2 - (8x)(4x)(x^2-1)}{(x^2-1)^4} = -\frac{8(x^2-1) - 32x^2}{(x^2-1)^3} = \frac{8(3x^2+1)}{(x^2-1)^3}$$

Evidently, the second order derivative is positive if $x^2 - 1 > 0$, that is, if $x > 1$. Thus, the function is convex for all $x > 1$ and is concave otherwise. Because of this, there is a local maxima at $x = 0$. Using the above results about the domain, the asymptotes and the properties of the derivatives, we can draw the graph as follows.

Calculus

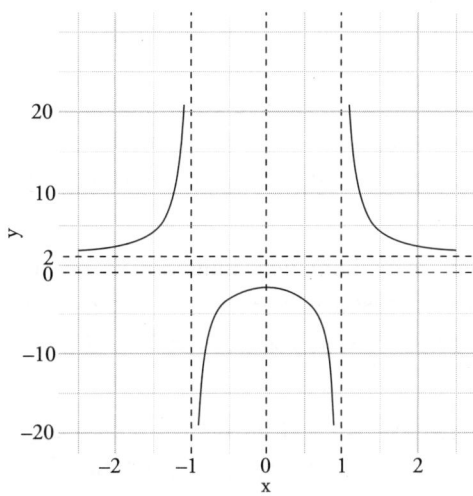

> **Useful Tip:** See the example of $f(x) = (5 - 3x^2)/(1 - x^2)$ at the beginning of the chapter, and observe how the graph in the above problem appears. Their similarity comes from the fact that both are location-scale transformed functions from $1/(1 - x^2)$. At times, it might be helpful to draw the graph of a simpler function and then carry out a location-scale transformation of the graph.

14. Let $f : \mathbb{N} + \{0\} \to \mathbb{N} + \{0\}$ be a function satisfying $f(0) = 0$, $f(1) = 1$ and $f(n) = f(n-1) + f(n-2)$ for $n > 2$. Show that the following results hold

    (i) $f(n)$ is increasing for all $n > 2$.

    (ii) The equation $f(f(n)) = f(n)$ is satisfied for exactly three positive integers.

    (iii) 5 divides $f(5n)$ for all $n \in \mathbb{N}$.

Solution:

(i) We can observe that $f(2) = 1$ and for all $n > 2$, $f(n) = f(n-1) + f(n-2)$, implying that $f(n)$ is strictly positive for all $n \geqslant 1$. Thus, for all $n > 2$, $f(n+1) = f(n) + f(n-1) > f(n)$.

(ii) It is easy to obtain the images for the first few positive integers:

$$f(1) = 1, f(2) = 1, f(3) = 2, f(4) = 3, f(5) = 5$$

Clearly, for $n = 1, 2, 5$, we get $f(f(n)) = f(n)$. We only have to prove that there is no other positive integer n that satisfies the condition.

For the given function, we have already shown that it is increasing for all $n > 2$. Subsequently, since $f(n)$ is a positive integer for $n \geqslant 1$, we can also deduce that once $f(m) > m$, for all $n > m$, $f(n)$ must be greater than n. Now, $f(6) = 8$, and so, for all $n \geqslant 6$, $f(n) > n$. Moreover, since f is strictly increasing, we get $f(f(n)) > f(n)$ for all $n \geqslant 6$. And hence, there exist precisely three positive integers for which $f(f(n)) = f(n)$.

(iii) We use the principles of mathematical induction to prove the required result. Note that $f(5) = 5$, and so, the result is true for $n = 1$. Suppose it is true for some m, that is, $f(5m)$ is divisible by 5. Note that $f(5m+5) = f(5m+4) + f(5m+3)$, and so, recursively

$$\begin{aligned} f(5m+5) &= 2f(5m+3) + f(5m+2) \\ &= 3f(5m+2) + 2f(5m+1) \\ &= 5f(5m+1) + 3f(5m) \end{aligned}$$

Clearly, both of the above terms are multiples of 5, and so, $f(5m+5)$ is a multiple of 5 as well. Hence, we can see that $f(5n)$ is divisible by 5 for all $n \in \mathbb{N}$.

15. Let f be a real-valued differentiable function with the domain $[1, \infty)$, such that

$$f'(x) = \frac{1}{x^2 + f^2(x)}.$$

If $f(1) = 1$, show that $f(x) \leqslant 1 + \pi/4$ for $x \geqslant 1$.

Solution: Since f is a real-valued function, we can say that $x^2 + f^2(x) > 0$ for all $x \geqslant 1$, and so, f must be a strictly increasing function on $[1, \infty)$. We can then say that $f(x) \geqslant f(1) = 1$ for all x. It further implies that for all x

$$f'(x) = \frac{1}{x^2 + f^2(x)} \leqslant \frac{1}{x^2 + 1}$$

Now, using the above results and the properties of integral calculus

$$f(x) - 1 = \int_1^x f'(x)\, dx \leqslant \int_1^\infty f'(x)\, dx \leqslant \int_1^\infty \frac{1}{x^2+1}\, dx = \left[\tan^{-1} x\right]_1^\infty = \frac{\pi}{4}$$

Hence, $f(x) \leqslant 1 + \pi/4$ for every $x \geqslant 1$.

16. Prove that the function $f : \mathbb{R} \to \mathbb{R}$ defined by

$$f(x) = \cos x + \cos\left(\frac{\sqrt{3}x}{2}\right)$$

Calculus

is not periodic.

Solution: Assume that the given function is periodic with fundamental period a. Then, $f(x+a) = f(x)$ for all real x, and so

$$g_a(x) = \cos(x+a) + \cos\left(\frac{\sqrt{3}(x+a)}{2}\right) - \cos x - \cos\left(\frac{\sqrt{3}x}{2}\right)$$

is identically zero for all real x.

We know that $\cos C - \cos D = 2\sin((C+D)/2)\sin((D-C)/2)$, and using this, we can simplify g_a as

$$g_a(x) = -2\sin\left(x + \frac{a}{2}\right)\sin\left(\frac{a}{2}\right) - 2\sin\left(\frac{\sqrt{3}x}{2} + \frac{\sqrt{3}a}{4}\right)\sin\left(\frac{\sqrt{3}a}{4}\right)$$

The above is identically 0 for all x. Then, using $x = 0$, we get $\sin^2(a/2) + \sin^2(\sqrt{3}a/4) = 0$. Clearly, both the terms must be equal to 0 and we obtain the following:

$$\sin\left(\frac{a}{2}\right) = 0, \ \sin\left(\frac{\sqrt{3}a}{4}\right) = 0 \implies \frac{a}{2} = n\pi, \ \frac{\sqrt{3}a}{4} = m\pi \ (n, m \in \mathbb{Z})$$

The above implies $\sqrt{3}n = 2m$ for some integers m, n, which is impossible unless $a = 0$. Hence, our assumption is wrong, proving that the function is not periodic.

> **Useful Tip:** This technique of checking for periodicity is useful for similar problems. For example, try to find out if $f(x) = [\sqrt{x}]$ is a periodic function or not.

17. Let $f : \mathbb{R} \to \mathbb{R}$ be defined by $f(x) = x^4 + bx^3 + cx^2 + dx + e$, where b, c, d, e are real numbers and $3b^2 < 8c$. Prove that f has a unique local minimum.

Solution: For the given function $f(x) = x^4 + bx^3 + cx^2 + dx + e$, we can write the following:

$$f'(x) = 4x^3 + 3bx^2 + 2cx + d, \ f''(x) = 12x^2 + 6bx + 2c$$

Now, for the second order derivative, we have a quadratic equation. The discriminant of this equation is

$$D = (6b)^2 - 4(12)(2c) = 36b^2 - 96c = 12(3b^2 - 8c) < 0$$

So, the second order derivative cannot have any real root, and since the leading coefficient is positive, this derivative is always positive. Thus, any solution of $f'(x) = 0$ is a local minima for the given function.

However, since $f''(x) > 0$ for all x, we can also say that $f'(x)$ is an increasing function for all x. Since it is a cubic polynomial, the ever-increasing nature implies that it has exactly one real root, and based on what we found above, that root must be a local minima for $f(x)$. Hence, the function f has a unique minimum.

18. Consider the sequence $1, 2^{1/2}, 3^{1/3}, 4^{1/4}, \ldots$. What is the maximum value in this sequence?

Solution: Let us consider the function $y = f(x) = x^{1/x}$ for $x > 0$. Clearly, $\ln y = (\ln x)/x$. Taking the derivative with respect to x, we get

$$\frac{1}{y}\frac{dy}{dx} = \frac{1}{x^2} - \frac{\ln x}{x^2} \implies \frac{dy}{dx} = \frac{y(1-\ln x)}{x^2}$$

Now, $y > 0$ for all $x > 0$ and so is x^2. Thus, the above first order derivative is positive when $1 - \ln x > 0$, that is, for $x < e$, and is negative otherwise.

Clearly, $f(x)$ is increasing for $x < e$ and is decreasing for $x > e$, thereby implying that it attains its global maximum at $x = e$. We also know that e is a number between 2 and 3. And therefore, because of the above property of $f(x)$, we can write the following:

$$f(1) < f(2) < f(e) > f(3) > f(4) > \ldots$$

Hence, the maximum of the given sequence is attained at either $x = 2$ or at $x = 3$. Since $2^3 < 3^2$, we can write that $2^{1/2} < 3^{1/3}$. Therefore, the maximum in the given sequence is $3^{1/3}$.

19. Define a sequence $\{x_n\}$ as

$$x_1 = \frac{1}{2}\left(a + \frac{5}{a}\right), \quad x_{n+1} = \frac{1}{2}\left(x_n + \frac{5}{x_n}\right) \text{ for all } n \geq 2,$$

where a is a positive real constant. Now, show that for all $n \geq 1$,

$$\frac{x_n - \sqrt{5}}{x_n + \sqrt{5}} = \left(\frac{a - \sqrt{5}}{a + \sqrt{5}}\right)^{2^n}.$$

Using the above or otherwise, find $\lim_{n \to \infty} x_n$.

Solution: For the first part, we use the principles of mathematical induction. Note that for $n = 1$

$$\frac{x_1 - \sqrt{5}}{x_1 + \sqrt{5}} = \frac{\frac{1}{2}\left(a + \frac{5}{a}\right) - \sqrt{5}}{\frac{1}{2}\left(a + \frac{5}{a}\right) + \sqrt{5}} = \frac{a^2 + 5 - 2\sqrt{5}x}{a^2 + 5 + 2\sqrt{5}a} = \left(\frac{a - \sqrt{5}}{a + \sqrt{5}}\right)^2$$

Thus, the given relation is true for $n = 1$. Now, let us assume that it is true for some $n = k$. In order to prove that it is true for $n = k+1$, we first use the recursion relation to write

$$\frac{x_{k+1} - \sqrt{5}}{x_{k+1} + \sqrt{5}} = \frac{\frac{1}{2}\left(x_k + \frac{5}{x_k}\right) - \sqrt{5}}{\frac{1}{2}\left(x_k + \frac{5}{x_k}\right) + \sqrt{5}} = \frac{x_k^2 + 5 - 2\sqrt{5}x_k}{x_k^2 + 5 + 2\sqrt{5}x_k} = \left(\frac{x_k - \sqrt{5}}{x_k + \sqrt{5}}\right)^2$$

Next, using the induction hypothesis, the above is equal to

$$\left[\left(\frac{a - \sqrt{5}}{a + \sqrt{5}}\right)^{2^k}\right]^2 = \left(\frac{a - \sqrt{5}}{a + \sqrt{5}}\right)^{2^{k+1}},$$

which indicates that the result is true for $n = k+1$. Hence, the required relationship is true for all $n \geq 1$.

Since a is a positive real number, we can say that $\left|\frac{a - \sqrt{5}}{a + \sqrt{5}}\right| < 1$, and so

$$\lim_{n \to \infty} \left(\frac{a - \sqrt{5}}{a + \sqrt{5}}\right)^{2^n} = 0 \implies \lim_{n \to \infty} \frac{x_n - \sqrt{5}}{x_n + \sqrt{5}} = 0$$

From the above, it is clear that $\lim_{n \to \infty} x_n = \sqrt{5}$.

> **Useful Tip:** In the earlier chapters, we saw that recursion relations are useful in solving complicated problems. This strategy can often be the best approach to find out the limit of a sequence.

20. Consider a decreasing sequence of positive real numbers $\{x_n\}$ such that $x_1 = \tan^{-1} 2$, and that for $n \geq 1$,

$$\sin(x_{n+1} - x_n) + 2^{-(n+1)} \sin x_n \sin x_{n+1} = 0.$$

Prove that $\lim_{n \to \infty} x_n = \frac{\pi}{4}$.

Solution: Note that the given equation can be simplified as

$$\sin x_{n+1} \cos x_n - \cos x_{n+1} \sin x_n + 2^{-(n+1)} \sin x_n \sin x_{n+1} = 0$$

Since all x_ns are positive real numbers less than $\tan^{-1} 2$, $\sin x_n \neq 0$ for all n. Dividing the above equation by $\sin x_n \sin x_{n+1}$, we obtain the following recursion relation:

$$\cot x_{n+1} = \cot x_n + 2^{-(n+1)}$$

We can use the above recursion sequentially to obtain the following:

$$\cot x_{n+1} = \cot x_1 + 2^{-2} + \ldots + 2^{-n} + 2^{-(n+1)}$$

Noting that $\cot x_1 = 1/2$, the above implies that

$$\cot x_n = 2^{-1} + 2^{-2} + \ldots + 2^{-n} = \left(\frac{1}{2}\right)\left(\frac{1-2^{-n}}{1-1/2}\right) = 1 - 2^{-n}$$

Subsequently, $x_n = \cot^{-1}(1-2^{-n})$, and hence, after taking the limit as $n \to \infty$, we get

$$\lim_{n \to \infty} x_n = \lim_{n \to \infty} \cot^{-1}(1-2^{-n}) = \cot^{-1} 1 = \frac{\pi}{4}$$

21. Let $f : [0, \infty) \to \mathbb{R}$ be a non-decreasing continuous function. For positive real numbers x, y, z satisfying $x < y < z$, prove that

$$(z-x) \int_y^z f(u)\, du \geq (z-y) \int_x^z f(u)\, du.$$

Solution: Let us define a new function g on $[0, z)$ by the following:

$$g(t) = \frac{1}{z-t} \int_t^z f(u)\, du$$

It is clear that g is differentiable. Then, using the Fundamental Theorem of Calculus and integration by parts, we can write

$$g'(t) = -\frac{f(t)}{z-t} + \frac{1}{(z-t)^2} \int_t^z f(u)\, du$$

Since f is a non-decreasing function, for $u \in [t, z]$, $f(u) \geq f(t)$, implying that $\int_t^z f(u)\, du \geq f(t)(z-t)$. Thus, from the above equation

$$g'(t) \geq \frac{f(t) - f(t)}{z-t} = 0$$

Therefore, g is also a non-decreasing function, and so, $g(y) \geq g(x)$ (since $x < y$). Hence

$$\frac{1}{z-y} \int_y^z f(u)\, du \geq \frac{1}{z-x} \int_x^z f(u)\, du \implies (z-x) \int_y^z f(u)\, du \geq (z-y) \int_x^z f(u)\, du$$

Calculus

22. Find the maximum and minimum of $f(x) = x^2 - x\sin x$ for $0 \leqslant x \leqslant \pi/2$.

Solution: Taking the first order derivative of the function with respect to x

$$f'(x) = 2x - x\cos x - \sin x$$

Since we are restricting ourselves to the interval $[0, \pi/2]$, we can further say that $1 \leqslant 2 - \cos x \leqslant 2$. Thus

$$f'(x) = x(2 - \cos x) - \sin x \geqslant x - \sin x$$

Letting $g(x) = x - \sin x$, we get $g'(x) = 1 - \cos x \geqslant 0$ for all $x \in [0, \pi/2]$. Therefore, $g(x)$ is an increasing function in the interval. It implies that $g(x) \geqslant g(0) = 0$ for all x.

Combining the above, $f'(x) \geqslant 0$ for all $x \in [0, \pi/2]$, thereby proving that f is an increasing function. Clearly, the minimum and maximum are attained at the two end-points. Hence

$$\min_{0 \leqslant x \leqslant \pi/2} f(x) = f(0) = 0, \quad \min_{0 \leqslant x \leqslant \pi/2} f(x) = f\left(\frac{\pi}{2}\right) = \frac{\pi^2}{4} - \frac{\pi}{2}$$

23. Compute the value of

$$\lim_{n \to \infty} \left\{ \left(1 + \frac{1}{2n}\right) \left(1 + \frac{3}{2n}\right) \left(1 + \frac{5}{2n}\right) \cdots \left(1 + \frac{2n-1}{2n}\right) \right\}^{1/2n}.$$

Solution: From the first principle of definite integral, $\lim_{n \to \infty} \frac{1}{n} \sum_{r=1}^{n} f(r/n) = \int_0^1 f(x)\, dx$.

Let us denote the limiting value of the given expression as A. Taking logarithm, we get

$$\log A = \lim_{n \to \infty} \frac{1}{2n} \sum_{r=1}^{n} \log\left(1 + \frac{2r-1}{2n}\right)$$

Clearly, the above is the sum of $\log(1 + j/2n)$ for all odd $j \leqslant 2n$. Thus, we can express the above as

$$\log A = \lim_{n \to \infty} \frac{1}{2n} \sum_{j=1}^{2n} \log\left(1 + \frac{j}{2n}\right) - \frac{1}{2} \lim_{n \to \infty} \frac{1}{n} \sum_{j=1}^{n} \log\left(1 + \frac{j}{n}\right)$$

Next, applying the first principle of definite integral, the above can be simplified to the following:

$$\int_0^1 \log(1+x)\, dx - \frac{1}{2} \int_0^1 \log(1+x)\, dx = \frac{1}{2} \int_1^2 \log x\, dx = \frac{1}{2} [x\log x - x]_1^2 = \log 2 - \frac{1}{2}$$

Hence, $\log A = \log 2 - \log e^{1/2}$, which implies that the required answer is $2e^{-1/2}$.

Useful Tip: For exercises related to finding the limits of infinite sums or products, most often it is useful to apply the first principle of definite integral.

24. If $A = \int_0^\pi \frac{\cos x}{(x+2)^2}\, dx$, prove the following identity

$$\int_0^{\pi/2} \frac{\sin x \cos x}{(x+1)}\, dx = \frac{1}{2}\left(\frac{1}{2} + \frac{1}{\pi+2} - A\right).$$

Solution: Using $\sin 2x = 2\sin x \cos x$, we can simplify the given integral as

$$\int_0^{\pi/2} \frac{\sin x \cos x}{(x+1)}\, dx = \int_0^{\pi/2} \frac{\sin 2x}{2x+2}\, dx = \frac{1}{2}\int_0^\pi \frac{\sin y}{y+2}\, dy$$

For convenience, let us denote the above integral as I. Next, using the concept of integration by parts

$$2I = \left[\frac{1}{y+2}\int \sin y\, dy\right]_0^\pi - \int_0^\pi \left(\frac{d}{dy}\left(\frac{1}{y+2}\right)\int \sin y\, dy\right)dy$$

$$= \left[-\frac{\cos y}{y+2}\right]_0^\pi - \int_0^\pi \frac{\cos y}{(y+2)^2}\, dy$$

$$= \frac{1}{\pi+2} + \frac{1}{2} - A$$

It is straightforward to obtain the required result from the above.

25. For all integers $n \geqslant 1$, show that

$$\frac{1}{n+1} \leqslant \log\left(1+\frac{1}{n}\right) \leqslant \frac{1}{n}.$$

You can use the identity $\log x = \int_1^x \frac{dt}{t}, x > 0$.

Solution: Using the given identity

$$\log\left(1+\frac{1}{n}\right) = \log(n+1) - \log n = \int_1^{n+1} \frac{dt}{t} - \int_1^n \frac{dt}{t} = \int_n^{n+1} \frac{dt}{t}$$

Now, for $t \in [n, n+1]$, we can say that

$$\frac{1}{n+1} \leqslant \frac{1}{t} \leqslant \frac{1}{n},$$

and using this in the previous equality, we get

$$\frac{1}{n+1}\int_n^{n+1} dt \leqslant \log\left(1+\frac{1}{n}\right) \leqslant \frac{1}{n}\int_n^{n+1} dt$$

It is easy to note that the value of the integral in the above inequality is equal to 1. Hence, we obtain our required result.

> **Useful Tip:** In the following problem, we use the fact that the equation of the form $y = ax^2 + bx + c$ represents a parabola. It is advisable to revise the concepts of coordinate geometry before reading the solution. Alternatively, one can draw the graph of the equation using the method discussed previously.

26. Calculate the area of the region bounded by the curves $y^3 = x^2$ and $y = 2 - x^2$.

Solution: The graph of $y^3 = x^2$ is symmetric about the y-axis and it should look similar to the graph of $y = x^{2/3}$. The other function represents the equation of a parabola. Simple calculations show that the axis of the parabola coincides with the y-axis and the vertex of the parabola is at $(0, 2)$. Thus, the graphs of the two functions are as shown in the figure below.

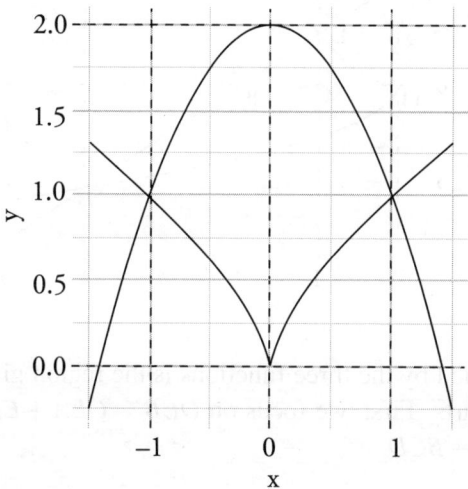

The points of intersection can be found out by solving the equation $y = 2 - y^3$. Note that $y^3 + y - 2 = y^3 - y^2 + y^2 - y + 2y - 2 = (y-1)(y^2 + y + 2)$, which implies that the solution is $y = 1$, further giving us $x^2 = 1$. Therefore, the two curves intersect at $(-1, 1)$ and $(1, 1)$, which are denoted in the graph as well.

Now, both the curves are symmetric about the y-axis, and therefore, it is enough to find the area enclosed by the curves for $x \geqslant 0$. It can be evaluated in the following way:

$$\int_0^1 (2-x^2)\,dx - \int_0^1 x^{2/3}\,dx = \left[2x - \frac{x^3}{3}\right]_0^1 - \left[\frac{x^{5/3}}{5/3}\right]_0^1 = 2 - \frac{1}{3} - \frac{1}{5/3} = \frac{16}{15}$$

The required area is double the above, and hence, it is $\frac{32}{15}$.

27. Calculate the area of the region bounded by the curves $y = x^2$, $x+y = 2$ and $y = -\sqrt{x}$.

Solution: First, we note that the common domain for the given functions is the positive real line, and we restrict ourselves to $x \geqslant 0$. Next, observe that $y = x^2$ denotes a parabola with vertex at the origin and with a positive y-axis as its axis. The second equation describes a straight line with slope -1 and intercept 2 while the third is the bottom part of a parabola with the origin as its vertex and a positive x-axis as its axis. So, the graph can be drawn as shown below.

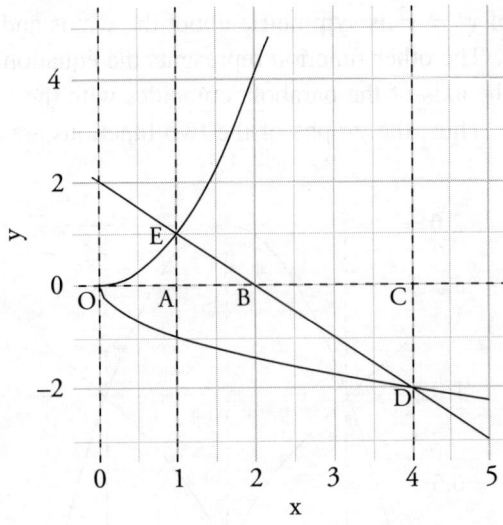

Clearly, the region bounded by the three functions is the region given by OED. We aim to obtain this area in two parts. First, we focus on $OEB = OEA + EAB$ and then we find out the area of $OBD = OCD - BCD$.

To find out the point of intersection E, we solve $y = x^2$ and $x + y = 2$ together. It implies $x^2 + x - 2 = 0$, that is, $(x-1)(x+2) = 0$. Since x is not negative here, the only possible solution is $x = 1$. Thus, the coordinates of E are $(1,1)$. Similarly, to obtain D, we need to solve $y = -\sqrt{x}$ and $x + y = 2$ together. Combining the two, we get $x = (2-x)^2$, which implies $x^2 - 5x + 4 = 0$. This factorizes into $(x-1)(x-4)$. Straightforward calculations then tell us that the point D is $(4,-2)$. We also find out that $A = (1,0)$, $B = (2,0)$ and $C = (4,0)$.

Using the coordinates, the area of the triangle EAB is $1/2$ while the same for the triangle BCD is 2.

Next, note that the area of the region OEA can be computed as

$$\int_0^1 x^2\,dx = \left[\frac{x^3}{3}\right]_0^1 = \frac{1}{3}$$

Using the above, $OEB = 1/3 + 1/2 = 5/6$. On the other hand, the area of the region OCD can be computed as

$$\left|\int_0^4 (-\sqrt{x})\,dx\right| = \left|\left[-\frac{x^{3/2}}{3/2}\right]_0^4\right| = \frac{2}{3} \times 4^{3/2} = \frac{16}{3}$$

It implies that $OBD = 16/3 - 2 = 10/3$. Hence, the required area is $5/6 + 10/3 = \frac{25}{6}$.

> **Useful Tip:** Finding the area under the curve is one of the most popular applications of definite integrals. These problems are commonly encountered in various competitive examinations. A common mistake is to not consider the absolute value of the integral when the region is in the negative side of the x-axis.

28. Suppose that a sector with central angle θ is cut out from a circular sheet of paper of radius a and is folded into the shape of a conical funnel. Find the value of θ for which the volume of the funnel is maximum.

Solution: For a circle with radius a, the length of an arc with central angle θ is given by $a\theta$. Now, since a sector with central angle θ is cut out and folded into the shape of a cone, the perimeter of the base of the cone is $a\theta$. Let the radius and the height of the cone be r and h, respectively. Then, it is easy to conclude that $2\pi r = a\theta$. Further, we know that the radius of the original circle lies along the side of the cone, and therefore, $h = \sqrt{a^2 - r^2}$.

Using the above relations, the volume of the cone can be written as

$$\frac{1}{3}\pi r^2 h = \frac{1}{3}\pi r^2 \sqrt{a^2 - r^2} = \frac{1}{3}\pi f(r),$$

where $f(r) = r^2 \sqrt{a^2 - r^2}$.

In order to find out the maximum value of the volume, we take the first order derivative of $f(r)$ and get

$$f'(r) = 2r\sqrt{a^2 - r^2} - r^2 \times \frac{r}{\sqrt{a^2 - r^2}} = \frac{r}{\sqrt{a^2 - r^2}}(2a^2 - 3r^2)$$

We know that r cannot be negative. Thus, $f'(r) = 0$ if $r = a\sqrt{2/3}$. Now, if $r^2 < 2a^2/3$, $f(r)$ is increasing and if $r^2 > 2a^2/3$, the function is decreasing. This implies that at $r = a\sqrt{2/3}$, the function attains its maximum. So, using $2\pi r = a\theta$, we can see that the volume is maximum when

$$\theta = \frac{2\pi a \sqrt{\frac{2}{3}}}{a} = 2\pi \sqrt{\frac{2}{3}}$$

29. Let $f : \mathbb{R} \to \mathbb{R}$ be a continuous function and let $[\cdot]$ denote the greatest integer function. Prove that for any $x > 1$,

$$\int_1^x [u]([u]+1) f(u)\, du = 2 \sum_{i=1}^{[x]} i \int_i^x f(u)\, du.$$

Solution: Observe that for a real number u, if it lies between integers k and $k+1$, then $[u] = k$. So, we can proceed as follows:

$$\int_1^x [u]([u]+1) f(u)\, du = \sum_{i=1}^{[x]-1} \int_i^{i+1} [u]([u]+1) f(u)\, du + \int_{[x]}^x [u]([u]+1) f(u)\, du$$

Note that the first term can be simplified as

$$\sum_{i=1}^{[x]-1} \int_i^{i+1} i(i+1) f(u)\, du = \sum_{i=1}^{[x]-1} \left[i(i+1) \int_i^x f(u)\, du - i(i+1) \int_{i+1}^x f(u)\, du \right]$$

$$= \sum_{i=1}^{[x]-1} i(i+1) \int_i^x f(u)\, du - \sum_{i=1}^{[x]-1} i(i+1) \int_{i+1}^x f(u)\, du$$

$$= \sum_{i=1}^{[x]-1} i(i+1) \int_i^x f(u)\, du - \sum_{j=2}^{[x]} j(j-1) \int_j^x f(u)\, du$$

Note that the second term in the first equation above is equal to $[x]([x]+1) \int_{[x]}^x f(u)\, du$. Using that along with the previous derivation, we get

$$\int_1^x [u]([u]+1) f(u)\, du = \sum_{i=1}^{[x]} i(i+1) \int_i^x f(u)\, du - \sum_{j=2}^{[x]} j(j-1) \int_j^x f(u)\, du$$

$$= 2 \int_1^x f(u)\, du + \sum_{i=2}^{[x]} \{i(i+1) - i(i-1)\} \int_i^x f(u)\, du$$

$$= 2 \sum_{i=1}^{[x]} i \int_i^x f(u)\, du,$$

and the proof is complete.

Calculus

30. Let $f(x)$ be a function such that $xf(x) = \log x$ for all $x > 0$. If $f^{(n)}(x)$ denotes the nth derivative of f, prove that

$$f^{(n)}(1) = (-1)^{n+1} n! \left(1 + \frac{1}{2} + \cdots + \frac{1}{n} \right).$$

Solution: Taking the first order derivative for both sides in $xf(x) = \log x$

$$f(x) + xf'(x) = \frac{1}{x} \implies xf'(x) = \frac{1}{x} - f(x)$$

Differentiating the above with respect to x once again, we get

$$f'(x) + xf''(x) = -\frac{1}{x^2} - f'(x) \implies xf''(x) = -\frac{1}{x^2} - 2f'(x)$$

Now, based on the above, we hypothesize that the following recursion is true for all $n \geq 1$:

$$xf^{(n)}(x) = \frac{(-1)^{n-1}(n-1)!}{x^n} + (-n) f^{(n-1)}(x)$$

To prove the above, we first note that the relationship is true for $n = 1$ and $n = 2$. Assuming that it is true for $n = k$, we can show that

$$xf^{(k+1)}(x) + f^{(k)}(x) = (-1)^{k-1}(k-1)! \left(\frac{-k}{x^{k+1}} \right) + (-k) f^{(k)}(x),$$

which implies

$$xf^{(k+1)}(x) = \frac{(-1)^k k!}{x^{k+1}} + (-(k+1)) f^{(k)}(x)$$

Then, using the principles of mathematical induction, we can argue that the above recursion relation is true. Now, using $x = 1$

$$f^{(n)}(1) = (-1)^{n-1}(n-1)! + (-n) f^{(n-1)}(1)$$

We can now use the above equation recursively to write the following:

$$\begin{aligned}
f^{(n)}(1) &= (-1)^{n-1}(n-1)! + (-1)^{n-1} n(n-2)! + (-1)^2 n(n-1) f^{(n-2)}(1) \\
&= (-1)^{n-1} n! \left(\frac{1}{n} + \frac{1}{n-1} \right) + (-1)^{n-1} \frac{n!}{n-2} + (-1)^3 n(n-1)(n-2) f^{(n-3)}(1) \\
&= \cdots \\
&= (-1)^{n-1} n! \left(\frac{1}{n} + \frac{1}{n-1} + \cdots + \frac{1}{2} \right) + (-1)^{n-1} \{ n(n-1) \ldots 2 \} f^{(1)}(1)
\end{aligned}$$

$$= (-1)^{n-1} n! \left(\frac{1}{n} + \frac{1}{n-1} + \cdots + \frac{1}{2} + f^{(1)}(1) \right)$$

Finally, from the original equation and its first derivative, we get $f(1) = 0$ and $f'(1) = 1$. Also, note that $(n-1)$ and $(n+1)$ have the same parity, which implies that

$$f^{(n)}(1) = (-1)^{n+1} n! \left(1 + \frac{1}{2} + \cdots + \frac{1}{n} \right)$$

Multiple Choice Questions

1. Consider the function

$$f(x) = \begin{cases} e^x & \text{if } x < 1, \\ \log x + ax^2 + bx & \text{if } x \geqslant 1, \end{cases}$$

where a, b are real numbers. Which of the following is true regarding the differentiability of f at $x = 1$?

(a) f is differentiable at $x = 1$ for all choices of a, b.
(b) f is differentiable at $x = 1$ for a unique choice of a, b.
(c) f is differentiable at $x = 1$ only when $a + b$ is constant.
(d) f is not differentiable at $x = 1$ for any choice of a, b.

Solution: (b)

In order to be differentiable, $f(x)$ must be continuous at $x = 1$. The left-hand limit of $f(x)$ at $x = 1$ is e, whereas the right-hand limit is $a + b$. Thus, f is continuous at $x = 1$ if and only if $a + b = e$.

Next, considering the differentiability of the individual functions, and applying the first principle of derivative, we can show that the left-hand derivative of $f(x)$ is e, whereas the right-hand derivative is $1 + 2a + b$. Clearly, f will be differentiable at $x = 1$ if and only if $2a + b + 1 = e$. It subsequently implies that the only possible choice is $a = -1$, $b = e + 1$.

2. Find the limit of the sequence $\sqrt{2}, \sqrt{2\sqrt{2}}, \sqrt{2\sqrt{2}\sqrt{2}}, \ldots$.

(a) 2   (b) $2\sqrt{2}$ (c) 4   (d) ∞

Solution: (a)

Let us denote the nth term of the given sequence as x_n. It is then easy to deduce that for all $n > 1$, $x_n^2 = 2x_{n-1}$. Thus, if the limit of the sequence is finite and is L, then it must satisfy $L^2 = 2L$. However, as L cannot be 0, we can argue that the limit must be 2.

3. If θ is an acute angle, then the maximum possible value of $3\sin\theta + 4\cos\theta$ is

(a) 4   (b) $3\left(1+\frac{\sqrt{3}}{2}\right)$ (c) $5\sqrt{2}$ (d) 5

Solution: (d)

For an acute angle θ, $\sin\theta$ lies between 0 and 1. Now, denoting it as x, the given function can be written as $f(x) = 3x + 4\sqrt{1-x^2}$. Taking the first derivative with respect to x

$$f'(x) = 3 + 4 \times \frac{1}{2}\frac{-2x}{\sqrt{1-x^2}} = 3 - \frac{4x}{\sqrt{1-x^2}}$$

The above is equal to 0 if and only if $9(1-x^2) = 16x^2$, that is, for $x = 3/5$. Differentiating the above function one more time, we get

$$f''(x) = -\frac{4}{\sqrt{1-x^2}} + (4x)\left(\frac{1}{2}\right)(1-x^2)^{-3/2} = \frac{-4(1-x^2)+2x}{(1-x^2)^{3/2}}$$

One may observe that $f''(3/5) < 0$, and hence, the function attains its maximum at $x = 3/5$. The corresponding value is

$$f\left(\frac{3}{5}\right) = \frac{9}{5} + 4\sqrt{1-\frac{9}{25}} = 5$$

4. Which of the following is not an odd function?

(a) A function f such that $f(x+y) = f(x) + f(y)$ for all x, y
(b) $f(x) = \frac{xe^{x/2}}{1+e^x}$
(c) $f(x) = x - [x]$, where $[\cdot]$ is the greatest integer function
(d) $f(x) = x^2 \sin x + x^3 \cos x$

Solution: (c)

For the function given in (a), using $x = y = 0$, we can write $f(0) = 2f(0)$, and hence, $f(0) = 0$. Now, putting $y = -x$, we get $f(0) = f(x) + f(-x)$, and therefore, $f(-x) = -f(x)$, implying that it is an odd function.

For the second function, note that

$$f(-x) = \frac{(-x)e^{-x/2}}{1+e^{-x}} = -\frac{xe^{x/2}}{e^x+1} = -f(x),$$

implying that it is an odd function.

To confirm that (d) is an odd function, observe that

$$f(-x) = (-x)^2 \sin(-x) + (-x)^3 \cos(-x) = x^2(-\sin x) - x^3 \cos x = -f(x)$$

Hence, (c) is not an odd function. In fact, one can see that $x - [x]$ is a strictly positive function.

5. Compute the limit of $\dfrac{1}{n^4} \sum_{k=1}^{n} k(k+2)(k+4)$, as $n \to \infty$.

(a) 1/4   (b) 1/8   (c) 0   (d) Does not exist

Solution: (a)

We can use the concepts of sums of the sequences $\{k\}_{k \geq 1}$, $\{k^2\}_{k \geq 1}$ and $\{k^3\}_{k \geq 1}$ to solve this problem. Note that the given expression can be written as

$$\frac{1}{n^4} \sum_{k=1}^{n} k(k+2)(k+4) = \frac{1}{n^4} \sum_{k=1}^{n} (k^3 + 6k^2 + 8k)$$

$$= \frac{1}{n^4} \left[\frac{n^2(n+1)^2}{4} + n(n+1)(2n+1) + 4n(n+1) \right]$$

$$= \frac{1}{4}\left(1 + \frac{1}{n}\right)^2 + \frac{g(n)}{n^4}$$

In the above expression, $g(n)$ is a cubic polynomial, and hence, $g(n)/n^4 \to 0$ as $n \to \infty$. The first term, on the other hand, converges to $1/4$, and hence, that is the required answer.

6. The value of the integral $\int_1^2 [x^2] \, dx$ is

(a) 1   (b) $6 - 2\sqrt{3}$ (c) $5 - \sqrt{2} - \sqrt{3}$ (d) None of these

Solution: (c)

Note that the function $[x^2]$ takes value 1 in the interval $(1, \sqrt{2})$, the value 2 in $(\sqrt{2}, \sqrt{3})$, and the value 3 in $(\sqrt{3}, 2)$. Dividing the integral in this manner, we can write

$$\int_1^2 [x^2] \, dx = \int_1^{\sqrt{2}} dx + \int_{\sqrt{2}}^{\sqrt{3}} 2 \, dx + \int_{\sqrt{3}}^{2} 3 \, dx$$

$$= \left(\sqrt{2} - 1\right) + 2\left(\sqrt{3} - \sqrt{2}\right) + 3\left(2 - \sqrt{3}\right)$$

$$= 5 - \sqrt{2} - \sqrt{3}$$

Calculus

7. Define the function
$$f(x) = \begin{cases} ax^2 e^x & \text{if } x \geq 0 \\ xe^{-x} & \text{if } x < 0, \end{cases}$$
for some unknown real number a. Which one of the following is true?

(a) f is not continuous everywhere.
(b) f is continuous, but not differentiable everywhere.
(c) f is differentiable everywhere.
(d) It cannot be answered without knowing the value of a.

Solution: (b)

We can obtain the right- and left-hand limits of $f(x)$ at $x = 0$ as
$$\lim_{x \to 0+} f(x) = 0, \ \lim_{x \to 0-} f(x) = 0$$

Clearly, f is continuous everywhere. For differentiability, the left- and right-hand derivatives at $x = 0$ can be computed as
$$\lim_{x \to 0+} f'(x) = 2axe^x + ax^2 e^x = 0, \ \lim_{x \to 0-} e^{-x} - xe^{-x} = 1$$

Evidently, irrespective of the value of a, the function is continuous everywhere, but not differentiable at $x = 0$.

For the next three questions, consider a continuous function $f : \mathbb{R} \to \mathbb{R}$ satisfying $f(1) = 1$, $f(2) = 4$, $f(3) = 9$, $f(4) = 16$.

8. Which one of the following statements is true?

(a) The range of f must include both 5 and 25.
(b) The range of f must include 5, but not necessarily 25.
(c) The range of f must include 25, but not necessarily 5.
(d) The range of f may not include either 5 or 25.

Solution: (b)

f is a continuous function and it takes the values 4 and 9 at $x = 2$ and $x = 3$. Thus, by intermediate value theorem, there exists $\xi \in (2, 3)$ such that $f(\xi) = 5$. Similar arguments do not necessarily hold for 25.

9. If it is further mentioned that f is differentiable everywhere, then which of the following intervals must contain x such that $f'(x) = 2x$?

(a) $(1,2)$ (b) $(2,3)$ (c) $(3,4)$ (d) All of them

Solution: (d)

Consider the function $g(x) = f(x) - x^2$. From the given information, we know that g is differentiable everywhere, $g(x) = 0$ for $x = 1, 2, 3, 4$, and $g'(x) = f'(x) - 2x$. Applying Rolle's Theorem for the intervals $(1,2)$, $(2,3)$ and $(3,4)$, one can now argue that each of the intervals contains at least one x for which $g'(x) = 0$. Thus, the correct answer is (d).

10. If f is a polynomial, what is the minimum possible degree of it?

(a) 1   (b) 2   (c) 3   (d) 4

Solution: (d)

As in the last part, we can write $g(x) = f(x) - x^2$ such that 1, 2, 3, 4 are the roots of the polynomial $g(x)$. Then, $(x-1)(x-2)(x-3)(x-4)$ divides $g(x)$, implying that $f(x)$ must be a fourth-degree polynomial.

Exercises

1. Let $f : \mathbb{R} \to \mathbb{R}$ be a function such that $f'(x)$ takes both positive and negative values. If $f''(x)$ is always positive, show that there exists $p \in \mathbb{R}$ such that $f(x)$ is increasing for $x \geqslant p$.

2. Let $k \in \mathbb{N}$ be odd. If $x, y \in \mathbb{N} + \{0\}$ satisfy $x + y = k$, what is the minimum value of $x^2 + y^2$?

3. If $0 \leqslant \theta \leqslant \pi/2$, show that $\pi \sin \theta \geqslant 2\theta$.

4. Find the domain of the function
$$f(x) = \frac{x+1}{(x-1)(x-7)}.$$
Now, study the derivatives of $f(x)$ and use that information to draw a rough sketch of $f(x)$.

5. Let f be a twice-differentiable continuous function on the domain $[0, 2\pi]$. If $f''(x)$ is continuous and non-negative everywhere, prove that
$$\int_0^{2\pi} f(x) \cos x \, dx \geqslant 0.$$

6. Let $f : \mathbb{R} \to \mathbb{R}^+$ be a continuously differentiable function. If $f'(x) \geqslant \sqrt{f(x)}$ for all $x \in \mathbb{R}$, then prove that for all $x \geqslant 1$
$$\sqrt{f(x)} \geqslant \sqrt{f(1)} + \frac{1}{2}(x-1).$$

7. Let $n \in \mathbb{N}$ and consider an $(n+1)$-times differentiable function $f : \mathbb{R} \to \mathbb{R}$, with the ith derivative denoted by $f^{(i)}$. If
$$f(1) = f(0) = f^{(1)}(0) = \ldots = f^{(n)}(0) = 0,$$
show that there exists $x \in (0,1)$ such that $f^{(n+1)}(x) = 0$.

8. Let f be a function defined on $(0, \infty)$ as follows:
$$f(x) = \lim_{n \to \infty} \frac{\log(2+x) - x^{2n} \sin x}{1 + x^{2n}}.$$
Prove that $f(x)$ is not continuous at $x = 1$. Find out how many roots $f(x)$ has in the interval $0 \leqslant x \leqslant \pi/2$.

9. Let $a_0, b_0 \in \mathbb{N}$ and define a_n, b_n, c_n for $n \geqslant 1$ as $a_n = a_{n-1} + 2b_{n-1}$, $b_n = a_{n-1} + b_{n-1}$ and $c_n = a_n/b_n$. For $n = 0, 1, 2, \ldots$, show that
$$\left|\sqrt{2} - c_{n+1}\right| < \frac{1}{1+\sqrt{2}}\left|\sqrt{2} - c_n\right|.$$
Compute the value of $\lim_{n \to \infty} c_n$.

10. For every integer $n \geqslant 0$, prove that
$$\int_0^{\pi/2} \frac{\sin(2n+1)x}{\sin x} dx = \frac{\pi}{2}.$$

11. For $n \in \mathbb{N}$, prove that
$$\int_0^\pi \left|\frac{\sin nx}{x}\right| dx \geqslant \frac{2}{\pi}\left(1 + \frac{1}{2} + \ldots + \frac{1}{n}\right).$$

12. Evaluate the following:
$$\lim_{n \to \infty} \frac{1}{2n} \log\binom{2n}{n}.$$

13. Let $g : \mathbb{R} \to \mathbb{R}$ be a function defined as
$$g(x) = (\alpha + |x|)^2 \exp\{(5 - |x|)^2\}.$$
Find α such that $g(x)$ is continuous and differentiable everywhere.

14. Consider a function $f: \mathbb{R} \to \mathbb{R}$ satisfying the following for all $(x,y) \in \mathbb{R}^2$:
$$|f(x+y) - f(x-y) - y| \leq y^2.$$
Prove that f is of the form $f(x) = x/2 + c$, where c is a real constant.

15. How many positive real numbers $x \neq 2$ are there that satisfy $\log_2 x = x/2$? Further, obtain the set of real numbers a such that
$$\frac{\log_2 x}{x} = a$$
has exactly one real solution.

16. Let $f: \mathbb{R} \to \mathbb{R}$ be a function defined as $f(x) = \int_0^1 |t-x| t \, dt$. Draw a rough sketch of $f(x)$.

17. Let $f: \mathbb{R}^+ \to \mathbb{R}^+$ be a function defined as $f(x) = x + 1/x$. For $x \in (0,1)$, let $h(x) = x^4/(1-x)^6$. Now, define a composite function g for all $x \in (0,1)$ as $g(x) = f(h(x))$. Prove that there exists a real number $x_0 \in (0,1)$ such that g is strictly decreasing for $x \leq x_0$ and is strictly increasing otherwise.

18. Draw the graphs of $y = x-1, y = x, y = x+1$ and $y = xe^{-1/|x|}$ for $-\infty < x < \infty$ using the same X and Y axes.

19. Suppose that a cow is tied to a pole with a rope 10 metres long. There are two walls perpendicular to each other. One of them is at a distance of 5 metres to the east of the pole and the other at a distance of $5\sqrt{2}$ metres to the north of the pole. If the cow is allowed to graze with the rope always tied to the pole, what is the total area it can cover?

20. Find the ratio of the two areas in which the curve $y^2 = 12x$ divides the circle $x^2 + y^2 = 64$.

Hints

1. Since the second order derivative is always positive, $f'(x)$ is a strictly increasing function. Now, let p be a real number such that $f'(p) > 0$, and it would imply that $f'(x) > 0$ for all $x > p$. Thus, $f(x)$ is an increasing function of x for all $x \geq p$.

2. Considering $y = k - x$, define the function $f(x) = x^2 + (k-x)^2$. One can show that this function is decreasing for $x < k/2$, is minimized at $x = k/2$ and is increasing for $x > k/2$. As k is odd, to obtain the minimum value, x must be $(k+1)/2$ or $(k-1)/2$ and the corresponding minimum value is $(k^2+1)/2$.

3. Consider the function $f(x) = \pi \sin x - 2x$ for $x \in [0, \pi/2]$. Taking the first two derivatives, we get $f'(x) = \pi \cos x - 2$, $f''(x) = -\pi \sin x < 0 \,\forall\, x \in (0, \pi/2)$. Using

these, it can be shown that a local maxima exists at $x = \cos^{-1}(2/\pi)$ and that the minimum value is attained at the end-points of the domain. Subsequently, it implies that $f(x) \geqslant 0$ for all x.

4. Note that the given function can be written as

$$f(x) = -\frac{1}{3(x-1)} + \frac{4}{3(x-7)},$$

which implies that the domain is $\mathbb{R} - \{1, 7\}$. Further observe that the function is positive for $x \in (-1, 1) \cup (7, \infty)$, -1 is a root of the function and as x approaches ∞ or $-\infty$, $f(x) \to 0$. The limits of the function as $x \to 1$ and $x \to 7$ imply that at $x = 1, 7$, there are two asymptotes. Next, taking the first and second order derivatives, show that the function is increasing for $x \in (-5, 3)$ and is decreasing otherwise; and that there is a local minima at $x = -5$ and a local maxima at $x = 3$. Also find the regions of convexity and concavity. Then, combine all of the above findings to draw a rough sketch of the function.

5. Use the concept of integration by parts twice to show that

$$\int f(x) \cos x \, dx = f(x) \sin x - f'(x) \cos x - \int f''(x) \cos x \, dx$$

Next, using the limits 0 and 2π, one can argue that the following is true:

$$\int_0^{2\pi} f(x) \cos x \, dx = \int_0^{2\pi} f''(x)(1 - \cos x) \, dx$$

Since both $f''(x) \geqslant 0$ and $1 - \cos x \geqslant 0$ for all $x \in [0, 2\pi]$, the result follows.

6. Consider the derivative of $g(x) = \sqrt{f(x)}$. Since $f(x)$ is always positive, using the given condition, one can argue that $g'(x) \geqslant 1/2$. Now, integrating $g(x)$ in $[1, x]$ and using the previous inequality, the proof can be completed.

7. Application of Rolle's Theorem suggests that for the given f, there is some point $\xi_1 \in (0, 1)$ such that $f^{(1)}(\xi_1) = 0$. Use the theorem repeatedly on $f^{(1)}, \ldots, f^{(n)}$ to show that there exists $x \in (0, 1)$ satisfying $f^{(n+1)}(x) = 0$.

8. Show that the function can be simplified as

$$f(x) = \begin{cases} \log(2+x) & \text{for } 0 < x < 1 \\ \frac{\log 3 - \sin 1}{2} & \text{for } x = 1 \\ -\sin x & \text{for } x > 1 \end{cases}$$

It is now straightforward to argue that f is not continuous at $x = 1$ and that $f(x)$ does not have any root in the interval $[0, \pi/2]$.

9. First, show that $\sqrt{2} - c_{n+1} = \sqrt{2} - 1 - 1/(c_n + 1)$. Next, write $c_n + 1 = (\sqrt{2}+1) - (\sqrt{2} - c_n)$ to obtain the following:

$$\sqrt{2} - c_{n+1} = \frac{(\sqrt{2}-1)(\sqrt{2}-c_n)}{(\sqrt{2}-c_n)-(\sqrt{2}+1)}$$

Note that a_n, b_n, c_n are positive for all n, and so, $|c_n + 1| > 1$. This, along with the above recursion relation and through algebraic manipulation, leads to the result of the first part. Now using that inequality recursively, we can write

$$\left|\sqrt{2}-c_{n+1}\right| < \frac{1}{(1+\sqrt{2})^n}\left|\sqrt{2}-c_1\right|$$

From the above, it is easy to show that $\lim_{n\to\infty} c_n = \sqrt{2}$.

10. One can use the principle of mathematical induction to prove this. Let A_n denote the integral for n. For $n = 0$, it is easy to show that $A_0 = \pi/2$. Next, assume that the result is true for $n = k$, that is, $A_k = \pi/2$. For $n = k+1$, use trigonometric identities to prove that

$$A_{k+1} = \int_0^{\pi/2} \left[\frac{\sin\{(2k+1)x\}}{\sin x} + 2\cos\{(2k+2)x\}\right] dx$$

The first integral in the above equation is equal to A_k. For the second integral, direct calculations show that the value is 0. Hence, by mathematical induction, the result is proved for all $n \geq 0$.

11. The integral is taken for $x \in [0, \pi]$. So, the function $|\sin nx|$ is non-negative for $x \in [0, \pi/n]$, negative for $x \in (\pi/n, 2\pi/n)$, and so on. Next, dividing the interval $[0, \pi]$ into n equal parts, we can write the following:

$$\int_0^\pi \left|\frac{\sin nx}{x}\right| dx = \sum_{r=0}^{n-1} \int_{r\pi/n}^{(r+1)\pi/n} \left|\frac{\sin nx}{x}\right| dx$$

The following result is easy to obtain:

$$\int_{r\pi/n}^{(r+1)\pi/n} |\sin nx|\, dx = \begin{cases} \left[\frac{-\cos nx}{n}\right]_{r\pi/n}^{(r+1)\pi/n} & \text{for even } r \\ \left[\frac{\cos nx}{n}\right]_{r\pi/n}^{(r+1)\pi/n} & \text{for odd } r \end{cases}$$

Now, for the interval $(r\pi/n, (r+1)\pi/n)$, $1/x \geq n/(r+1)\pi$. Use that along with the above result to show that

$$\int_{r\pi/n}^{(r+1)\pi/n} \left|\frac{\sin nx}{x}\right| dx \geq \frac{2}{(r+1)\pi}$$

The required result immediately follows from the above.

12. Using the properties of binomial coefficients and logarithms, prove that

$$\lim_{n\to\infty} \frac{1}{2n} \log \binom{2n}{n} = \lim_{n\to\infty} \frac{1}{2n} \sum_{r=1}^{n} \log \frac{n+r}{r}$$

Next, using the first principle of definite integral, the above can be shown to be equal to $\frac{1}{2}\int_0^1 \log(1+x)\,dx - \frac{1}{2}\int_0^1 \log x\, dx$. The first term here simplifies to $\log 2 - 1/2$. The second term is an improper integral. Using the concept of limits, argue that $\int_0^1 \log x\, dx = -1$, which subsequently would imply that the required answer is $\log 2$.

13. Observe that

$$g(x) = \begin{cases} (\alpha-x)^2 \exp\{(5+x)^2\} & \text{if } x \leq 0 \\ (\alpha+x)^2 \exp\{(5-x)^2\} & \text{if } x > 0 \end{cases}$$

Now, $g(x)$ is clearly continuous for $x \neq 0$ as it is a product of two continuous functions in this domain. Using the left-hand and right-hand limits at $x = 0$ using the above forms, one can show that $g(x)$ is continuous at all $x \in \mathbb{R}$. Using similar logic, one can check the differentiability at $x = 0$. Using the first principle, argue that g is differentiable at 0 if and only if $2\alpha - 10\alpha^2 = 0$. Hence, the given function is continuous and differentiable everywhere for $\alpha \in \{0, 1/5\}$.

14. Letting $g(x) = f(x) - x/2$, for all $(x,y) \in \mathbb{R}^2$, the given condition becomes $|g(x+y) - g(x-y)| \leq y^2$. Next, setting $x+y = m$ and $x-y = n$, for $(m,n) \in \mathbb{R}^2$, one can rewrite the above condition as

$$|g(m) - g(n)| \leq \frac{(m-n)^2}{4}$$

Further, repeated use of the triangle inequality on the above (with necessary transformation) implies that

$$|g(m) - g(n)| \leq \frac{(m-n)^2}{2^k}$$

Thus, for any $(m,n) \in \mathbb{R}^2$, given any $\varepsilon > 0$, we can show that $|g(m) - g(n)| < \varepsilon$, and hence, $g(x)$ is a constant function, which subsequently proves that $f(x)$ is of the form $x/2 + c$.

15. Consider the function $f(x) = \log_2 x - x/2$ for $x > 0$. Taking the first order derivative, $f'(x) = (\log_2 e)/x - 1/2$. It implies that f is strictly increasing in $(0, 2\log_2 e)$ and strictly decreasing elsewhere. Since both $\lim_{x\to 0} f(x) = -\infty$ and $\lim_{x\to\infty} f(x) = -\infty$, it is easy to conclude that the function has exactly two roots if $f(2\log_2 e) > 0$, exactly one root if $f(2\log_2 e) = 0$ and has no real root if $f(2\log_2 e) < 0$. Finding the value

of $f(2\log_2 e)$, one can argue that there is exactly one real solution other than 2 that satisfies the given equation.

For the second part, consider the function $g(x) = \log_2 x - ax$. If $a > 0$, using similar techniques as above, it can be shown that the equation $g(x) = 0$ has only one real solution if and only if $g((\log_2 e)/a) = 0$, which implies that $a = \log_2 e/e$. Next, for $a < 0$, $g'(x) = (\log_2 e)/x - a > 0$ for all $x \in (0, \infty)$, and thus, it is a strictly increasing function. It helps to prove that the function has exactly one real solution for all $a < 0$. Finally, for $a = 0$, it is obvious that $g(x) = 0$ only when $x = 1$. Hence, the set of real numbers a that satisfies the given condition is $(-\infty, 0] \cup \{\log_2 e/e\}$.

16. One can calculate $f(x)$ for three different parts and obtain the following:

$$f(x) = \begin{cases} 1/3 - x/2 & \text{if } x < 0 \\ (2x^3 - 3x + 2)/6 & \text{if } 0 \leqslant x \leqslant 1 \\ x/2 - 1/3 & \text{if } x > 1 \end{cases}$$

Note that the function is continuous everywhere. For both $x < 0$ and $x > 1$, the function is linear in x. Next, using $g(x) = (2x^3 - 3x + 2)/6$, $g'(x) = x^2 - 1/2$, implying that the function is decreasing for $x \in [0, 1/\sqrt{2}]$ and is increasing for $x \in [1/\sqrt{2}, 1]$. The second order derivative of the function is $g''(x) = 2x > 0$ for all $0 \leqslant x \leqslant 1$. So, it is a convex function. It would also suggest that the function has a local minima at $x = 1/\sqrt{2}$, which can be evaluated as $g(1/\sqrt{2}) = (2 - \sqrt{2})/6$. Since the minimum value in that interval is positive, we can further say that $f(x)$ does not have any root in $[0, 1]$. Using these facts, one can easily draw a rough sketch of the graph of $f(x)$.

17. In order to check the increasing and decreasing nature of $g(\cdot)$, one should consider its derivatives. Since $f'(x) = 1 - 1/x^2$, the first order derivative of $g(\cdot)$ can be written as

$$g'(x) = f'(h(x))h'(x) = h'(x)\left(1 - \frac{1}{h(x)^2}\right)$$

Now, taking the first order derivative of $h(\cdot)$, for x between 0 and 1, it can be shown that h is a strictly increasing function. Thus, the sign of $g'(x)$ depends on the value of $h(x)$. More specifically, if $h(x) < 1$, $g'(x) < 0$ and if $h(x) > 1$, $g'(x) > 0$. Therefore, it suffices to prove that there is a real number $x_0 \in (0, 1)$ such that $h(x) < 1$ when $x < x_0$ and $h(x) > 1$ when $x > x_0$, because that would imply $g(x)$ is decreasing for $x < x_0$ and increasing for $x > x_0$. This can be shown using $\lim_{x \to 0} h(x) = 0$ and $\lim_{x \to 1} h(x) = +\infty$.

18. Observe that $y = x - 1$, $y = x$ and $y = x + 1$ are parallel straight lines. Next, note that $y = xe^{-1/|x|}$ is an odd function, and so, it is symmetric about the origin. It is therefore

Calculus

enough to understand the nature of the function for the positive real values of x. So, consider $f(x) = xe^{-1/x}$ for $x > 0$. Using standard calculus ideas, one can show that the derivative of $e^{-1/x}$ is $e^{-1/x}/x^2$. Subsequently, $f'(x) = 1 - (1 + 1/x)e^{-1/x}$. Now, using the exponential series for $x \in (0, \infty)$

$$e^{1/x} = 1 + \frac{1}{x} + \frac{1}{x^2 \, 2!} + \frac{1}{x^3 \, 3!} + \cdots \implies 1 + \frac{1}{x} < e^{1/x},$$

which further implies that $f'(x) > 0$. Thus, $f(x)$ is a strictly increasing function.

Next, taking the second order derivative, show that $f(x)$ is a convex function for all $x > 0$. Also, using the exponential series again, it can be shown that $f(x)$ lies below $y = x$. It is also easy to argue that $\lim_{x \to 0} f(x) = 0$, $\lim_{x \to \infty} f(x) = \infty$. Combining the above, one can draw the graph of $f(x)$ for $x > 0$. For $x < 0$, one simply needs to draw a curve that is symmetric about the origin.

19. In the XY-plane, denote the pole by the origin. Then, the cow can travel anywhere within the circle of radius 10 metres, centred at the origin. The equation of this circle is given by $x^2 + y^2 = 100$. However, two walls are described in the problem. Thus, according to the following figure, the area the cow can graze on is given by the larger area inside the circle bounded by the three points A, B, C. Using the equation of the circle, the coordinates of these three points can be found as $A = (5, 5\sqrt{2}), B = (5, -\sqrt{75}), C = (-5\sqrt{2}, 5\sqrt{2})$.

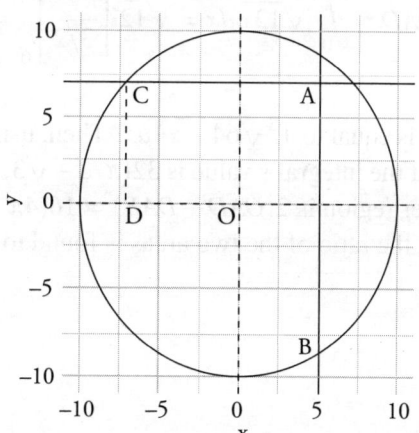

Thus, the required area can be determined by adding the area under the curve $y = \sqrt{100 - x^2}$ from $x = -10$ to $x = -5\sqrt{2}$, the area of the rectangle with length $(5\sqrt{2} + 5)$ and width $5\sqrt{2}$, and the area under the curve $y = \sqrt{100 - x^2}$ from $x = -10$ to $x = 5$. Denote these three areas as A_1, A_2, A_3, respectively. Then, $A_2 = 5\sqrt{2}(5\sqrt{2} + 5) = 50 + 25\sqrt{2}$. $A_1 = \int_{-10}^{-5\sqrt{2}} \sqrt{100 - x^2} \, dx$ and it can be computed using the polar transformation. Similarly, A_2 can be computed as well.

20. Drawing the curves together is helpful in this problem as well. Note that $y^2 = 12x$ describes a parabola with the vertex at the origin. The two curves are shown in the following figure:

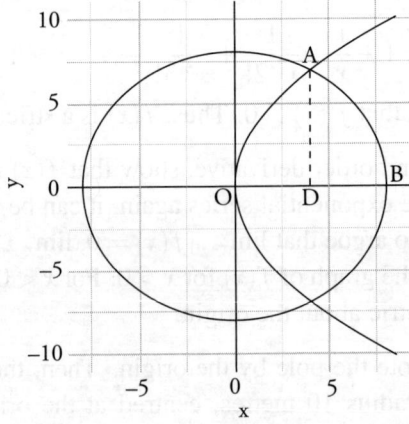

Solve the two equations to argue that the intersection points in the graph are $A = (4, \sqrt{48})$, $B = (8,0)$, $D = (4,0)$. Next, observe that the smaller area is two times the sum of the two areas OAD and DAB. The first one can be evaluated as follows:

$$OAD = \int_0^4 \sqrt{12x}\, dx = \sqrt{12} \left[\frac{x^{3/2}}{3/2}\right]_0^4 = \frac{32\sqrt{3}}{3}$$

For DAB, note that it is equal to $\int_4^8 \sqrt{64 - x^2}\, dx$. Then, using the polar transformation $x = 8\cos\theta$, prove that the integral's value is $32(\pi/3 - \sqrt{3}/4)$. One can then show that the area of the smaller region is $2(OAD + DAB) = 16(4\pi + \sqrt{3})/3$. Since the area of the full circle is 64π, the ratio of the two areas is found to be $(8\pi - \sqrt{3}) : (4\pi + \sqrt{3})$.

5
Euclidean Geometry

"Where there is matter, there is geometry."

Johannes Kepler, the German astronomer and mathematician, averred the importance of geometry in the world through the above words. It goes without saying that the world revolves around geometrical shapes and related concepts. In its literal meaning though, the word 'geometry' comes from the Greek words for earth and measurement. It is in Egypt where we can first see the application of geometry in the pages of history. Later, the Greeks developed the theoretical underpinnings of the topics which cumulated in Euclid's *The Elements*, circa 300 BCE.

The methods in this branch of geometry consist of a set of intuitively appealing axioms, which are helpful to prove many other propositions and theorems. While many of the results were stated by other mathematicians, Euclid was the first to bring them together into a comprehensive deductive and logical system, thereby ushering in the term Euclidean geometry.

In this chapter, we will focus on the problems related to Euclidean geometry, while in the next one, we will note the connections and differences in the concepts of coordinate geometry.

KEY RESULTS

Euclidean geometry revolves around structures and their relationships. We start with the notion of directed line segments, which denote the length between two points on a plane and take the direction into account as well. For example, in the figure below, AB and BA are two line segments with equal length but in opposite directions. Typically, one writes $AB = -BA$. Further, a point P on AB is said to divide the segment internally and AP/PB is positive; whereas Q on the extended AB is said to divide the segment externally and AQ/QB is considered to be a negative quantity.

Recall that polygons are closed geometric structures formed of line segments. The most commonly studied polygons are triangles and quadrilaterals such as squares, rectangles, parallelograms and rhombuses. We will not discuss the definitions of these structures; it is assumed that the reader is aware of the basics. Below, we focus on some important properties and results of different polygons.

Definition 5.1 (Similar Polygons): Two polygons are said to be similar if one can draw a direct one-to-one correspondence between the set of vertices in such a way that the corresponding angles are equal and the corresponding sides are proportional.

For example, let us look at two similar triangles ABC and DEF, as shown in the figure below. Following the definition, one can say that $AB/DE = BC/EF = CA/FD$.

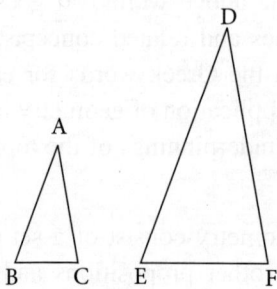

Theorem 5.1: Let ABC be a triangle. The following important results are connected to the notion of similarity defined above.

- If D and E are the midpoints of AB and BC, respectively, then DE is parallel to CA and $DE = CA/2$.

- Any straight line parallel to BC cuts AB and CA (possibly extended) proportionally. The converse is true as well.

- If a straight line is drawn through the midpoint of AB and is parallel to BC, then it must pass through the midpoint of CA.

- Recall that the area of a triangle is given by half of the product of the base and the altitude. Thus, the areas of triangles with equal bases are proportional to their heights. Further, the ratio of the areas of two similar triangles is equal to the square of the ratio of their bases.

- If the internal bisector of $\angle A$ cuts the opposite side BC at D, then $BD/DC = AB/AC$. Similarly, if the external bisector of $\angle A$ cuts BC externally at X, then $BX/XC = -AB/AC$.

Next, we focus on a few vital theorems related to triangles. Hereafter and conventionally, a, b, c are used to denote, respectively, the sides BC, CA, AB of the triangle ABC, while the angles are denoted using the uppercase letters A, B, C.

Theorem 5.2 (Pythagorean Theorem): If ABC is a right-angled triangle with $C = 90°$, then $a^2 + b^2 = c^2$. Any such triplet (a, b, c) is known as a Pythagorean triplet.

Theorem 5.3 (Menelaus' Theorem): Suppose that a straight line cuts the sides BC, CA, AB (suitably extended) of triangle ABC at three point D, E, F, respectively. Then

$$\left(\frac{BD}{DC}\right)\left(\frac{CE}{EA}\right)\left(\frac{AF}{FB}\right) = -1$$

Conversely, if three points D, E, F are taken on the three sides of the triangle such that the above equation holds, then D, E, F must be collinear.

Theorem 5.4 (Ceva's Theorem): Let D, E, F be three points, respectively, on the sides BC, CA, AB of triangle ABC such that AD, BE, CF are concurrent at O. Then

$$\left(\frac{BD}{DC}\right)\left(\frac{CE}{EA}\right)\left(\frac{AF}{FB}\right) = 1$$

Conversely, if three points D, E, F are taken on the three sides of the triangle such that the above equation holds, then AD, BE, CF must be concurrent.

> **Useful Tip:** One can show that the above equation is equivalent to the following trigonometric form:
>
> $$\left(\frac{\sin \angle BAD}{\sin \angle DAC}\right)\left(\frac{\sin \angle CBE}{\sin \angle EBA}\right)\left(\frac{\sin \angle ACF}{\sin \angle FCB}\right) = 1$$

A few important corollaries to Ceva's Theorem are that in any triangle, the medians are concurrent, the perpendicular bisectors of the three sides are concurrent, the altitudes are concurrent, and the internal bisectors of the three angles are concurrent. These results are left as exercises to the reader. Note that these points of concurrence are, respectively, known as the centroid, circumcentre, orthocentre and incentre of a circle. It is important to remember the various properties of these points.

Before discussing these results, we recall that a polygon is called cyclic if there is a circle that passes through all the vertices of the polygon. A triangle is always cyclic, with its centre at the circumcentre. Such a circle is known as the circumcircle of the triangle. On a related note, a circle centred at the incentre with radius equal to the length of the perpendicular from the incentre onto any side is called an incircle. Every side of the triangle serves as a tangent to the incircle. The figures below show the four types of concurrence for triangle ABC.

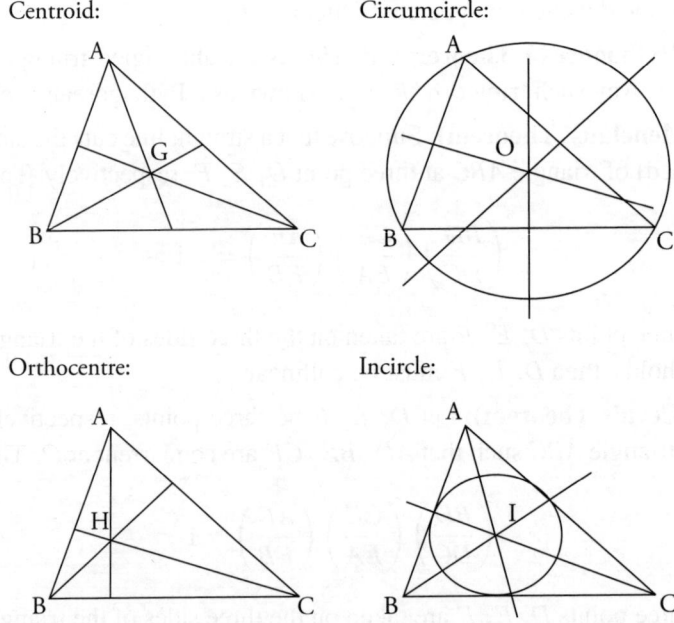

We now turn our attention to the properties that are crucial in many exercises.

Theorem 5.5 (Sine Rule for Triangles): If R is the circumradius, that is, the radius of the circumcircle, of a triangle ABC, then

$$\frac{a}{\sin A} = \frac{b}{\sin B} = \frac{c}{\sin C} = 2R$$

Theorem 5.6 (Euler Line): Let O, H, G denote, respectively, the circumcentre, orthocentre and centroid of a non-equilateral triangle. Then, $GH = 2(OG)$ and the three points are collinear. This common line is known as the Euler line.

Theorem 5.7 (Euler's Theorem): For a triangle ABC, let O and I be the circumcentre and incentre, respectively. If the corresponding radii are denoted by R and r, then $OI^2 = R^2 - 2Rr$.

Theorem 5.8 (Area of a Triangle): Let ABC be any triangle with the lengths of the sides a, b, c and angles A, B, C, as mentioned earlier. Then, the area of the triangle (say Δ) can be calculated by the following formulae:

- $\Delta = \frac{1}{2}bc\sin A = \frac{1}{2}ca\sin B = \frac{1}{2}ab\sin C$
- $\Delta = rs$, where r is the inradius and $s = (a+b+c)/2$ is the semiperimeter
- Heron's formula: $\Delta = \sqrt{s(s-a)(s-b)(s-c)}$

Theorem 5.9: The opposite angles of a quadrilateral inscribed in a circle add up to 180°. Conversely, if the opposite angles of a quadrilateral are supplementary (that is, the sum is 180°), then it is cyclic.

Theorem 5.10 (Ptolemy's Theorem): For a cyclic quadrilateral $ABCD$, if AC and BD indicate the two diagonals, then $(AC)(BD) = (AB)(CD) + (AD)(BC)$.

> **Useful Tip:** A useful corollary of the above is that for any equilateral triangle, if we take a point on the circumcircle, then its distance to the farthest vertex is equal to the sum of the distances from the other two vertices. One should also note that if $ABCD$ is not a cyclic quadrilateral, then $(AC)(BD) < (AB)(CD) + (AD)(BC)$.

Theorem 5.11: The angles in the same segment of a circle are equal, and the value is equal to half of the angle subtended at the centre. In the figure below, $\angle APB = \angle AQB = \angle AOB/2$.

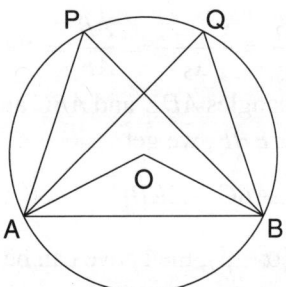

Conversely, if a chord AB subtends equal angles at two points P, Q on the same side of it, then $ABPQ$ is a cyclic quadrilateral.

Theorem 5.12 (Brahmagupta's Theorem): For a triangle ABC, let $AD \perp BC$ such that D lies on BC and let AE be a diameter of the circumcircle of the triangle. Then, $(AB)(AC) = (AD)(AE)$.

Theorem 5.13: If AB and $A'B'$ are two chords of a circle such that they intersect at P inside the circle, then $(PA)(PA') = (PB)(PB')$.

> **Useful Tip:** Both of the above theorems can be proved using the properties of similar triangles. Another interesting exercise would be to find out what happens in Theorem 5.13 if AB and $A'B'$ intersect each other outside the circle.

Solved Examples

1. Let *ABC* be any triangle, right angled at *A*, with *D* as any point on the side *AB*. The line *DE* is drawn parallel to *BC* to meet the side *AC* at the point *E*. *F* is the foot of the perpendicular drawn from *E* to *BC*. If $AD = x_1, DB = x_2, BF = x_3, EF = x_4$ and $AE = x_5$, then show that

$$\frac{x_1}{x_5} + \frac{x_2}{x_5} = \frac{x_1 x_3 + x_4 x_5}{x_3 x_5 - x_1 x_4}.$$

Solution: The figure described in the question is shown below. We also join *E* and *B*.

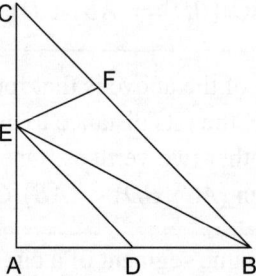

Using $AD - x_1, DB = x_2, AE = x_5$, the left-hand side in the given equation can be simplified as

$$\frac{x_1}{x_5} + \frac{x_2}{x_5} = \frac{x_1 + x_2}{x_5} = \frac{AB}{AE} = \cot \angle ABE$$

Since *DE* is parallel to *BC*, the triangles *ADE* and *ABC* are similar. Thus, $\angle ADE = \angle ABC$. Now, writing $\angle ABE = \angle ABC - \angle EBF$, we get

$$\frac{x_1}{x_5} + \frac{x_2}{x_5} = \cot(\angle ABC - \angle EBF) = \cot(\angle ADE - \angle EBF)$$

Next, using the expansion of $\cot(\alpha - \beta)$, the above can be further simplified as follows:

$$\frac{x_1}{x_5} + \frac{x_2}{x_5} = \frac{\cot \angle ADE \cot \angle EBF + 1}{\cot \angle EBF - \cot \angle ADE} = \frac{(x_1/x_5)(x_3/x_4) + 1}{x_3/x_4 - x_1/x_5} = \frac{x_1 x_3 + x_4 x_5}{x_3 x_5 - x_1 x_4},$$

and that proves the required result.

> **Useful Tip:** We use trigonometric identities to solve this problem. A similar approach is very useful when the required result is an algebraic expression. In particular, you would find that the law of sines is one of the most valuable identities in geometry exercises.

2. For a triangle *ABC*, let $\angle B$ be twice $\angle C$ and suppose $CD = AB$. Consider a point *D* on *BC* such that *AD* is the internal bisector of $\angle A$. Find the value of $\angle A$.

Solution: Let us draw the figure described in the question.

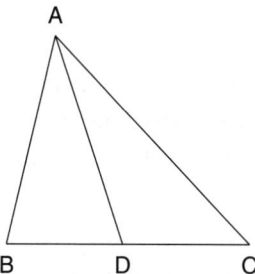

Using the sine rule for triangles *ABD* and *ADC*, we get the following:

$$\frac{AB}{\sin \angle ADB} = \frac{AD}{\sin \angle B} = \frac{BD}{\sin \frac{1}{2}\angle A}, \frac{AD}{\sin \angle C} = \frac{CD}{\sin \frac{1}{2}\angle A} = \frac{AC}{\sin \angle ADC}$$

For notational convenience, we remove the angle signs for the above terms. Since $CD = AB$, from the above, we can write the equality $\sin(ADB)/\sin B = \sin(A/2)/\sin C$. Further, using $B = 2C$ and observing $ADB = 180° - ADC = C + A/2$, we get

$$\sin\left(C + \frac{A}{2}\right) = \frac{\sin\frac{A}{2}\sin B}{\sin C} = 2\sin\frac{A}{2}\cos C$$

The above implies

$$\sin C \cos\frac{A}{2} + \cos C \sin\frac{A}{2} = 2\sin\frac{A}{2}\cos C \implies \sin\left(C - \frac{A}{2}\right) = 0$$

In view of the fact that A, B, C are the angles of a triangle, it is now easy to argue that $A = 2C$, which would also suggest that $5C = 180°$. Thus, $C = 36°$, implying that $\angle A = 72°$.

3. Suppose *ABC* is a triangle where *BC* is twice the length of *AB*. Let *D* be the midpoint of *BC* and *E* be the midpoint of *BD*. Prove that *AD* is the angle bisector of $\angle CAE$.

Solution: In order to leverage the properties of parallel straight lines, draw *DF* parallel to *AC*, where *F* lies on the side *AB*.

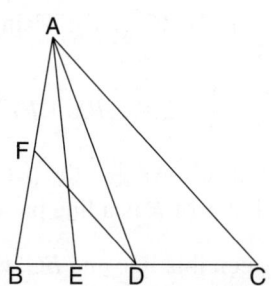

As $DF \parallel AC$, it is easy to argue that F is the midpoint of AB and $\angle ADF = \angle DAC$. Also, the condition $2AB = BC$ implies that $AB = BD$, $BF = BE$. Thus, for triangles ABE and DBF, we have the required conditions to infer that these are congruent triangles. Therefore, $\angle BAE = \angle FDB$. Further, using $AB = BD$, one can write $\angle BAD = \angle ADB$. Subtracting these two equations, we get $\angle EAD = \angle ADF$. However, the latter has already been shown to be equal to $\angle DAC$. Hence, AD bisects $\angle CAE$.

> **Useful Tip:** We utilized an appropriate construction technique to arrive at the result. Often, the trick is to identify whether any such construction, most commonly parallel lines or perpendiculars, are vital in the context of the problem. Consider another example below.

4. Consider an isosceles triangle ABC such that $AB = AC = 20$. Find the locus of all points P inside the triangle ABC such that the sum of the distances of P to AB and that of P to AC is 1.

Solution: The following figure shows the triangle and the given points. We also plot X and Y, the feet of the perpendiculars from P on AB, AC, respectively.

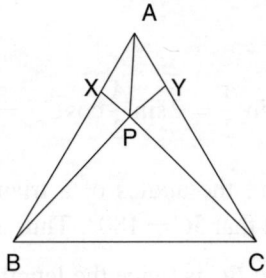

According to the given conditions, $PX + PY = 1$ and $AB = AC = 20$. Now, considering the area of triangles ABP, BCP and ACP, one can write that $[\triangle BCP] = [\triangle ABC] - ([\triangle ABP] + [\triangle ACP])$. The second term (within parentheses) of the expression on the right-hand side can be computed as $(1/2)(AB)(PX) + (1/2)(AC)(PY)$. Using the aforementioned conditions, we get

$$[\triangle BCP] = [\triangle ABC] - \frac{1}{2} \times 20 \times (PX + PY) = [\triangle ABC] - 10,$$

which is a constant quantity. Thus, it follows that the perpendicular distance from P to BC must be fixed. In other words, the locus of P is a line parallel to BC.

In order to obtain the distance between this line and BC, we need to know the length of BC. Suppose $BC = 2a$ and the distance of A from BC is h. Then, the area of triangle ABC is ah, and therefore, the area of *BPC* is $(ah-10)$, implying that the perpendicular distance from P to BC must be $(h-10/a)$.

Hence, the locus of P is a straight line parallel to BC, situated at a distance $(h-20/BC)$ units from BC (where h is the distance from A to BC).

5. Consider a quadrilateral *ABCD* such that the sum of a pair of opposite sides (say, $AB+CD$) equals the sum of the other two sides (respectively, $AD+BC$). Show that the two circles inscribed in triangles *ABC* and *ACD* are tangents to each other.

Solution: The following figure shows the quadrilateral, along with one inscribed circle.

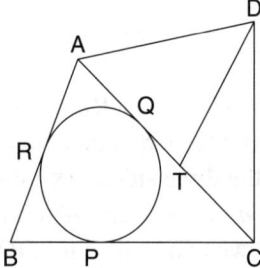

Suppose that the incircle to the triangle *ABC* touches the three sides at P, Q, R and that the incircle to the triangle *ACD* touches *AC* at T. If we can show that T and Q are essentially the same points, that would mean *AC* is tangent to both the incircles, thereby giving us the required result.

It is easy to note that $AR=AQ$, $BR=BP$ and $CP=CQ$. Then, $AR+BP+CQ=AQ+BR+CP=(AB+BC+CA)/2$. From the second equation and using $BR=BP$, we get

$$AQ = \frac{1}{2}(AB+BC+CA) - (BP+CP) = \frac{1}{2}(AB+BC+CA) - BC$$

Next, from the relationship $AB+CD=AD+BC$, we can write

$$AQ = \frac{1}{2}(AD+BC-CD+CA-BC) = \frac{1}{2}(AD+CA+CD) - CD$$

Now, if we consider the incircle to triangle *ACD*, using similar arguments as above, we can show that the last term is actually equal to AT. Thus, we get $AQ=AT$, that is, Q and T are the same points and it completes the proof.

6. Consider a triangle *ABC* such that a, b and c are the lengths of the sides BC, CA and AB, respectively. Let p_1, p_2, p_3 be the lengths of the perpendiculars drawn from the circumcentre to the sides BC, CA and AB. Prove that

$$\frac{a}{p_1} + \frac{b}{p_2} + \frac{c}{p_3} = \frac{abc}{4p_1 p_2 p_3}.$$

Solution: Let O be the circumcentre and let D, E, F be the feet of the perpendiculars on the three sides. The figure is given below.

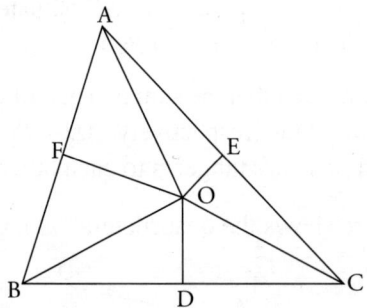

It is given that $BC = a, CA = b, AB = c$; $OD = p_1, OE = p_2, OF = p_3$. Since the circumcentre is obtained by taking the perpendicular bisectors of the sides, we can say that D, E, F are the midpoints of the three sides. Assume that the circumradius is R. Then, using the sine rule for the triangle, $a/\sin A = 2R$, which implies that $(a/2)/R = \sin A$. Note that $DC = a/2$ and $OC = R$. Thus, we can write $\sin \angle DOC = \sin A$, that is, $\angle DOC = A$.

Using the above

$$\tan A = \frac{DC}{OD} = \frac{a}{2p_1}$$

We can obtain similar expressions for $\tan B$, $\tan C$. We can then perform the following:

$$\begin{aligned}
\frac{a}{p_1} + \frac{b}{p_2} + \frac{c}{p_3} &= 2(\tan A + \tan B + \tan C) \\
&= 2\left[\frac{\sin A}{\cos A} + \frac{\sin B}{\cos B} + \tan(\pi - A - B)\right] \\
&= 2\left[\frac{\sin A \cos B + \cos A \sin B}{\cos A \cos B} - \tan(A + B)\right] \\
&= 2\left[\frac{\sin(A+B)}{\cos A \cos B} - \frac{\sin(A+B)}{\cos(A+B)}\right] \\
&= 2\sin(A+B)\left[\frac{\cos(A+B) - \cos A \cos B}{\cos A \cos B \cos(A+B)}\right] \\
&= 2\sin(\pi - C) \cdot \frac{\cos A \cos B - \sin A \sin B - \cos A \cos B}{\cos A \cos B \cos(\pi - C)} \\
&= 2\tan A \tan B \tan C
\end{aligned}$$

Finally, replacing the expressions obtained earlier for $\tan A$, $\tan B$, $\tan C$, we can write
$$\frac{a}{p_1}+\frac{b}{p_2}+\frac{c}{p_3}=\frac{abc}{4p_1p_2p_3},$$
and that completes the proof.

7. Consider an equilateral triangle ABC. Let PD, PE and PF be the perpendiculars from an arbitrary point P to the sides BC, CA and AB, respectively. Prove that the value of
$$\frac{PD+PE+PF}{BD+CE+AF}$$
is independent of the choice of P.

Solution: The figure, according to the given conditions, is shown below.

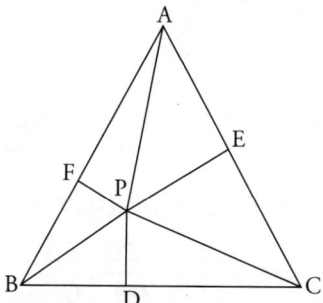

Let the sides of the triangle be a. Now, PB is a perpendicular on BC, and so, $PB^2 - BD^2 = PC^2 - DC^2$. Applying the Pythagorean Theorem for triangles PBF and PCE, we obtain the equation
$$PF^2 + BF^2 - BD^2 = PE^2 + CE^2 - DC^2$$

Once again, we can apply the Pythagorean Theorem for triangles PFA and PEA and obtain $PA^2 - AF^2 + BF^2 - BD^2 = PA^2 - AE^2 + CE^2 - DC^2$. Rearranging the terms, we get $BD^2 + CE^2 + AF^2 = BF^2 + CD^2 + AE^2$. Next, using the fact that it is an equilateral triangle, we can write $BF = a - AF$, $CD = a - BD$ and $AE = a - CE$. Straightforward algebraic manipulations then lead to the following:
$$2a(BD+CE+AF) = 3a^2 \implies BD+CE+AF = \frac{3a}{2}$$

On the other hand, the area of the triangle is $\sqrt{3}a^2/4$ and considering the triangles BPC, CPA and APB, we can write
$$\frac{1}{2}(PD)(BC)+\frac{1}{2}(PE)(CA)+\frac{1}{2}(PF)(AB) = \frac{\sqrt{3}a^2}{4} \implies PD+PE+PF = \frac{\sqrt{3}a}{2}$$

Combining the above, we obtain the required ratio as $1/\sqrt{3}$, which does not depend on the choice of P.

8. Consider a triangle ABC with an interior point P. Draw the line segments AP, BP and CP and extend them to meet the opposite sides BC, CA and AB at D, E and F, respectively. Prove that
$$\frac{AF}{FB} + \frac{AE}{EC} = \frac{AP}{PD}.$$

Solution: The required figure is shown below.

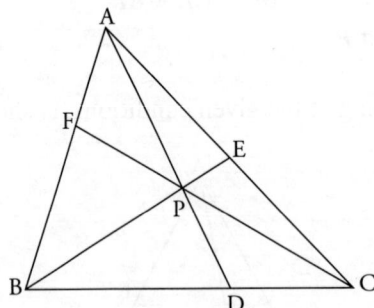

At first, consider the triangle ADC and the transversal BPE. By Menelaus' Theorem
$$\frac{DB}{BC} \cdot \frac{CE}{EA} \cdot \frac{AP}{PD} = -1 \implies \frac{AP}{PD} = \frac{-BC}{DB} \cdot \frac{EA}{CE} \implies \frac{AP}{PD} = \frac{CB}{DB} \cdot \frac{AE}{EC}$$

On the other hand, in triangle ABC, by Ceva's Theorem
$$\frac{BD}{DC} \cdot \frac{CE}{EA} \cdot \frac{AF}{FB} = 1 \implies \frac{AF}{FB} = \frac{EA}{CE} \cdot \frac{DC}{BD} \implies \frac{AF}{FB} = \frac{AE}{EC} \cdot \frac{CD}{DB}$$

Now, using the above two relations
$$\frac{AF}{FB} + \frac{AE}{EC} = \frac{AE}{EC} \cdot \frac{CD}{DB} + \frac{AE}{EC} = \frac{AE}{EC}\left[\frac{CD}{DB} + 1\right] = \frac{CB}{DB} \cdot \frac{AE}{EC} = \frac{AP}{PD},$$

and the proof is complete.

Useful Tip: Remember that Ceva's Theorem and Menelaus' Theorem deal with concurrent lines, and hence, they should be utilized in similar problems.

9. Let $ABCD$ be a cyclic quadrilateral with $AB = p$, $BC = q$, $CD = r$, $DA = s$. Prove that
$$\frac{AC}{BD} = \frac{ps + qr}{pq + rs}.$$

Solution: The given conditions are provided in the following figure:

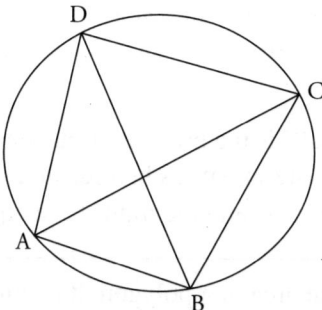

Recall that in a cyclic quadrilateral *ABCD*, opposite angles are supplementary, that is, $A = \pi - C$, $B = \pi - D$ (and, therefore, have a common sine). Also, as a consequence of the law of sines, a triangle *XYZ* inscribed in a circle of diameter d has side length

$$YZ = d\sin X,\ ZX = d\sin Y,\ XY = d\sin Z$$

Thus, for the given quadrilateral *ABCD*, if the circle has a diameter d, then we can write

$$BD = d\sin A = d\sin C,\ AC = d\sin B = d\sin D$$

Now, if the area of the quadrilateral is M, then, using the above, we get

$$ps + qr = \frac{2}{(BD/d)}\left(\frac{1}{2}ps\sin A + \frac{1}{2}qr\sin C\right) = \frac{2d}{BD}(\triangle ABD + \triangle BCD) = \frac{2dM}{BD}$$

We can follow the same procedure to show that $pq + rs = 2dM/AC$, and then, taking the ratio of the above two expressions, we can obtain our required result.

10. Consider two parallelograms *ABCD* and *EFGH* such that *E* is on the side *AB* and *C* is on the side *FG*. Prove that the two parallelograms have equal area.

Solution: The required figure is given below and we also join *E* and *C*.

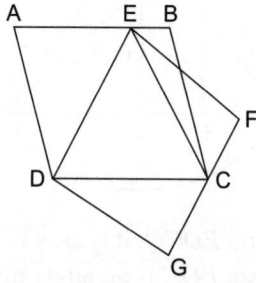

Since AB and CD are parallel, the area of the parallelogram $ABCD$ is equal to the product of the length of DC and the height from E to DC. Thus, we can argue that the area of the triangle EDC is half that of $ABCD$.

On the other hand, the area of EDC is the product of the length of ED and the height from C to ED. Clearly, using identical arguments as before, we can infer that the area of $EFGH$ is twice that of EDC. Hence, the two parallelograms have equal area.

> **Useful Tip:** While finding the area of a polygon, it is often most useful to construct the appropriate triangles, as formulae can be applied directly and conveniently for triangles. Keeping that in mind, work out the above problem to show that the proposition is true even if E lies on the extension of AB through B.

11. Let AB be a chord of a circle C. For which point P on the circumference of C is the value of $(PA)(PB)$ the maximum?

Solution: Let the area of the triangle inscribed in the circle be Δ and the radius of the circle be r. Then

$$\Delta = \frac{1}{2}(PA)(PB)\sin P \implies (PA)(PB) = \frac{2\Delta}{\sin P}$$

For any chord AB, we know that the angle it makes at any point on the circumference is the same, and so, $\sin P$ is constant. Thus, $(PA)(PB)$ attains its maximum value when the area of the triangle is the greatest. Since AB is fixed, it essentially means that P is a point such that the length of the perpendicular from P to AB is the maximum. Now, suppose PD is the perpendicular on AB.

Let us now drop a perpendicular from the centre (O) of the circle to the chord AB and extend it to the other side so that it intersects the circle at a point Q. The required figure is shown below.

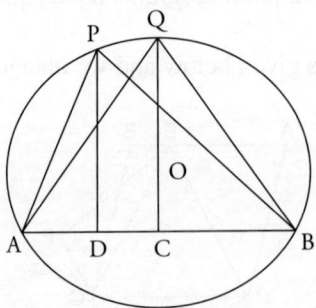

Then, if we consider the quadrilateral $PDCQ$, it is easy to observe that PD is parallel to QC, implying that it is a trapezium. Also, PQC is an angle made at the circumference by some chord (say, PX, where X is a point where the extended QC intersects with the circle) and so, it must be an acute angle. Thus, we can say that $PD < QC$.

Hence, $(PA)(PB)$ is maximum when we choose P to be the same as Q in the above figure, that is, we need to drop a perpendicular from the centre of the circle on the chord AB and extend it to the other side so that it intersects the circle at a point Q.

12. Let ABC be an equilateral triangle with an altitude of 3 cm. A circle is inscribed in this triangle. Next, another circle is drawn in such a way that it is tangent to the earlier circle as well as to the sides AB and AC.

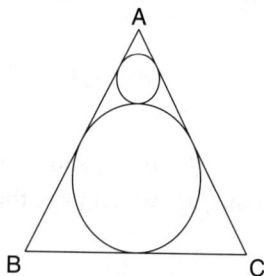

Now, suppose that infinitely many such circles are drawn following the idea that each is tangent to the previous circle and to the sides AB and AC. Compute the sum of the areas of all such circles.

Solution: Let the radii of all these circles be denoted by $r_1, r_2, \ldots$. Since the altitude of the triangle is 3 cm, the length of each side is $2\sqrt{3}$ cm. Further, recall that for an equilateral triangle, the centroid, circumcentre and incentre coincide. Hence, it is possible to show that the inradius is one-third the median. Therefore, $r_1 = 1$.

As the second circle touches the first circle, if we draw the tangent line such that it cuts AB and AC at D and E, respectively, then ADE is an equilateral triangle with altitude equal to 1 cm. Then, using identical arguments as before, we can say that the radius of the second circle must be $1/3$. Proceeding in this way, we obtain $r_k = 1/3^k$. Hence, the sum of the areas of all such circles, in sq. cm, is

$$\Delta = \sum_{k=1}^{\infty} \frac{\pi}{3^{2k}} = \frac{\pi}{1 - 1/9} = \frac{9\pi}{8}$$

13. What is the maximum area of a rectangle that can be inscribed in a triangle of area Δ?

Solution: Suppose the three sides of the triangle are $a, b,$ and c, respectively, and the length of the perpendicular from A to BC is d. Also, suppose k is the length of the rectangle and h is the height. Thus, in the figure below, $BC = a, CA = b, AB = c, AD = d, PQ = h, QR = k$.

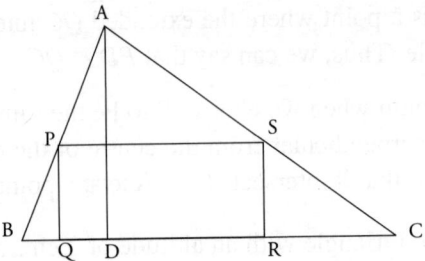

Since triangles BPQ and ABD are similar, we can write that $BQ/BD = PQ/AD = h/d$. Similarly, from triangles ACD and RCS, $RC/DC = h/d$. Thus

$$BQ + RC = \frac{h}{d}(BD + DC) \implies BC - QR = \frac{ha}{d} \implies QR = \frac{a(d-h)}{d}$$

So, the area of the rectangle is $hk = ah(d-h)/d$, and thus, it is maximum when $h(d-h)$ is maximized. Using the AM-GM inequality, we can say that

$$h(d-h) \leqslant \left(\frac{h+(d-h)}{2}\right)^2 = \frac{d^2}{4},$$

and the equality holds when $h = d/2$.

Thus, the area of the rectangle is $ah(d-h)/d = ad/4$ and since $\Delta = ad/2$, we can say that the maximum possible area of the rectangle inscribed in a triangle of area Δ is $\Delta/2$.

14. Consider an isosceles triangle ABC such that $AB = BC = 1$ cm and $\angle A = 30°$. Compute the volume of the solid that can be obtained by revolving the triangle about the line AB.

Solution: It is evident that the solid formed by revolving the triangle about the line AB is a right-circular cone, the height and radius of which are given by AD and DC in the following figure.

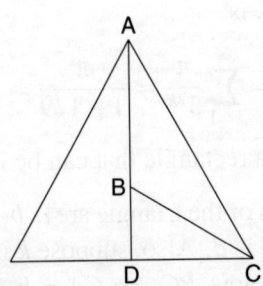

Let $AD = h$ cm, $DC = r$ cm. Then, the required volume is $\pi r^2 h/3$ cu. cm. Since $\angle BAC = 30°$ and ADC is a right-angled triangle, we get $\angle ACD = 60°$. So

$$\frac{AD}{DC} = \tan 60° \implies h = r\sqrt{3}$$

Also, using the isosceles property of ABC, we can say that $\angle ACB = 30°$, implying that $\angle BCD = 30°$. Then, as before, $BD = DC \tan 30°$, that is, $\sqrt{3}(h-1) = r$. Combining it with what we obtained earlier

$$\sqrt{3}(h-1) = \frac{h}{\sqrt{3}} \implies 3h - 3 = h \implies h = \frac{3}{2}, \ r = \frac{\sqrt{3}}{2}$$

Hence, the volume of the solid is $\pi r^2 h/3 = 3\pi/8$ cu. cm.

15. Let $ABCD$ be a trapezium such that AB is parallel to DC and $AB/DC = \alpha > 1$. Let P and Q be two points on AC and BD, respectively, such that

$$\frac{AP}{AC} = \frac{BQ}{BD} = \frac{\alpha - 1}{\alpha + 1}.$$

Show that $PQCD$ is a parallelogram.

Solution: Let AC and BD intersect at K. Given that $\dfrac{AP}{AC} = \dfrac{BQ}{BD} = \dfrac{\alpha - 1}{\alpha + 1}$, it can be rewritten as

$$\frac{DQ}{BD} = \frac{PC}{AC} = \frac{2}{\alpha + 1}$$

Now, the triangles DKC and AKB are similar. So, using the properties of similar triangles, we get

$$\alpha = \frac{BK}{DK} = \frac{AK}{CK} \implies \alpha + 1 = \frac{BD}{DK} = \frac{AC}{CK}$$

Earlier, it was found that $DQ/BD = 2/(\alpha + 1)$. From these two relations, we can conclude that $DQ = 2(DK)$, that is, $DK = KQ$, and similarly, it can be shown that $PK = KC$. Hence, $PQCD$ is a parallelogram.

16. A train is passing along a train line that intersects another line at a junction at an acute angle θ. Suppose that the train subtends an angle α at a station on the other line when the front of the train is at the junction. On the other hand, when its rear is at the junction, it subtends an angle β at the same station. If $\beta < \alpha$, prove that

$$\tan \theta = \frac{2 \sin \alpha \sin \beta}{\sin(\alpha - \beta)}.$$

Solution: In the figure shown below, AB and MN are the two lines, and let us suppose that the train is going along BA. Let O be the junction and let S be the said station on the other line, PO is the position of the train when the front is at the junction and OQ is the position when the rear is at the junction. From these conditions, we have $\angle POS = \theta$, $\angle OSP = \alpha$, $\angle OSQ = \beta < \alpha$.

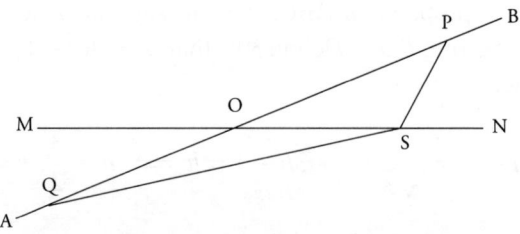

From the $\cot(m-n)$ theorem, we know that if D is a point on side BC of a triangle ABC such that $BD:DC = m:n$, then $(m+n)\cot\angle ADC = m\angle BAD - n\angle CAD$. For our problem, we have $m = n = 1$ since both OP and OQ are the lengths of the train. So, using the above theorem, we can say that $2\cot\angle POS = \cot\angle OSQ - \cot\angle OSP$. Thus

$$\tan\theta = \frac{2}{2\cot\angle POS} = \frac{2}{\cot\beta - \cot\alpha}$$

Substituting $\cot\theta = \cos\theta/\sin\theta$, the above leads to the required result as

$$\tan\theta = \frac{2\sin\alpha\sin\beta}{\cos\beta\sin\alpha - \cos\alpha\sin\beta} = \frac{2\sin\alpha\sin\beta}{\sin(\alpha-\beta)}$$

17. Consider a right-angled triangle ABC with $BC = AC = 1$, and let P be a point on AB. Let PQ and PR be two perpendiculars on AC and BC, respectively. If $\Delta(X)$ denotes the area of a geometric figure X, then find the minimum possible value of $\max\{\Delta(BPR), \Delta(APQ), \Delta(PQCR)\}$.

Solution: Let us draw the required figure.

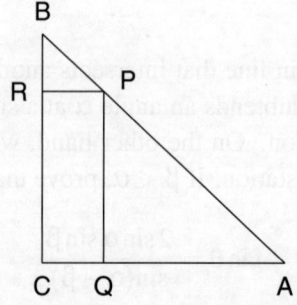

Consider that $PR = x$. Then, $AQ = 1 - x$. Also, since $\angle BAC = 45°$, we can say that $BR = x$, $RC = 1 - x$. Define M to be the maximum of the following three areas:

$$BPR = \frac{x^2}{2}, \quad APQ = \frac{(1-x)^2}{2}, \quad PQCR = x(1-x)$$

Now, $x^2 > (1-x)^2$ if $x > 1/2$. On the other hand, since $x > 0$, $x^2 > 2x(1-x)$ implies $x(3x - 2) > 0$, that is, $x > 2/3$.

Similarly, since $x < 1$, $(1-x)^2 > 2x(1-x)$ if $x < 1/3$. Thus

$$2M = \begin{cases} (1-x)^2 & \text{if } x \leqslant 1/3 \\ 2x(1-x) & \text{if } 1/3 < x < 2/3 \\ x^2 & \text{if } x \geqslant 2/3 \end{cases}$$

Subsequently, the above implies the following:

$$\min_{x \in (0,1)} 2M = \min \left\{ \min_{x \leqslant 1/3} (1-x)^2, \min_{1/3 < x < 2/3} 2x(1-x), \min_{x \geqslant 2/3} x^2 \right\}$$

$$= \min \left\{ \frac{4}{9}, \min_{1/3 < x < 2/3} 2x(1-x), \frac{4}{9} \right\}$$

Now, the function $x(1-x)$ is continuous everywhere, is increasing for $x < 1/2$, attains its maximum at $x = 1/2$ and decreases afterwards. Thus, in the above interval, the minimum is attained at $x = 1/3$ or at $x = 2/3$. And we can check that for both, the value of $2x(1-x)$ is $4/9$.

Hence, the minimum possible value of $2M$ is $4/9$, implying that the minimum possible value of M is $2/9$.

18. A rectangular parallelepiped needs to be enclosed in a cylindrical container with a hemispherical lid. Let the height of the container from the base to the top of the lid be 60 cm and the radius of its base be 30 cm. What is the volume of the largest parallelepiped that can be completely enclosed inside the container with the lid on?

Solution: Suppose the parallelepiped is placed in such a way that its bottom makes an angle θ ($\angle QPB$ in the figure) with the base of the container.

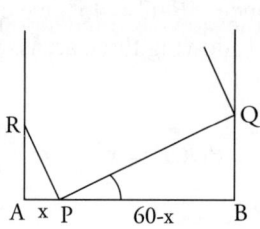
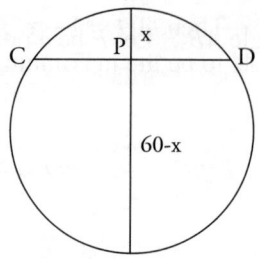

Then, the length of the parallelepiped (given by QP) is $(60-x)\sec\theta$, the height (given by RP) is $x\csc\theta$.

On the other hand, from the figure on the right, $PD = \sqrt{x(60-x)}$ (based on the properties of the chord of a circle). Hence, the length, breadth and height of the parallelepiped are $\sqrt{x(60-x)}, (60-x)\sec\theta$ and $x\csc\theta$, respectively. So, the volume of the parallelepiped is $V = \{x(60-x)\}^{3/2}\cot\theta$.

It is now easy to observe that for a given x, the volume is maximum when θ is minimum, and thus, we can see that the base of the parallelepiped should be along the base of the container. And so, the bottom of the container should appear as shown in the figure below.

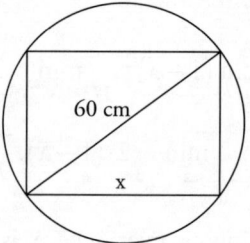

Clearly, the length, breadth and height of the rectangular parallelepiped should be $x, \sqrt{60^2 - x^2}$ and 60 cm, respectively. And so, the volume is maximized when $x\sqrt{3600 - x^2}$ is maximum. Let us denote it by $f(x)$. Taking the first derivative

$$f'(x) = \sqrt{3600 - x^2} + x \times \frac{(-2x)}{2\sqrt{3600-x^2}} = \frac{3600 - 2x^2}{\sqrt{3600-x^2}}$$

The above is 0 for $x = \pm\sqrt{1800} = \pm 30\sqrt{2}$. Taking the second order derivative of $f(x)$, we obtain

$$f''(x) = -\frac{4x}{\sqrt{3600-x^2}} + (3600 - 2x^2) \times \frac{d}{dx}\frac{1}{\sqrt{3600-x^2}},$$

which is less than 0 for $x = 30\sqrt{2}$. Thus, the function has a maxima at $x = 30\sqrt{2}$ and the maximum possible volume is $(30\sqrt{2}) \times \sqrt{3600 - 1800} \times 60$ cm^3, which is equal to 0.108 cu. m.

Euclidean Geometry

19. Consider a triangle *ABC*. Let *P* be a point on the side *AB*. Find a point *E* on the side *AC* such that the area of the quadrilateral *BPEC* is half that of the triangle.

Solution: We need to find *E* such that *BPEC* is half the area of the triangle *ABC*. Now, the quadrilateral can be written as $\triangle PEC + \triangle PBC$. To make computations more tractable, if we can find a point *D* such that $\triangle PEC = \triangle PDC$, then the area of the quadrilateral *BPEC* can be shown to be equal to $\triangle BDC$. Our aim is to first show that this can be achieved by drawing *ED* parallel to *CP*.

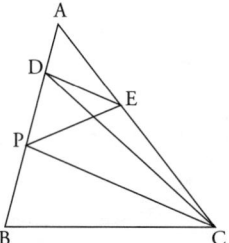

Since *PC* is the common side for both triangles *PEC* and *PDC*, and because $DE \parallel PC$, the lengths of the perpendiculars on *PC* from *D* and *E* are equal. Clearly, $\triangle PEC = \triangle PDC$, subsequently suggesting that the area of *BPEC* is equal to that of *BDC*. Now, if we can choose *D* in such a way that $\triangle BDC = \triangle ABC/2$, then that would ensure what we require.

Hence, one can choose *D* as the midpoint of *AB*, join *PC* and draw *DE* parallel to *PC*. The point *E* obtained in this way, because of the earlier discussions, guarantees that the area of the quadrilateral is half that of the triangle.

> **Useful Tip:** This is an interesting problem of construction to achieve a required condition. Follow similar ideas to trisect a given quadrilateral by means of two straight lines drawn from one of its vertices.

20. Consider a circle as shown in the figure below. Let *E* be the midpoint of the arc *ABEC*. The segment *ED* is perpendicular to the chord *BC*. Find the length of *BC* if the length of the chord *AB* is l_1 and that of the segment *BD* is l_2.

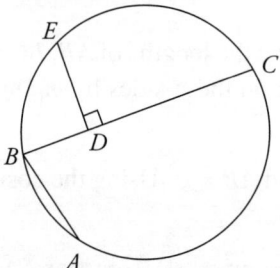

Solution: We can use the concept of rotation to solve this problem. At first, rotate the triangle EDC about point E such that EC falls along EA. The corresponding figure is shown below. We see that $ED'A$ is the rotated form of EDC. We first claim that B lies on the line $D'A$.

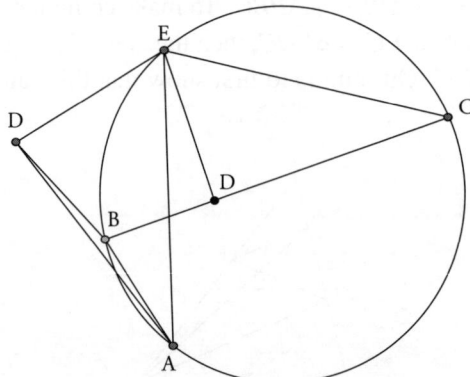

Since E is the midpoint of the arc $ABEC$, EC must be equal to EA. It suffices to show that $\angle D'AE = \angle BAE$. Now, due to rotation, we can say that $\angle D'AE = \angle DCE = \angle BCE$. However, $\angle BCE = \angle BAE$ as they are the angles subtended by the same segment BE. Thus, we have $\angle D'AE = \angle BAE$, implying that B falls on $D'A$.

Now, observe that because of rotation, we can say $ED = ED'$ and $\angle ED'A = \angle EDC = 90°$. Due to the first relation, if we draw the triangle EDD', we get $\angle ED'D = \angle EDD'$, and so, combining that with what we obtained earlier, we get

$$\angle BD'D = \angle ED'A - \angle ED'D = 90° - \angle EDD' = \angle EDB - \angle EDD' = \angle BDD'$$

Clearly, we must have $BD' = BD = l_2$. Since $AD' = DC$ (from rotation) and $AB = l_1$, we can now say that the length of DC is equal to $AB + BD'$, that is, $(l_1 + l_2)$. Thus, the length of BC is $(l_1 + 2l_2)$.

21. Prove that it is impossible to have a triangle with lengths of the sides as a, b and c such that the medians have lengths $2a/3$, $2b/3$ and $4c/5$.

Solution: Conventionally, we take the lengths of AB, BC and CA to be c, a, b, respectively. Let us denote the medians drawn on these sides by m_c, m_a and m_b. These are displayed in the figure.

Note that $AD = m_a$, $DB = a/2$ and $AB = c$. Using the cosine rule for triangle ADB, one can easily say that

$$c^2 = m_a^2 + \frac{a^2}{4} - am_a \cos \angle ADB$$

Euclidean Geometry

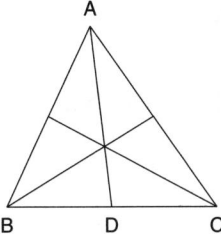

Similarly, since $\angle ADC = 180° - \angle ADB$, from triangle ADC

$$b^2 = m_a^2 + \frac{a^2}{4} - am_a \cos \angle ADC = m_a^2 + \frac{a^2}{4} + am_a \cos \angle ADB$$

So, adding the above two equations, one can get $2m_a^2 = b^2 + c^2 - a^2/2$. Similar results hold for m_b and m_c. Therefore

$$2(m_a^2 + m_b^2 + m_c^2) = \left(b^2 + c^2 - \frac{a^2}{2}\right) + \left(a^2 + c^2 - \frac{b^2}{2}\right) + \left(a^2 + b^2 - \frac{c^2}{2}\right)$$

$$\implies m_a^2 + m_b^2 + m_c^2 = \frac{3}{4}(a^2 + b^2 + c^2)$$

Thus, if the lengths of the medians are $2a/3, 2b/3$ and $4c/5$, then we must have

$$\left(\frac{2a}{3}\right)^2 + \left(\frac{2b}{3}\right)^2 + \left(\frac{4c}{5}\right)^2 - \frac{3}{4}(a^2 + b^2 + c^2) = 0,$$

which can be simplified to

$$\frac{11}{36}a^2 + \frac{11}{36}b^2 + \frac{11}{100}c^2 = 0$$

The above is impossible since the square of a non-zero real number must always be positive. Hence, it is not possible to have a triangle with sides a, b, c whose medians have lengths $2a/3, 2b/3, 4c/5$.

22. Consider a square $ABCD$ with E as the intersection point of the two diagonals. Now, if N is any point on AE, prove that $AB^2 - BN^2 = (AN)(NC)$.

Solution: The required figure is shown below.

Note that the diagonals of a square are perpendicular to each other and also bisect one another. Thus, $AE = EC$. Now, the term AB^2 can be expressed in terms of AN and BN

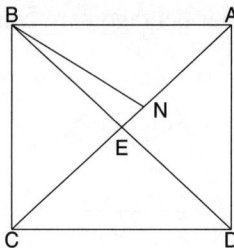

using the cosine rule on triangle ABN. Further, using the fact that $\angle BEN = \angle BEC$ is a right angle, we can argue that

$$AB^2 = BN^2 + AN^2 + 2(AN)(NE) \implies AB^2 - BN^2 = AN^2 + 2(AN)(NE)$$

The right-hand side of the above equation is simplified to $AN(AN + 2NE)$. Then, one can write $AN + 2NE = AE + NE = EC + NE = NC$, which proves the required result.

> **Useful Tip:** The above problem leads to an important corollary about isosceles triangles. One can say that if ABC is a triangle with $AB = AC$, $\angle A \neq 90°$ and D is a point on BC, then $AB^2 - AD^2 = (BD)(DC)$. An application of this result is shown in the problem below.

23. Let ABC be an isosceles triangle with $AB = AC$. Can you find the point D on BC such that if E is taken on AC to ensure $DE \perp BC$, then $AD^2 + DE^2 = AC^2$.

Solution: Suppose D is the required point (see figure) and E is drawn accordingly.

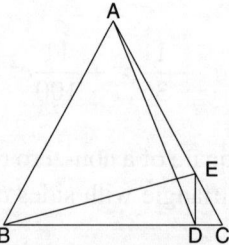

The given condition suggests that $AD^2 + DE^2 = AC^2$ must hold. However, following the result from the previous problem, one can argue that $AC^2 - AD^2 = (BD)(DC)$. Clearly, what we require is to have D such that $DE^2 = (BD)(DC)$. This is only true if $\angle EBC$ is a right angle. Therefore, the required construction is to draw perpendicular BE on AC and then drop perpendicular ED on to BC. The point D obtained in this way is the required point.

24. Prove that all the vertices of a regular pentagon are concyclic. What is the radius of this circumcircle?

Solution: Let us consider that the length of each side of the pentagon is x units. For a regular pentagon, we know that each angle is $108°$. Let us now draw the pentagon $ABCDE$ and also draw the angle bisector of $\angle A$ that intersects CD at P. It is evident that the triangle ACD is isosceles with $AC = AD$. This follows from the fact that ABC and ADE are congruent (AB, AC, AE, DE are of length x units and $\angle ABC = \angle AED = 108°$).

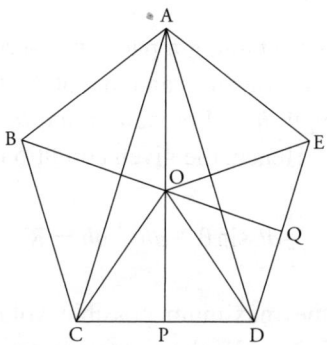

Since $\angle AED = 108°$ and $AE = DE$, we get $\angle ADE = \angle DAE = 36°$. Similarly, $\angle BCA = \angle CAB = 36°$.

The above implies that $\angle CAD = 36°, \angle ACD = \angle ADC = 72°$. Let us now draw an angle of $54°$ on top of CD. Suppose the line cuts AP at O. From the construction, it can be said that $OC = OD$. On the other hand, we know that AP is the angle bisector, and so, $\angle CAO = 18°$. However, from the construction, $\angle ACO = 18°$ (since $\angle ACD = 72°$). Thus, $OA = OC = OD$.

We now join B and O and extend it to cut DE at Q. For triangles BAO and BCO, note the following:
$$BC = AB, OA = OC, \angle BAO = \angle BCO$$

So, these two triangles are congruent, implying that BQ is the angle bisector of $\angle B$. Since $\angle ODE = \angle ODA + \angle ADE = 54°$, using similar arguments as before, we can prove that $OB = OD = OE$.

Hence, for the point O, we get $OA = OB = OC = OD = OE$, proving that the vertices of the pentagon are concyclic and the circumcircle is centred at the point O.

In order to find the circumradius R, for triangle OCD, we can apply the cosine rule. Then, $x^2 = R^2 + R^2 - 2(R)(R) \cos 72°$, which can be simplified to
$$2R^2(1 - \cos 72°) = 2R^2(2\sin^2 36°)$$

Hence, the circumradius is $x/(2\sin 36°)$, where x is the length of each side.

25. Consider a prism with triangular base, and let A be a particular vertex. If the total area of the three faces containing A is K, find the maximum possible volume of the prism.

Solution: Let us assume that the two sides of the triangular base, adjacent to the mentioned vertex, are of a and b units and the height is h units. Also, let us assume that the angle between the two sides of the triangular base is θ. Then, the area of the base is $\Delta = ab\sin\theta/2$ and the volume of the prism is $h\Delta$.

The total area of the three faces containing a particular vertex is given as K, which means that the sum of the area of the two side faces and that of the triangular base is K. Since each side is a parallelogram with length h and breadth a and b, the area of these two sides are equal to ah and bh, respectively. Hence, the given condition gives us the equation

$$\frac{1}{2}ab\sin\theta + ah + bh = K$$

Clearly, in order to find out the maximum possible volume of the prism, we need to maximize the quantity $abh\sin\theta/2$, under the above constraint.

First, it is obvious that for any given h, the volume is maximized when the area of the triangular base is maximum, and that happens if $\theta = \pi/2$. Considering that, the above problem reduces to the following:

$$\text{maximize } \frac{1}{2}abh, \text{ under the constraint } \frac{1}{2}ab + ah + bh = K$$

Once again, since the condition is symmetric in a and b, in order to maximize $abh/2$, we must have $a = b$. So, $a^2 + 4ah = 2K$, that is, $h = (2K - a^2)/4a$ and we need to maximize $a^2h/2 = (2Ka - a^3)/8$. Taking the derivative with respect to a and setting it to 0, we get $2K - 3a^2 = 0$, which implies

$$a = \pm\sqrt{2K/3}$$

Since the second order derivative is negative whenever a is positive, we can say that the maximum is attained for $a = \sqrt{2K/3}$. Thus, the maximum possible volume is

$$\frac{1}{8}a(2K - a^2) = \frac{1}{8}\sqrt{\frac{2K}{3}}\left(2K - \frac{2K}{3}\right) = \frac{K}{6}\sqrt{\frac{2K}{3}} = \sqrt{\frac{K^3}{54}}$$

26. Among all triangles with perimeter K, which one has the maximum area?

Solution: Suppose the lengths of the three sides of the triangle are a, b, c. Let p denote the semiperimeter of the triangle, that is, $p = K/2$. Then, using Heron's formula, we get the area as
$$\Delta = \sqrt{p(p-a)(p-b)(p-c)}$$
Now, $p-a=(b+c-a)/2, p-b=(c+a-b)/2, p-c=(a+b-c)/2$, which leads to the equation
$$\Delta = \frac{\sqrt{K}}{4}\{(b+c-a)(c+a-b)(a+b-c)\}^{1/2}$$
Since a, b, c are the sides of a triangle, we can say that each of the terms in the right-hand side of the above are positive, and so, we can use the AM-GM inequality to obtain
$$\Delta \leqslant \frac{\sqrt{K}}{4}\left\{\frac{(b+c-a)+(c+a-b)+(a+b-c)}{3}\right\}^{3/2}$$
$$= \frac{\sqrt{K}}{4}\left\{\frac{a+b+c}{3}\right\}^{3/2}$$
$$= \frac{\sqrt{K}}{4} \times \frac{K^{3/2}}{3^{3/2}} = \frac{K^2}{12\sqrt{3}}$$

Thus, the maximum possible area is $K^2/12\sqrt{3}$ and it occurs when the equality holds in the above AM-GM inequality, that is, when $b+c-a=c+a-b=a+b-c$, or in other words, $a=b=c$.

Hence, the triangle with the maximum area is the equilateral triangle, with each side of length $K/3$ units and with an area of $K^2/12\sqrt{3}$ sq. units.

27. Prove that amongst all quadrilaterals having perimeter K, the square has the maximum area.

Solution: Let the sides of the quadrilateral be denoted as a, b, c and d. Then, $K = (a+b+c+d)$ is the perimeter of the quadrilateral.

If we denote the area of the quadrilateral as Δ, then it can be expressed as the sum of the two triangles obtained by drawing one diagonal. Further, using the sine rule for the area of a triangle, and using $\sin\alpha \leqslant 1$ for all angles, we can show that
$$\Delta \leqslant \frac{ab}{2} + \frac{cd}{2}$$
Similarly, by drawing the other diagonal, it can be shown that
$$\Delta \leqslant \frac{ad}{2} + \frac{bc}{2}$$

We then combine the two inequalities, $4\Delta \leqslant (a+c)(b+d)$. Now, applying the AM-GM inequality on $(a+c)$ and $(b+d)$, we get

$$4\Delta \leqslant \frac{(a+b+c+d)^2}{4} = \frac{K^2}{4}$$

Now, the equality in the AM-GM inequality holds if and only if $a+c=b+d$. On the other hand, the equality sines in the earlier inequalities on Δ hold if and only if the sines of all the angles are 1, which happens only for a rectangle. Combining these two results, the proof follows.

> **Useful Tip:** An alternative solution to this problem can be worked out based on the earlier result from Problem 26. It is left as an exercise to the student.

28. In a triangle ABC, the bisector of $\angle A$ meets the opposite side at D and the bisector of $\angle B$ meets AC at point E. If $DE \parallel AB$, show that the triangle is isosceles.

Solution: The required figure is shown below.

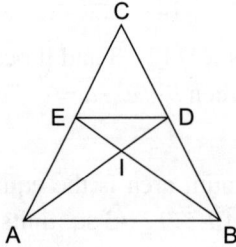

Since AD is the angle bisector, using $DE \parallel AB$, we can write

$$\angle EAD = \angle DAB = \angle EDA$$

Thus, the triangle EAD is isosceles with $EA = ED$. In a similar fashion, we can also prove that EBD is isosceles with $ED = DB$. Therefore, $EA = DB$. Further, using the parallel lines assumption, we can write

$$\frac{CE}{EA} = \frac{CD}{DB},$$

which subsequently implies $CE = CD$. Hence, $CA = CE + EA = CD + DB = CB$, implying that the triangle ABC is isosceles.

29. Let ABC be a triangle with inradius r. Suppose that the incircle touches the sides BC, CA and AB at D, E and F, respectively. Further, let $BD = x$, $CE = y$ and $AF = z$. Prove that

$$r^2 = \frac{xyz}{x+y+z}.$$

Solution: Let us denote the incentre by I and let us join this to the three points D, E, F. Observe that for triangles BID and BIF, we have $ID = IF = r$, $\angle IBD = \angle IBF$ (since I is the incentre) and $\angle IFB = \angle IDB = 90°$, as the inradius is perpendicular to the sides, which are tangents to the incircle. And thus, the two triangles are congruent, thereby giving us $BD = BF = x$, $CD = CE = y$, $AE = AF = z$.

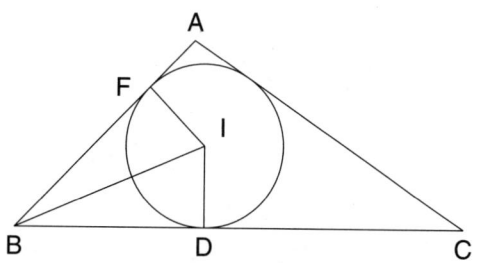

From the above discussion, we also get $a = x+y, b = y+z, c = z+x$. So, the perimeter of the triangle is $2(x+y+z)$ and the semiperimeter is $s = x+y+z$. Now, the area of the triangle (say, Δ) can be computed from the inradius–semiperimeter relationship as well as Heron's formula, as follows:

$$\Delta = rs = r(x+y+z), \quad \Delta = \sqrt{s(s-a)(s-b)(s-c)} = \sqrt{(x+y+z)xyz}$$

Equating the above expressions

$$r^2(x+y+z)^2 = xyz(x+y+z),$$

and that leads to the required result.

30. Consider a rectangle $ABCD$ with a point E on the side DA satisfying $DE = 6, DA = 8, DC = 6$. Extend the line segment CE to meet the circumcircle at F. Calculate the length of the chord DF.

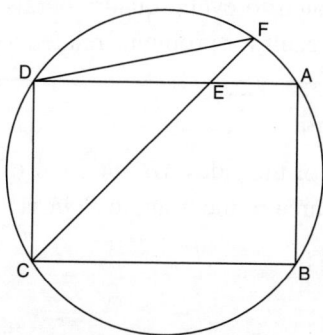

Solution: We aim to use Ptolemy's Theorem and to that end, draw the line segments AF and AC.

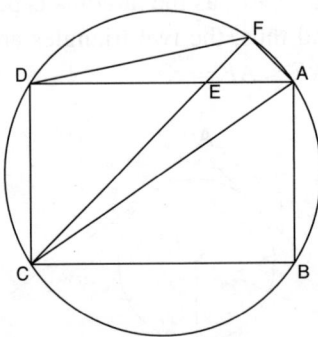

Ptolemy's Theorem suggests that for a cyclic quadrilateral, the product of the diagonals equals the sum of the products of the opposite sides. Therefore, for $AFDC$, $(DA)(CF) = (AF)(DC) + (DF)(AC)$. Using the given values and applying the Pythagorean Theorem

$$8(CF) = 6(AF) + \sqrt{6^2 + 8^2}(DF) \implies 4(CF) = 3(AF) + 5(DF)$$

Further, $DC = DE = 6$ suggests that $\angle DCE = 45°$. On the other hand, CA is a diameter of the circle, and therefore, $\angle CFA = 90°$. Thus, $CF^2 + AF^2 = 100$. Further, $\cos \angle DCA = 6/10 = 3/5$, thereby implying

$$\cos \angle FCA = \cos \angle DCA \cos \angle DCE + \sin \angle DCA \sin \angle DCE = \frac{7}{5\sqrt{2}}$$

However, $\cos \angle FCA = CF/AC$, indicating $CF = 7\sqrt{2}$. Subsequently, we obtain $AF = \sqrt{2}$. Now, combining these with the earlier equation, $5(DF) = 28\sqrt{2} - 3\sqrt{2}$, which implies that the length of the chord DF is $5\sqrt{2}$ units.

> **Useful Tip:** Ptolemy's Theorem serves as an excellent result to determine the length of a line segment related to cyclic quadrilaterals. Students should look for opportunities to exploit this result for problems related to circumcircles.

Multiple Choice Questions

1. Let P, Q, R be the midpoints of the sides AB, BC, CA of a triangle ABC. If the area of the triangle ABC is 20, then the area of the triangle PQR is

(a) 4 (b) 5 (c) 6 (d) 8

Solution: (b)

Since P, Q, R are the midpoints of the three sides, it can be shown that the area of the triangle PQR is one-fourth the entire triangle, and hence, the required answer is 5.

2. ABC is a right-angled triangle with the right angle at B and D is a point lying on AC such that $AD = 2$ cm, $\angle ABD = 45°$, $AC = 6$ cm. The length of AB is

(a) $\dfrac{6}{\sqrt{5}}$ cm (b) $3\sqrt{2}$ cm (c) $\dfrac{12}{\sqrt{5}}$ cm (d) 2 cm

Solution: (a)

We know that $\angle ABD = \angle CBD = 45°$. From triangles ABD and ADC, applying the sine rule, we can write

$$\frac{AD}{\sin 45°} = \frac{BD}{\sin A} \text{ and } \frac{DC}{\sin 45°} = \frac{BD}{\sin C} = \frac{BD}{\sin(90° - A)} = \frac{BD}{\cos A}$$

Using $AD = 2$, $DC = 4$, the above leads to the condition $2\cos A = \sin A$. Thus, $4\cos^2 A = \sin^2 A = 1 - \cos^2 A$, which implies that $\cos^2 A = 1/5$. Subsequently

$$\cos^2 A = \frac{AB^2}{AC^2} \implies AB^2 = \frac{6^2}{5} \implies AB = \frac{6}{\sqrt{5}}$$

3. A rectangle $ABCD$ is inscribed in a circle, with PQ being a diameter parallel to the side AB. If $\angle BPC = 30°$, then the ratio of the area of the circle to that of the rectangle is

(a) $\dfrac{\pi}{2}$ (b) $\dfrac{\sqrt{3}\pi}{2}$ (c) $\dfrac{\pi}{\sqrt{3}}$ (d) $\dfrac{2\pi}{\sqrt{3}}$

Solution: (c)

We draw the following figure and connect B and C to the centre of the circle O.

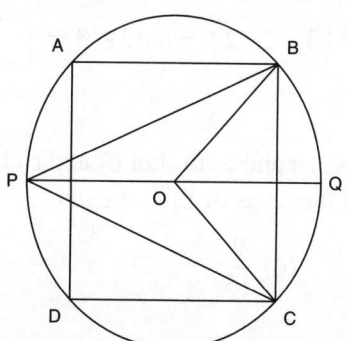

Since $\angle BPC = 30°$, the angle made at the centre $\angle BOC = 60°$. It is easy to show that the triangle BOC is equilateral with side equal to the radius of the circle (call it r).

Next, considering the diagonal AC, we know that the centre of the circle should lie on it, and thus, we can say that $\angle AOB = 180° - 60° = 120°$. Then, for the triangle AOB

$$\frac{AB/2}{OB} = \cos \angle OBA = \cos 30° \implies AB = OB\sqrt{3}$$

Clearly, the two sides of the rectangle are r and $r\sqrt{3}$. Hence, the required ratio is $\pi r^2 / \sqrt{3} r^2 = \pi/\sqrt{3}$.

4. A square with side 2 metres has its corners cut in such a way that the resulting figure is a regular octagon. Then, the area of the octagon, in square metres, is

(a) 2   (b) $\dfrac{8}{1+\sqrt{2}}$ (c) $4(3-2\sqrt{2})$ (d) None of the foregoing numbers

Solution: (b)

Assume that the corners are cut at x metres from each vertex. For a regular octagon, each angle must be $1080°/8 = 135°$, which means that the region cut from each corner forms an isosceles right-angled triangle with the two equal sides being x cm each. Thus, the length of each side of the octagon must be $x\sqrt{2}$, implying that

$$2x + x\sqrt{2} = 2 \implies x = \frac{2}{2+\sqrt{2}}$$

Therefore, the total area of the four regions cut from the four corners is

$$\frac{4x^2}{2} = \frac{8}{(2+\sqrt{2})^2} = \frac{4}{3+2\sqrt{2}} = 4(3-2\sqrt{2})$$

Hence, the area of the octagon is

$$4 - 4(3 - 2\sqrt{2}) = 8\sqrt{2} - 8 = \frac{8}{1+\sqrt{2}}$$

5. Consider a triangle with sides 3, 4 and 5 cm. Let C_1 and C_2 be its incircle and circumcircle, respectively. Then, the ratio of the areas of C_1 and C_2 is

(a) $\dfrac{16}{25}$ (b) $\dfrac{4}{25}$ (c) $\dfrac{9}{25}$ (d) $\dfrac{9}{16}$

Solution: (b)

Since the sides are 3, 4 and 5 cm, it can be argued that the triangle is a right-angled triangle with the right angle being at the opposite vertex of the side with length 5 cm. Using the sine rule, we can now say that $2R = 5$, where R is the circumradius.

On the other hand, the area of the triangle is $\frac{1}{2} \times 3 \times 4 = 6$ square cm, and thus, if r and s are the inradius and the semiperimeter, then $rs = 6$. We can compute s to be 6 cm, indicating that $r = 1$ cm. Hence, the ratio of the areas of C_1 and C_2 is $r^2/R^2 = 4/25$.

6. A girl finds that at a point south of a tower, the angle of elevation of the tower is $60°$. She then walks $10\sqrt{6}$ metres on a horizontal plane towards the west, and finds that the new angle of elevation is $30°$. What was the original distance (in metres) of the girl from the tower?

(a) $5\sqrt{3}$ (b) $15\sqrt{3}$ (c) 15   (d) 75

Solution: (a)

Let us assume that the girl is originally standing at a distance d metres from the tower and let the height of the tower be h metres. Then, the first condition suggests that $\tan 60° = h/d$, that is, $h = d\sqrt{3}$.

After walking $10\sqrt{6}$ metres on a horizontal plane towards the west, the distance of the girl from the tower is $\sqrt{600 + d^2}$. Therefore, from the second condition, we can write

$$\tan 30° = \frac{h}{\sqrt{600+d^2}} \implies \frac{1}{\sqrt{3}} = \frac{d\sqrt{3}}{\sqrt{600+d^2}} \implies 600 + d^2 = 9d^2$$

Hence, $d^2 = 75$, indicating that the original distance was $5\sqrt{3}$ metres.

7. For a triangle ABC, let BF and CG be any two lines drawn from B and C to AC and AB, respectively. If these two lines intersect in H, then

(a) $AF + AG = HF + HG$ (b) $AF + AG < HF + HG$

(c) $AF + AG > HF + HG$ (d) None of the foregoing statements is necessarily true

Solution: (c)

The given conditions are shown in the following figure. We also draw HD and HE parallel to AB and AC, respectively.

Because of the constructions, we can say that $ADHE$ is a parallelogram, that is, $AD = EH$ and $AE = DH$. Now, from triangle DHF, $DH + DF > HF$, which implies that $AE + DF > HF$.

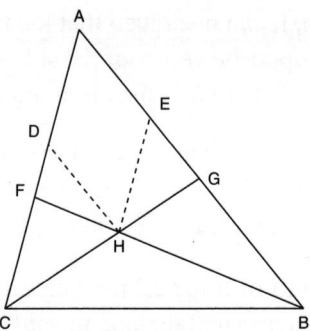

Similarly, from triangle EGH, we can write $EH + EG > HG$, which leads to the inequality $AD + EG > HG$. Adding this inequality to the one obtained earlier, we get $AE + EG + AD + DF > HF + HG$. It is now easy to conclude that (c) must be true.

8. Let $ABCD$ be a cyclic quadrilateral within a circle of radius r. The bisectors of the angles A and C cut the circle at points P and Q, respectively. Then, which of the following must be true?

(a) $AP = 2r$ (b) $PQ = 2r$ (c) $BQ = DP$ (d) $PQ = AP$

Solution: (b)

Let us draw the given quadrilateral along with the angle bisectors.

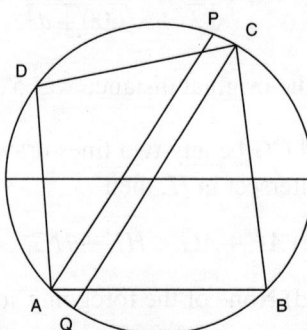

Since $ABCD$ is a cyclic quadrilateral, we know that the opposite angles are supplementary, that is, the sum of the angles at the two vertices A and C is $180°$. Considering the angle bisectors, we can then say that $\angle PAB + \angle BCQ = 90°$. Further, since angles in the segment of a circle are equal, $\angle BCQ = \angle BAQ$.

Combining the above two relations, we can also say that $\angle PAB + \angle BAQ = 90°$. From triangle APQ, it is straightforward to note that the angle made by the segment PQ is a right angle, suggesting that PQ is a diameter of the circle. Hence, (b) must be true.

For the next two questions, let A_n be the area of a regular n-sided polygon inscribed in a circle of radius 1.

9. What is the value of A_4?

(a) 4   (b) 3   (c) 2   (d) 1

Solution: (c)

Assume that the side of the polygon is a. If the polygon is divided into n triangles by joining the centre to each of the vertices, then each such triangle is an isosceles triangle with two equal sides having length 1 and the third side having length a. Further, the angle made by the the two equal sides is $2\pi/n$. Let the length of the perpendicular drawn from the centre of the circle on any side of the polygon be d. Then, using the above, it is easy to show that

$$\frac{a}{2} = \sin\left(\frac{\pi}{n}\right), \; d = \cos\left(\frac{\pi}{n}\right)$$

Thus, the area of each such triangle is

$$\frac{1}{2} \times a \times d = \sin\left(\frac{\pi}{n}\right)\cos\left(\frac{\pi}{n}\right) = \frac{1}{2}\sin\left(\frac{2\pi}{n}\right),$$

which further implies that the area of a regular n-sided polygon inscribed in a circle of radius 1 is

$$A_n = \frac{n}{2}\sin\left(\frac{2\pi}{n}\right) \implies A_4 = \frac{4}{2}\sin\left(\frac{\pi}{2}\right) = 2$$

10. If $[\cdot]$ denotes the greatest integer function, then the value of $\lim_{n\to\infty}[A_n]$ is

(a) 1   (b) 2   (c) 3   (d) 4

Solution: (c)

Let us use $x = 2\pi/n$. Then

$$\lim_{n\to\infty}[A_n] = \lim_{n\to\infty}\left[\frac{n}{2}\sin\left(\frac{2\pi}{n}\right)\right] = \lim_{x\to 0}\left[\frac{\pi\sin x}{x}\right]$$

We note that $\sin x/x$ converges to 1 as $x \to 0$, and thus, the required limit is $[\pi] = 3$.

Exercises

1. Prove that a convex polygon can have at most three acute angles.

2. Let a, b, c be three positive real numbers such that a, b, c are the sides of a right-angled triangle (say, T_1), while $1/a, 1/b, 1/c$ are also the sides of a right-angled triangle (say, T_2). If θ is the smallest angle of T_1, prove that $\sin\theta = \frac{\sqrt{5}-1}{2}$.

3. Consider a circle C of radius r. Let AD be a diameter and B, C be two other points on C satisfying $AB = BC = r/2$. Calculate the value of CD.

4. For positive integers n, if $A + B + C = n\pi$, prove that

$$\sin 2A + \sin 2B + \sin 2C = (-1)^{n-1} 4\sin A \sin B \sin C.$$

5. Consider two disjoint circles C_1 and C_2 with centres P and Q, respectively, such that P lies outside C_2 and Q lies outside C_1. Draw two tangents from P to C_2 and assume that they intersect C_1 at A and B. Similarly, two tangents are drawn from Q to C_1, which intersect C_2 at M and N. Prove that $AB = MN$.

6. Consider two triangles ABC and DEF that are inscribed in the same circle. If the two triangles have equal perimeters, then show that

$$\sin A + \sin B + \sin C = \sin D + \sin E + \sin F.$$

Further prove that the converse is also true.

7. Consider a line segment AB with a point X on it such that $AB \cdot BX = AX^2$. Draw a circle with the centre at A and with radius AB. Let C be a point on the circumference of the circle such that $BC = AX$ (see the figure below). Prove that angle BAC is equal to $36°$.

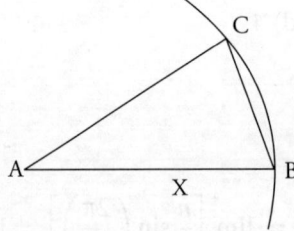

8. Let AB be a chord of a circle C. For which point P on the circumference of C is the value of $PA + PB$ the maximum?

9. Consider a regular heptagon $ABCDEFG$ as shown in the figure.

Euclidean Geometry

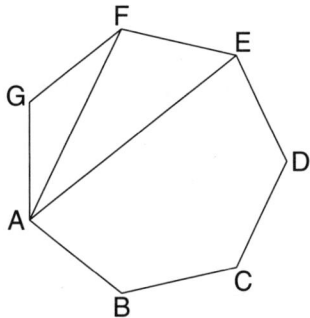

Prove the following:

$$\frac{1}{\sin\frac{\pi}{7}} = \frac{1}{\sin\frac{2\pi}{7}} + \frac{1}{\sin\frac{3\pi}{7}}.$$

Using the above or otherwise, further prove that

$$\frac{1}{AG} = \frac{1}{AF} + \frac{1}{AE}.$$

10. Consider triangle ABC with the angles satisfying the equality

$$\frac{\sin^2 A + \sin^2 B + \sin^2 C}{\cos^2 A + \cos^2 B + \cos^2 C} = 2.$$

Prove that ABC is right angled.

11. Consider a function $f : \mathbb{R}^2 \to \mathbb{R}^2$ with the following property: for any two points A and B in $\mathbb{R}^2$, the distance between A and B is the same as that between $f(A)$ and $f(B)$. Let the unique straight line passing through A and B be denoted by $\ell(A,B)$.

   (a) For two points C, D in $\mathbb{R}^2$, if X is a point on the line $\ell(C,D)$, show that $f(X)$ is a point on the line $\ell(f(C), f(D))$.

   (b) Let E and F be two more points in $\mathbb{R}^2$ and let α be the angle at which $\ell(E,F)$ intersects $\ell(C,D)$. Prove that the line $\ell(f(C), f(D))$ intersects $\ell(f(E), f(F))$ at an angle α.

   (c) In the above set-up, what would happen if the two lines $\ell(C,D)$ and $\ell(E,F)$ do not intersect?

12. If an isosceles triangle ABC (with $AB = AC$) is inscribed in a circle and if P is a point on the arc BC, prove that the quantity $PA/(PB+PC)$ is always a constant.

13. Let A, B and C be three points on the circumference of a circle with radius R. Find the condition under which the area of the triangle ABC is maximum.

14. Consider a triangle ABC with points D, E, F on the sides BC, CA, AB, respectively, such that $BD = CE = AF = x$. Suppose that the lines drawn through D, E, F and parallel to the three sides form a triangle GHK.

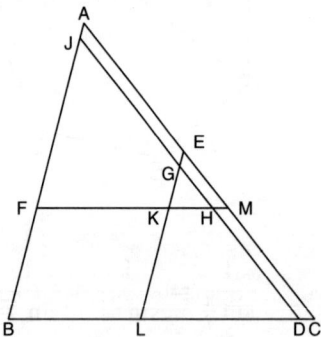

Prove that the ratio of the area of the triangles GHK and ABC is $\{2-(x/a+x/b+x/c)\}^2$, where a, b, c are the lengths of BC, CA, AB, respectively.

15. Let ABC be a right-angled triangle with $\angle A = 90°$. If AD is a perpendicular on the hypotenuse, with D being on the side BC, then show that

$$\frac{1}{AD^2} = \frac{1}{AB^2} + \frac{1}{AC^2}.$$

16. A 40-foot-high television is placed on a wall 10 feet above eye level. Find the distance at which one should stand to maximize the angle subtended by the screen at the eye?

17. Compute the area of a triangle ABC if $BC = \sqrt{6}$, $AB + AC = 3 + \sqrt{3}$ and $\angle A = 60°$.

18. In the given figure, CZ is perpendicular to XY and the ratio of AZ to ZB is 1 : 2. If the angle ACX is α and the angle BCY is β, find an expression for the angle AZC.

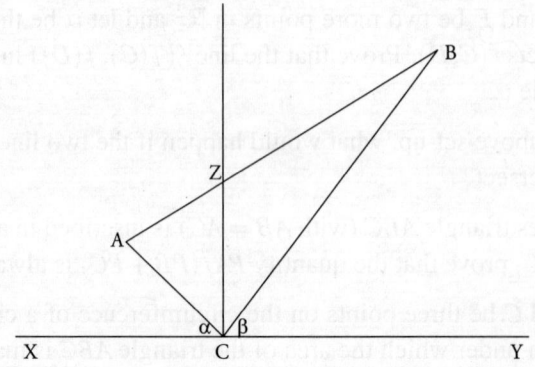

19. If X, Y, Z are the three angles of a triangle, prove that

$$\tan\frac{X}{2}\tan\frac{Y}{2}+\tan\frac{Y}{2}\tan\frac{Z}{2}+\tan\frac{Z}{2}\tan\frac{X}{2}=1.$$

Hence or otherwise, show that

$$\tan\frac{X}{2}\tan\frac{Y}{2}\tan\frac{Z}{2}\leqslant\frac{1}{3\sqrt{3}}.$$

20. Let PQR be an acute-angled triangle with circumcentre C, incentre I and orthocentre O. If $\angle QCR$, $\angle QIR$ and $\angle QOR$ are α, β, γ (measured in degrees), respectively, prove that

$$\frac{1}{\alpha}+\frac{1}{\beta}+\frac{1}{\gamma}>\frac{1}{45}.$$

Hints

1. Let us denote the polygon as $A_1 A_2 \ldots A_n$. Assume that it has four acute angles, and let the corresponding vertices be A_i, A_j, A_k, A_ℓ. Clearly, $A_i A_j A_k A_\ell$ form a convex quadrilateral. However, due to the fact that the given polygon is convex, one can argue that the segments $A_i A_j$, $A_j A_k$, $A_k A_\ell$ and $A_\ell A_i$ are strictly inside the initial polygon. Therefore, the angles of the quadrilateral $A_i A_j A_k A_\ell$ must be acute, which is absurd as the sum of the four angles must be $360°$.

2. Without loss of generality, assume that $a < b < c$, which implies $1/c < 1/b < 1/a$. Then, using the Pythagorean Theorem, show that $a^2 + b^2 = c^2$ and $a^2 c^2 = b^4$. Now, since a is the smallest side in $\mathcal{T}_1$ and θ is its opposite angle, one can write $\sin\theta = a/c$. These conditions together would lead to the equation $\sin^2\theta + \sin\theta - 1 = 0$, which can be solved using Sridhar Acharya's formula.

3. Let O be the centre of the circle. Join O with B and C, and let $\angle AOB = \theta$. Then, one can argue that $\angle BOC = \theta$, $\angle OAB = 90° - \theta/2$. Subsequently, applying the sine rule for triangle AOB, it can be shown that $\sin(\theta/2) = 1/4$, $\cos(\theta/2) = \sqrt{15}/4$ and therefore

$$\sin\theta = 2\sin\left(\frac{\theta}{2}\right)\cos\left(\frac{\theta}{2}\right) = \frac{\sqrt{15}}{8}, \quad \cos\theta = \frac{7}{8}.$$

Then, using $\angle COD = 180° - 2\theta$, and applying the sine rule in the triangle COD, one can obtain the final solution.

4. Using $A + B + C = n\pi$, first show that $\sin 2C = -\sin(2A + 2B)$ and $\sin C = (-1)^{n-1}\sin(A+B)$. Then, use these identities to prove the required result.

5. The required figure is shown below, along with the necessary constructions.

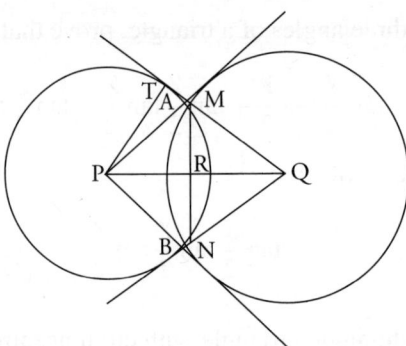

First, argue that $MR = RN$ and $\angle MRQ = 90°$. Then, show that the triangles MRQ and PTQ are similar and therefore

$$\frac{MR}{MQ} = \frac{PC}{PQ} \implies MN = \frac{2r_1 r_2}{PQ},$$

where r_1, r_2 are the radii of the two circles. Using the same method for the line segment AB, one can also obtain $AB = 2r_1 r_2/PQ$, which completes the proof.

6. Both results can be proved directly using the law of sines, which says that twice the circumradius is equal to the ratio of the length of a side and the sine of the opposite angle.

7. Without loss of generality, assume $AB = AC = 1$, and let $AX = x$ units. Then, the problem suggests $x^2 = 1(1-x)$, which further implies $x = (-1+\sqrt{5})/2$. Now, let $\angle BAC = \theta$. Then, using the cosine rule for triangle ABC, one can argue that $\theta = 2\sin^{-1}(x/2)$.

Next, take $y = 18°$ and write $\sin(3y) = \sin(90° - 2y)$. It can be simplified to $(\sin y - 1)(4\sin^2 y + 2\sin y - 1) = 0$. Since the first term cannot be 0, y must satisfy $4\sin^2 y + 2\sin y - 1 = 0$. Simple application of Sridhar Acharya's formula then leads to the solution, $\sin y = x/2$, and hence, θ must be $36°$.

8. Since the triangle ABP is inscribed in C, we can say that $PA + PB = 2r(\sin A + \sin B)$. For any chord AB, we can also argue that $\sin P$ is constant, and $A + B = \pi - P$. Thus, we need to maximize $\sin A + \sin B$ under the restriction that $A + B$ is fixed (call it θ). In other words, it is a maximization problem for the function $f(x) = \sin x + \sin(\theta - x)$, $0 < x < \theta$. One can then easily show that P must be a point on the circumference of C such that $\angle PAB = \angle PBA$.

9. The first part can be proved by starting from the expression on the right-hand side of the equation and by making use of the identity $\sin\theta = \cos(\pi/2 - \theta)$. For the second part, draw the segments AF and AE, and observe that the triangles AGF and AFE

Euclidean Geometry 5.41

must have the same circumradius. Now, use the law of sines to prove the require result.

10. Using $\sin^2\theta+\cos^2\theta=1$, the given condition can be rewritten as

$$\frac{3-(\cos^2 A+\cos^2 B+\cos^2 C)}{\cos^2 A+\cos^2 B+\cos^2 C}=2,$$

which can be simplified to $\cos^2 A+\cos^2 B+\cos^2 C=1$. Subsequently, repeated use of the identity $\cos 2\theta=2\cos^2\theta-1$ would lead to the equality $\cos(A-B)=\cos C$. Then, using the fact that $A+B+C=\pi$, one can easily show that the triangle is right-angled.

11. Let $d(Y,Z)$ denote the distance between two points Y and Z. Then, if X lies on the segment CD, we can say that $d(C,X)+d(X,D)=d(CD)$. We can use this along with the given property of f to prove the first part. For part (b), consider T to be the point of intersection of EF and CD. Next, apply the result from part (a) to argue that $\ell(f(E),f(F))$ and $\ell(f(C),f(D))$ intersect at $f(T)$. The rest of the proof can be completed by noting that the two triangles formed by these line segments are similar. Finally, for part (c), one can use similar arguments as above to show that $\ell(f(C),f(D))$ is parallel to $\ell(f(E),f(F))$.

12. Join P with B and C and make use of Ptolemy's Theorem on $ABPC$, which is a cyclic quadrilateral. Since $AB=AC$, one can show that the ratio $PA/(PB+PC)=AB/BC$, which is independent of P.

13. Join the centre of the circle (call it O) to the three vertices of the triangle. The law of sines and the fact that the area of a triangle can be computed by $(ab\sin\theta/2)$, where a and b are two sides of the triangle and θ is the angle made by those two sides, can be used in this problem. First, use the second property separately for the triangles AOC, BOC and AOB, to show that the area of the triangle ABC is $(\sin(2A)+\sin(2B)+\sin(2C))/2$. Next, assume that one of the angles, say A, is fixed. Writing $C=\pi-A-B$, the problem reduces to minimizing the expression $\cos(A+2B)\sin A$, for fixed A. This is achieved if $B=C$.

Thus, whenever we fix an angle, the area of the triangle is maximum if the other two are equal. It implies that the area of the triangle is maximum when the triangle is equilateral.

14. Using the fact that the lines FM, DJ and EL are parallel to the sides BC, CA, AB, respectively, argue that the triangle GHK is similar to ABC. Then, the ratio of the heights of the two triangles is equal to KH/BC, which subsequently implies that the ratio of the areas of the two triangles is equal to $(KH/BC)^2$. Now, one can express x/c as FM/BC and then subsequently show that it is equal to $(BL+KH+CD)/BC$.

Similarly, show that $x/b = (CD + DL)/BC$. Then, straightforward computations would lead to the required result.

15. The area of the triangle can be calculated in two ways: $2\triangle ABC = (AD)(BC) = (AB)(AC)$. Clearly, $AD^2 = (AB^2)(AC^2)/(BC^2)$. Then, using the Pythagorean identity, the proof can be completed.

16. Suppose that one is standing at a distance of h feet from the wall. Let θ be the angle subtended by the screen, from top to bottom. Then, the objective is to find h that maximizes θ. One can make use of the fact that

$$\tan\theta = \frac{30h}{h^2 + 400}$$

The above is a function of h, and it is a straightforward exercise to maximize $\tan\theta$. The answer would be obtained as 20 feet from the wall.

17. Using the rule of cosines for a triangle, one can write $a^2 = b^2 + c^2 - 2bc\cos 60°$, which implies $6 = (3 + \sqrt{3})^2 - 3bc$ for this problem. Subsequently, one can obtain $bc = 2(1 + \sqrt{3})$. Thus, utilizing the concepts of quadratic equations, it is easy to argue that b, c are the roots of the quadratic equation $x^2 - (3+\sqrt{3})x + 2(1+\sqrt{3}) = 0$. Sridhar Acharya's formula can then be applied to obtain the solutions $2, 1 + \sqrt{3}$ as the lengths of the two sides AB and AC. Heron's formula can then be used to compute the area.

18. As constructions, drop perpendiculars on CZ from A and B. Now, letting $\angle AZC = \theta$ and $AZ = t$, one can write $\angle QBZ = 90° - \theta$, $\angle QBC = \beta$, $\angle PAC = \alpha$, $ZB = 2t$. Then, derive appropriate expressions for QZ, ZP, PC, QC and use the equation $QC = QZ + ZP + PC$ to obtain the equation $2\sin\theta\tan\beta = 3\cos\theta + \sin\theta\tan\alpha$. The proof can be completed through straightforward trigonometric manipulations.

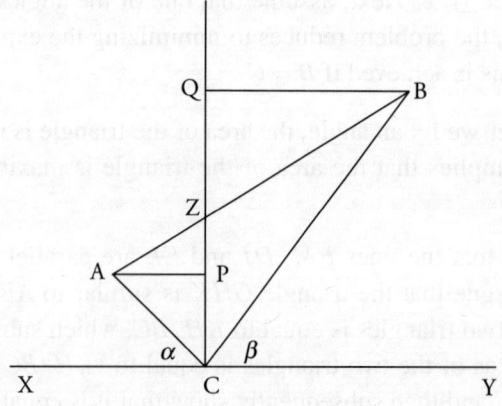

Euclidean Geometry

19. If X, Y, Z are the angles of a triangle,

$$\frac{X}{2} + \frac{Y}{2} = \frac{\pi}{2} - \frac{Z}{2}$$

Then, taking $\tan(\cdot)$ of both sides, straightforward algebraic manipulation would lead to the first part. For the second part, observe that $\tan\frac{X}{2}, \tan\frac{Y}{2}, \tan\frac{Z}{2} > 0$. Then, use the AM-GM inequality on the three terms from the first part to show that the inequality holds for all triangles.

20. The required figure is shown below. Here, C, I and O are the circumcentre, incentre and orthocentre of the triangle. For convenience, denote $\angle QPR, \angle PQR$ and $\angle PRQ$ by P, Q, R, respectively.

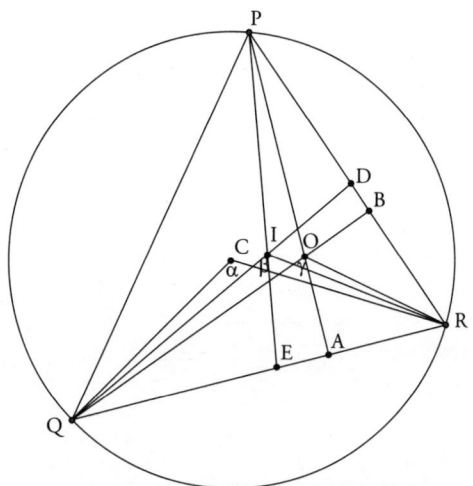

Observe that $\alpha = 2P$ and $\beta = 180° - (R+Q)/2$. Next, one can show that $\angle OQR = 90° - R$ and $\angle ORQ = 90° - Q$. Thus, $\gamma = R + Q$. Further, considering that $P + Q + R = 180°$, the above equations imply $\alpha = 2P, \beta = 90° + P/2, \gamma = 180° - P$. Finally, apply the AM-HM inequality for α, β, γ and use the fact that P is an acute angle to obtain the required result.

6
Coordinate Geometry

"Such [ecstatic] moments are also granted to students in the abstract regions of thought, and high among them must be placed the morning when Descartes lay in bed and invented the method of co-ordinate geometry."

The previous chapter focused on the nuances of Euclidean geometry. The system of coordinates is designed to visualize geometric shapes and phenomena using the concepts of algebra. In other words, coordinate geometry (also known as analytic geometry) describes the link between geometry and algebra. On the one hand, it provides geometric aspects in algebra by presenting every number as a coordinate in a plane, while on the other, it enables us to solve geometric problems using algebraic theorems and relationships. It is well known that French philosopher and mathematician René Descartes pioneered this branch of mathematics and it is therefore also known as Cartesian geometry. The quote above by the famous English mathematician and philosopher Alfred North Whitehead clearly shows how important and fascinating this branch of mathematics is.

KEY RESULTS

Throughout this chapter, the following notations are used:
N = the set of natural numbers   Z = the set of integers
R = the set of real numbers   C = the set of complex numbers

At this level, we primarily deal with coordinate geometry problems in the two-dimensional plane. The concepts can be naturally extended to higher dimensional spaces as well. We start with two axes in a plane, and the system of coordinates is defined relative to these two axes. In the figure below, the two axes are shown with dotted lines and O is the origin.

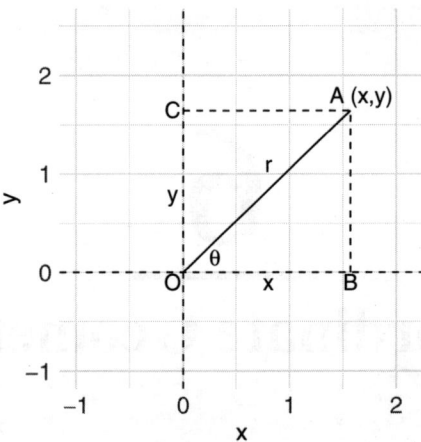

Here, a point A is denoted by the coordinates (x,y), where the two numbers represent the distances from the x- and y-axis, respectively. Thus, if perpendiculars are dropped from A onto the two axes, we can argue that $OB = CA = x$ and $OC = BC = y$. This is known as the Cartesian system.

Another convention in coordinate geometry is to use the polar system, where each point is denoted using (r, θ), where r denotes the distance from the origin and θ indicates the angle made with the positive x-axis.

> **Useful Tip:** Note that the polar system and the Cartesian system are connected by the relationships $r^2 = x^2 + y^2$ and $\tan \theta = y/x$.

Theorem 6.1 (Rotation of Axes): If the two axes are rotated anticlockwise by an angle θ, such that the coordinates of a point $P(x,y)$ change to (x', y'), then

$$x' = x\cos\theta + y\sin\theta, \qquad y' = y\cos\theta - x\sin\theta$$
$$x = x'\cos\theta - y'\sin\theta, \qquad y = y'\cos\theta + x'\sin\theta$$

The following figure illustrates this concept. The student is advised to verify the above results for better understanding of the concept.

> **Useful Tip:** Translation of axes is a topic that occurs frequently in the exam. If the origin is shifted to a point that was (a,b) in the previous system and if the two axes remain parallel to the previous axes, then the new coordinates (x', y') of a point $P(x,y)$ would satisfy $x' = x - a$, $y' = y - b$.

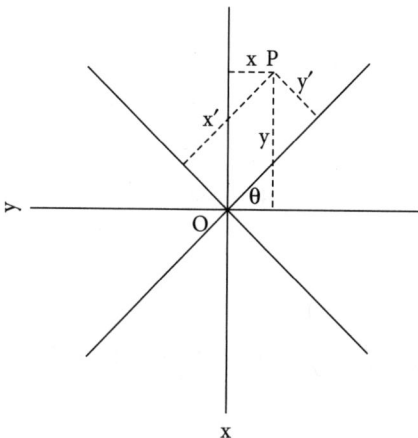

Theorem 6.2 (Shoelace Theorem): If the vertices of a polygon, taken in an anticlockwise order, are at the points $(x_1, y_1), (x_2, y_2), \ldots, (x_n, y_n)$, then the area of the polygon is given by

$$\Delta = \frac{1}{2} |(x_1 y_2 - y_1 x_2) + (x_2 y_3 - y_2 x_3) + \ldots + (x_n y_1 - y_n x_1)|$$

Theorem 6.3: Consider two points $P_1 \equiv (x_1, y_1)$ and $P_2 \equiv (x_2, y_2)$. The following are true about the line segment $P_1 P_2$:

- The coordinates of the point that divides $P_1 P_2$ in the ratio $r_1 : r_2$ are given by

$$\left(\frac{r_2 x_1 + r_1 x_2}{r_1 + r_2}, \frac{r_2 y_1 + r_1 y_2}{r_1 + r_2} \right)$$

  Thus, the midpoint of $P_1 P_2$ is $((x_1 + x_2)/2, (y_1 + y_2)/2)$.
- The length of the line segment is $\sqrt{(x_2 - x_1)^2 + (y_2 - y_1)^2}$.
- The gradient of the line segment is $(y_2 - y_1)/(x_2 - x_1)$.

The last result from the previous theorem is directly connected to the equation of a straight line in coordinate geometry. Note that any straight line in the Cartesian plane can be expressed as $ax + by + c = 0$, while a more conventional way is the slope-intercept form of $y = mx + c$, where m is the gradient or slope of the straight line and c is the y-intercept. If the straight line makes an angle θ with the positive x-axis, then $m = \tan \theta$. Combining these concepts, one can say that the equation of a straight line passing through $P_1 (x_1, y_1)$ and $P_2 (x_2, y_2)$ is

$$\frac{y - y_1}{x - x_1} = \frac{y_2 - y_1}{x_2 - x_1}$$

This can also be written using the parametric form. Assume that a straight line passes through (x_1, y_1) and makes an angle θ with the positive x-axis. If r is a parameter denoting the distance between (x, y) and (x_1, y_1), then the equation of the line is given by

$$\frac{x - x_1}{\cos \theta} = \frac{y - y_1}{\sin \theta} = r$$

Theorem 6.4: The following results are instrumental in solving problems related to straight lines

- The length of the perpendicular from a point (x_1, y_1) to a straight line $ax + by + c = 0$ is

$$\left| \frac{ax_1 + by_1 + c}{\sqrt{a^2 + b^2}} \right|$$

- Three straight lines $a_1 x + b_1 y + c_1 = 0$, $a_2 x + b_2 y + c_2 = 0$ and $a_3 x + b_3 y + c_3 = 0$ are concurrent if and only if

$$a_3(b_1 c_2 - b_2 c_1) + b_3(c_1 a_2 - c_2 a_1) + c_3(a_1 b_2 - a_2 b_1) = 0$$

- If the angle between two straight lines $y = m_1 x + c_1$ and $y = m_2 x + c_2$ is θ, then

$$\tan \theta = \frac{m_1 - m_2}{1 + m_1 m_2}$$

- Two straight lines with gradients m_1 and m_2 are parallel to each other if and only if $m_1 = m_2$.

- Two straight lines with gradients m_1 and m_2 are perpendicular to each other if and only if $m_1 m_2 = -1$.

- The distance between two parallel straight lines $ax + by + c_1 = 0$ and $ax + by + c_2 = 0$ is

$$\left| \frac{c_1 - c_2}{\sqrt{a^2 + b^2}} \right|$$

- The points $P(x_1, y_1)$ and $Q(x_2, y_2)$ lie on the same (or opposite) side of the line $ax + by + c = 0$ if $ax_1 + by_1 + c$ and $ax_2 + by_2 + c$ have the same (or opposite) sign.

- Consider two intersecting straight lines $L_1 = a_1 x + b_1 y + c_1 = 0$ and $L_2 = a_2 x + b_2 y + c_2 = 0$. Any straight line passing through the point of intersection of L_1, L_2 is of the form $L_1 + \lambda L_2 = 0$, for some parameter $\lambda \in \mathbb{R}$.

- The equation of the two angle bisectors of the pair of straight lines $a_1x+b_1y+c_1=0$ and $a_2x+b_2y+c_2=0$ is given by

$$\frac{a_1x+b_1y+c_1}{\sqrt{a_1^2+b_1^2}}=\pm\frac{a_2x+b_2y+c_2}{\sqrt{a_2^2+b_2^2}}$$

Theorem 6.5 (Properties of a Triangle): Consider a triangle ABC such that the vertices are at $A\ (x_1,y_1),\ B\ (x_2,y_2),\ C\ (x_3,y_3)$. Let the angles be denoted by A,B,C, while the lengths of the sides BC,CA,AB are denoted by a,b,c, respectively.

- The coordinates of the circumcentre are given by

$$O \equiv \left(\frac{x_1\sin 2A + x_2\sin 2B + x_3\sin 2C}{\sin 2A + \sin 2B + \sin 2C},\ \frac{y_1\sin 2A + y_2\sin 2B + y_3\sin 2C}{\sin 2A + \sin 2B + \sin 2C}\right)$$

- The coordinates of the centroid are given by

$$G \equiv \left(\frac{x_1+x_2+x_3}{3},\ \frac{y_1+y_2+y_3}{3}\right)$$

- The coordinates of the incentre are given by

$$I \equiv \left(\frac{ax_1+bx_2+cx_3}{a+b+c},\ \frac{ay_1+by_2+cy_3}{a+b+c}\right)$$

- The coordinates of the orthocentre are given by

$$H \equiv \left(\frac{x_1\tan A + x_2\tan B + x_3\tan C}{\tan A + \tan B + \tan C},\ \frac{y_1\tan A + y_2\tan B + y_3\tan C}{\tan A + \tan B + \tan C}\right)$$

> **Useful Tip:** Though the above formulae can be directly used to find the coordinates of these special points, it is often computationally easier to use the concepts related to straight lines. For example, to find the orthocentre, one can find out the equations of the straight lines perpendicular to BC and CA, passing through A and B, respectively, and then find out where these two lines intersect. This would obviate the need to compute the angles, which is required in the aforementioned formula.

In coordinate geometry, another pivotal concept is that of a locus, a term used to indicate the path traced by a moving point that is subject to some restriction. One can also interpret it as an infinite set of points that satisfies a certain condition. The concept of locus allows us to interpret such conditions in a more convenient way. For example, the locus of a moving point in a plane equidistant from two fixed points P_1 and P_2 in the same plane is essentially the perpendicular bisector of the line segment $P_1 P_2$.

We next turn our attention to the equations of a conic section, all of which are quadratic in x and y. The general equation of a conic section is $ax^2 + 2hxy + by^2 + 2gx + 2fy + c = 0$. Special cases are discussed below:

- If $(gh - af)^2 = (h^2 - ab)(g^2 - ac)$, then the equation can be factored as a product of two linear equations in x and y. This is known as a pair of straight lines.

- If $a = b$ and $h = 0$, one can write the general equation in the form

$$(x - x_0)^2 + (y - y_0)^2 = r^2,$$

  and it denotes a circle. It can also be thought of as the locus of a moving point that is at a fixed distance r from the point (x_0, y_0).

- If there is a moving point such that its distance from a fixed point F is always the same from a straight line L, then the locus is known as the parabola. A parabola is symmetric about a straight line perpendicular to the directrix. The point of intersection of the parabola and this line of symmetry is called the vertex of the parabola; the point F is the focus and the straight line L is known as the directrix. In its simplest form, if $F \equiv (a, 0)$, and the directrix is the line $x = -a$, then the equation of the parabola is

$$y^2 = 4ax$$

  Its vertex is at the origin and it is symmetric about the x-axis. One can use the concepts of rotation and translation to find out the equation of any parabola. Remember that the general equation of the conic section indicates a parabola if it is a second degree equation such that $h^2 = ab$.

- Consider two fixed points F_1 and F_2, and two parallel lines L_1 and L_2. As before, each of the points is called a focus and the lines are the directrices. If there is a moving point such that the ratio of the distances from a focus and its corresponding directrix is a constant value less than 1, then it is called an ellipse. This curve is symmetric about two lines, one perpendicular to the directrix and another parallel and in the middle of the two directrices. These two lines of symmetry are known as the major axis and the minor axis. In the simplest case, if an ellipse has the x- and y-axis as the major and minor axes, then the equation of the ellipse is

$$\frac{x^2}{a^2} + \frac{y^2}{b^2} = 1$$

  As before, rotation and translation can be used to find the equation of any ellipse. In the general form of a conic section, $h^2 < ab$ corresponds to an ellipse.

- In a similar set-up as in the ellipse, if there is a moving point such that the ratio of the distances from a focus and its corresponding directrix is a constant value greater than 1, then it is called a hyperbola. The ideas of symmetry, major axis and minor axis are similar to the above. For a hyperbola with the *x*- and *y*-axis as the major and minor axes, the equation is

$$\frac{x^2}{a^2} - \frac{y^2}{b^2} = 1$$

It can be shown that the two lines $y = \pm bx/a$ are two asymptotes to the above hyperbola. One can use the concepts of rotation and translation here as well; and in the conic section equation, a hyperbola corresponds to the condition $h^2 < ab$. Note that the equation of a hyperbola with major and minor axes reversed is

$$\frac{y^2}{b^2} - \frac{x^2}{a^2} = 1$$

Definition 6.1 (Eccentricity): An important property of ellipse, parabola and hyperbola is the ratio of the distance from the focus and the distance from the directrix. This constant is known as the eccentricity. Its value is 1, < 1 and > 1, for parabola, ellipse and hyperbola, respectively.

The figures given below help us to visualize the notion of eccentricity. In the case of the parabola, $FP/PD = 1$. For ellipse, the eccentricity is $PF1/PD1 = PF2/PD2 < 1$, whereas the same quantity is greater than 1 for hyperbola.

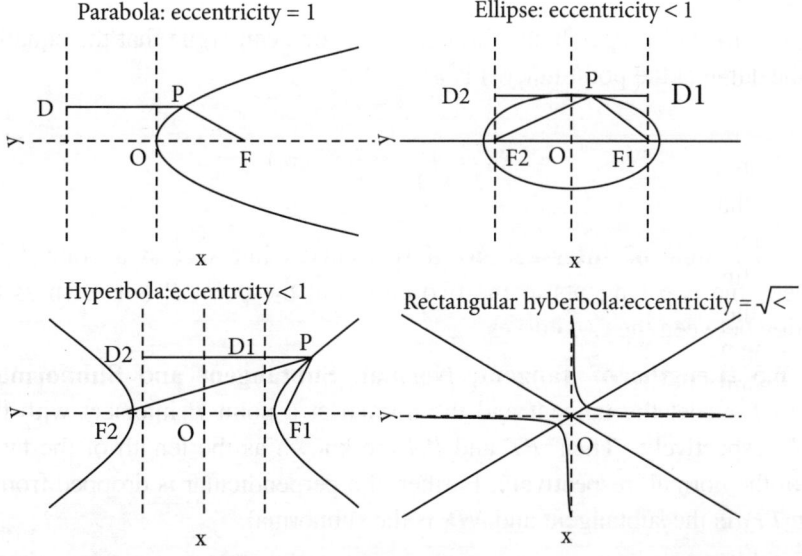

Definition 6.2 (Rectangular Hyperbola): It is a special case of hyperbolic equations, where $a = b$, that is, the standard form becomes $x^2 - y^2 = a^2$. In this case, the two asymptotes, given by $y = \pm x$, are perpendicular to each other. If this hyperbola is rotated in such a way that the asymptotes become the two axes, then the equation of the rectangular hyperbola is of the form $xy = c^2$. Its eccentricity is $\sqrt{2}$.

For the equations of different conic sections, an effective trick is to use the parametric form; that is, to use a general form defined as a function of an unknown parameter for all the points on the curve. For example, any point on the circle $(x - x_0)^2 + (y - y_0)^2 = r^2$ can be written as $(x_0 + r\cos\theta, y_0 + r\sin\theta)$, where θ is the parameter. For the parabola $y^2 = 4ax$, the parametric form is $(at^2, 2at)$ for $t \in \mathbb{R}$. For the ellipse $x^2/a^2 + y^2/b^2 = 1$, any point can be written as $(a\cos\theta, b\sin\theta)$, while the parametric form of a point on the hyperbola $x^2/a^2 - y^2/b^2 = 1$ is $(a\sec\theta, b\tan\theta)$. In both cases, θ is the parameter and it is imperative to point out that the value of θ, in the parameterization of both the ellipse and the hyperbola, is called the eccentric angle of a point. For the rectangular hyperbola $xy = c^2$, the parametric form is $(ct, c/t)$.

Definition 6.3 (Tangency): If a straight line touches a curve at a point (h, k), then it is called a tangent to the curve at that point. The straight line perpendicular to a tangent is called a normal to the curve at that point.

Theorem 6.6: Consider a curve given by the equation $y = f(x) = 0$. The equation of a tangent to this curve at the point (x_0, y_0) is

$$y - y_0 = f'(x_0)(x - x_0)$$

Using the properties of perpendicular straight lines, one can argue that the equation of the normal to the curve at the point (x_0, y_0) is

$$y - y_0 = -\frac{1}{f'(x_0)}(x - x_0)$$

Definition 6.4 (Angle of Intersection): If two curves intersect at a point P, then the angle between the two tangents to the two curves at the point P is known as the angle of intersection between the two curves.

Definition 6.5 (Lengths of Tangent, Normal, Subtangent and Subnormal): For a function $y = f(x)$, let the tangent and the normal at a point P intersect with the x-axis at T and N, respectively. Then, PT and PN are known as the length of the tangent and the length of the normal, respectively. Further, if a perpendicular is dropped from P to the x-axis, then TP_1 is the subtangent and NP_1 is the subnormal.

Theorem 6.7: The following are some important points regarding tangents and normals:

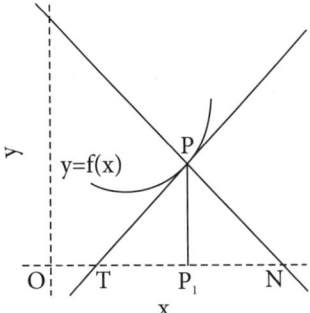

- If dy/dx is 0 at some point, then the tangent at that point is parallel to the x-axis, and vice-versa. Similarly, if $dx/dy = 0$ at some point, then the tangent is perpendicular to the y-axis, and vice-versa.
- If a tangent is parallel to the straight line $ax + by + c = 0$, then dy/dx at the point of tangency is $(-a/b)$.
- If the tangent at a point is equally inclined to the two axes, then dy/dx at that point is ± 1. In this case, the tangent intersects the two axes at equal distance from the origin.

As the final topic of this chapter, we return to the complex numbers introduced in Chapter 3. French mathematician Argand connected the concepts of coordinate geometry and complex numbers by noticing that each complex number can be presented conveniently in the Cartesian system, if the x-axis corresponds to the real part and the y-axis corresponds to the imaginary part of the number. This representation, in mathematics, is known as the Argand diagram. Thus, the number $z = x + \iota y$ is geometrically denoted by the point (x, y). Further, it is easy to observe that the polar transformation $(x, y) \to (r, \theta)$ provides the modulus and argument of a complex number.

> **Useful Tip:** Each concept and result related to complex numbers, as discussed in Chapter 3, can be visualized and proved using coordinate geometry. It is often a smarter way to solve an algebraic problem. For example, the set of complex numbers z satisfying $|z+1| + |z-1| = 8$ represents all points $P = (x, y)$ in the plane, such that $AP + BP = 8$, where $A = (1, 0)$ and $B = (-1, 0)$. Clearly, it represents an ellipse and one can compute the corresponding set of complex numbers easily.

Definition 6.6 (nth Roots of Unity): Any solution to the equation $x^n = 1$ is called an nth root of unity.

Following the theory discussed in Chapter 3, one can argue that there are exactly n number of nth roots of unity, one or two of which are real (depending on whether n is odd or even). In the Argand diagram, all these roots of unity lie on the unit circle, and the corresponding points can be represented as

$$A_k = \left(\cos\frac{2k\pi}{n}, \sin\frac{2k\pi}{n}\right) \equiv e^{i2k\pi/n}, \text{ for } k = 0, 1, \ldots, n-1$$

Theorem 6.8: If $A_0, A_1, \ldots, A_{n-1}$ are the points in the Argand diagram corresponding to the nth roots of unity, then $A_0 A_1 \ldots A_{n-1}$ is a regular n-gon.

> **Useful Tip:** One should note the geometric interpretation of De Moivre's Theorem and utilize the equivalence of nth roots of unity and regular polygons wisely while solving related problems.

Solved Examples

1. In what conditions for a and b will the system of equations $x + y = 2, ax + y = b$ have exactly one solution?

Solution: To find out the number of solutions of a given system of equations, we need to look at the slope and intercept of the two straight lines. For $x + y = 2$, the slope is -1 and the intercept is 2. For the second equation, similarly, the slope is $-a$ and the intercept is b.

Now, the system has exactly one solution when the two straight lines intersect at exactly one point. This takes places when the slopes of the two lines are different. Thus, the required condition is $a \neq 1$.

> **Useful Tip:** In the above problem, one should also know when two equations have infinitely many solutions or no solution. The latter takes place if the two lines are parallel. So, this happens when the slopes are the same but the intercepts are different. For the above problem, the corresponding condition is $a = 1, b \neq 2$. On the other hand, the system has more than one solution only if both the slope and the intercept are the same, implying that the lines coincide. In this problem, that would happen if $a = 1$ and $b = 2$.

2. Consider the following three straight lines for $a, b \in \mathbb{R}$:

$$ax + by = a + b, \quad bx - (a+b)y = -a, \quad (a+b)x - ay = b.$$

If two of the above three lines intersect each other, prove that all three lines are concurrent.

Solution: For the given three straight lines, we have the following:

Equation 1: $ax + by = a + b$, $\quad$ Slope: $-\dfrac{a}{b}$, $\quad$ Intercept: $\dfrac{a+b}{b}$

Equation 2: $bx - (a+b)y = -a$, $\quad$ Slope: $\dfrac{b}{a+b}$, $\quad$ Intercept: $\dfrac{a}{a+b}$

Coordinate Geometry

Equation 3: $(a+b)x - ay = b$,   Slope: $\dfrac{a+b}{a}$,   Intercept: $-\dfrac{b}{a}$

It is easy to obtain the solution of the first pair of equations as $x = 1, y = 1$. Thus, the two lines intersect at $(1,1)$. Substituting these values in the third equation, we can see that $(1,1)$ is on that line too. Clearly, the three lines are concurrent, and not identical, if a and b are appropriately chosen.

Now, if the first two lines intersect, their slopes cannot be equal, that is, $-a/b \neq b/(a+b)$, which can be simplified as $a^2 + ab + b^2 \neq 0$. Similarly, if the second and third equations intersect, we obtain the condition $b/(a+b) \neq (a+b)/a$. And if first and third lines intersect, we obtain $-a/b \neq (a+b)/a$. Both of these lead to the same condition as above, that is, $a^2 + ab + b^2 \neq 0$. Hence, if $a^2 + ab + b^2 \neq 0$, the three equations represent different straight lines that intersect at $(1,1)$.

Note that $a^2 + ab + b^2 = (a+b/2)^2 + 3b^2/4$. Since a and b are real numbers, $a^2 + ab + b^2 = 0$ if and only if $a = 0, b = 0$, in which case, the equations become trivial identities. Thus, for any real a, b, if the given three equations denote straight lines, then $a^2 + ab + b^2 \neq 0$ and that completes the proof.

> **Useful Tip:** Remember that two straight lines intersect each other if the corresponding two equations have a unique solution.

3. Find all the real values of k for which the straight line $(2x - y - 3) + k(x - y - 1) = 0$ is a tangent to the circle $x^2 + y^2 + 4x - 6y + 11 = 0$.

Solution: Suppose that the straight line (hereafter denoted as $\mathcal{L}$) is a tangent to the circle at the point (x_0, y_0). Then, the equation of $\mathcal{L}$ implies $(k+2)x_0 - (k+1)y_0 - (k+3) = 0$. On the other hand, the given circle can be rewritten as

$$(x+2)^2 + (y-3)^2 = 2,$$

and thus, it is centred at $(-2, 3)$ while the radius is $\sqrt{2}$. Note that the condition of tangency implies that the distance of the centre from $\mathcal{L}$ is equal to the radius of the circle. Therefore

$$\frac{\{(k+2)(-2) - 3(k+1) - (k+3)\}^2}{(k+2)^2 + (k+1)^2} = 2 \implies \frac{(6k+10)^2}{2k^2 + 6k + 5} = 2$$

Subsequently, we obtain $16k^2 + 54k + 45 = 0$, which can be solved using Sridhar Acharya's formula as follows:

$$k = \frac{-54 \pm \sqrt{54^2 - 4 \times 16 \times 45}}{32} = \frac{-54 \pm 6}{32}$$

Hence, the possible values of k are $-3/2$ and $-15/8$, respectively.

4. Prove the law of sines for a triangle using appropriate methods of coordinate geometry.

Solution: Let ABC be a triangle on the xy-plane such that $A = (0,0)$, $B = (b,0)$ and $C = (h,k)$.

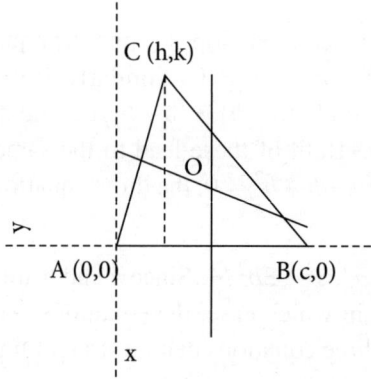

A perpendicular is dropped from C to the side AB. Since the length of AC is b, one can get $h = b\cos A$, $k = b\sin A$.

Let $O = (x_0, y_0)$ be the point of intersection of the perpendicular bisectors of AB and AC. The perpendicular bisctor of AB is clearly $x = c/2$. On the other hand, the equation of AC can be obtained as $hy = kx$, and thus, the equation of the perpendicular bisector, since it passes through the midpoint of AC, that is, $(h/2, k/2)$, is

$$\frac{y - k/2}{x - h/2} = -\frac{h}{k}$$

Therefore

$$x_0 = \frac{c}{2}, \quad y_0 = -\frac{h}{k}\left(\frac{c}{2} - \frac{h}{2}\right) + \frac{k}{2} = \frac{h^2 + k^2 - ch}{2k} = \frac{b - c\cos A}{2\sin A}$$

Using the above, the length of OA, OB, OC can be obtained as follows:

$$OA^2 = x_0^2 + y_0^2 = \frac{c^2}{4} + \left(\frac{b - c\cos A}{2\sin A}\right)^2$$

$$OB^2 = (x_0 - c)^2 + y_0^2 = \frac{c^2}{4} + \left(\frac{b - c\cos A}{2\sin A}\right)^2$$

$$OC^2 = (x_0 - h)^2 + (y_0 - k)^2$$

Coordinate Geometry

$$= \left(\frac{c}{2} - b\cos A\right)^2 + \left(\frac{b - c\cos A}{2\sin A} - b\sin A\right)^2$$

$$= \frac{c^2}{4} + \left(\frac{b - c\cos A}{2\sin A}\right)^2 - bc\cos A + b^2 - b(b - c\cos A)$$

Clearly, $OA = OB = OC$, thereby proving that O is the circumcentre. Let this length be R, which denotes the circumradius. Thus, we can write

$$4R^2 \sin^2 A = c^2 \sin^2 A + (b - c\cos A)^2 = b^2 + c^2 - 2bc\cos A = a^2$$

Hence, $a/\sin A = 2R$. In an exactly similar fashion, we can show that

$$\frac{a}{\sin A} = \frac{b}{\sin B} = \frac{c}{\sin C} = 2R,$$

and that completes the proof of the law of sines.

> **Useful Tip:** Other theorems we studied in the previous chapter can be proved using coordinate geometry as well. It would be a good exercise for the reader to attempt that.

5. Consider an isosceles triangle ABC such that the length of BC and the length of the perpendicular from A to BC are both 1 unit. Points D, E, F are chosen from BC, CA, AB, respectively, in such a way that $BDEF$ is a rhombus. Compute the length of each side of this rhombus.

Solution: In the xy-plane, let the coordinates of the three vertices of the triangle be denoted by $A = (0.5, 1)$, $B = (0, 0)$, $C = (1, 0)$. Let the coordinates of D be $(a, 0)$.

Since $BDEF$ is a rhombus, DE must be parallel to AB, the slope of which can be calculated to be $(1 - 0)/(0.5 - 0) = 2$. Thus, the equation of AB is $y = 2x$, and the equation of DE must be $y = 2x - 2a$. On the other hand, the equation of the straight line AC is

$$\frac{y - 0}{x - 1} = \frac{1 - 0}{0.5 - 1} \implies y = -2x + 2$$

Now, E is the point of intersection of the two straight lines $y = 2x - 2a$ and $y = -2x + 2$, and it is easy to find that $E = ((1 + a)/2, 1 - a)$. As $BDEF$ is a rhombus, DE must be equal to a, and therefore

$$\left(a - \frac{1 + a}{2}\right)^2 + (1 - a)^2 = a^2 \implies 5(1 - a)^2 = 4a^2 \implies a^2 - 10a + 5 = 0$$

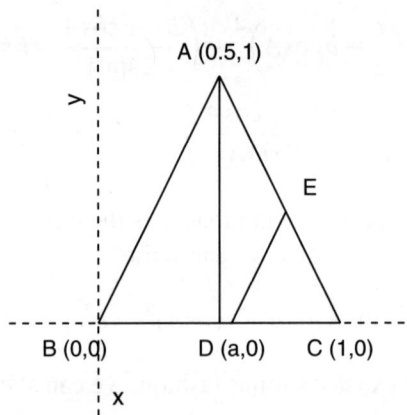

Solving the above, one can get $a = 5 \pm 2\sqrt{5}$. Since the length of each side of the rhombus is equal to a and it must be less than 1, the required answer is $5 - 2\sqrt{5}$.

> **Useful Tip:** One can also use concepts from Euclidean geometry, such as the properties of similar triangles, to solve the above problem.

6. Find the values of θ for which the equation
$$(x^2 + y^2)\cos 2\theta + 2xy = 0$$
represents a pair of straight lines. Compute the angle between these two lines.

Solution: We can start with the assumption that $\cos 2\theta \neq 0$. Recall that an equation of the form $ax^2 + 2hxy + by^2 + 2gx + 2fy + c = 0$ indicates a pair of straight lines only if $(gh - af)^2 = (h^2 - ab)(g^2 - ac)$. Now, in the given equation, we have $a = b = \cos 2\theta$, $h = 1$ and $g = f = c = 0$, which satisfy the condition. We can further argue that if it is a pair of straight lines, then both lines must pass through the origin. In that case, we can modify the given equation as
$$(x^2 + y^2)\cos 2\theta + 2xy = \cos 2\theta (y - m_1 x)(y - m_2 x)$$

Clearly, $m_1 m_2 = 1$ and $(m_1 + m_2)\cos 2\theta = 2$, which implies
$$m_1^2 \cos 2\theta - 2m_1 + \cos 2\theta = 0 \implies m_1 = \frac{2 \pm \sqrt{4 - 4\cos^2 2\theta}}{2\cos 2\theta} = \frac{1 \pm \sin 2\theta}{\cos 2\theta}$$

Then, using $\sin 2\theta = 2\sin\theta\cos\theta$ and $\cos 2\theta = \cos^2\theta - \sin^2\theta$, the above can be simplified as
$$m_1 = \frac{\cos\theta - \sin\theta}{\cos\theta + \sin\theta}, \quad m_2 = \frac{\cos\theta + \sin\theta}{\cos\theta - \sin\theta}$$

Coordinate Geometry

We can easily argue that for any θ satisfying $\cos 2\theta \neq 0$, the above two quantities are real numbers. Thus, the given equation represents a pair of straight lines for all such values of θ. Furthermore, if the angle between the two lines is ϕ, then

$$\tan\phi = \frac{1}{2}\left(\frac{\cos\theta - \sin\theta}{\cos\theta + \sin\theta} - \frac{\cos\theta + \sin\theta}{\cos\theta - \sin\theta}\right) = -\frac{4\sin\theta\cos\theta}{2(\cos^2\theta - \sin^2\theta)} = -\tan 2\theta$$

Hence, we can conclude that the two angles between the two lines must be 2θ and $(180° - 2\theta)$.

7. A circle C is given by the equation $(x-2)^2 + (y-8)^2 = 1$ and a parabola $\mathcal{P}$ is given by the equation $y^2 = 4x$. Let A be a moving point on C and B be a moving point on $\mathcal{P}$. What is the minimum value of the length of the line segment AB?

Solution: Any point on the circle C can be written in the parametric form $A = (2 + \cos\theta, 8 + \sin\theta)$, while any point on the parabola $\mathcal{P}$ has the parametric form $B = (t^2, 2t)$. Thus, if we consider the distance between A and B, we get

$$AB = (2 + \cos\theta - t^2)^2 + (8 + \sin\theta - 2t)^2 = f(\theta, t)$$

In order to minimize the above quantity, we can take the partial derivatives with respect to θ and t.

$$\frac{\partial f(\theta,t)}{\partial \theta} = -2\sin\theta(2 + \cos\theta - t^2) + 2\cos\theta(8 + \sin\theta - 2t),$$

$$\frac{\partial f(\theta,t)}{\partial t} = -4t(2 + \cos\theta - t^2) - 4(8 + \sin\theta - 2t)$$

Setting both of the above equations equal to 0, we get

$$\frac{2 + \cos\theta - t^2}{8 + \sin\theta - 2t} = \frac{\cos\theta}{\sin\theta} = \frac{-4}{4t},$$

which implies $t = -\tan\theta$.

Now, from the first equation, $-4\sin\theta + 2t^2\sin\theta + 16\cos\theta - 4t\cos\theta = 0$. Straightforward algebraic manipulation then leads us to the equation $\tan\theta(t^2 - 2) = 2(t - 4)$. Using the above identity, we now arrive at the equation

$$-t(t^2 - 2) = 2(t - 4) \implies t^3 - 8 = 0$$

Clearly, $t = 2$, and thus, $\tan\theta = -2$. Using this, we get $\sec^2\theta = 1 + \tan^2\theta = 5$. So, $\cos^2\theta = 1/5$ and $\sin^2\theta = 4/5$. Clearly, $\cos\theta$ and $\sin\theta$ can be either positive or negative and they are of different signs since $\tan\theta$ is negative.

Note that $2-t^2 = -2, 8-2t = 2$. So, AB is minimum if we use a positive value for $\cos\theta$ and a negative value for $\sin\theta$. Hence, the minimum possible value of AB is

$$AB_{\min} = \left(-2+\frac{1}{\sqrt{5}}\right)^2 + \left(2-\frac{1}{\sqrt{5}}\right)^2 = 2\left(2-\frac{1}{\sqrt{5}}\right)^2 = \frac{2}{5}\left(21-4\sqrt{5}\right)$$

Useful Tip: Using the parametric form of a point on a conic section is immensely useful in many applications. It provides tractable algebraic expressions to work with.

8. Consider two curves given parametrically by

$$x = 2k\cos t, y = k\sin t,$$
$$x = ct', y = \frac{c}{t'},$$

where k and c are two positive constants and t, t' are the parameters. Suppose that two of the points of intersection of the above curves lie on the straight line $y = x$. Find the relationship between c and k. Further prove that the two curves have four points of intersection and that they lie at the vertices of a parallelogram whose sides have lengths k and $3k$.

Solution: From the given parametric relationships, we can write the equations of the two curves as

$$\frac{x^2}{4k^2} + \frac{y^2}{k^2} = 1, \quad xy = c^2$$

Since each curve passes through two points on the straight line $y = x$, one can easily argue that those two points must be $(c,c), (-c,-c)$. Subsequently, using the equation of the first curve, we obtain that the relationship between c and k is given by $5c^2 = 4k^2$.

To prove the second part, let us find all the points of intersection. This can be done by substituting $y = c^2/x$ in the first equation. Using $5c^2 = 4k^2$, one can obtain

$$\frac{x^2}{5c^2} + \frac{4c^4}{5c^2 x^2} = 1 \implies \frac{x^2}{c^2} + \frac{4c^2}{x^2} = 5$$

Let $z = x^2/c^2$. Then, the above is equivalent to $z^2 - 5z + 4 = 0$, and thus, $z = 1, 4$. The solutions $x^2 = c^2$ have already been discussed to obtain the two points of intersection $A \equiv (c,c)$, $C \equiv (-c,-c)$. So, for the other two points of intersection, $x^2 = 4c^2$, that is, $x = \pm 2c$. Clearly, this leads to the solutions $(2c, c/2), (-2c, -c/2)$. Let us denote these two points of intersection as B and D, respectively. Then, $ABCD$ forms a quadrilateral, the lengths of the four sides being

$$AB = \sqrt{(c-2c)^2 + (c-c/2)^2} = \sqrt{5c^2/4} = k$$

$$BC = \sqrt{(2c+c)^2 + (c/2+c)^2} = \sqrt{45c^2/4} = 3k$$
$$CD = \sqrt{(-c+2c)^2 + (-c+c/2)^2} = \sqrt{5c^2/4} = k$$
$$DA = \sqrt{(-2c-c)^2 + (-c/2-c)^2} = \sqrt{45c^2/4} = 3k$$

It is now clear that the four points of intersection lie at the vertices of a parallelogram whose sides have lengths k and $3k$.

9. If the normal at the point P on $xy = c^2$ meets the hyperbola $x^2 - y^2 = a^2$ at two points Q and R, show that P is the midpoint of the line segment QR.

Solution: One can consider the parametric form of a point on $xy = c^2$ as $x = ct, y = c/t$. Now, taking the derivative with respect to x for the given equation, we obtain

$$\frac{dy}{dx} = -\frac{c^2}{x^2} \implies \left.\frac{dy}{dx}\right|_{x=ct} = -\frac{1}{t^2},$$

which implies that the slope of the normal at $(ct, c/t)$ must be equal to t^2. Thus, the equation of the normal at $P = (ct, c/t)$ is

$$\frac{y - c/t}{x - ct} = t^2 \implies y = t^2 x + \left(\frac{c}{t} - ct^3\right)$$

Since the normal cuts the hyperbola $x^2 - y^2 = a^2$ at Q and R, we can argue that the x-coordinates of Q and R are the two solutions of the equation

$$x^2 - \left[t^2 x + \left(\frac{c}{t} - ct^3\right)\right]^2 = a^2 \implies x^2(1 - t^4) - 2xct(1 - t^4) - \left[\left(\frac{c}{t} - ct^3\right)^2 + a^2\right] = 0$$

Let us now denote the coordinates as $Q = (x_1, y_1)$ and $R = (x_2, y_2)$. From the above equation and using the concepts of quadratic equations, we can say that $x_1 + x_2 = 2ct$. Subsequently, as these points lie on the normal, we can also obtain

$$y_1 + y_2 = t^2(x_1 + x_2) + \frac{2c}{t}(1 - t^4) = 2ct^3 + \frac{2c}{t}(1 - t^4) = \frac{2c}{t}$$

Finally, with $(x_1 + x_2)/2 = ct$, $(y_1 + y_2)/2 = c/t$, it is easy to conclude that $P = (ct, c/t)$ is the midpoint of the line segment QR.

10. Consider the set $S = \{(x, y) \mid x \in \mathbb{R}, y \in \mathbb{R}, (x+5)^2 + (y-12)^2 = 14\}$. Find the pair $(x, y) \in S$ for which $x^2 + y^2$ is the minimum.

Solution: Note that the given equation is of a circle. We can use the concepts of polar transformation. From $(x+5)^2 + (y-12)^2 = 14$, one can write $x = 14\cos\theta - 5, y = 14\sin\theta +$

12 for some θ. It can be used to express x^2+y^2 as a function of θ in the following way: $f(\theta) = (14\cos\theta - 5)^2 + (14\sin\theta + 12)^2$. Now, taking the first order derivatives of $f(\theta)$

$$f'(\theta) = -28\sin\theta(14\cos\theta - 5) + 28\cos\theta(14\sin\theta + 12) = 28(5\sin\theta + 12\cos\theta)$$

Subsequently, we get

$$f''(\theta) = 28(5\cos\theta - 12\sin\theta) = 28\cos\theta(5 - 12\tan\theta)$$

So, the first order derivative is when $5\sin\theta + 12\cos\theta = 0$, that is, when $\tan\theta = -12/5$, and for all such points, the second order derivative is positive if $\cos\theta > 0$. Thus, we can see that the minimum value is obtained for θ satisfying $\sin\theta = -12/13, \cos\theta = 5/13$.

Hence, the required minimum value is

$$\left(\frac{14\times 5}{13} - 5\right)^2 + \left(-\frac{14\times 12}{13} + 12\right)^2 = \left(\frac{5}{13}\right)^2 + \left(-\frac{12}{13}\right)^2 = 1$$

11. Consider the point $P = (a + 2at, at^2)$ on the parabola $(x-a)^2 = 4ay$. Find the equations of the tangent and the normal to the parabola at P. Further, if the tangent and the normal cut the positive x-axis at the points T and N, respectively, prove that

$$\frac{PT^2}{TN} = at.$$

Solution: Taking the derivative of the given equation with respect to x, we obtain

$$2(x-a) = 4a\frac{dy}{dx} \implies \frac{dy}{dx} = \frac{x-a}{2a}$$

The above can be used to compute the slope of the tangent, which, at $(a+2at, at^2)$, is equal to t. Therefore, the equation of the tangent at P must be

$$\frac{y - at^2}{x - a - 2at} = t \implies y = tx - (at + at^2)$$

Using the above, we can also argue that the slope of the normal at P is equal to $-1/t$, and thus, the corresponding equation is

$$\frac{y - at^2}{x - a - 2at} = -\frac{1}{t} \implies ty = -x + (a + 2at + at^3)$$

For the last part of the problem, to find out the coordinates of T and N, we can set $y = 0$ in the above equations. Then, we obtain $T = (a+at, 0)$, $N = (a+2at+at^3, 0)$. Thus, the length of TN is $(at + at^3)$. On the other hand

$$PT^2 = (a+2at-a-at)^2 + (at^2)^2 = a^2t^2 + a^2t^4$$

Hence

$$\frac{PT^2}{TN} = \frac{a^2t^2 + a^2t^4}{at+at^3} = at$$

12. Consider two circles given by the equations $x^2 + y^2 - 2cy - a^2 = 0$ and $x^2 + y^2 - 2bx + a^2 = 0$. Denote their centres by A and B, respectively. If the two circles intersect at P and Q, prove that the points A, B, P, Q and the origin lie on a circle.

Solution: The first equation can be written as $x^2 + (y-c)^2 = a^2 + c^2$, and so, its centre is $A = (0, c)$ and its radius is $\sqrt{a^2 + c^2}$. Similarly, the second equation can be written as $(x-b)^2 + y^2 = b^2 - a^2$. Thus, its centre is $B = (b, 0)$ and its radius is $\sqrt{b^2 - a^2}$.

In order to find the coordinates of the two intersection points, we can solve the two equations. Note that simultaneous solutions of the two equations lead to the equation $2x^2 + 2y^2 - 2bx - 2cy = 0$. Let us denote one solution of the two equations as $P = (\alpha, \beta)$. Then, we must have $\alpha^2 + \beta^2 - b\alpha - c\beta = 0$.

Now, consider the quadrilateral $OAPB$, where $O = (0, 0)$ is the origin. It is obvious that $\angle AOB = 90°$. The slope of the line AP is $(\beta - c)/\alpha$ while the slope of PB is $\beta/(\alpha - b)$. So, if $\angle APB = \theta$, then

$$|\tan\theta| = \left| \frac{(\beta-c)/\alpha - \beta/(\alpha-b)}{1 + \beta(\beta-c)/\alpha(\alpha-b)} \right| = \left| \frac{(\beta-c)(\alpha-b) - \alpha\beta}{\alpha^2 + \beta^2 - b\alpha - c\beta} \right|$$

Clearly, the denominator of the above equation is 0, and so, we can say that $\theta = 90°$, thereby proving that $\angle AOB + \angle APB = 180°$. So, $OAPB$ is a cyclic quadrilateral.

In an exactly similar fashion, one can show that $OAQB$ is a cyclic quadrilateral as well. Thus, combining the above two results, we get that A, B, P, Q and O lie on a circle.

> **Useful Tip:** The properties of intersecting circles, equations of tangents to circles and the concepts of orthogonal circles are crucial for many competitive examinations.

13. Recall that two intersecting circles are orthogonal to each other if the tangents to the two circles at any point of intersection are perpendicular to each other. Prove that every circle that passes through the points $(2, 0)$ and $(-2, 0)$ is orthogonal to the circle given by the equation $x^2 + y^2 - 5x + 4 = 0$.

Solution: Two intersecting circles are orthogonal if and only if $r_1^2 + r_2^2 = d^2$, where r_1, r_2 are the radii of the two circles and d is the distance between the two centres.

Now, the circle $x^2 + y^2 - 5x + 4 = 0$ can be written as $(x - 5/2)^2 + y^2 = 9/4$, and so, the centre is $(5/2, 0)$ while the radius is $3/2$. Let us now consider a circle C that passes through the points $(2, 0)$ and $(-2, 0)$. Suppose, its centre is (a, b). Then, the square of the radius of the circle is $(a - 2)^2 + b^2 = (a + 2)^2 + b^2$. Solving this equation, we get $4a = 0$, implying that the coordinates of the centre are $(0, b)$.

From the above, it is clear that the two circles have radii $r_1 = 3/2$ and $r_2 = \sqrt{b^2 + 4}$ and the coordinates of the two centres are $C_1 = (5/2, 0)$ and $C_2 = (0, b)$. Let the length of the line segment $C_1 C_2$ be denoted by ℓ. Then, it is enough to prove that $r_1^2 + r_2^2 = \ell^2$ and it can be shown in the following way:

$$r_1^2 + r_2^2 = \frac{9}{4} + b^2 + 4 = \frac{25}{4} + b^2 = \left(\frac{5}{2} - 0\right)^2 + (0 - b)^2 = \ell^2$$

Hence, any circle passing through $(2, 0)$ and $(-2, 0)$ is orthogonal to the given circle.

14. Let $x^2 + y^2 = r^2$ be a circle in the xy-plane such that $Z = (p, q)$ is a point outside the circle. Under what condition would Z lie outside the circle? In that case, there are two tangents that can be drawn from Z to the circle. Find the equation of AB, where A, B are the points of contact of these two tangents.

Solution: Let us use C to denote the given circle. Z lies outside the circle if and only if $p^2 + q^2 > r^2$. It is easy to understand that there are two tangents that can be drawn from Z to C. Suppose that these two tangents touch C at $A = (x_1, y_1)$ and $B = (x_2, y_2)$. To find the equation of PA and PB, note that for the given circle

$$\frac{dy}{dx} = -\frac{x}{y}$$

Thus, the equation of PA is

$$\frac{y - y_1}{x - x_1} = -\frac{x_1}{y_1} \implies yy_1 + xx_1 = x_1^2 + y_1^2 \implies xx_1 + yy_1 = r^2$$

Similarly, the equation of PB can be obtained as $xx_2 + yy_2 = r^2$. Now, P lies on both of these straight lines, and therefore

$$px_1 + py_1 = r^2, \quad px_2 + py_2 = r^2$$

Subsequently, we can infer that (x_1, y_1) and (x_2, y_2) lie on the straight line $px + qy = r^2$, which must be the equation of AB.

Coordinate Geometry

15. The equation $xy = c^2$ represents a rectangular hyperbola. Let $A = (ct_1, c/t_1)$ and $B = (ct_2, c/t_2)$ be two points on this hyperbola, such that the chord AB is of constant length a. As the position of the chord varies, let G be the moving point denoting the centroid of the triangle AOB, where O is the origin. Find the locus of G.

Solution: The coordinates of G are $(c(t_1+t_2)/3, c(1/t_1+1/t_2)/3)$. For convenience, let us denote it as (h, k). Since AB is of constant length, we can write

$$c^2(t_1-t_2)^2 + c^2\left(\frac{1}{t_1}-\frac{1}{t_2}\right)^2 = a^2 \implies c^2(t_1-t_2)^2(1+t_1^2t_2^2)/t_1^2t_2^2 = a^2$$

Now, $9(h^2+k^2) = c^2(t_1+t_2)^2(1+t_1^2t_2^2)/t_1^2t_2^2$. Substituting the expression from the above equation

$$9(h^2+k^2) = \frac{a^2(t_1+t_2)^2}{(t_1-t_2)^2} \implies \frac{a^2}{9(h^2+k^2)} = \frac{(t_1+t_2)^2 - 4t_1t_2}{(t_1+t_2)^2}$$

On the other hand, $9hk = c^2(t_1+t_2)^2/t_1t_2$, that is, $t_1t_2/(t_1+t_2)^2 = c^2/9hk$. Thus, from the previous equality, we can write

$$\frac{a^2}{9(h^2+k^2)} = 1 - \frac{4c^2}{9hk} \implies a^2 hk = (9hk - 4c^2)(h^2+k^2)$$

Hence, the locus of G is $(9xy - 4c^2)(x^2+y^2) = a^2xy$.

16. Suppose a circle C intersects the hyperbola $y = 1/x$ at four distinct points whose coordinates are given by (a_i, b_i), for $i = 1, 2, 3, 4$. Show that $a_1 a_2 = b_3 b_4$.

Solution: Suppose that the equation of C is $(x-a)^2 + (y-b)^2 = r^2$, that is, it has centre (a,b) and radius r. Since the circle intersects $y = 1/x$ at (a_i, b_i), the following condition holds:

$$(a_i - a)^2 + \left(\frac{1}{a_i} - b\right)^2 = r^2 \implies a_i^2(a_i-a)^2 + (1 - ba_i)^2 - r^2 a_i^2 = 0$$

As there are four distinct intersection points, the above 4-degree polynomial must have four distinct real roots. Now, both the leading coefficient and the constant term in the above polynomial is 1, and since their ratio denotes the product of the roots, we get $a_1 a_2 a_3 a_4 = 1$ (these are the roots of the equation). Further, using $b_3 = 1/a_3$ and $b_4 = 1/a_4$ (as these points lie on the given hyperbola), we get our desired result, that is, $a_1 a_2 = b_3 b_4$.

17. Assume that a straight line passing through A $(-5, -4)$ meets the lines $x+3y+2=0$, $2x+y+4=0$ and $x-y-5=0$ at B, C, D, respectively. If

$$\left(\frac{15}{AB}\right)^2 + \left(\frac{10}{AC}\right)^2 = \left(\frac{6}{AD}\right)^2,$$

find the equation of the line.

Solution: For convenience, let us use r_1, r_2, r_3 to denote the lengths of AB, AC, AD, respectively. We can use the parametric form of the equation of a straight line in this problem. For the line AB, it can be written as

$$\frac{x+5}{\cos\theta} = \frac{y+4}{\sin\theta} = r,$$

where r is the parameter indicating the distance of (x, y) from A. Now, if the length of the line segment AB is r_1, then the above implies that the coordinates of B are $(r_1\cos\theta - 5, r_1\sin\theta - 4)$. Further, as this point lies on the line $x + 3y + 2 = 0$

$$(r_1\cos\theta - 5) + 3(r_1\sin\theta - 4) + 2 = 0 \implies \frac{15}{r_1} = \cos\theta + 3\sin\theta$$

Following an identical procedure for AC and AD, we can show that

$$\frac{10}{r_2} = 2\cos\theta + \sin\theta, \quad \frac{6}{r_3} = \cos\theta - \sin\theta$$

Thus, based on the given relationship, we can write

$$(\cos\theta + 3\sin\theta)^2 + (2\cos\theta + \sin\theta)^2 = (\cos\theta - \sin\theta)^2,$$

which implies $9\sin^2\theta + 12\sin\theta\cos\theta + 4\cos^2\theta = 0$. This is equivalent to $3\sin\theta + 2\cos\theta = 0$, that is, $\tan\theta = -2/3$, which is in fact the slope of the straight line. Finally, since it passes through $(-5, -4)$, the equation of the line is

$$\frac{y+4}{x+5} = -\frac{2}{3} \implies 2x + 3y + 22 = 0$$

> **Useful Tip:** Here, we utilized the parametric form of a straight line. This technique is useful when some relationship with respect to the distance between two points on the same line is known. See another example below.

18. Find the equation(s) of a line drawn through the point A $(1, 2)$ so that its points of intersection with the line $x + y = 4$ is at a distance $\sqrt{2/3}$ from A.

Solution: Suppose that the required line makes an angle θ with the positive x-axis. Then, using the parameteric form of a straight line, we can write its equation as

$$\frac{x-1}{\cos\theta} = \frac{y-2}{\sin\theta} = r,$$

where the parameter r indicates the distance of a point (x,y) from A. Thus, if the point of intersection with $x+y=4$ is given by B, then its coordinates are

$$B = \left(\sqrt{\frac{2}{3}}\cos\theta + 1, \sqrt{\frac{2}{3}}\sin\theta + 2\right)$$

As B lies on $x+y=4$, we can further say that

$$\cos\theta + \sin\theta = \sqrt{\frac{3}{2}} \implies \frac{1}{\sqrt{2}}\cos\theta + \frac{1}{\sqrt{2}}\sin\theta = \frac{\sqrt{3}}{2}$$

Therefore, $\sin(\theta + 45°) = \sin 60°$, which implies $\theta = 15°$ or $75°$. Hence, the required equation of the line is

$$y = x\tan 15° + (2 - \tan 15°), \text{ or } y = x\tan 75° + (2 - \tan 75°)$$

19. A square $ABCD$ is such that the side AB lies on the line $y = x+8$, and the points C, D lie on the parabola $x^2 = y$. Find all the possible values of the length of the side of the square.

Solution: Let the coordinates of C and D be (c, c^2) and (d, d^2), respectively. As CD is parallel to AB, their slopes must be equal. It implies

$$\frac{d^2 - c^2}{d - c} = 1 \implies c + d = 1$$

Next, the length of CD is given by $|c - d|/\cos 45°$, that is, $CD = \sqrt{2}|c - d|$. As $ABCD$ is a square, the distance from C to AB must be equal to CD. This implies

$$\frac{|c - c^2 + 8|}{\sqrt{2}} = \sqrt{2}|c - d|$$

Using $1 - c = d$, the above implies $|cd + 8| = 2|c - d|$. Let us write $cd = p$. We can write $(c - d)^2 = (c + d)^2 - 4cd$. Then, from the above results, we obtain

$$(p + 8)^2 = 4(1 - 4p) \implies p^2 + 32p + 60 = 0$$

Clearly, the possible solutions are $p = -2$ or $p = -30$. Further, c and d must be the roots of the equation $t^2 - (c+d)t + p = 0$, that is, $t^2 - t + p = 0$. Now, for $p = -2$, the equation is $t^2 - t - 2 = 0$, which leads to the solutions $-1, 2$. For $p = -30$, on the other hand, one can obtain the solutions $-5, 6$. Since $CD = \sqrt{2}|c - d|$, we can conclude that the possible values of the lengths of the square are $\{3\sqrt{2}, 11\sqrt{2}\}$.

20. Consider an ellipse $\mathcal{E}$ with centre at origin O and with major and minor axes of length $2a$ and $2b$, respectively. Let $\mathcal{C}$ be a circle with centre at the origin. Suppose that θ is the acute angle at which $\mathcal{E}$ is cut by $\mathcal{C}$, that is, θ is the acute angle of intersection of their tangents at a point of intersection. What is the maximum possible value of θ?

Solution: The equation of the given ellipse is $x^2/a^2 + y^2/b^2 = 1$. Suppose the radius of the circle is r, that is, the equation of the circle is $x^2 + y^2 = r^2$. Now, if (h,k) is a point of intersection of the ellipse and the circle, then we must have

$$\frac{r^2 - k^2}{a^2} + \frac{k^2}{b^2} = 1,$$

which implies the following:

$$k^2 = \frac{b^2(a^2 - r^2)}{a^2 - b^2}, \quad h^2 = \frac{a^2(r^2 - b^2)}{a^2 - b^2}$$

Clearly, there are four intersection points, obtained by taking both positive and negative square roots of the above quantities. Because of symmetry, the angle θ is the same for all of the four. Let us consider the positive square roots without loss of generality, and let us denote that point as (x_0, y_0).

The equation of the tangent to the ellipse at (x_0, y_0) is $y - y_0 = -\frac{b^2 x_0}{a^2 y_0}(x - x_0)$ and the same to the circle is $y - y_0 = -\frac{x_0}{y_0}(x - x_0)$. Using the two slopes and the fact that the acute angle these two tangents make is θ, we get

$$\tan\theta = \left|\frac{-b^2 x_0/a^2 y_0 + x_0/y_0}{1 + b^2 x_0^2/a^2 y_0^2}\right| = \left|\frac{-b^2 x_0 y_0 + a^2 x_0 y_0}{a^2 y_0^2 + b^2 x_0^2}\right|$$

Since $x_0, y_0 > 0$, the above simplifies to $x_0 y_0 (a^2 - b^2)/(a^2 b^2)$, which further indicates

$$\tan\theta = \left(\frac{a^2 - b^2}{a^2 b^2}\right)\left(\frac{ab}{a^2 - b^2}\sqrt{(a^2 - r^2)(r^2 - b^2)}\right)$$

In view of the fact that $\tan\theta$ is an increasing function of θ, we can say that θ is maximized if the function $f(r) = (a^2 - r^2)(r^2 - b^2)$ is maximized. Since $f'(r) = 2r[(a^2 - r^2) - (r^2 - b^2)]$, it can be argued that this function is maximized when $r^2 = (a^2 + b^2)/2$, and then, we get $f(r) = (a^2 - b^2)^2/4$. Hence, the maximum possible value of $\tan\theta$ is $(a^2 - b^2)/2ab$, and we get

$$\theta_{\max} = \tan^{-1}\left(\frac{a^2 - b^2}{2ab}\right)$$

Coordinate Geometry

21. For the unit circle C centred at the origin, let AB be an arc subtending an angle θ at the centre. Determine the possible location(s) of an arbitrary point P on this arc, such that the product of the lengths of AP and PB is maximized.

Solution: We shall use complex number notations in this problem. Note that the equation of the unit circle centred at the origin is $x^2 + y^2 = 1$. Now, every point on this circle can be denoted as $e^{i\theta}$ for some $\theta \in (-\pi, \pi]$. Here, $e^{i\theta} = \cos\theta + i\sin\theta$. Also, note that

$$\left|e^{i\theta} - 1\right|^2 = (\cos\theta - 1)^2 + \sin^2\theta = 2 - 2\cos\theta$$

Since AB is an arc that makes an angle θ at the centre, we can consider, without loss of generality, that $A = 1$ and then, $B = e^{i\theta}$. Take an arbitrary point $P = e^{i\phi}$ on the arc, that is, let $0 < \phi < \theta$. Denoting the product of the lengths of AP and PB as ℓ, we get

$$\ell = \left|e^{i\phi} - 1\right| \cdot \left|e^{i\theta} - e^{i\phi}\right| = \left|e^{i\phi} - 1\right| \cdot \left|e^{i(\theta-\phi)} - 1\right|$$

Squaring both sides

$$\ell^2 = 4(1 - \cos\phi)(1 - \cos(\theta - \phi)) = 4f(\phi) \text{ (say)}$$

Thus, the product is maximized if the right-hand side is maximized with respect to ϕ. Taking the first and second order derivatives, we get

$$\begin{aligned} f'(\phi) &= \sin\phi(1 - \cos(\theta - \phi)) - \sin(\theta - \phi)(1 - \cos\phi) \\ &= \sin\phi - \sin(\theta - \phi) + \sin(\theta - 2\phi) \\ f''(\phi) &= \cos\phi + \cos(\theta - \phi) - 2\cos(\theta - 2\phi) \end{aligned}$$

Clearly, the first order derivative is 0 at $\phi = \theta/2$ and we can check that the second order derivative is negative at that point, implying that the quantity is maximized for $\phi = \theta/2$. Hence, in conclusion, the product is maximized when P is the midpoint of the arc AB.

22. Let $z_1, z_2, z_3, z_4 \in \mathbb{C}$ be distinct numbers satisfying

$$\text{Re}\left(\frac{z_2 - z_1}{z_4 - z_1}\right) = \text{Re}\left(\frac{z_2 - z_3}{z_4 - z_3}\right) = 0.$$

Find the set of real numbers x such that

$$|z_1 - z_2|^x + |z_1 - z_4|^x \leq |z_2 - z_4|^x \leq |z_2 - z_3|^x + |z_4 - z_3|^x.$$

Further, prove that $|z_3 - z_1| \leq |z_4 - z_2|$.

Solution: Let the points A, B, C, D denote the four complex numbers z_1, z_2, z_3, z_4 in the Argand plane. Then, the condition

$$\operatorname{Re}\left(\frac{z_2 - z_1}{z_4 - z_1}\right) = \operatorname{Re}\left(\frac{z_2 - z_3}{z_4 - z_3}\right) = 0$$

implies that both $\angle BAD$ and $\angle BCD$ are 90°. Now, the term $|z_1 - z_2|$ indicates the length of the side AB while $|z_1 - z_4|$ and $|z_2 - z_4|$ are, respectively, the lengths of AD and BD. Since BAD is a right-angled triangle with $\angle BAD = 90°$, we can say that $AB^x + AD^x \leqslant BD^x$ for all $x \geqslant 2$. In other words

$$|z_1 - z_2|^x + |z_1 - z_4|^x \leqslant |z_2 - z_4|^x$$

for all $x \geqslant 2$. In an exactly similar fashion, we can also argue that for all $x \leqslant 2$

$$|z_2 - z_3|^x + |z_4 - z_3|^x \geqslant |z_2 - z_4|^x$$

Thus, in order to have both inequalities to be true, the only possibility is $x = 2$.

For the second part of the problem, note that $|z_3 - z_1|$ is the length of AC while $|z_4 - z_2|$ is the length of BD. However, because $\angle BAD = \angle BCD = 90°$, $ABCD$ is a cyclic quadrilateral such that BD is the diameter. Clearly, AC, which is a chord of the circle, cannot be greater than BD. This completes the proof.

23. Consider two real positive numbers $a < b$. Prove that amongst all the triangles with perimeter $a + b$ and with one side equal to a, the triangle that has three sides of length $a, b/2, b/2$ has the maximum area.

Solution: Let BC be the side of the triangle that has length a, and let A be a moving point such that $AB + AC = b$. Obviously, the locus of A is an ellipse with foci at B and C. Let us drop a perpendicular from A to BC, and name its foot D.

Since the area of ABC is $(AD)(BC)/2$, the area is maximum when the distance from A to BC is maximum. This is attained when A lies on the perpendicular bisector of BC. The required result follows immediately.

> **Useful Tip:** A different version of the above problem was considered in the previous chapter and was solved using concepts from Euclidean geometry.

24. Let C be a unit-radius circle with centre at $(0, 1)$, and let P be the point on the circumference that is on the origin at this position. Suppose that C is rolled along the positive x-axis without slipping from the initial position. Find the locus of P.

Solution: Let us find the position of the point P after the circle travels t units along the positive x-axis. From the figures given below, it is clear that the new position of P is at a distance t from the axis, where the distance is calculated along the circumference.

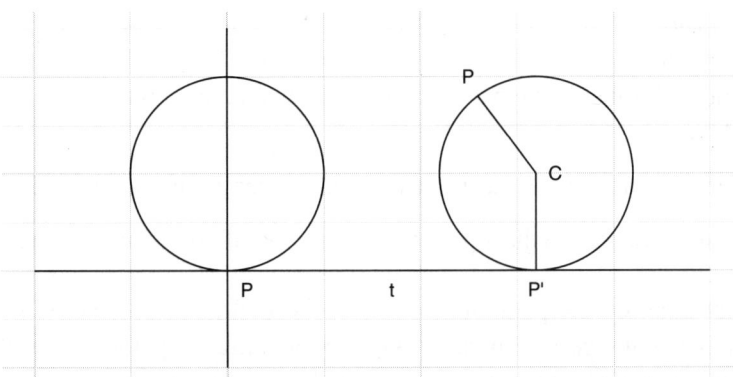

We use C to denote the centre of the circle at the new position, and P' is the point on the x-axis. Clearly, the length of the arc PP' is t units. We know that if s is the length of an arc that makes an angle θ at the centre, then $s = r\theta$, where r is the radius of the circle. Using this, we can say that $\angle PCP' = t$ (the radius of the circle is 1).

Since the circle is shifted by t units, the coordinates of the new position are $P' = (t,0), C = (t,1)$. Let us assume that $P = (x,y)$.

Now, $\angle PCP' = t$ and CP' is a perpendicular on the x-axis. Thus, the straight line PC, when extended, cuts the x-axis at an angle $t - \pi/2$, and so, the slope of PC is $(-\tan(t - \pi/2)) = \cot t$. On the other hand, the distance between P and C must be 1 unit. The above two conditions give us the following:

$$\frac{y-1}{x-t} = \cot t, \qquad (y-1)^2 + (x-t)^2 = 1$$

From the second equation, we get $x - t = \pm\sqrt{2y-y^2}$ and so, $t = x \pm \sqrt{2y-y^2}$. On the other hand, the first equation gives us

$$\tan^2 t = \frac{(x-t)^2}{(y-1)^2} = \frac{1-(y-1)^2}{(y-1)^2} = \frac{1}{(y-1)^2} - 1$$

The above can be further simplified to argue that $\cos^2 t = (y-1)^2$, that is, $\cos t = \pm(y-1)$. Subsequently, using the fact that $\cos^{-1}(-x) = \cos^{-1}(x)$, we obtain $t = \cos^{-1}(y-1)$. Hence, the required locus of the point is

$$(y-1)^2 + \left(x - \cos^{-1}(y-1)\right)^2 = 1$$

25. The region inside the parabola $y = x^2$ is the set of points (a,b) such that $b \geqslant a^2$. We define a 'bubble at a point P' on the graph of $y = x^2$ as the largest circle that contains P and has all the points on or inside the parabola. Assume that at any point on the parabola, there is a unique bubble.

(a) If a bubble at some point P has radius 1, find the centre of that bubble.

(b) Find the radius of the smallest possible bubble for all points on the parabola.

Solution: Any point on the parabola $y = x^2$ can be written in parametric form as (t, t^2). Note that a bubble at any point P must be a circle touching the parabola. Further, it is also possible to argue that the bubble at $P = (t, t^2)$ is the same as the one at $P' = (-t, t^2)$, that is, all bubbles are symmetric about the y-axis. Thus, the centre of the bubble at P is of the form $C = (0, k)$.

Now, consider the tangent to the parabola at point P. Due to the property discussed earlier, it is a tangent to the circle as well. Since $dy/dx = 2x$, the slope of the tangent at P is $2t$. Consequently, the slope of PC must be $(-1/2t)$.

(a) It is given that $PC = 1$. Construct the point $Q = (0, t^2)$ such that PCQ is a right-angled triangle with the right angle at the vertex Q. Then, $PC^2 = PQ^2 + QC^2$, that is, $t^2 = 1 - QC^2$. On the other hand, $QC = |PQ \tan \angle CPQ|$, and $\tan \angle CPQ$ is essentially the slope of PC. Thus, $QC = |(t)(-1/2t)| = 1/2$, which implies that $t^2 = 3/4$ and $Q = (0, 3/4)$. Hence, using $QC = 1/2$, we can conclude that the centre of the specified bubble is $(0, 5/4)$.

(b) We have already seen that for any P, the radius of the bubble satisfies the condition $PC^2 = t^2 + 1/4$. Clearly, the radius of the smallest possible bubble can be obtained for $t = 0$ (one can also show this using the continuity argument at $t \to 0$), and the value of that radius is $1/2$.

26. Let C_1 and C_2 be two circles, each with radius r. If the two circles pass through the centres of each other, prove that the area of the region common to them is $r^2(4\pi - \sqrt{27})/6$.

Solution: Without loss of generality, we can assume that the centres of C_1 and C_2 are $(0,0)$ and $(r,0)$, respectively. The corresponding equations of the circles are $x^2 + y^2 = r^2$ and $(x-r)^2 + y^2 = r^2$.

Coordinate Geometry

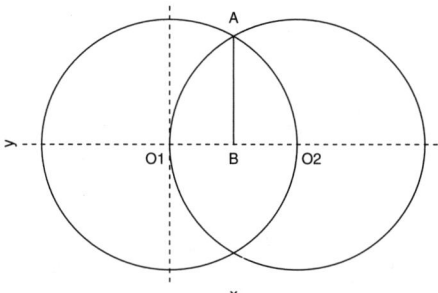

To find the point of intersection A, we can solve the above two equations and obtain the solution as $x = r/2, y = r\sqrt{3}/2$. Then, it is easy to argue that the area of the region common to the two circles is four times the area of $BAO2$ (denote it as Δ), which can be computed as follows.

$$\begin{aligned}
\Delta &= \int_{r/2}^{r} \sqrt{r^2 - x^2}\, dx \\
&= \left[\frac{x}{2}\sqrt{r^2-x^2} + \frac{r^2}{2}\sin^{-1}\left(\frac{x}{r}\right)\right]_{r/2}^{r} \\
&= \left[\frac{r^2}{2}\sin^{-1}(1) - \frac{\sqrt{3}r^2}{8} - \frac{r^2}{2}\sin^{-1}\left(\frac{1}{2}\right)\right] \\
&= \frac{r^2}{4}\left[\frac{2\pi}{3} - \frac{\sqrt{3}}{2}\right]
\end{aligned}$$

Multiplying the above by 4, we obtain the required result.

27. A curve is described by the equation $x^{2/3} + y^{2/3} = a^{2/3}$, where a is a positive real number. It is known that the normal to the curve at some particular point makes an angle θ with the X-axis. Prove that the corresponding equation of the normal is $y\cos\theta - x\sin\theta = a\cos 2\theta$.

Solution: The equation of the normal to a curve $y = f(x)$ at some point (h,k) is given by $y - k = -(x-h)/f'(h)$, which can be re-written as $y = x(-1/f'(h)) + k + h/f'(h)$. Also, recall that the equation of a straight line that makes an angle θ with the X-axis is of the form $y = x\tan\theta + c$.

We need to prove that the equation should be $y\cos\theta - x\sin\theta = a\cos 2\theta$, which is equivalent to the equation $y = x\tan\theta + a\cos 2\theta/\cos\theta$. Connecting it with the above, we need to show that if $\{-1/f'(h) = \tan\theta\}$, then $\{k + h/f'(h) = a\cos 2\theta/\cos\theta\}$ and that would give us our required result.

First, taking the derivative of the given equation with respect to x, we get

$$\frac{2}{3}x^{-1/3} + \frac{2}{3}y^{-1/3}\frac{dy}{dx} = 0 \implies -\frac{1}{dy/dx} = \frac{y^{-1/3}}{x^{-1/3}}$$

Thus

$$\tan\theta = -\frac{1}{f'(h)} = \frac{k^{-1/3}}{h^{-1/3}} = \frac{h^{1/3}}{k^{1/3}},$$

where $h^{2/3} + k^{2/3} = a^{2/3}$. Now

$$a\cos 2\theta / \cos\theta = a \times \frac{1-\tan^2\theta}{1+\tan^2\theta} \times \sqrt{1+\tan^2\theta}$$

Substituting the expression obtained previously for $\tan\theta$ and using the identity $h^{2/3} + k^{2/3} = a^{2/3}$, this can be simplified as

$$a\left(\frac{1 - h^{2/3}/k^{2/3}}{\sqrt{1 + h^{2/3}/k^{2/3}}}\right) = \frac{(h^{2/3}+k^{2/3})^{3/2}}{k^{1/3}}\left(\frac{k^{2/3} - h^{2/3}}{\sqrt{h^{2/3}+k^{2/3}}}\right) = \frac{k^{4/3} - h^{4/3}}{k^{1/3}}$$

This leads to the equation $a\cos 2\theta/\cos\theta = k - h^{4/3}/k^{1/3}$. Earlier, we found that $f'(h) = -k^{1/3}/h^{1/3}$, and thus, straightforward algebraic manipulation implies that $a\cos 2\theta/\cos\theta = k + h/f'(h)$, and that completes the proof.

28. Five points $P_0 = (0,0)$, $P_1 = (0,4)$, $P_2 = (4,0)$, $P_3 = (-2,-2)$, $P_4 = (3,3)$, $P_5 = (5,5)$ are given in a plane. Let R be the region consisting of all points P in the xy-plane such that the distance of P from P_0 is smaller than that from any other P_i, $i = 1,2,3,4,5$. Find the perimeter of the region R.

Solution: We shall denote the distance between two points A and B as $d(A,B)$. Let us consider a point $S \equiv (x,y)$, which is in the region R. Then, $d(S,P_0) < d(S,P_1)$ implies

$$x^2 + y^2 < x^2 + (y-4)^2 \implies y < 2$$

Similarly, from $d(S,P_0) < d(S,P_2)$, we can get $x < 2$. Now, for the other three points, note that each is of the form (a,a). So, for these three points, in general, we have

$$x^2 + y^2 < (x-a)^2 + (y-a)^2 \implies x+y \begin{cases} < a & \text{if } a > 0 \\ > -a & \text{if } a < 0 \end{cases}$$

Thus, the following conditions are satisfied for the region R:

$$x < 2, y < 2, x+y > 2, x+y < 3, x+y < 5$$

This region is displayed in the following figure (the shaded portion represents the region R).

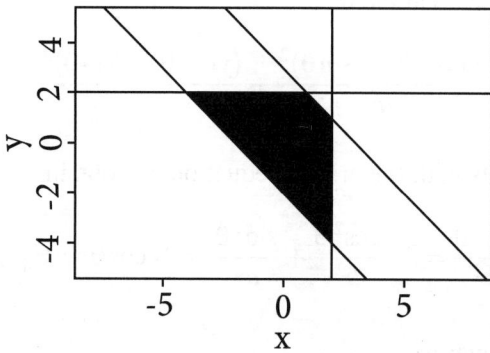

Note that it is an isosceles trapezium, for which the end-points are $(2,-4)$, $(2,1)$, $(-4,2)$ and $(1,2)$. So, the lengths of the parallel sides are the distances between $(2,-4),(-4,2)$ and $(2,1),(1,2)$. These are $\sqrt{(2+4)^2+(-4-2)^2}=6\sqrt{2}$ and $\sqrt{(2-1)^2+(1-2)^2}=\sqrt{2}$, respectively. On the other hand, the length of each of the other two sides is 5 units. Hence, the perimeter of the region R is the sum of the lengths of the four sides and it is $10+7\sqrt{2}$ units.

29. Consider the region

$$A = \{(x,y) : x = u+v, y = v, u^2 + v^2 \leqslant 1\}.$$

Find the length of the longest line segment that can be enclosed in the region A.

Solution: Note that the region A describes the set of all (x,y) satisfying

$$x^2 + 2y^2 - 2xy - 1 \leqslant 0$$

Let S denote the curve $x^2 + 2y^2 - 2xy - 1 = 0$. It is clearly in the form of a conic section, and using the rule of $h^2 < ab$, one can confirm that S represents an ellipse. Thus, the longest line segment that can be enclosed in A is the same as the major axis of the ellipse.

Now, solving

$$\frac{\partial S}{\partial x} = 0, \quad \frac{\partial S}{\partial y} = 0$$

one can obtain that the centre of S is at the origin. However, the equation also suggests that the axes of the ellipse are not parallel to the axes of the coordinate system. Let us assume that the major axis of S forms an angle of θ with the positive x-axis.

Consider a new axis system $(x,y) \to (u,v)$ obtained by rotating the axes by an angle θ, and let the equation of S be $u^2/a^2 + v^2/b^2 = 1$ in the new system. Then, using the rule of rotation of axes, it is easy to argue that

$$\frac{(x\cos\theta + y\sin\theta)^2}{a^2} + \frac{(y\cos\theta - x\sin\theta)^2}{b^2} = 1$$

Equating the coefficients with the original equation, we obtain

$$\frac{\cos^2\theta}{a^2} + \frac{\sin^2\theta}{b^2} = 1, \quad \frac{\cos^2\theta}{b^2} + \frac{\sin^2\theta}{a^2} = 2, \quad \cos\theta\sin\theta\left(\frac{1}{b^2} - \frac{1}{a^2}\right) = 1$$

Adding the first two equations

$$\frac{1}{a^2} + \frac{1}{b^2} = 3$$

Then, subtracting the second equation from the first

$$-\frac{\cos^2\theta}{\cos\theta\sin\theta} + \frac{\sin^2\theta}{\cos\theta\sin\theta} = -1 \implies \tan^2\theta + \tan\theta - 1 = 0 \implies \tan\theta = \frac{-1 \pm \sqrt{5}}{2}$$

Taking the positive sign

$$\sin 2\theta = \frac{-1 + \sqrt{5}}{1 + 6/4 - \sqrt{5}/2} = \frac{2}{\sqrt{5}}.$$

The above implies, from the conditions before, that

$$\frac{1}{b^2} - \frac{1}{a^2} = \sqrt{5}$$

This, in conjunction with $1/a^2 + 1/b^2 = 3$, leads to the result

$$a^2 = \frac{2}{3 - \sqrt{5}} = \frac{4}{(\sqrt{5} - 1)^2} \implies a = \frac{2}{\sqrt{5} - 1} = \frac{\sqrt{5} + 1}{2}$$

Since the above is the semi-major axis, the length of the major axis of the ellipse S, that is, the length of the longest segment that can be enclosed in A, is $(\sqrt{5} + 1)$ units.

30. Let PQR be a triangle, with a point A on or inside the triangle. Let $f(x,y) = ax+by+c$. Show that $f(A) \leq \max\{f(P), f(Q), f(R)\}$.

Solution: First, we consider that A is on the triangle and without loss of generality, assume that it is on the side QR (refer to the figure on the left).

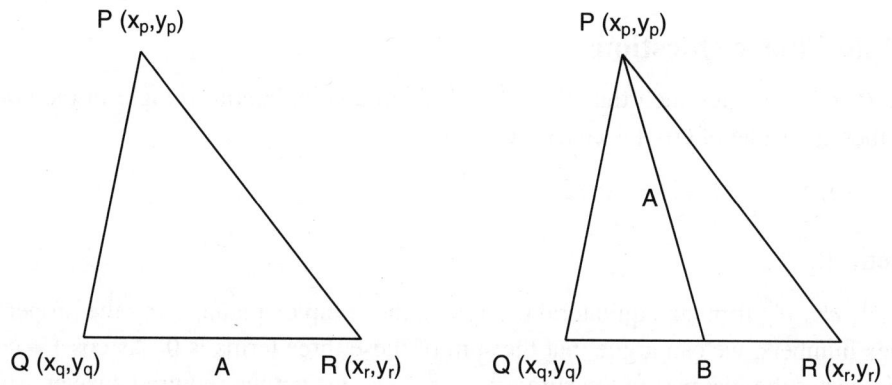

Suppose the coordinates of Q and R are (x_q, y_q) and (x_r, y_r), respectively. Also, let us assume that A has coordinates (x, y) and it divides the side QR in the ratio $m:n$ (m,n are positive real numbers). Then

$$x = \frac{mx_q + nx_r}{m+n}, \quad y = \frac{my_q + ny_r}{m+n}$$

Now, observe that

$$f(A) - f(Q) = a(x - x_q) + b(y - y_q) = \frac{an(x_r - x_q)}{m+n} + \frac{bn(y_r - y_q)}{m+n}$$

Similarly, we can show that

$$f(A) - f(R) = \frac{am(x_q - x_r)}{m+n} + \frac{bm(y_q - y_r)}{m+n} = -\frac{m}{n}\{f(A) - f(Q)\}$$

And hence, $f(A) - f(Q)$ and $f(A) - f(R)$ are of different signs. So, $f(A)$ cannot be greater than both and we can say that $f(A) \leq \max\{f(Q), f(R)\}$.

We can extend the above result to the case when A is inside the triangle (refer to the figure on the right). Let us simply join P and A and extend it to QR. Suppose it intersects QR at B. Then, from the triangle PQB, using the above result, we can say that $f(A) \leq \max\{f(P), f(B)\}$.

Next, since B is on QR, we can use the above result once again and get $f(B) \leqslant \max\{f(Q), f(R)\}$. Hence, combining these two inequalities, we obtain the required result, that is

$$f(A) \leqslant \max\{f(P), f(Q), f(R)\}$$

Multiple Choice Questions

1. If A, B, C are angles such that $e^{\iota A}$, $e^{\iota B}$, $e^{\iota C}$ form an equilateral triangle in the complex plane, then the value of $\cos A + \cos B + \cos C$ is

(a) 0   (b) 1   (c) -1 (d) 3/2

Solution: (a)

Since $e^{\iota A}$, $e^{\iota B}$, $e^{\iota C}$ form an equilateral triangle in the complex plane, using the properties of complex numbers, we can argue that the sum of these three terms is 0. As $\cos A + \cos B + \cos C$ indicates the real part of the sum $e^{\iota A} + e^{\iota B} + e^{\iota C}$, we get the required answer as 0.

2. Let L denote a straight line tangent to the graph of $y = x^3$ and passing through the point $(0, 2000)$. What is the slope of L?

(a) -10 (b) 100   (c) -30 (d) 300

Solution: (d)

With $dy/dx = 3x^2$, the equation of any tangent to the given curve is of the form

$$y - h^3 = 3h^2(x - h)$$

As L passes through $(0, 2022)$, we have $2000 = -2h^3$, that is, $h = -10$. Thus, L is the tangent at the point $(-10, -1000)$ and its slope is $3(-10)^2 = 300$.

3. If $\iota = \sqrt{-1}$, and z and w represent the two diagonally opposite vertices of a square, then the other two vertices are given by

(a) $w + \iota z$ and $w - \iota z$
(b) $\frac{1}{2}(w+z) + \frac{1}{2}\iota(w+z)$ and $\frac{1}{2}(w+z) - \frac{1}{2}\iota(w+z)$
(c) $\frac{1}{2}(w-z) + \frac{1}{2}\iota(w-z)$ and $\frac{1}{2}(w-z) - \frac{1}{2}\iota(w-z)$
(d) $\frac{1}{2}(w+z) + \frac{1}{2}\iota(w-z)$ and $\frac{1}{2}(w+z) - \frac{1}{2}\iota(w-z)$

Solution: (d)

Note that the centre of the square (call it C) is $(w+z)/2$ and that if we imagine a circle centred at C, then the radius of the circle is $|(w-z)/2|$. Since the other two vertices are on the perpendicular with respect to the diagonal and must be at distance $|(w-z)/2|$ from C, the coordinates must be

$$\frac{1}{2}(w+z) + \frac{1}{2}\iota(w-z) \text{ and } \frac{1}{2}(w+z) - \frac{1}{2}\iota(w-z)$$

4. The curve in the complex plane given by the equation $\text{Re}(1/z) = 1/4$, where $\text{Re}(\cdot)$ denotes the real part of a complex number, is a

(a) straight line not passing through the origin;
(b) straight line passing through the origin;
(c) circle with radius 2;
(d) circle with radius 1.

Solution: (c)

Let $z = x + \iota y$. Then, the given equation can be rewritten as

$$\text{Re}\left(\frac{x - \iota y}{x^2 + y^2}\right) = \frac{1}{4} \implies 4x = x^2 + y^2$$

The above leads to the equation $(x-2)^2 + y^2 = 4$, which is the equation of a circle centred at $(2,0)$ and with radius 2.

5. A circle of radius $\sqrt{3}-1$ units, with both coordinates of the centre being negative, touches the straight lines $y - \sqrt{3}x = 0$ and $x - \sqrt{3}y = 0$. The equation of the circle is

(a) $x^2 + y^2 + 2(x+y) + (\sqrt{3}-1)^2 = 0$
(b) $x^2 + y^2 + 2(x+y) + (\sqrt{3}+1)^2 = 0$
(c) $x^2 + y^2 + 4(x+y) + (\sqrt{3}-1)^2 = 0$
(d) $x^2 + y^2 + 4(x+y) + (\sqrt{3}+1)^2 = 0$

Solution: (d)

Note that the angle made by the two given lines with the positive x-axis are $60°$ and $30°$, respectively. Thus, the equation of the angle bisector of the two lines is $y = x$. Since the centre of the circle must lie on this angle bisector, let the equation of the circle be $(x+a)^2 + (y+a)^2 = (\sqrt{3}-1)^2$, where $a > 0$.

Let us use O to denote the origin in the coordinate plane, C to denote the centre of the circle and let D be the point of tangency of the circle with the straight line $x - \sqrt{3}y = 0$. It is obvious that OCD is a right-angled triangle, with $CO = a\sqrt{2}$, $CD = \sqrt{3}-1$ and $\angle COD = 15°$. Clearly

$$\sin 15° = \frac{\sqrt{3}-1}{a\sqrt{2}} \implies \cos 30° = 1 - 2\sin^2 15° = 1 - \frac{(\sqrt{3}-1)^2}{a^2}$$

The above leads to the equation

$$\frac{(\sqrt{3}-1)^2}{a^2} = \frac{4-2\sqrt{3}}{4} \implies a = 2,$$

and hence, the equation of the circle must be $x^2 + y^2 + 4(x+y) + (\sqrt{3}+1)^2 = 0$.

6. A rectangle $PQRS$ joins the points $P \equiv (2,3)$, $Q \equiv (x_1, y_1)$, $R \equiv (8, 11)$ and $S \equiv (x_2, y_2)$, where QS is known to be parallel to the y-axis. What are the coordinates of Q and S?

(a) $(0,7)$ and $(10,7)$
(b) $(5,2)$ and $(5,12)$
(c) $(7,6)$ and $(7,10)$
(d) None of the above

Solution: (b)

Since QS is parallel to the y-axis, the x-coordinates of the two points must be the same, and therefore, the length of QS is $y_2 - y_1$ (assuming $y_1 < y_2$ without loss of generality). Furthermore, $PQRS$ is a rectangle, and the lengths of the diagonals PR and QS must be the same, implying that

$$(y_2 - y_1)^2 = (8-2)^2 + (11-3)^2 = 100 \implies y_2 = y_1 + 10$$

On the other hand, the midpoint of the diagonal PR is $(5,7)$. Since it must coincide with the midpoint of QS, which is $(x_1, (y_1+y_2)/2)$, we can write $x_1 = x_2 = 5$ and $y_1 + y_2 = 14$. This helps us in obtaining the required answer

$$Q \equiv (5,2), \ S \equiv (5,12)$$

7. If the point z in the complex plane describes a circle of radius 2 with centre at the origin, then the point $z + 1/z$ describes

(a) a circle   (b) a parabola   (c) an ellipse   (d) a hyperbola

Solution: (c)

Letting $z = x + \iota y$, the given condition can be written as $x^2 + y^2 = 4$. Now, $1/z = \bar{z}/|z|^2 = x/4 - \iota y/4$. Thus, $z + 1/z$ describes the equation

$$\frac{5x}{4} + \iota \frac{3y}{4} = h + \iota k, \text{ (say)}$$

Coordinate Geometry

It is then easy to see that
$$\frac{h^2}{5^2} + \frac{k^2}{3^2} = \frac{1}{16}(x^2+y^2) = \frac{1}{4},$$
which describes an ellipse.

8. The vertices of a triangle are the points $(0,0)$, $(4,4)$ and $(0,8)$. The circumradius of the triangle is

(a) $3\sqrt{2}$ (b) $2\sqrt{2}$ (c) 3 (d) 4

Solution: (d)

The circumcentre (call it O) must be equidistant from the three vertices A, B, C. If the coordinates of O are (h,k), then using $OA = OC$, we get
$$h^2 + k^2 = h^2 + (k-8)^2 \implies k = 8 - k \implies k = 4$$
Then, using $OA = OB$
$$h^2 + 4^2 = (h-4)^2 \implies h = 0$$
Hence, the circumradius is the distance between O and A, which is equal to 4.

9. Consider the ellipse $9x^2 + 16y^2 = 144$, and let r be the length of the chord intercepted by it on the line $3x + 4y = 12$. Then, the value of r is

(a) 3 (b) 5 (c) 7 (d) $\sqrt{7}$

Solution: (b)

Let the point of intersection of the ellipse and the given line be (h,k). Then, we can write
$$(12-4k)^2 + 16k^2 = 144 \implies 32k^2 - 96k = 0 \implies k = 0, 3,$$
and correspondingly, $h = 4, 0$. Thus, the two points of intersection are $(4,0)$ and $(0,3)$, and hence, the length of the chord intercepted between these two points is 5 units.

10. In the coordinate plane, a straight line passes through $(8,4)$ and cuts the x- and y-axes at points N and M, respectively (shown in the figure below).

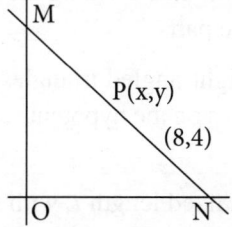

What is the locus of the midpoint P of the segment MN?

(a) $xy - 4x - 2y + 8 = 0$ (b) $xy + 2x + 4y = 64$
(c) $xy - 2x - 4y = 0$ (d) $xy + 4x + 2y = 72$

Solution: (c)

Since the coordinates of P are (x,y), we can write $M = (0, 2y)$, $N = (2x, 0)$. If the point $(8, 4)$ is denoted by A, then the slopes of AN and AM must be equal, which implies that

$$\frac{4}{8-2x} = \frac{4-2y}{8} \implies 8 = (4-x)(2-y) \implies xy - 2x - 4y = 0$$

Exercises

1. What type of geometric structure does the equation $y = \cos x \, \cos(x+2) - \cos^2(x+1)$ represent?

2. Show that the locus of the point that divides the line joining $A\,(1,0)$ and $(2\cos\theta, 2\sin\theta)$ internally in the ratio $2:3$ for all θ is a circle. Can you draw a tangent from A to this circle?

3. For a non-zero complex number a ($|a| \neq 1$), let P and Q denote the points a and $1/\bar{a}$, respectively. We say that two circles orthogonally intersect each other if the tangents at the point of intersection for the two circles are perpendicular to each other. If C_1 is the unit circle on the complex plane and C_2 is any circle passing through P and Q, prove that C_1 and C_2 orthogonally intersect each other.

4. Let $a, b, c \in \mathbb{R} - \{0\}$. Prove that the straight line $ax + by + c = 0$ passes through the first quadrant if and only if either $ac < 0$ or $bc < 0$.

5. In the xy-plane, denote the point $(3,4)$ as P. Let Q be the point $(x, \sqrt{25-x^2})$, and let $M(x)$ be the slope of the straight line joining P and Q. What is the value of $\lim_{x \to 3} M(x)$?

6. Consider a rectangle $OACB$ with the two axes as two sides, and with the length OA being four times the width OB. A circle is drawn passing through the points B and C and touching OA at its midpoint, thus dividing the rectangle into three parts. Find the ratio of the areas of these three parts.

7. Find the vertices of the two right-angled triangles, each having area 18 square units and such that the point $(2,4)$ lies on the hypotenuse and the other two sides are formed by the x and y axes.

8. Let PQ be a line segment of a fixed length L with its two ends P and Q sliding along the X-axis and Y-axis, respectively. Complete the rectangle $OPRQ$, where O is the

origin. Show that the locus of the foot of the perpendicular drawn from R on PQ is given by
$$x^{2/3} + y^{2/3} = L^{2/3}.$$

9. Define a function $f : \mathbb{R} \to \mathbb{R}$, such that $f(x) = x^2 + ax + b$ for two real numbers a, b. If the graph of f intersects the two axes in three distinct points, prove that the circle passing through these three points also passes through $(0, 1)$.

10. Consider the function $f : \mathbb{R} \times \mathbb{R} \to \mathbb{R}$ defined as $f(x, y) = x^2 + y^2$. Let D denote the region enclosed by $y \leqslant x/2, y \geqslant -x/2$ and $x \leqslant y^2 + 1$. What is the maximum value of $f(x, y)$ for $(x, y) \in D$?

11. Consider a point $P = (a, b)$ inside the parabola $y^2 = 4x$. If F is the focus of the parabola, deduce the point Q on the parabola such that $FQ + QP$ is minimum. Further prove that the normal to the parabola at Q bisects the angle FQP.

12. Let Γ_1, Γ_2 be two circles centred at the points $(a, 0), (b, 0)$, $0 < a < b$ and having radii a, b, respectively. Let Γ be the circle touching Γ_1 externally and Γ_2 internally. Find the locus of the centre of Γ.

13. Tangents are drawn to a given circle from a point on a given straight line, which does not meet the given circle. Prove that the locus of the midpoint of the chord joining the two points of contact of the tangents with the circle is a circle.

14. Three circles C_1, C_2 and C_3 with radii 1, 2 and 3, respectively, touch each other externally. The centres of C_1 and C_2 lie on the x-axis, while C_3 touches them from the top. Find the ordinate of the centre of the circle that lies in the region enclosed by the circles C_1, C_2 and C_3 and touches all of them.

15. Consider a triangle ABC in the xy-plane. Find the locus of all points M that satisfy
$$\text{Area}(ABM) = \text{Area}(ACM).$$

16. Let $ABCD$ be a square with two adjacent vertices A and B on the positive x-axis and positive y-axis, respectively. If $C = (u, v)$ lies on the first quadrant, find the area of $ABCD$ in terms of u and v.

17. Find the coordinates of the point at which the normal to the parabola $y^2 = 4x$ at the point $(t^2, 2t)$ meets the curve again. Hence or otherwise, deduce the locus of the midpoints of all normal chords of the parabola.

18. Consider an infinite sequence of circles $\{C_n\}$, all of which are in the positive quadrant of the XY-plane. Assume that the sequence has strictly decreasing radii, each C_n touches both the axes, and for all $n \geqslant 1$, the circle C_{n+1} touches C_n externally. If the radius of C_1 is 10 cm, show that the sum of the areas of all the circles in the sequence is $\dfrac{25\pi}{3\sqrt{2}-4}$ sq. cm.

19. Consider four points $E = (0,0)$, $F = (0,-1)$, $G = (1,-1)$, $H = (1,0)$. Find all the points $A = (p,q)$ with $p > 0, q > 0$ so that E, F, G, H are the midpoints of, respectively, the sides AB, BC, CD, DA of a convex quadrilateral $ABCD$.

20. Let P and Q be two points on the rectangular hyperbola $xy = c^2$. Suppose that the line PQ meets the x-axis at N. If M is the midpoint of PQ and O is the origin, prove that $OM = MN$.

Hints

1. We can write $\cos x \cos(x+2)$ as $\cos((x+1) - 1)\cos((x+1) + 1)$ and simplify the given expression as $y = -\sin^2 1$. Hence, the given equation represents a straight line parallel to the x-axis at a distance $\sin^2 1$ units below the origin.

2. If the coordinates of the point are (h,k), then for all θ
$$h = \frac{3 + 4\cos\theta}{5}, \frac{4\sin\theta}{5}$$

   Eliminating θ from the above, one can show that the locus is $(5x-3)^2 + (5y)^2 = 16$, that is, it is a circle with centre at $(3/5, 0)$ and with radius $4/5$. It is also easy to find that $(1,0)$ lies inside the circle, and hence, one cannot draw a tangent from A to this circle.

3. Recall that two circles of radii r_1 and r_2 whose centres are a distance d apart are orthogonal if $r_1^2 + r_2^2 = d^2$. Therefore, if the centre of C_2 is c, the radius of the circle C_2 is $|c - a| = |c - 1/\bar{a}|$, thereby indicating that the two circles would orthogonally intersect each other if $1 + |c - a|^2 = |c|^2$. Using the properties of complex numbers, one can show that the above takes place if $a\bar{c} + c\bar{a} = 1 + |a|^2$. This can be proved by starting from $|c - a| = |c - 1/\bar{a}|$ and writing

$$(c-a)\overline{(c-a)} = \left(c - \frac{1}{\bar{a}}\right)\overline{\left(c - \frac{1}{\bar{a}}\right)}$$

4. Since $c \neq 0$, for any point (x,y) on the line, we must have $acx + bcy < 0$. Now, the line passes through the first quadrant if and only if there is a point (x,y) with positive coordinates that satisfy the above condition. Clearly, when both x, y are positive, in order to satisfy the above condition, at least one of acx and bcy must be negative. Thus, the necessary condition is either $ac < 0$ or $bc < 0$. To prove that it is a sufficient condition, write the equation as $y = -ax/b - c/b$, and analyze the signs of the slope and the intercept based on the values of a, b, c.

Coordinate Geometry

5. $M(x)$ is the slope of the line PQ, that is, $M(x) = (\sqrt{25-x^2}-4)/(x-3)$. Note that both numerator and denominator approach 0 as $x \to 3$ and both are differentiable functions. Then, use L'Hospital Rule to show that $\lim_{x \to 3} M(x) = -3/4$.

6. Without loss of generality, suppose the length of OB to be 1 unit. Then, the coordinates of the four vertices are $O = (0,0)$, $A = (4,0)$, $C = (4,1)$, $B = (0,1)$. Let the centre of the circle be $P = (h,k)$. Using $PB = PC$, argue that $h = 2$. Next, since the circle touches the x-axis, argue that the equation of the circle is $(x-2)^2 + (y-k)^2 = k^2$. Further, as $(0,1)$ lies on the circle, one can show that $k = 2.5$.

    To find the required ratio, one has to find the three areas OBD, BDC and DAC. It is easy to note that $DAC = OBD$, and $BDC = 4 - OBD - DAC$. Now, solve the integral

    $$OBD = \int_0^2 \left[2.5 - \sqrt{(2.5)^2 - (x-2)^2} \right] dx$$

    to obtain the values of each area, which would subsequently lead to the answer.

7. Suppose the two vertices are $(0,a)$ and $(b,0)$. Since $(2,4)$ lies on the hypotenuse, a,b are positive. Observing that the equation of the hypotenuse is $y - a = -ax/b$ and that $(2,4)$ lies on this line, one can show that $a^2 - 18a + 72 = 0$. Straightforward calculations then show that the vertices of the two right-angled triangles are $(0,0), (0,6), (0,6)$ and $(0,0), (0,12), (3,0)$.

8. Let the coordinate of P be $(a,0)$. Then, $Q = (0, \sqrt{L^2 - a^2})$, $R = (a, \sqrt{L^2 - a^2})$, and the slope of the line PQ is $-\sqrt{L^2 - a^2}/a$. Clearly, the equation of the perpendicular from R on PQ is

    $$y - \sqrt{L^2 - a^2} = \frac{a}{\sqrt{L^2 - a^2}} (x - a),$$

    while the equation of PQ is

    $$y = -\frac{\sqrt{L^2 - a^2}}{a}(x - a)$$

    Solving the above two equations, we can find that the two lines intersect at

    $$y = (L^2 - a^2)^{3/2}/L^2, \quad x = \frac{a^3}{L^2}$$

    It is now straightforward to find the locus by eliminating a from the above system of equations.

9. Since the graph of f intersects the two axes at three distinct points, one can say that $b \neq 0$ and that the equation has two distinct real roots, that is, $a^2 - 4b > 0$. In that

case, the three points of intersection are

$$A = (0,b),\ B = \left(\frac{-a+\sqrt{a^2-4b}}{2}, 0\right),\ C = \left(\frac{-a-\sqrt{a^2-4b}}{2}, 0\right)$$

Now, we can argue that the circumradius is of the form $O = (-a/2, k)$. Then, use $OA^2 = OB^2$ to show that the equation of the circle passing through the three points is

$$\left(x+\frac{a}{2}\right)^2 + \left(y-\frac{1+b}{2}\right)^2 = \frac{a^2}{4} + \frac{(1-b)^2}{4}$$

The above automatically indicates that the circle passes through $(0,1)$.

10. Note that $y = x/2$ and $y = -x/2$ are straight lines while $x = y^2 + 1$ is a parabola, and that $f(x,y)$ denotes the distance of a point (x,y) from the origin in a plane. Draw the graphs of the three equations to find the region D, and observe that $\max f(x,y)$ is attained for the points at which the straight lines intersect the parabola. Solving the two systems of equations, one can see that $f(x,y)$ is maximized for $(x,y) = (1,2)$ or $(-1,-2)$, and that the corresponding maximum value is 5.

11. Let N be the foot of the perpendicular drawn from Q to the directrix of the parabola. Using $FQ = QN$, one can argue that $FQ + QP$ is minimum if P, Q, N lie on the same line. Thus, Q is the point at which the perpendicular from P to the directrix intersects the parabola. The coordinate of Q can then be written as $(b^2/4, b)$. For the second part, show that the equation of the normal at Q (let us denote it as QZ) must have slope $m = -b/2$. Then, find out the slopes of FQ and PQ, and show that $\tan \angle FQZ = \tan \angle PQZ$, which subsequently implies that QZ is the bisector of $\angle FQP$.

12. Denote $(a,0), (b,0)$ as A, B, let the centre of Γ be O, and let its radius be r. Then, $OA = a + r$, $OB = b - r$, which implies $OA + OB = a + b$. Recall that the locus of a point whose sum of distances from two given points is constant is an ellipse and those two points are the two foci of that ellipse. Thus, from the above condition, we can say that the locus of the centre of Γ is an ellipse with foci at A and B.

13. Without loss of generality, consider the circle $x^2 + y^2 = 1$ and the straight line $y = mx + c$. Suppose that tangents are drawn from the point $P = (p,q)$ to the circle. Let the points of contact at the circle be denoted as $A = (x_1, y_1)$ and $B = (x_2, y_2)$. Then, we can prove (see Question 14 in Solved Examples) that the equations of PA, PB, AB are as follows:

$$PA: xx_1 + yy_1 = 1,\ PB: xx_2 + yy_2 = 1,\ AB: px + qy = 1$$

Let the midpoint of AB be $M = (h,k)$. Show that the equation $hx + ky = h^2 + k^2$ represents the line passing through two points on the circle for which the midpoint is M. Subsequently, one can argue that the equation of AB can also be written as $hx + ky = h^2 + k^2$. Therefore

$$\frac{p}{h} = \frac{mp+c}{k} = \frac{1}{h^2+k^2},$$

from which one can deduce that the locus of M is given by the equation $c(x^2 + y^2) + mx - y = 0$.

14. First, observe that the ordinate of the circle that lies in the enclosed region will be the same, irrespective of the centre of C_1. So, without loss of generality, assume that C_1 is centred at the origin. Since the three circles touch each other externally, the distance between the centres of two circles is the sum of their radii. As the centre of C_2 lies on the x-axis, using the information of the radii, one can argue that C_2 is centred at $(3,0)$. Further, if the centre of C_3 is (h,k), we can also write $h^2 + k^2 = 16$, $(h-3)^2 + k^2 = 25$. Subsequently, the solution would be $h = 0, k = 4$.

Now, assume that the coordinates of the centre of the circle that lies in the region enclosed by the three circles and touches all of them are (p,q), and let the radius be r units. Then, we can obtain the following system of equations:

$$p^2 + q^2 = (1+r)^2, \quad (p-3)^2 + q^2 = (2+r)^2, \quad p^2 + (q-4)^2 = (3+r)^2$$

Solve the above to show that the ordinate of the centre of the circle is $\frac{20}{23}$.

15. Design the coordinate axes in such a way that the vertices of the triangle ABC are $A = (0,0)$, $B = (r,s)$, $C = (0,t)$. Suppose that the coordinated of M are (x,y). Clearly, r,s,t,x,y are all positive. Next, use the formula for the area of a triangle using coordinates to show that the given condition leads to $|ry - xs| = xt$. Subsequently, argue that the locus of the point M is a straight line.

16. Let $A = (a,0)$, $B = (0,b)$, thereby implying that the length of the side of the square is $\sqrt{a^2 + b^2}$. Note that the slope of AB is $(-b/a)$, and therefore, the slope of BC must be a/b. Then, for the line BC, using r as the distance between B and C and considering that $\tan\theta = a/b$, use the parametric form of a straight line and write the equation of BC as

$$\frac{\sqrt{a^2+b^2}(x-0)}{b} = \frac{\sqrt{a^2+b^2}(y-b)}{a} = \sqrt{a^2+b^2}$$

Since the above line passes through (u,v), it is easy to argue that $u = b$, $v = a+b$. Hence, the area of the square is $a^2 + b^2 = (v-u)^2 + u^2$.

17. First, show that the slope of the normal at the point $(t^2, 2t)$ is $(-t)$. Then, the equation of the normal is $tx + y = t^3 + 2t$. To find out the coordinates of the point (call it Q) at which the normal meets the curve again, substitute $y = t^3 + 2t - tx$ in $y^2 = 4x$, note

that $x = t^2$ is a solution to this equation, and obtain that in the other solution, that is, the x coordinate of the other point of intersection is $(t^2+2)^2/t^2$. Now, let the midpoint of the normal chord be $M = (h,k)$. Then

$$h = \frac{t^4+2t^2+2}{t^2}, \quad k = -\frac{2}{t},$$

which subsequently implies $t^2 = 4/k^2$. Substituting this expression of t^2 in the first equation, we can obtain the required locus.

18. Suppose that the radius of the circle C_n is r_n. Consider C_{n+1} and C_n and aim to find a recursion relation. First, note that any circle touching both the axes has the same intercepts in both the axes, and therefore, the centres lie on the straight line $y = x$. So, the coordinates of the two centres are $A = (r_{n+1}, r_{n+1}), B = (r_n, r_n)$. Then, using the fact that the two circles touch each other externally, argue that $AB = r_{n+1} + r_n$ and $(r_{n+1}-r_n)^2 + (r_{n+1}-r_n)^2 = (r_{n+1}+r_n)^2$. Subsequently, show that $r_{n+1} = r_n(3-\sqrt{8}) = r_1(3-\sqrt{8})^n$. Next, apply the concept of infinite geometric series to compute the required answer.

19. Using the given conditions, one can show that $B = (-p,-q)$, $C = (p, q-2)$ and $D = (2-p,-q)$. Therefore, the diagonals of the quadrilateral, that is, AC and BD, lie on the straight lines $x = p$ and $y = -q$, respectively. Moreover, in order for $ABCD$ to be a convex quadrilateral, A,C must lie on two different sides of the diagonal BD and B,D should also lie on two different sides of AC. Using this, argue that $A = (p,q)$ must satisfy $0 < p, q < 1$ and that would allow for a convex quadrilateral $ABCD$ with the required conditions.

20. Use the parametric form of a rectangular hyperbola and write $P = (ct_1, c/t_1)$, $Q = (ct_2, c/t_2)$. Then

$$M = \left(\frac{ct_1+ct_2}{2}, \frac{ct_1+ct_2}{2t_1t_2}\right)$$

Next, find the equation of the line PQ and show that $N = (ct_1+ct_2, 0)$. The required result then follows immediately from computing the values of OM and MN.

7
Probability and Statistics

> *"The most important questions of life are, for the most part,
> really only problems of probability."*
>
> –Pierre-Simon Laplace

Over the last couple of decades, probability and statistics have become instrumental parts of many disciplines, ranging from economics to social sciences, archaeology to medicine, sports to political sciences, and so on.

This chapter aims to provide basic knowledge about probability and statistics and to build the foundation for pursuing more advanced theory in undergraduate studies. Note that problems related to probability are commonly encountered in ISI, CMI and engineering entrance tests, while statistics problems can appear in the IIT-JEE and AIEEE exams.

KEY RESULTS

In probability, we treat a random phenomenon as the outcome of an experiment in a very general sense. All possible outcomes constitute a set known as the sample space (Ω). Any subset of Ω is called an event. We assign probability, that is, a number in the closed interval $[0,1]$, to every event and it denotes the likelihood of the occurrence of the event. For example, the most common probability experiment is the one where we consider tossing a coin. Clearly, the outcomes are heads and tails. We can denote them as H/T or can assign numbers such as 1 and 0 (you can interpret it as the number of heads in one toss). Thus, $\Omega = \{0,1\}$ and any subset of it is an event. Further, if we assume that the probability of getting a head is 0.3 (it indicates that the coin is not fair), then the entire probability distribution can be written as

$$P(\phi) = 0,\ P(\{0\}) = 0.7,\ P(\{1\}) = 0.3,\ P(\{0,1\}) = 1$$

The empty set is commonly denoted by ϕ and is known as the null event, while the full sample space is called a sure event. Typically, the notation $P(A)$ is used to quantify the probability of the occurrence of an event A. Adopting set theoretic notations, we use A^c, $A \cup B$ and $A \cap B$ to indicate the complement, union and intersection of events. Now, formally, the following provides the definition of a probability function.

Definition 7.1 (Fundamental Laws of Probability): A probability function P on a finite or countably infinite sample space Ω assigns to each event A in Ω a number $P(A) \in [0,1]$ such that the following are satisfied:

- $P(\Omega) = 1, P(\phi) = 0$
- $P(A^c) = 1 - P(A)$ for all A
- If $\{A_1, A_2, \cdots\}$ is a countably infinite or finite collection of disjoint events, then $P(A_1 \cup A_2 \cdots) = P(A_1) + P(A_2) + \cdots$

In probability, set theoretic results and combinatorial arguments are used extensively. In fact, the most common way to calculate the probability of an event is to find the number of favourable outcomes for the event, and take its ratio with respect to the total number of possible outcomes. A few other key definitions and results are listed below.

Definition 7.2 (Equally Likely and Mutually Exclusive Events): All outcomes of an experiment are said to be equally likely if the probability of each outcome is the same. Two events are said to be mutually exclusive or disjoint if they cannot appear together. In set theoretic notations, if A and B are mutually exclusive, $P(A \cap B) = 0$.

> **Useful Tip:** The concept of equally likely events is directly connected to the concept of random sampling in statistics.

Theorem 7.1 (De Morgan's Laws): For any two events A and B, $(A \cup B)^c = A^c \cap B^c$ and $(A \cap B)^c = A^c \cup B^c$.

Theorem 7.2: For any two events A and B, we have $P(A \cup B) = P(A) + P(B) - P(A \cap B)$. A generalization of this result is given by the principle of inclusion-exclusion, which states that for n number of events $A_1, A_2, \ldots, A_n$,

$$P\left(\bigcup_{i=1}^{n} A_i\right) = \sum_{k=1}^{n} (-1)^k \sum_{\substack{i_1,\ldots,i_k=1 \\ i_1 < \cdots < i_k}}^{n} P\left(\bigcap_{j=1}^{k} A_{i_j}\right)$$

Sometimes we want to calculate the probability of an event A given that an event C has already occurred. This is termed conditional probability. This also leads to the notion of independent events.

Definition 7.3: Assume that C is an event such that $P(C) > 0$. Then, the conditional probability of A given C is given by

$$P(A|C) = \frac{P(A \cap C)}{P(C)}$$

Definition 7.4 (Independence): An event A is said to be independent of an event B if $P(A|B) = P(A)$ and $P(B|A) = P(B)$, which is equivalent to $P(A \cap B) = P(A)P(B)$. More generally, a collection of events $A_1, A_2, \cdots, A_m$ is said to be independent if and only if

$$P\left(\bigcap_{k=1}^{m} A_k\right) = \prod_{k=1}^{m} P(A_i)$$

The above statement also holds if the A_ks are replaced by their complements.

Theorem 7.3 (The Law of Total Probability): Suppose that $C_1, C_2, \cdots, C_m$ are disjoint events such that $C_1 \cup C_2 \cup \cdots \cup C_m = \Omega$. Then, the probability of an arbitrary event A can be written as

$$P(A) = \sum_{k=1}^{m} P(A \cap C_k) = \sum_{k=1}^{m} P(A|C_k)P(C_k)$$

Theorem 7.4 (Bayes' Rule): Suppose that $C_1, C_2, \cdots, C_m$ are disjoint events such that $C_1 \cup C_2 \cup \cdots \cup C_m = \Omega$. Then, the conditional probability of C_i given an arbitrary event A can be written as

$$P(C_i|A) = \frac{P(A|C_i)P(C_i)}{\sum_{k=1}^{m} P(A|C_k)P(C_k)}$$

> **Useful Tip:** Conditional probability, independence and Bayes' rule are immensely useful concepts for solving probability problems.

We next turn our attention to the concept of random variables, which forms the backbone of advanced probability theory. A random variable, in the naivest sense, is a numerical description of the outcome of an experiment. Refer to the coin toss example we discussed at the beginning. There, a random variable is the number of heads in the random experiment of a single toss of a coin. Random variables can be categorical (for example, the quality of a student), discrete (for example, the number of heads in 10 tosses, the size of a household) or continuous (for example, the price of petrol, the time taken to finish this book). At this level, the focus would be restricted to discrete random variables.

Definition 7.5 (Discrete Random Variable): For a sample space Ω, a discrete random variable is defined as a function $X : \Omega \to \mathbb{R}$ that takes on a finite or countably infinite number of values.

Definition 7.6 (Probability Distribution, Expectation and Variance): Consider a discrete random variable X taking values in the set $\{a_1, a_2, \cdots\}$. Then, the probability distribution of X is given by the probabilities $P(a_1), P(a_2), \cdots$, such that they satisfy the fundamental laws. Further, the expectation, also known as the population mean, of X is defined as

$$E(X) = \sum_k a_k P(a_k)$$

Along similar lines, the population variance is defined as

$$\text{Var}(X) = \sum_k (a_k - E(X))^2 P(a_k),$$

and the population standard deviation is defined as $\sqrt{\text{Var}(x)}$.

Theorem 7.5: Some important properties of expectation are as follows:

- It is a linear relationship, that is, for any two random variables X, Y and for two real constants a, b, $E(aX + bY) = aE(X) + bE(Y)$.
- If X, Y are two independent random variables, then $E(XY) = E(X)E(Y)$.

> **Useful Tip:** Population mean is a representative value of the centre of the probability distribution, whereas variance is a measure of the spread of the distribution.

For a real dataset, the true probability distribution and the true measures of centre and spread would be unknown. This necessitates the use of statistics, where the objective is often to identify the underlying true distribution and its properties by virtue of a sample of observations.

Definition 7.7 (Sample Mean and Variance): Suppose we have n number of independent observations in the dataset $\{x_1, x_2, \ldots, x_n\}$. Then, the sample mean ($\bar{x}$) and sample variance (S_x^2) are defined as

$$\bar{x} = \frac{1}{n} \sum_{i=1}^{n} x_i, \quad S_x^2 = \frac{1}{n-1} \sum_{i=1}^{n} (x_i - \bar{x})^2$$

The quantity S_x is called the standard deviation of the sample.

As before, $\bar{x}$ and S_x help us in understanding the centre and spread of the sample. There are a few other quantities that are also used to better analyze the centre, spread and shape of a sample.

Definition 7.8: Consider the sample $\{x_1, x_2, \ldots, x_n\}$, with mean $\bar{x}$ and standard deviation S_x.

- The value that appears the most number of times in a sample is called the mode.
- The middlemost value of an ordered sample is known as the median.

- If the sample is sorted in increasing order, the values that divide the dataset into four equal parts are called the quartiles, and they are typically denoted by Q_1, Q_2, Q_3. Note that Q_2 is the median.
- The difference between the maximum and minimum values of a sample is called the range.
- If x_m denotes the median of the sample, then the mean deviation about the mean and the same about the median are, respectively, given by

$$\mathrm{MD}(\bar{x}) = \frac{1}{n} \sum_{i=1}^{n} |x_i - \bar{x}|, \quad \mathrm{MD}(x_m) = \frac{1}{n} \sum_{i=1}^{n} |x_i - x_m|$$

- The coefficient of variation is given by $100 S_x / \bar{x}$. It is a unit-free measure.
- A distribution is symmetric when mean, median and mode are all equal. A measure of asymmetry is given by the quantity $(\bar{x} - \text{mode})/S_x$. It is also known as a measure of skewness.

Useful Tip: Note that median and mode provide ideas about the centre, while the range, quartiles, mean deviation and coefficient of variation are indicative of the spread. Measures of skewness are representative of the shape of a distribution.

Theorem 7.6 (Location–Scale Shift): If we consider a sample $\{y_1, \ldots, y_n\}$ obtained from $\{x_1, \ldots, x_n\}$ by considering the transformation $y_i = a x_i + b$ for all i (a and b are real constants), then the mean and variance of the two samples are related as $\bar{y} = a \bar{x} + b$ and $S_y^2 = a^2 S_x^2$.

Useful Tip: The above result is vital in statistics problems related to change of unit. The reader is further instructed to identify how a location and scale shift would affect the other measures discussed earlier.

Definition 7.9 (Covariance and Correlation): For two random variables X and Y, the population covariance is defined as $\mathrm{Cov}(X,Y) = E[(X - E(X))(Y - E(Y))]$. In a similar fashion, for a sample of paired observations $(x_1, y_1), (x_2, y_2), \ldots, (x_n, y_n)$, the sample covariance is defined as

$$S_{xy} = \frac{1}{n-1} \sum_{i=1}^{n} (x_i - \bar{x})(y_i - \bar{y})$$

The population and sample correlation coefficients are then defined as

$$\mathrm{Cor}(X,Y) = \frac{\mathrm{Cov}(X,Y)}{\sqrt{\mathrm{Var}(X)\,\mathrm{Var}(Y)}}, \quad r_{xy} = \frac{S_{xy}}{S_x S_y}$$

Theorem 7.7: The sample and population correlation coefficients always lie between $[-1,1]$. They take the value ± 1 when the two samples (or the random variables) are perfectly related by the linear function $y_i = ax_i + b$, where a and b are real constants ($a > 0$ leads to coefficient 1 while $a < 0$ corresponds to correlation coefficient -1).

Definition 7.10 (Simple Linear Regression): For bivariate data $(x_1, y_1), (x_2, y_2), \ldots, (x_n, y_n)$, a simple linear regression model assumes that $y_i = \alpha + \beta x_i + \varepsilon_i$ for $i = 1, 2, \ldots, n$, where $\varepsilon_1, \ldots, \varepsilon_n$ are random error terms. Here, y_is are typically denoted as dependent variables and x_is as independent variables. The line $y = \alpha + \beta x$ is called the regression line, where α is the intercept and β is the slope.

Theorem 7.8 (Least Squares Regression): For the simple linear regression model, if we minimize the sum of squared errors with respect to α and β, then the following are obtained:

$$\hat{\beta}_{yx} = \frac{S_{xy}}{S_x^2}, \quad \hat{\alpha}_{yx} = \bar{y} - \hat{\beta}_{yx}\bar{x}$$

The line $y = \hat{\alpha}_{yx} + \hat{\beta}_{yx}x$ is known as the least squares regression line of y on x. An important property is that the regression line always passes through the point with means of the variables, that is, $(\bar{x}, \bar{y})$.

> **Useful Tip:** If we switch the roles of x and y in the simple linear regression model, the new estimates of regression coefficients would be obtained as $\hat{\beta}_{xy} = S_{xy}/S_y^2$, $\hat{\alpha}_{xy} = \bar{x} - \hat{\beta}_{xy}\bar{y}$. The corresponding line is called the regression line of x on y.

Solved Examples

1. In a friendly league, the main and reserve squads of two soccer teams play each other once every week until one of the matches ends in a result (that is, win/loss and not a draw). The probability of a match ending in a result is p. Supposing that the outcomes of the matches between the main and reserve squads are independent and also on different weeks, what is the probability that the league ends in week n?

Solution: The event that the league ends in week n is equivalent to observing draws in the first $(n-1)$ weeks for both matches and observing a result in at least one of the games in the nth week. As the outcomes of the games between the main and reserve squads are independent, the probability that both matches end in a draw in any week is $(1-p)^2$.

Let A denote the event that we observe a draw in the first $(n-1)$ consecutive weeks. The outcomes are independent, and thus, $P(A) = (1-p)^{2(n-1)}$.

Let B denote the event that we observe a result in the nth week. Then, $P(B) = (1-(1-p)^2)$. We are seeking the value of $P(A \cap B)$, that is, the probability that the matches in the first

$(n-1)$ weeks end in draws and there is a result in the nth week. Since events A and B are independent

$$P(A \cap B) = P(A)P(B) = (1-(1-p)^2)(1-p)^{2(n-1)}$$

2. Urn I has 3 red balls and 2 green balls, and urn II contains 1 red ball and 5 green balls. A ball is drawn at random from urn I and placed in urn II. Then, we draw a ball randomly from urn II.

   (a) What is the probability that the ball drawn from urn II is red?

   (b) Given that the ball drawn from urn II is red, what is the probability that the transferred ball was red?

Solution: Let us define the events $T_r = \{$Red ball transferred$\}$, $T_g = \{$Green ball transferred$\}$ and $R = \{$The ball drawn from urn II is red$\}$.

   (a) We want to find $P(R)$, which is equal to $P(R \cap T_g) + P(R \cap T_r)$. Now, applying the concepts of conditional probability, we can obtain

$$P(R) = P(R|T_g)P(T_g) + P(R|T_r)P(T_r) = \left(\frac{1}{6}\right)\left(\frac{2}{5}\right) + \left(\frac{2}{6}\right)\left(\frac{3}{5}\right) = \frac{4}{15}$$

   (b) Here also, we need to use the concepts of conditional probability. Using identical arguments as above, we can obtain

$$P(T_r|R) = \frac{P(T_r \cap R)}{P(R)} = \frac{\frac{2}{6} \times \frac{3}{5}}{\frac{4}{15}} = \frac{3}{4}$$

3. A certain mango variety is grown in two regions (Malda, Murshidabad) in West Bengal. Both areas are infested from time to time with parasites that damage the fruit. Let A be the event that Malda is infested with parasites and B that Murshidabad is infested. Suppose $P(A) = 3/4$, $P(B) = 2/5$ and $P(A \cup B) = 4/5$. If the food inspector detects the parasite in a freight carrying mangoes from Malda, what is the probability that Murshidabad is infested as well?

Solution: We are asked to find the probability $P(B|A)$. Using the concepts of conditional probability, it can be wriiten as $P(A \cap B)/P(A)$. Now

$$P(A \cap B) = P(A) + P(B) - P(A \cup B) = \frac{3}{4} + \frac{2}{5} - \frac{4}{5} = \frac{7}{20}$$

Hence, it is straightforward to find that

$$P(B|A) = \frac{7/20}{3/4} = \frac{7}{15}$$

4. In "Random Walk" school, every student starts at grade 1 and graduates after grade 10. The grade changes take place once a year. A student always moves to grade 2 from grade 1 after 1 year. Whenever students are in grades 2 to 9, they move one grade up or one grade down, each with probability 0.5 after 1 year. The student always graduates 1 year after reaching grade 10. What is the expected number (average number) of years a student takes to graduate in "Random Walk" school after being admitted in grade 1?

Solution: Let S_n be the number of years a student takes to graduate from grade n. Observe that $S_{10} = 1, S_2 = S_1 - 1$. Now, for $2 \leqslant n \leqslant 9$

$$S_n = \frac{S_{n-1} + S_{n+1}}{2} + 1,$$

because at grade n, the student either moves to grade $(n-1)$ or $(n+1)$ with probability 0.5, and with the cost of 1 year.

Observe that $S_2 = (S_3 + S_1)/2 + 1$, which implies that $S_3 = S_1 - 4$. Continuing in this manner, we obtain the sequence $S_4 = S_1 - 9, S_5 = S_1 - 16, \ldots, S_{10} = S_1 - 81$. Notice that the corresponding recursion equation can be written as

$$S_n = S_1 - (n-1)^2$$

Hence, for $n = 10$, since the assumption guarantees that $S_{10} = 1$, we can write $S_1 = 81 + 1 = 82$, and thus, the expected number of years a student takes to graduate from the school after being admitted is 82.

> **Useful Tip:** Recall the notions of recursion relation used in earlier chapters. In the above problem, we identify the nature of the recursion relation and utilize it to obtain the answer. As an exercise, rework the above problem assuming that the probability to move one grade up or one grade down are not equal.

5. Let $S = \{(x,y) : x, y \in \mathbb{Z}, |x| \leqslant 5, |y| \leqslant 5\}$, where $\mathbb{Z}$ is the set of integers. We pick three random points A, B, C with replacement and independently from S, and construct the triangle ABC. Let M denote the area of the (can be degenerate) triangle ABC. What is the expected value (average value) of M^2?

Solution: Let $A = (x_1, y_1), B = (x_2, y_2), C = (x_3, y_3)$. Then, by the Shoelace Theorem in coordinate geometry, the area of the triangle ABC is

$$M = \frac{1}{2}(x_1 y_2 + x_2 y_3 + x_3 y_1 - x_2 y_1 - x_3 y_2 - x_1 y_3)$$

Squaring the above equation

$$M^2 = \frac{1}{4}(x_1^2 y_2^2 + x_2^2 y_3^2 + x_3^2 y_1^2 + x_2^2 y_1^2 + x_3^2 y_2^2 + x_1^2 y_3^2 + \text{cross product terms})$$

Note that the cross-product terms involve at least one variable that is linear, for example, $2x_1^2y_2y_3$, $2x_1x_2y_1y_2$, etc. Next, observe that $E(x_i) = E(y_i) = 0$ for all i, because they are chosen uniformly from $\{-5, -4, \ldots, 0, \ldots, 4, 5\}$, a set of integers symmetric around 0. Moreover, since x_i, y_is are chosen independently and since there is at least one linear term, any cross-product term must have expectation 0. For example

$$E(x_1^2 y_2 y_3) = E(x_1^2)E(y_2)E(y_3) = 0$$

Noting that all points are chosen identically and independently, we can write

$$E(M^2) = \frac{1}{4}\left[E(x_1^2y_2^2 + x_2^2y_3^2 + x_3^2y_1^2 + x_2^2y_1^2 + x_3^2y_2^2 + x_1^2y_3^2)\right] = \frac{6}{4}E(x_1^2y_2^2) = \frac{3}{2}E(x_1^2)^2$$

Now

$$E(x_1^2) = \frac{(-5)^2 + (-4)^2 + \cdots + 4^2 + 5^2}{11} = \frac{2 \times 55}{11} = 10$$

Combining the above, the expected value of M^2 can be computed to be 150.

6. Positive integers a, b, possibly equal, are chosen independently and randomly (that is, all numbers can be chosen with equal probability) from the set $\{n : n \in \mathbb{N}, n \mid 400\}$, where $\mathbb{N}$ is the set of natural numbers. What is the probability that $gcd(a,b) = 1$ and $lcm(a,b) = 400$.

Solution: Note that any divisor of 400 is of the form $2^a 5^b$, where $0 \leq a \leq 4$, $0 \leq b \leq 2$. Thus, the set of positive divisors of 400 has $(4+1)(2+1) = 15$ numbers. Clearly, in order to ensure $gcd(a, b) = 1$, a and b cannot have 2 or 5 as their common factors. Further, since $lcm(a, b)$ is desired to be 1, the choice must be of the form $(a, 400/a)$.

From the above, one can argue that the possible choices that satisfy the required conditions are $(1, 400)$, $(2^4, 5^2)$, and their ordered pairs. That is, only four combinations are favourable.

Now, since a, b are chosen independently and randomly, there are $15^2 = 225$ possible combinations, each with equal probability of being selected. Hence, the probability that $gcd(a,b) = 1$ and $lcm(a,b) = 400$ is $4/225$.

7. We have a special sequence of five real numbers 20, 100, 200, 60 and x, whose average (arithmetic mean) is equal to the median. Find the median of all the possible values of x.

Solution: The mean of the numbers in the given sequence is $(380 + x)/5$. The numbers in this sequence (excluding x) in order are $20, 60, 100, 200$. Obviously, there are three possible cases.

Case 1 : $x \leq 60$. Here, the median is 60 and solving $(380 + x)/5 = 60$, we obtain $x = -80$.

Case 2 : $60 \leqslant x < 100$. Here, the median is x. Once again, solving $(380+x)/5 = x$ gives us $x = 95$.

Case 3 : $x \geqslant 100$. In this case, the median is 100. Then, equating the mean and median, we get $x = 120$.

Combining the above, the median of the possible values of x is found out to be 95.

8. On an entrance exam, 10% of the students got 70 points, 25% got 80 points, 20% got 85 points, 15% got 90 points, and the rest got 95 points. Find the difference between the mean and the median score on this exam.

Solution: First, notice that the remaining 30% of students got 95 points. Since 15% got 90 points, it is clear that the 45th to 65th percentile of numbers is 85. This makes the median 85.

The mean, on the other hand, can be calculated as

$$\frac{70(10) + 80(25) + 85(20) + 90(15) + 95(30)}{100} = \frac{1720}{20} = 86$$

The difference between the mean and median, therefore, is 1.

9. The game of backgammon involves a six-faced die inscribed with the numbers $2, 2^2, 2^3, 2^4, 2^5$ and 2^6, respectively. Let a, b, c, d be the values of four consecutive and independent rolls of the die. Find the probability of $\frac{a+b}{c+d}$ being the average of $\frac{a}{c}$ and $\frac{b}{d}$?

Solution: Let us first work out the conditions required for $\frac{a+b}{c+d}$ to be the average of $\frac{a}{c}$ and $\frac{b}{d}$. Note that the condition can be written as

$$\frac{a+b}{c+d} = \frac{ad+bc}{2cd} \implies 2acd + 2bcd = acd + bc^2 + ad^2 + bcd$$

The above simplifies to $acd + bcd - bc^2 - ad^2 = 0$, which can be factorized as

$$(ad - bc)(d - c) = 0$$

Therefore, either $ad = bc$ or $d = c$. Let us denote these events as $E_1 = \{ad = bc\}, E_2 = \{d = c\}$. We want to find $P(E_1 \cup E_2)$.

The expression ad or bc can take values of the form 2^j, for $j = 2, 3, \ldots, 12$. Since all faces are equally likely, it is easy to argue that these values are obtained with probabilities $\frac{1}{36}, \frac{2}{36}, \frac{3}{36}, \frac{4}{36}, \frac{5}{36}, \frac{6}{36}, \frac{5}{36}, \frac{4}{36}, \frac{3}{36}, \frac{2}{36}, \frac{1}{36}$, respectively.

On the other hand, ad and bc are obtained independently. So

$$P(E_1) = \sum_{j=2}^{12} P(ad = 2^j)P(bc = 2^j) = \frac{1^2 + 2^2 + \cdots + 6^2 + 5^2 + \ldots + 1^2}{36^2} = \frac{146}{1296}$$

For the other event, it is easy to argue that $P(E_2) = P(\{c = d\}) = 1/6$. Further

$$P(E_1 \cap E_2) = P(\{ad = bc\} \cap \{c = d\}) = P(\{a = b, c = d\}) = \frac{1}{36}$$

Hence, using the law of probability, we obtain

$$P(E_1 \cup E_2) = \frac{146}{1296} + \frac{1}{6} - \frac{1}{36} = \frac{163}{648}$$

10. Bob and Alice throw two standard dice, one each, independently. Alice gets the numbers A (first throw) and B (second throw) and plots the line $Ax + By = 2020$. Similarly, Bob gets C and D and then draws the line $Cx + Dy = 2021$. What is the probability that the two lines are parallel?

Solution: The slope of Alice's line is $(-A/B)$ and the slope of Bob's line is $(-C/D)$. In the event of two lines being parallel, the slopes must be equal, and one should get $AD = BC$. Now, A, B, C, D are all numbers from independent dice throws and can take values $1, \ldots, 6$ with probability $1/6$.

	1	2	3	4	5	6
1	1	2	3	4	5	6
2	2	4	6	8	10	12
3	3	6	9	12	15	18
4	4	8	12	16	20	24
5	5	10	15	20	25	30
6	6	12	18	24	30	36

In the above table, we present the possible values of AD or BC. We see 5 numbers $(1, 9, 16, 25,$ and $36)$ appear once each, 10 numbers $(2, 3, 5, 8, 10, 15, 18, 20, 24,$ and $30)$ appear 2 times each, 1 number (4) that appears 3 times, and 2 numbers $(6$ and $12)$ that appear 4 times each. Hence

$$P(AD = BC) = 5\left(\frac{1}{36}\right)^2 + 10\left(\frac{2}{36}\right)^2 + 1\left(\frac{3}{36}\right)^2 + 2\left(\frac{4}{36}\right)^2 = \frac{43}{648},$$

and that is the required answer.

Useful Tip: Enumerating all possible scenarios is often convenient and the easiest way to solve probability problems when the sample space is a small discrete set.

11. A tick walks randomly on the faces of a cube. From one face, the tick moves to four of its neighbouring faces with equal probability. What is the expected number of steps that the tick needs to take to reach the opposite face of its starting location?

Solution: Let $A_1, A_2, A_3, A_4, A_5, A_6$ be the six faces of the cube, with (A_1, A_6), (A_3, A_4), and (A_2, A_5) being the pairs of opposite faces.

Without loss of generality, assume that the tick starts at A_1 and that we want to calculate the expected number of steps it needs to take to reach A_6. Let us denote u as the expected number of steps for the tick to reach A_6 from A_1 and v as the expected number of steps for the tick to reach A_6 from A_2. By symmetry, v is also the expected number of steps for the tick to reach A_6 from A_3 or A_4 or A_5.

Starting from A_1, the tick will be at either A_2 or A_3 or A_4 or A_5 after one step. Hence, $u = 1 + v$. Similarly, from A_2, the tick can move to A_1 with probability $1/4$, to A_3 or A_4 with probability $1/2$, and to A_6 with probability $1/4$. Subsequently, we can argue that the expected number of steps the tick needs to take to reach A_6 from A_2 is $(u/4 + v/2 + 1)$. Since this is equal to v, we obtain $u = 2v - 4$.

The two equations $u = 1 + v$ and $u = 2v - 4$ lead to the solution $u = 6, v = 5$. Hence, the expected number of steps that the tick needs to take to reach its opposite face is 6.

12. If we pick a random element from the set $S = \{(b,c) : |b|, |c| \leqslant 6\}$, what is the probability that the two roots of the quadratic $x^2 + bx + c$ are consecutive integers?

Solution: If the quadratic $x^2 + bx + c$ has consecutive integers as roots, then there exists an integer a such that

$$(x^2 + bx + c) = (x - a)(x - (a+1)) = x^2 - (2a+1)x + a(a+1)$$

Equating the coefficients of the two expressions, we can say that the value of a must satisfy $|2a+1| \leqslant 6$ and $|a(a+1)| \leqslant 6$ simultaneously. Thus, a can take 6 possible values: $\{-3, -2, -1, 0, 1, 2\}$. Further, for each choice of a, the numbers b and c can be picked in a unique way.

Since the total number of elements in the set S is $13^2 = 169$, and of them 6 possible pairs of (b, c) can satisfy our condition, the required probability is $6/169$.

13. Let A, B and C be three vertices (can be the same) chosen independently from a cube. Should one bet in favour of A, B, C sharing a common face?

Probability and Statistics

Solution: A cube has 8 vertices, and hence, any vertex has probability $1/8$ to be chosen as the first vertex A.

For the next vertex B, we can have four cases: (i) $A = B$ with probability $1/8$, (ii) A and B are connected by an edge and that can occur with probability $3/8$, (iii) A and B are diagonals of a face that occurs with probability $3/8$; and finally, (iv) A and B are diagonally across the cube with probability $1/8$.

Let us now look into the possibilities of the three vertices sharing a common face, under the above cases.

Case (i): If C is chosen as the point diagonally across the cube from A, the three vertices will not share the same face. So, the conditional probability for our event is $7/8$.

Case (ii): The only two points that do not share a common face with A, B is the edge opposite the edge AB across the cube. So, the conditional probability for our event is $6/8$.

Case (iii): In order to satisfy the required condition, C must be one of the the four points that the faces A and B share. The corresponding probability is $4/8$.

Case (iv): There is no possible way C can be chosen so that A, B, C share a common face. Hence, the conditional probability in this case is 0.

Combining the above, the probability that A, B, C are contained in a common face is calculated as
$$8 \times \frac{1}{8}\left(\frac{1}{8} \times \frac{7}{8} + \frac{3}{8} \times \frac{6}{8} + \frac{3}{8} \times \frac{4}{8} + \frac{1}{8} \times 0\right) = \frac{37}{64}$$

Since the above is greater than 0.5, it makes sense to bet in favour of the event.

> **Useful Tip:** A very common problem in the betting context is the birthday problem, which asks for the minimum value of n for which one should bet in favour of the event that in a set of n randomly chosen people, at least two will share a birthday. Try to solve this on your own.

14. In a class, there are k students including Bob. n identical chocolates are distributed among the students one by one, such that at every step, each student is equally likely to get the chocolate. Thus, a student can get more than one chocolate. Compute the probability that Bob gets at least one chocolate. What would be the answer if you assume that the chocolates are distributed at once, and that all distributions are equally likely?

Solution: For the first part, in every turn, every student gets a chocolate with probability $1/k$. Thus, if Bob does not get a chocolate in a turn, it is $(k-1)/k$. Since all chocolates are distributed one by one independently, the overall probability that Bob does not get any chocolate is $(k-1)^n/k^n$. Hence, the probability that Bob gets at least one chocolate is

$$1 - \left(\frac{k-1}{k}\right)^n$$

In the second part, the total number of possible distributions is the same as the number of non-negative integer solutions of the equation $x_1 + x_2 + \ldots + x_k = n$. We know that it is equal to $\binom{n+k-1}{n}$.

Using similar arguments, we can say that the number of distributions in which Bob gets at least one chocolate is the same as the number of non-negative integer solutions to the equation $x_1 + x_2 + \ldots + x_k = n - 1$. This is equal to $\binom{n+k-2}{n-1}$.

Now, since all distributions are equally likely, the required probability is

$$\frac{\binom{n+k-2}{n-1}}{\binom{n+k-1}{n}} = \frac{(n+k-2)!}{(n-1)!(k-1)!} \times \frac{n!(k-1)!}{(n+k-1)!} = \frac{n}{n+k-1}$$

> **Useful Tip:** The above is a direct application of combinatorial results to calculate probability. Similar problems are commonly encountered in the CMI and IIT-JEE entrance tests.

15. Joseph is asked to frame a random mathematical expression containing three single-digit positive integers with an addition sign (+) or a subtraction sign (−) between each pair of adjacent digits. For example, the expression can be $4 + 5 - 3$, with value 6. Each choice of positive digit and sign is equally likely and they are chosen independently. Find the expected value of the expression.

Solution: First, let us look at the possibilities for the sign. For the three chosen digits x, y, z, we can have 4 possible expressions, namely, $x+y+z$, $x+y-z$, $x-y+z$ and $x-y-z$, each being equally likely (with probability 1/4). Thus, the required expected values can be calculated as

$$\frac{1}{4}[E(x+y+z) + E(x+y-z) + E(x-y+z) + E(x-y-z)],$$

which, using the linearity property of expectation, simplifies to

$$\frac{1}{4} \times 4E(x) = E(x)$$

Now, (x, y, z) are chosen from the set $\{1, 2, \cdots, 9\}$, where each number can be picked with equal probability. So, the expected value of x is equal to the average of these nine numbers.

Hence, the expected value of the expression is 5.

16. Professor Gambledoor enrolls in a lottery. Each ticket has 6 distinct numbers chosen from 1 to 49, and written in increasing order. The Professor picks his ticket so that the sum of the base-ten logarithms of his six numbers is an integer. Magically, the integers on the winning ticket also have the same property. What is the probability that Professor Gambledoor holds the winning ticket?

Solution: Remember that the sum of the logarithm of some numbers is the logarithm of the product of those numbers. Thus, the base-ten logarithm of the product of six integers in the winning ticket (and also in the Professor's ticket) is an integer.

In order to ensure that the above occurs, every number should be of the form $2^a 5^b$. Let us then denote the six numbers as $n_i = 2^{a_i} 5^{b_i}$, which implies that the product is of the form

$$2^{\sum_{i=1}^{6} a_i} 5^{\sum_{i=1}^{6} b_i} = 10^{\sum_{i=1}^{6} b_i} 5^{\sum_{i=1}^{6}(a_i - b_i)}$$

Clearly, we want to choose the integers such that $\sum_{i=1}^{6}(a_i - b_i) = 0$.

The possible numbers from 1 to 49 that are of the form $2^a 5^b$ are 1, 2, 4, 5, 8, 10, 16, 20, 25, 32, 40 and the corresponding values of $(a - b)$ are $0, 1, 2, -1, 3, 0, 4, 1, -2, 5, 2$. Since the numbers are distinct, the only possible choices for the six values of $(a - b)$ to satisfy $\sum_{i=1}^{6}(a_i - b_i) = 0$ are $-2, -1, 0, 0, 1, 2$.

Among these possible values, 0 appears twice and there are two choices only. Similarly, (-1) and (-2) can also be obtained in a unique way. Therefore, the only choice comes from 1 and 2, each of which occurs twice. Clearly, there are $2 \times 2 = 4$ possible choices for the Professor to pick a ticket, and out of that, 1 ticket would be the winning one. Hence, the probability that Professor Gambledoor holds the winning ticket is $1/4$.

17. Bob and Alice play a numbers game. Bob goes first, and randomly selects two numbers (can be equal) from the set $\{1, 2, 3, 4, 5\}$, while Alice randomly selects a number from the set $\{1, 2, \ldots, 10\}$. Alice wins if her number is greater than the sum of the two numbers chosen by Bob. What is the probability that Alice wins?

Solution: Let S denote Bob's sum, and let T denote Alice's number. By symmetry, for $i = 2, 3, \ldots, 10$, $P(S = i) = P(S = 12 - i)$.

If Bob's sum is i, then the probability that Alice's number is larger than i is $(10-i)/10$. Thus, the probability that Alice wins is

$$P(S > T) = \sum_{i=2}^{10} P(T = i) \times \frac{10-i}{10}$$

Using the symmetry argument, we can also write the above sum as

$$P(S > T) = \sum_{i=2}^{10} P(T = 12 - i) \times \frac{10-i}{10} = \sum_{j=2}^{10} P(T = j) \times \frac{j-2}{10}$$

Adding the above two equivalent expressions, we get

$$2P(S > T) = \sum_{i=2}^{10} P(T = i) \times \left(\frac{10-i}{10} + \frac{i-2}{10}\right) = \frac{4}{5} \sum_{i=2}^{10} P(T = i) = \frac{4}{5}$$

Hence, the probability of Alice winning is $2/5$.

18. Select two numbers a and b randomly and independently between 0 and 1. Let c denote their sum. If A, B, C denote the nearest integers to a, b and c, respectively, find the probability that $A + B = C$.

Solution: Consider the unit square with values of a on the x-axis and b on the y-axis. The conditions under which $A + B = C$ holds true are as follows:

(a) If $a + b < 1/2$, then $A = B = C = 0$. Area of the corresponding region is $1/8$.

(b) If $a \geqslant 1/2$ and $b < 1/2$, then $B = 0$ and $A = C = 1$. The corresponding area is $1/4$.

(c) If $a < 1/2$ and $b \geqslant 1/2$, then $A = 0$ and $B = C = 1$. As before, the area is $1/4$.

(d) If $a + b \geqslant 3/2$, then $A = B = 1$ and $C = 2$. The area of this region is $1/8$.

Thus, the total area producing the desired result is $3/4$. Since the area of the unit square is 1, the required probability is $3/4$.

> **Useful Tip:** We use the concept of areas to solve the above problem. In similar exercises related to probability, one can leverage geometric concepts to calculate the area of the favourable region and divide it by the total area. Some more examples are provided below.

19. We choose three random points independently on a circle. Find the probability that all three pairwise distances between the points are less than the radius of the circle?

Solution: Without loss of generality, we consider a unit circle, and refer to each point by the angle (in radians) it makes with the real axis in an Argand diagram. Note that the first point can be chosen anywhere. After that, each point must be chosen $\pi/3$ or less away from each other.

Let x be the amount of radians the second point is away from the first and y be the amount of radians the third point is away from the first. We notice that x and y can take values in $[-\pi, \pi]$. Then, for our condition, we must have

$$|x| \leqslant \frac{\pi}{3}, \ |y| \leqslant \frac{\pi}{3}, \ |x-y| \leqslant \frac{\pi}{3}$$

We can calculate the area bounded by the lines $|x| = \pi/3, |y| = \pi/3$ and $|x-y| = \pi/3$, and obtain it as $\pi^2/3$. On the other hand, the area encompassed by all possible choices of x and y is the region bounded by $|x| \leqslant \pi, |y| \leqslant \pi$, and that is calculated as $(2\pi)^2$.

Thus, the required probability is $\frac{(\pi^2/3)}{(2\pi)^2} = 1/12$.

20. A regular polygon with 100 sides is inscribed in a circle. We want to choose three vertices at random, each choice being equally likely. What is the probability that we can form a right-angled triangle with the three chosen points?

Solution: Let us denote the polygon by $A_1 A_2 \ldots A_{100}$, and suppose that $A_i A_j A_k$ is the triangle formed by the three chosen vertices. There are a total of $\binom{100}{3}$ choices for the triangle.

Under the favourable condition (when the triangle is right angled), without loss of generality, let the right angle be formed at the vertex A_i. We know that the angle formed by a chord at the circumference is half the angle formed by the same chord at the centre. Thus, $A_j A_k$ must be a diameter of the circle.

Since the polygon is 100-sided, A_j, A_k can be chosen in 50 ways. Then, for every such choice, A_i can be chosen in 98 ways. Hence, the probability that a right-angled triangle can be formed from the three chosen points is

$$\frac{50 \times 98}{\binom{100}{3}} = \frac{50 \times 98 \times 3!}{100 \times 99 \times 98} = \frac{1}{33}$$

> **Useful Tip:** A different version of this problem, using a 20-sided polygon, was asked in ISI Admission Test (2017).

21. For each real number $a \in [0,1]$, let us choose two numbers x and y independently at random from the intervals $[0,a]$ and $[0,1]$, respectively. Denote $P(a)$ as the probability that

$$\sin^2(\pi x) + \sin^2(\pi y) > 1.$$

Find the maximum value of $P(a)$.

Solution: We proceed by simplifying the inequality $\sin^2(\pi x) + \sin^2(\pi y) > 1$ as

$$\sin^2(\pi x) > 1 - \sin^2(\pi y) = \cos^2(\pi y)$$

The boundary of this region is given by $\sin(\pi x) = \cos(\pi y)$ and $\sin(\pi x) = -\cos(\pi y)$. This is equivalent to $\sin(\pi x) = \cos(\pi y) = \sin(\pi/2 \pm \pi y)$. Solutions to these equations are

$$y = \frac{1}{2} - x, \quad y = x - \frac{1}{2}, \quad \text{or}$$
$$y = x + \frac{1}{2}, \quad y = \frac{3}{2} - x$$

The region bounded by these lines is the grey shaded region in the figure below.

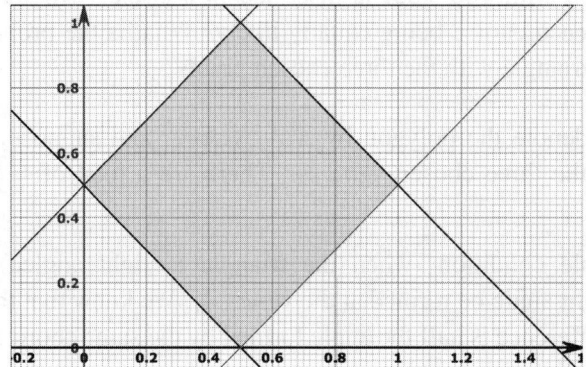

Now, let us call $Q(a)$ as the area of the region intersected by the line $x = a$. Then, $P(a) = Q(a)/a$, that is, the total area for possible (x, y), would be a (it is the rectangle formed by $y = 0$, $y = 1$, $x = 0$ and $x = a$).

Case 1: If $a \leqslant 1/2$, the region for $Q(a)$ consists of a triangle with height a and base $2a$, and hence, $Q(a) = a^2$ and $P(a) = a$. So, the maximum would be at $a = 1/2$.

Case 2: For $a > 1/2$, $Q(a)$ consists of a triangle with area $1/4$ and a trapezoid with bases 1 and $(2 - 2a)$ and height $(a - 1/2)$. Thus

$$P(a) = \frac{1}{a}\left(\frac{1}{4} + \frac{(a - 1/2)(3 - 2a)}{2}\right)$$

After simplifying, we get $P(a) = (-4a^2 + 8a - 2)/4a = 2 - a - 1/2a$. In order to maximize $P(a)$, we need to minimize $a + 1/2a$.

By the AM-GM inequality, $a + 1/2a \geq 2\sqrt{a/2a} = \sqrt{2}$, which can achieve equality when $a = 1/\sqrt{2}$. Hence, in this case, the maximum value of $P(a)$ is $2 - \sqrt{2} > 1/2$, thereby implying that the overall maximum value of $P(a)$ is $2 - \sqrt{2}$.

22. Rashida and Rahul run on a circular track. Rashida runs counter-clockwise and completes a lap every 90 seconds, whereas Rahul runs clockwise and completes a lap every 80 seconds. Both start from the starting line at the same time. At some random time between 10 minutes and 11 minutes after they begin to run, a photographer standing inside the track takes a picture that shows one-fourth of the track, centred on the starting line. Find the probability that both Rashida and Rahul are in the picture.

Solution: After 10 minutes (600 seconds), Rashida would have completed 6 laps and be 30 seconds from completing her seventh lap. Remember that Rashida runs one-fourth of a lap in 22.5 seconds. Hence, she will be in the picture between 18.75 seconds and 41.25 seconds of the tenth minute.

On the other hand, after 10 minutes, Rahul will have completed 7 laps and be 40 seconds from completing his eighth lap. Because Rahul runs one-fourth of a lap in 20 seconds, he will be in the picture between 30 seconds and 50 seconds of the tenth minute.

Taking the intersection of their time ranges, both Rashida and Rahul will be in the picture if it is taken between 30 seconds and 41.25 seconds of the 11th minute. Therefore, the probability that both runners are in the picture is

$$\frac{41.25 - 30}{60} = \frac{3}{16}$$

23. We throw a dart randomly into a rectangular region with vertices $(0,0)$, $(2,0)$, $(2,1)$ and $(0,1)$. What is the probability that the dart lands closer to the origin than to the point $(3,1)$?

Solution: Let us assume that the dart lands at point P. If we assume that P is randomly chosen within the rectangle with vertices $(0,0)$, $(3,0)$, $(3,1)$, $(0,1)$, then the region for P to be closer to the origin than to point $(3,1)$ is exactly $1/2$ of the area of the rectangle, or 1.5 square units.

If P is within the square with vertices $(2,0)$, $(3,0)$, $(3,1)$, $(2,1)$, which has area 1 square unit, it is definitely closer to $(3,1)$.

Now, the given rectangle has vertices $(0,0)$, $(2,0)$, $(2,1)$ and $(0,1)$. Clearly, it is the rectangle with vertices $(0,0)$, $(3,0)$, $(3,1)$, $(0,1)$ minus the square with vertices $(2,0)$, $(3,0)$, $(3,1)$ and $(2,1)$. Hence, in this case, the area for P to be closer to $(3,1)$ is decreased by 1 square unit, and we are left with only 0.5 square units.

Since the total area of the given rectangle is 2 square units, the probability that the dart lands closer to $(3,1)$ is $0.5/2 = \frac{1}{4}$ and the probability of the dart landing closer to the origin is $3/4$.

24. Fourteen students are taking a test. Of them, 5 are well prepared, 6 are adequately prepared and 3 are poorly prepared. There are 10 questions on the test. A well prepared student can answer 9 questions correctly, an adequately prepared student can answer 6 questions correctly and a poorly prepared student can answer 3 questions correctly. Assume that the question numbers matter in this case.

(a) If a randomly chosen student is asked to answer two distinct questions from the test, chosen randomly and independently of the student, what is the probability that the student can answer both questions correctly?

(b) Assume that a randomly chosen student has answered two randomly chosen questions from the test correctly. What is the probability that it was a well prepared student?

Solution: Let A, B and C, respectively, denote the event that the selected student is well prepared, adequately prepared and poorly prepared. Then

$$P(A) = \frac{5}{14}, P(B) = \frac{6}{14}, P(A) = \frac{3}{14}$$

(a) Let S denote the event of correctly answering the two questions. Using the given information, we can write

$$P(S|A) = \frac{\binom{9}{2}}{\binom{10}{2}} = \frac{4}{5}, P(S|B) = \frac{\binom{6}{2}}{\binom{10}{2}} = \frac{1}{3}, P(S|C) = \frac{\binom{3}{2}}{\binom{10}{2}} = \frac{1}{15}$$

Since the two questions are chosen randomly and independently of the student, to find $P(S)$, we can use the concept of conditional probability as follows:

$$P(S) = P(S|A)P(A) + P(S|B)P(B) + P(S|C)P(C) = \frac{5 \times 12 + 6 \times 5 + 3 \times 1}{14 \times 15} = \frac{31}{70},$$

and that is the required answer.

(b) The probability that the student is well prepared if both questions are answered correctly is given by $P(A|S)$. Using the rule of conditional probability, we can write it as

$$\frac{P(S|A)P(A)}{P(S)} = \frac{(4/5) \times (5/14)}{(31/70)} = \frac{20}{31}$$

Useful Tip: A common possible mistake here is to consider all questions to be identical and replaceable, that is, to assume that a well prepared student can answer any question with probability 9/10 and, thereby, answer any two questions with probability $(9/10)^2$.

25. Let R be the range of a dataset $x_1,\ldots,x_n$, and let S_x be the standard deviation defined by

$$S_x = \sqrt{\frac{1}{n-1}\sum_{i=1}^{n}(x_i-\bar{x})^2},$$

where $\bar{x}$ is the mean of the observations. Prove that

$$\frac{S_x}{R} \leq \sqrt{\frac{n-1}{n}}.$$

Solution: The range can be written as

$$R = \max_{i,j}|x_i-x_j|$$

Recall that $\bar{x} = (x_1 + \ldots + x_n)/n$. Then

$$(x_i-\bar{x})^2 = \frac{1}{n^2}[(x_i-x_1)+(x_i-x_2)+\ldots+(x_i-x_n)]^2 \leq \frac{1}{n^2}\left[\sum_{\substack{j=1\\j\neq i}}^{n}|x_i-x_j|\right]^2$$

Since each summand in the above expression (right-hand side) is less than or equal to R, we can write

$$(x_i-\bar{x})^2 \leq \frac{(n-1)^2R^2}{n^2}$$

Taking the sum over all such expressions for $i=1,\ldots,n$, we obtain

$$S_x^2 \leq \frac{n}{n-1} \times \frac{(n-1)^2R^2}{n^2} = \frac{(n-1)R^2}{n}$$

The above automatically leads to the required inequality.

26. The mean temperature (measured in degree Celsius) in New York City during the month of July is 25. The corresponding variance is equal to 5. What is the mean and variance of the temperature if measured on a Fahrenheit scale? The relation of Celsius (C) and Fahrenheit (F) is given by:

$$\frac{C}{5} = \frac{F-32}{9}.$$

Solution: This is a problem of location–scale shift of a dataset. Let us use $\bar{C}$ and V_C to denote the mean and variance in the Celsius scale. $\bar{F}$ and V_F are used accordingly for the Fahrenheit scale. Then, using the known relationships, we can write

$$\frac{\bar{C}}{5} = \frac{\bar{F}-32}{9}, \quad \frac{V_C}{25} = \frac{V_F}{81}$$

Now, $\bar{C} = 25$, which implies $\bar{F} - 32 = 45$, that is, $\bar{F} = 77$. On the other hand, V_F can be computed in a straightforward way as $81/5 = 16.2$. Thus, the mean and variance of the temperature if measured on a Fahrenheit scale are 77 and 16.2, respectively.

27. Alice is interested in the average temperature of New York City over the summer (May to July). She finds the following measures for the three months:

	May	June	July
Mean	20.72	24.67	27.31
Median	20.15	25.75	28.72
Standard deviation	4.07	4.33	4.67

Can she compute the overall mean, median and standard deviation of the three months?

Solution: Let us use $x_1, \ldots, x_{n_1}$ to denote the dataset for May. The corresponding mean and standard deviation are indicated by $\bar{x}$ and s_x. Similarly, the dataset for June is taken as $y_1, \ldots, y_{n_2}$ and the same for July is $z_1, \ldots, z_{n_3}$. The means and standard deviations of these two months, in the same spirit as before, are denoted by $\bar{y}, s_y, \bar{z},$ and s_z. Also, observe that $n_1 = 31, n_2 = 30, n_3 = 31$.

The overall mean (m) can be computed as follows.

$$m = \frac{1}{n_1+n_2+n_3}\left(\sum_{i=1}^{n_1} x_i + \sum_{i=1}^{n_2} y_i + \sum_{i=1}^{n_3} z_i\right) = \frac{n_1\bar{x}+n_2\bar{y}+n_3\bar{z}}{n_1+n_2+n_3}$$

Using the given values of the means, one can find that the overall mean is 24.23 (rounded off to two digits).

In order to evaluate the median, the distribution of the individual observation in each dataset is required. With only the given information, it is impossible for Alice to find the overall median.

For calculating the overall standard deviation(s), the following formula is required:

$$s^2 = \frac{1}{n_1+n_2+n_3-1}\left(\sum_{i=1}^{n_1}(x_i-m)^2 + \sum_{i=1}^{n_2}(y_i-m)^2 + \sum_{i=1}^{n_3}(z_i-m)^2\right)$$

Next, we note that $(n_1-1)s_x^2 = \sum_{i=1}^{n_1} x_i^2 - n_1 \bar{x}^2$. Using this, the first sum from the above expression can be simplified as

$$\sum_{i=1}^{n_1}(x_i-m)^2 = \sum_{i=1}^{n_1} x_i^2 - 2mn_1\bar{x} + n_1 m^2 = (n_1-1)s_x^2 + n_1(\bar{x}^2 + m^2) - 2mn_1\bar{x}$$

We can obtain similar expressions for the other two sums as well. Then, using the values from above, one would obtain (all numbers are rounded off to second digits)

$$s^2 = \frac{878.56 + 549.56 + 948.62}{n_1 + n_2 + n_3 - 1} = 26.12$$

Taking the square root, the overall standard deviation is found out to be approximately 5.11.

> **Useful Tip:** The above is a classic case of combining multiple samples to calculate overall mean and standard deviation. It is regularly encountered in real statistical studies.

28. Consider two variables Y and X, and we calculate the lines of regression of Y on X (call it L_1) and that of X on Y (call it L_2). When presented in a coordinate plane together, L_1 and L_2 make angles of $30°$ and $60°$, respectively, with the positive x-axis. What is the correlation coefficient between the two variables?

Solution: The slope of the regression line of Y on X is given by

$$m(Y,X) = \frac{\text{Cov}(X,Y)}{\text{Var}(X)}$$

Since this line makes an angle of $30°$ with the positive x-axis, it is easy to argue that

$$\frac{\text{Cov}(X,Y)}{\text{Var}(X)} = \tan 30° = \frac{1}{\sqrt{3}}$$

Using similar arguments for the regression line of X on Y, we obtain

$$\frac{\text{Var}(Y)}{\text{Cov}(X,Y)} = \tan 60° = \sqrt{3}$$

Combining the two equations

$$\frac{\text{Cov}(X,Y)^2}{\text{Var}(X)\text{Var}(Y)} = \left(\frac{1}{\sqrt{3}}\right)^2$$

Taking the square root of the above equation, we obtain the correlation coefficient between the two variables as $1/\sqrt{3}$.

29. In an attempt to understand how studying habits influence the results, Bob and Alice collect data on three variables – GPA (G), hours spent in the library (L), hours spent on studying at home (H) – for 100 students. Bob finds that the regression line $G = 0.2H + 2.5$ best explains the relationship between these two variables, while Alice finds that the regression line of G on L has the same intercept as the above line but is rotated by 15° anticlockwise. If the dataset shows that the mean of L is 3, what is the average number of hours spent on studying at home?

Solution: Let us first find the regression line of G on L. From the given information, it is of the form $G = mL + 2.5$, such that $m = \tan(\tan^{-1} 0.2 + \pi/12)$. Here, we use the fact that 15° is equivalent to $\pi/12$ radians.

Using the expansion of $\tan(A+B)$

$$m = \frac{\tan(\tan^{-1} 0.2) + \tan(\pi/12)}{1 - \tan(\tan^{-1} 0.2)\tan(\pi/12)} = \frac{0.2 + \tan(\pi/12)}{1 - 0.2\tan(\pi/12)}$$

Letting $\theta = \pi/12$, we note that $\tan(2\theta) = 1/\sqrt{3}$. Thus

$$\frac{2\tan\theta}{1-\tan^2\theta} = \frac{1}{\sqrt{3}} \implies \tan^2\theta + 2\sqrt{3}\tan\theta - 1 = 0 \implies \tan\theta = 2 - \sqrt{3}$$

Substituting this in the previous expression, we obtain

$$m = \frac{2.2 - \sqrt{3}}{0.6 + 0.2\sqrt{3}}$$

Now, we know that any regression line passes through the mean of the two variables. Clearly, if we denote the three averages as $\bar{G}, \bar{H}, \bar{L}$, we can write

$$\bar{G} = 0.2\bar{H} + 2.5, \quad \bar{G} = m\bar{L} + 2.5,$$

which implies that $\bar{H} = 3m/0.2 = 15m$. Then, using the value of m obtained above, we obtain that, on average, 7.42 hours are spent on studying at home.

30. We construct two circles of radius 1 as follows. The centre of circle A is chosen uniformly and at random on the line segment joining $(0,0)$ and $(2,0)$. The centre of circle B is chosen uniformly and at random, and independently of the first choice, on the line segment joining $(0,1)$ to $(2,1)$. Find the probability that circles A and B intersect.

Solution: Circles centred at A and B will only overlap if A and B are closer to each other than if the circles were tangent. Now, the circles are tangent to each other when the distance between their centres is equal to the sum of their radii. Thus, the distance from A to B must be 2.

Let us denote A_x, B_x as the x-coordinates and A_y, B_y as the y-coordinates of the centres of circles A and B, respectively. Observe that $|A_y - B_y| = 1$. Hence, for A and B to be tangent, $|A_x - B_x|$ needs to be equal to $\sqrt{3}$. And if $|A_x - B_x| < \sqrt{3}$, the circles intersect.

Notice that A_x and B_x are chosen independently and uniformly from $(0,2)$. We split the scenarios into three cases.

(a) $A_x \in (0, 2-\sqrt{3})$. The probability that B_x falls within the desired range for a given A_x is $(A_x + \sqrt{3})/2$. The total probability for this range of (A_x, B_x) values is the sum of all these probabilities of B_x (over the range of A_x) divided by the total range of A_x (which is 2). Thus, the total probability for this interval is

$$\frac{1}{2}\left(\int_0^{2-\sqrt{3}} \frac{x+\sqrt{3}}{2}\,dx\right) = \frac{1}{2}\left(\frac{x^2}{4} + \frac{x\sqrt{3}}{2}\right)\Big|_0^{2-\sqrt{3}} = \frac{1}{2}\left(\frac{4-4\sqrt{3}+3}{4} + \sqrt{3} - \frac{3}{2}\right)$$

The above simplifies to $1/8$.

(b) $A_x \in (2-\sqrt{3}, \sqrt{3})$. In this case, any value of B_x satisfies our condition. So, the probability for the interval is simply $(\sqrt{3} - (2-\sqrt{3}))/2 = \sqrt{3} - 1$.

(c) $A_x \in (\sqrt{3}, 2)$. This is identical, by symmetry, to case (a), and hence, the probability is $1/8$.

Hence, we can conclude that the probability of the two circles intersecting is

$$\sqrt{3} - 1 + 2 \times \frac{1}{8} = \frac{4\sqrt{3}-3}{4}$$

Multiple Choice Questions

1. A survey revealed that during the last 12 months, 45.8% of people rented a car for business purposes, 54% rented a car for personal reasons, whereas 30% rented a car for both business and personal reasons. If we pick two random individuals from the same population, what is the chance (select the closest value) that during the last 12 months, neither of them rented a car at all?

(a) 5%   (b) 10%   (c) 20%   (d) 30%

Solution: (b)

If A and B, respectively, denote the events of renting a car for personal reasons and for business purposes, then

$$P(A) = 0.54, \ P(B) = 0.458, \ P(A \cap B) = 0.3$$

Then, from the laws of probability

$$P(A \cup B) = P(A) + P(B) - P(A \cap B) = 0.54 + 0.458 - 0.3 = 0.698$$

Hence, the probability that each individual did not rent a car is 0.312. Since we need the probability of both individuals not renting a car, assuming independence, we can obtain the solution as $0.312^2 \approx 0.097$, that is, almost 10%.

2. Ms. Gupta writes a 50-digit number N such that all the digits except the 26th from the right are 1. What is the probability that N is divisible by 13?

(a) $\dfrac{1}{9}$ (b) 0.1   (c) $\dfrac{2}{9}$ (d) 0.3

Solution: (b)

Assume that the 26th digit from the right is d. We know that $111111 \equiv 0 \pmod{13}$, implying that the number formed by the 24 digits on the left is divisible by 13, and that the number formed by the rightmost 24 digits is also divisible by 13. Thus, N is divisible by 13 if and only if the number formed by the digits $d, 1$; that is, the number $10d + 1$ is divisible by 13. This is possible if and only if $d = 9$. As there are 10 possible choices for d, the required probability is $1/10$.

3. If a fair coin is tossed 100 times, what is the probability of getting at least one head?

(a) $\dfrac{100}{2^{100}}$ (b) $\dfrac{99}{100}$ (c) $1 - \dfrac{1}{100!}$ (d) $1 - \dfrac{1}{2^{100}}$

Solution: (d)

The probability of getting at least one head is the same as $1 -$ probability of getting all tails. Since the coin is fair, the probability of getting 100 tails is $1/2^{100}$. Thus, the required answer is (d).

4. Let us call a statistical measure *robust* if it is less affected by outliers. What is the correct increasing order of robustness (starting with the least robust measure) for the three measures of dispersion: standard deviation, range and IQR?

(a) Range < Standard deviation < IQR (b) Standard deviation < IQR < Range
(c) Range < IQR < Standard deviation (d) Standard deviation < Range < IQR

Solution: (a)

Since outliers impact the two tails, quartiles are typically not impacted by them. Thus, inter-quartile range (IQR) is the least affected. Range will always be impacted by the outliers, whereas standard deviation depends on how many and how large the outliers are. Thus, it is less affected than the range.

For the next three questions, consider a dataset with observations $x_1, x_2, \ldots, x_{500}$, which indicate the income (in thousands of rupees) of 500 randomly selected households in a city. Let $y_1, y_2, \ldots, y_{500}$ denote the corresponding expenditure (in thousands of rupees) of the households. Following are some summary statistics of the two variables.

	Income (x)	Expenditure (y)
Mean	45.3	27.1
Median	38.0	25.0
Variance	7.5	4.8

5. Which of the following must be true about the covariance between income and expenditure?

(a) It cannot be zero.
(b) It must be between 0 and 7.5.
(c) It must be less than 6.
(d) It can be anything, but must be positive.

Solution: (c)

We know that the correlation coefficient between two datasets must be between $[-1, 1]$. Thus, if S_{xy} is the covariance between the two variables, then

$$|S_{xy}| \leq \sqrt{(7.5)(4.8)} = 6$$

6. Assume that the correlation coefficient between the two variables is 0.5. Then, the least square regression line explaining the relationship of expenditure on income is

(a) $y = 27.1 + 0.5x$ (b) $y = 8.98 + 0.25x$ (c) $y = 8.98 + 0.4x$ (d) $y = 27.1 + 18.2x$

Solution: (c)

The sample means of the two variables are $\bar{y} = 27.1$, $\bar{x} = 45.3$. Let the covariance be denoted as S_{xy} and the two variances are $S_x^2 = 7.5$, $S_y^2 = 4.8$. Now, if the regression line is of the form $y = \alpha + \beta x$, then we know that the least square estimates are

$$\hat{\beta} = \frac{S_{xy}}{S_x^2} = \frac{(0.5)S_y}{S_x} = (0.5)\sqrt{\frac{48}{75}} = 0.4, \quad \hat{\alpha} = \bar{y} - \hat{\beta}\bar{x} = 27.1 - 0.4 \times 45.3 = 8.98$$

Hence, the least square regression line is $y = 8.98 + 0.4x$.

7. If due to COVID-19, the incomes of the 100 households who are in the bottom 20% in terms of the income level in the sample are reduced by Rs 10,000 each, then what are the new mean and median income of the sample?

(a) Mean is 35.3 and median is 28
(b) Mean is 43.3 and median is 36
(c) Mean is 35.3 and median is 38
(d) Mean is 43.3 and median is 38

Solution: (d)

Without loss of generality, let us assume that $x_1, x_2, \ldots, x_{500}$ are in increasing order. Then, the new values of the income variable are $x_1 - 10, \ldots, x_{100} - 10, x_{101}, \ldots, x_{500}$. Clearly, the median remains unchanged. To compute the new mean, if the new values are denoted as $z_1, \ldots, z_{500}$, then we note that

$$\bar{z} = \frac{1}{500}\sum_{i=1}^{500} z_i = \frac{1}{500}\left(\sum_{i=1}^{100}(x_i - 10) + \sum_{i=101}^{500} x_i\right) = \frac{1}{500}\left(\sum_{i=1}^{500} x_i - 1000\right) = \bar{x} - 2$$

For the next three questions, consider the quadratic equation $x^2 + bx + c = 0$ and assume that b and c are chosen randomly from the interval $[0, 1]$ with the probability uniformly distributed over all pairs (b, c). Let $f(b)$ be the function for the given (fixed) value of b, denoting the probability that the given equation has a real solution.

8. The value of $f(0.5)$ is

(a) 1/16   (b) 1/8   (c) 1/4   (d) 1/2

Solution: (a)

The equation $x^2 + bx + c = 0$ has a real solution if and only if $b^2 - 4c \geq 0$. Thus, for $b = 0.5$, the set of favourable outcomes is $c \leq 1/16$. Since c is uniformly distributed in the interval $[0, 1]$, it implies that the probability $f(0.5)$ is 1/16.

9. As a function of b, $f(b)$ is

(a) always increasing
(b) always decreasing
(c) first increasing then decreasing
(d) first decreasing then increasing

Solution: (a)

Similar to the previous part, we note that for a fixed value of b, the given equation has a real solution if and only if $c \leqslant b^2/4$. Since c is uniformly selected from the unit interval, it implies that $f(b) = b^2/4$, a strictly increasing function in b.

10. As b and c both vary, what is the probability that the given equation has a real solution?

(a) 1/2   (b) 2/3   (c) 1/12   (d) 5/18

Solution: (c)

First, observe that the pair (b,c) is chosen uniformly from the unit square $[0,1] \times [0,1]$. Now, the equation has a real solution if and only if $b^2 - 4c \geqslant 0$, which means that the required probability is the area under the parabola $y = x^2/4$, between $x = 0$ and $x = 1$. This can be computed as

$$\int_0^1 \frac{x^2}{4} dx = \frac{1}{12}$$

Exercises

1. We choose a point P randomly in the interior of an equilateral triangle ABC. Find the probability that the triangle ABP has a greater area than each of ACP and BCP.

2. Denote S as the set of permutations of the sequence 1, 2, 3, 4, 5 such that the first term is not 1. We choose a permutation randomly from S. What is the probability that the second term is 2?

3. An object moves 5 cm in a straight line from A to B, and turns at an angle α, measured in radians and chosen at random from the interval $(0, \pi)$, and then moves 8 cm in a straight line to C. Find the probability that $AC < 7$.

4. Let X be a variable taking values only in the interval $[0,1]$. Show that, irrespective of the sample space or the probability distribution of X,

$$\text{Var}(X) \leqslant \frac{1}{4}.$$

5. If we choose two distinct numbers a, b from the set $\{2, 2^2, 2^3, \ldots, 2^{25}\}$, find the probability that $\log_a b$ is an integer.

6. Let D denote the event of a patient getting infected with COVID-19 and T denote the probability of the RTPCR test detecting it. Assume that $P(T|D) = 0.99$, $P(T^c|D^c) = 0.95$ and that 60% of the entire population has the disease.

    (a) A patient tests positive for COVID-19. What is the chance that the patient really has the disease?

    (b) Suppose that the patient does a second RTPCR test and tests positive again. Assuming that all tests are independent, how would you change your answer to the previous part?

7. The final scores of the students in a course are evaluated as the weighted sum of the scores from three tests. The weights are assigned as 40% to the score in Test A, 40% to Test B and 20% to Test C. Suppose that the results of Test A have mean 59 and standard deviation 10, while the results of Test B have a mean of 67 and a standard deviation of 13. If the overall average and standard deviation of the final scores are 65 and 7, respectively, find the mean and standard deviation of the results from Test C. You can assume that the covariance between the scores in any two tests is zero.

8. Suppose that we are throwing balls into bins numbered with positive integers so that for each ball, the probability that it is tossed into bin i is 2^{-i} for $i = 1, 2, \ldots$. After three balls are randomly and independently tossed, find the probability that the balls end up evenly spaced in distinct bins. For example, the balls are evenly spaced if they are tossed into bins 5, 16 and 11. Assume that more than one ball is allowed in each bin.

9. Roger and Rafael are playing a tennis match. It is deuce (scores are level at 40-40) currently, so, if anyone wins the next two rallies, the game is over. If they each win a rally, it is deuce again. Suppose that the outcomes of the rallies are independent and that Roger wins a rally with probability p. Let us denote F as the event that Roger wins the game, and G as the event that the game ends after the next two rallies. Let D be the event of deuce again.

    Find $P(F|G)$ and show that $P(F) = p^2 + 2p(1-p)P(F|D)$. Hence or otherwise, determine the value of $P(F)$.

10. Bob and Alice are fighting over a concert ticket. Alice proposes a game. She will toss a coin until heads appears. If the number of tosses required is odd, she will take the ticket, otherwise Bob can take it. Let the probability of heads be p, where $0 < p < 1$. Should Bob agree to play the game?

11. Rachel has two bags X and Y. The first bag contains m white marbles, while the second one contains $(m-1)$ white marbles and 1 blue marble. She chooses a bag with probability 0.5 and removes a random marble from that bag, each marble being equally likely. If she continues these steps in a similar way until one of the bags becomes empty, find the probability that the blue marble is still in bag Y.

12. In a parking lot, a sedan requires one space to be parked and an SUV needs two adjacent spaces. The parking lot has 16 spaces in a single row. When a car arrives at the lot, it chooses its space randomly from the available ones. Twelve sedans have already arrived at the lot since morning. What is the probability that a newly arriving SUV can find a place to park?

13. Bowley's measure of skewness is defined as
$$S_k(B) = \frac{Q_3 + Q_1 - 2M_d}{Q_3 - Q_1},$$
where Q_1, Q_3 are the first and the third quarttiles, and M_d is the median. Show that $|S_k(B)| \leq 1$. When does it attain equality?

14. The mean deviation about the median for the numbers $a, 2a, \ldots, 50a$ is 50. Find all possible values of a.

15. A magic sequence of 8 integers has their mean, median, unique mode and range all equal to 8. Find the largest integer that can be an element of this sequence.

16. Imagine that the city of Gotham is broken down into grids in the coordinate plane. Batman and Joker move simultaneously in Gotham via a sequence of steps, each of length 1. Batman starts at $(0,0)$ and moves either right or up with equal probability in each step. Joker starts at $(6,8)$ and is equally likely to move left or down in each step. Find the probability that Batman and Joker meet.

17. Ronald plays a game of dice. He starts with one die. At each step, he rolls all the dice available to him and if all of them show 6, he places another die on the table. Let D be the number of dice on the table after 2022 steps. Find the expected value of 6^D. You can use the fact that $E(E(X|Y)) = E(X)$.

18. Saleem rolls a fair tetrahedral die whose faces are numbered 1, 2, 3 and 4. He records the number on the bottom face of the die and creates a sequence. He discards any roll if the number from that roll would result in two consecutive terms in the sequence summing to 5. Further, Saleem stops rolling once all four numbers have appeared in the sequence. What is the expected (average) number of terms in the sequence?

19. A class has n boys and n girls. They play a game in the probability class. Each of the boys and girls is asked to choose a random number from the set $\{1,2,3,4,5\}$,

uniformly and independently. Denote p_n as the probability that every boy chooses a different number than every girl. Find the limiting value of $\sqrt[n]{p_n}$ as $n \to \infty$.

20. Pacman hops on a 3×3 grid of squares, moving one square on each hop. It can only move in the up, down, left or right directions, with each being equally likely. Pacman is forbidden to hop diagonally. If the direction of a hop would take it off the grid, it "wraps around" and jumps to the opposite edge. For example, suppose that Pacman starts in the centre square and makes two hops up. The first move would place it in the top row middle square, and in the second hop, Pacman would jump to the opposite edge, thus arriving in the bottom row middle square. Assume that Pacman always starts from the centre square, makes at most four hops at random, and stops moving if it lands on a corner square. Find the probability that it reaches a corner square on one of the four hops.

Hints

1. Once we pick the point P, by symmetry, the probability that ACP is the greatest area, or ABP or BCP, are all the same. Since they all add up to 1, the probability that ACP has the greatest area is $1/3$.

2. We have 4 choices for the first element of S, and for each of these choices, there are $4!$ ways to arrange the remaining elements. If the second element is 2, then we are left with only 3 choices for the first element and $3!$ ways to arrange the remaining elements. Combine the above to show that the required probability is $3/16$.

3. Use the law of cosines on the triangle ABC to show that the event $(AC < 7)$ is equivalent to $(0 < \alpha < \pi/3)$. Then, using the assumption that α is picked following a uniform distribution over $(0, \pi)$, argue that the answer is $1/3$.

4. Irrespective of the sample space or the probability distribution of X, one can write $\mathrm{Var}(X) = E(X^2) - E(X)^2$. Further, since X always takes values in the interval $[0, 1]$, using the properties of expectation, $E(X^2) < E(X)$, $0 \leqslant E(X) \leqslant 1$. Combine this information, along with the AM-GM inequality, to show that $\mathrm{Var}(X) \leqslant E(X)[1 - E(X)] \leqslant 1/4$.

5. Define $a = 2^x$, $b = 2^y$. Then, $\log_a b = z$ implies that x divides y. So, the largest possible value of x is 12. Now, argue that there are $\lfloor 25/x - 1 \rfloor$ possible choices for y, given the value of x. Here, $\lfloor \cdot \rfloor$ denotes the floor function. Thus, the total number of possible choices can be calculated as 62. Since the total number of ways to pick two distinct numbers (the ordering is important here) from the given set is $25 \times 24 = 600$, the required probability is $62/600$.

6. In part (a), one can use Bayes' Theorem to determine

$$P(D|T) = \frac{P(T|D)P(D)}{P(T|D)P(D) + P(T^c|D^c)P(D^c)}$$

The answer would be obtained as 0.967. Then, for part (b), let us define S to denote the event of testing positive on the second test. We need to calculate $P(D|T \cap S)$, and we can follow a similar procedure as above. One needs to use the fact that the two tests are independent to compute $P(T \cap S|D) = P(T|D) \times P(S|D)$.

7. Assume that there are n students. Let us use x_i to denote the final score of the student. Then, $x_i = 0.4a_i + 0.4b_i + 0.2c_i$, where a_i, b_i, c_i are the scores from the three tests. Next, one can argue that $\bar{x} = 0.4\bar{a} + 0.4\bar{b} + 0.2\bar{c}$, and $s_x^2 = 0.4^2 s_a^2 + 0.4^2 s_b^2 + 0.2^2 s_c^2$. Here, $\bar{a}$ and s_a denote the mean and standard deviation of the scores in test A (similarly for B and C). Subsequently, using the given information, it is possible to obtain the mean and standard deviation of the results from Test C as 73 and 12.21 (rounded off to two digits), respectively.

8. To obtain "evenly spaced" bins, the numbers on the bins need to form an arithmetic progression. If the middle bin in the sequence is numbered x, then there are $x - 1$ different possibilities for the first bin, and these two bins would uniquely determine the final bin. Now, suppose that the first bin is numbered $x - a$ and the other bin is numbered $x + a$ for some non-negative integer a. Then, one can show that the probability of getting $(x-a), x, (x+a)$ as the bins from the first three throws is

$$\binom{3}{2}(x-1)\left(\frac{1}{2^{x-a+x+x+a}}\right) = \frac{6(x-1)}{8^x}$$

Since x can be any positive integer greater than 1, the total probability can be obtained by summing over all x. Applying the concepts of infinite geometric series, the answer would be found to be 6/49.

9. Observe that $P(G) = p^2 + (1-p)^2$ and $P(D) = 2p(1-p)$. Then, use the formula $P(F|G) = P(F \cap G)/P(G)$ to find the conditional probability. Next, one can use $P(F) = P(F \cap G) + P(F \cap D)$ to complete the second part. Finally, observe that the event of deuce resets the game to a deuce again, and thus, $P(F) = P(F|D)$. Substituting this in the previous equation, one can calculate the value of $P(F)$.

10. Notice that the probability of Alice getting the ticket can be simplified as

$$\sum_{m=0}^{\infty}(1-p)^{2m}p = \frac{p}{1-(1-p)^2}$$

Subsequently, the probability of Bob getting the ticket can be computed as $p(1-p)/(1-(1-p)^2)$. Compare these two probabilities to argue if Bob should agree to this game.

11. For $1 \leqslant k \leqslant m$, first compute the probability that at the end there are exactly k marbles in bag Y. Observe that final marble removed must have been from bag X. The probability that at the end there are exactly k marbles in bag Y can be calculated as $\binom{2m-1-k}{m-1}/2^{2m-k}$. Use these probabilities to find the expected number of balls in bag Y at the end to be

$$\sum_{k=1}^{m} \frac{\binom{2m-1-k}{m-1} 2^k}{2^{2m}} k = \frac{m\binom{2m}{m}}{2^{2m}}$$

Since the blue marble is 1 out of m marbles in bag Y initially, the desired probability is computed as $\binom{2m}{m}/2^{2m}$.

12. A newly arrived SUV will not be able to park only when none of the four available spots are adjacent. We consider this a complement event. Let us use 1s in a sequence to denote the 12 cars that are already parked. We know that 4 spaces must be left empty, and we need arrangements where no empty spaces are adjacent to one another. Observe that this is simply the number of ways to put four 0s into 13 slots and this can be done in $\binom{13}{4}$ ways. Hence, the probability of the said event is $\binom{13}{4}/\binom{16}{4} = 11/28$.

13. Note the natural ordering of $Q_1 \leqslant M_d \leqslant Q_3$. Now, the numerator in the expression of $S_k(B)$ can be rewritten as $(Q_3 - M_d) - (M_d - Q_1)$. Then, using $M_d - Q_1 \geqslant 0$ and $Q_3 - M_d \leqslant Q_3 - Q_1$, one can argue that $S_k(B) \leqslant 1$. Similar arguments can be used to prove that $S_k(B) \geqslant -1$. It also shows that equality occurs if $M_d = Q_1$ (leads to the value 1) or if $M_d = Q_3$ (leads to the value -1).

14. Note that a must be non-zero. Assume that a is positive. Since the numbers form a strictly increasing sequence, the median is $51a/2$. Thus, the mean deviation about the median is

$$\frac{1}{50} \sum_{k=1}^{50} \left| ka - \frac{51a}{2} \right|$$

One can show that the above simplifies to $25a/2$. Equating it to the given information, one can prove that $a = 4$. In an exactly similar fashion, if a is negative, the only possible value of a can be obtained as (-4).

15. Denote the integers in an increasing order as $a_1, a_2, \ldots, a_8$. Based on the given information, argue that $a_4 = a_5 = 8$. This further implies that $2a_1 + a_2 + a_3 + a_6 + a_7 = 40$. Now, use appropriate justifications to deduce that a_1 must be less than 7. Subsequently, show that all conditions are satisfied for the sequence $\{6, 6, 6, 8, 8, 8, 8, 14\}$. Hence, the largest integer to ensure the given conditions is 14.

Probability and Statistics 7.35

16. If Batman and Joker meet, their paths must connect the points $(0,0)$ and $(6,8)$. So, we need to find out all possible paths from $(0,0)$ to $(6,8)$. Using the concept of generating function (refer to Chapter 2), argue that the number of possible paths is equal to the coefficient of x^6 in the generating function $f(x) = (x+1)^{14}$. This gives us the total number of paths so that they meet as $\binom{14}{6}$. Now, the number of all possible paths for the two of them after 7 steps is $2^7 \times 2^7$. Hence, the probability of Batman and Joker meeting is $3003/2^{14}$, which is approximately equal to 0.18.

17. Let us define D_n as the number of dice on the table after n steps, for any non-negative integer n. Observe that $D_0 = 1$ and

$$D_{n+1} = \begin{cases} D_n + 1, & \text{with probability } 6^{-D_n} \\ D_n, & \text{with probability } (1 - 6^{-D_n}) \end{cases}$$

The above conditional probability distribution helps in computing the conditional expectation, $E(6^{D_{n+1}}|D_n)$ as $5 + 6^{D_n}$. Using the given rule, one can then obtain the recursion relation $E(6^{D_{n+1}}) = E(6^{D_n}) + 5$. Solve this recursion to show that the required answer is 10116.

18. Let x_k be the expected number of terms needed to complete the sequence when Saleem already has k different terms in his sequence. We need to find x_0. First, observe that $x_0 = x_1 + 1$ and $x_4 = 0$. Then, using the rules of the game, show that

$$x_1 = \frac{1}{3}x_1 + \frac{2}{3}x_2 + 1, \quad x_2 = \frac{2}{3}x_2 + \frac{1}{3}x_3 + 1$$

Now, without loss of generality, assume that the first three distinct values are 1, 2 and 3. Then, there are two "sub-cases" for x_3: (a) the last roll was 1 (the number which would add up to 5 with the remaining distinct number 4), and (b) the last roll was 2 or 3 (one of the already paired numbers that add up to 5 with each other). Denoting e and f as the expected number of moves required to finish for the two sub-cases, show that

$$e = \frac{1}{3}e + \frac{2}{3}f + 1, \quad f = \frac{1}{3}e + \frac{1}{3}f + \frac{1}{3}x_4 + 1$$

One can solve the above using $x_4 = 0$ to obtain $e = 6, f = 9/2$, which subsequently implies $x_3 = 9/2, x_2 = 15/2, x_1 = 9$ and $x_0 = 10$.

19. Let E denote the event that every boy chooses a different number than every girl. Further, for any $A \subset \{1,2,3,4,5\}$, let E_A denote the event that the n boys choose something from A and the n girls choose something from the A^c. Then, taking $A' := \{1,2,3\}$, argue that $E_{A'} \subset E \subset \cup_A E_A$, which would imply

$$P(E_{A'}) \leqslant p_n \leqslant \sum_A P(E_A)$$

Note that $P(E_A)$ can only take the values $0, (4/25)^n, (6/25)^n$ and that there are 32 possible subsets for A. Then, using the Sandwich Theorem for limits

$$\left(\frac{6}{25}\right)^n \leqslant p_n \leqslant 32\left(\frac{6}{25}\right)^n \implies \lim_{n\to\infty} \sqrt[n]{p_n} = \frac{6}{25}$$

20. At any time-point, we can denote the state of Pacman as follows: centre (C), edge (E) and corner (R). There are only a few ways it can reach a corner in four or fewer moves. We can look at the sequence of the state Pacman lands in those situations. They are $ER, EER, EEER, ECER$. Calculating the probabilities of each of these moves occurring show that the answer is 25/32.

8
Miscellaneous

"There should be no such thing as boring mathematics."
–Edsger W Dijkstra

The previous chapters aptly characterize the most common problems encountered in the competitive exams at high school level. There are a few other topics that are relevant at this level, and these are discussed here in appropriate detail. While the primary focus of this chapter is on differential equations, matrices and determinants (typically termed linear algebra), three-dimensional geometry and vectors, we shall also discuss some problems that are of general nature and can be solved by a combination of techniques from multiple topics studied thus far.

KEY RESULTS

> Throughout this chapter, the following notations are used:
> $\mathbb{N}$ = the set of natural numbers $\qquad$ $\mathbb{Z}$ = the set of integers
> $\mathbb{R}$ = the set of real numbers $\qquad$ $\mathbb{Q}$ = the set of rational numbers
> $\mathbb{C}$ = the set of complex numbers

DIFFERENTIAL EQUATIONS

Definition 8.1 (Ordinary Differential Equations (ODE)): Ordinary differential equations (ODE) are those involving unknown functions of a single independent variable and its derivatives. An ODE of order n can be written as an equation of the form $G(x, y, y^{(1)}, \ldots, y^{(n)}) = 0$, where $y = f(x)$ for some unknown f and $y^{(j)}$ denotes the jth derivative of y with respect to x.

Theorem 8.1 (Solving ODE by Inspection): If a differential equation is of the form $\sum_{k=1}^{m} \phi_k(f_k(x,y)) d(f_k(x,y)) = 0$, then one can solve it by integrating each term.

For example, consider the differential equation $y(1+xy)dx = xdy$. Observe that it can be rewritten as $xy^2 dx + (ydx - xdy) = 0$. Clearly, one can write

$$xdx + \frac{ydx - xdy}{y^2} = 0 \implies xdx + d\left(\frac{x}{y}\right) = 0$$

One can directly solve the above by integrating each term, and obtain the solution $x^2/2 + x/y = c$, for some integrating constant c.

> **Useful Tip:** Unless some condition is provided, one must write the integration constant while solving differential equations.

Theorem 8.2 (Solving ODE by Variable Separation): If an ODE can be written such that variables are separated for integration, then the equation can be solved by separate integrations. For example, the solution to the ODE $f(x)dx + g(y)dy = 0$ is $\int f(x)dx + \int g(y)dy = 0$.

Theorem 8.3 (Solving ODE Using Homogeneous Equations): An equation of the form $dy/dx = f(x,y)/\phi(x,y)$ is called a homogeneous differential equation. Here, f and ϕ are homogeneous functions, that is, $f(\lambda x, \lambda y) = \lambda^k f(x,y)$ for some k. Usually, this type of equation can be solved by replacement of the variable, typically by putting $y = vx$. An example is the equation $x^2 dy + y(x+y)dx = 0$, which can be expressed using homogeneous functions as

$$\frac{dy}{dx} = \frac{-y(x+y)}{x^2}$$

Substituting $y = vx$, one would obtain $dy/dx = v + x\,dv/dx$, which implies that

$$v + x\frac{dv}{dx} = -\frac{vx^2 + v^2 x^2}{x^2} \implies \int \frac{dv}{v^2 + 2v} = -\int \frac{dx}{x}$$

The above can be solved directly using integration techniques.

> **Useful Tip:** If a differential equation is of the form $\frac{dy}{dx} = \frac{f(x,y)+a_1}{\phi(x,y)+a_2}$, where f and ϕ are homogeneous equations, then one can look for a transformation of the variable from (x,y) to (x',y') such that the equation transforms into a homogeneous differential equation. The concepts of rotation and translation of axes can be utilized in this aspect.

Theorem 8.4 (Solving Linear ODE by Integrating Factor): Linear differential equations are of the form $\frac{dy}{dx} + P(x)y = Q(x)$, where $P(x), Q(x)$ are functions of only x. In other words, in a linear ODE, the dependent variable y and its derivatives always appear only in the first degree. We solve such types of equations as

$$\exp\left(\int P(x)dx\right)\left(\frac{dy}{dx}+P(x)y\right) = Q(x)\exp\left(\int P(x)dx\right),$$

which implies

$$\frac{d}{dx}\left\{y\exp\left(\int P(x)dx\right)\right\} = Q(x)\exp\left(\int P(x)dx\right)$$

Subsequently, the solution is

$$y\exp\left(\int P(x)dx\right) = \int Q(x)\exp\left(\int P(x)dx\right)dx + c$$

In the above solution, the term $\exp(\int P(x)dx)$ is called the integrating factor (IF).

MATRICES AND DETERMINANTS

Definition 8.2 (Vectors and Matrices): A matrix is defined as an array of $m \times n$ numbers arranged in a rectangular formation along m rows and n columns. For example, a matrix of order $m \times n$ can be written as

$$A = \begin{bmatrix} a_{11} & a_{12} & \cdots & a_{1n} \\ a_{21} & a_{22} & \cdots & a_{2n} \\ \vdots & \vdots & \ddots & \vdots \\ a_{m1} & a_{m2} & \cdots & a_{mn} \end{bmatrix}$$

If $m = 1$, then A is commonly called a row vector of dimension n, whereas for $n = 1$, A would be called a column vector of dimension n. If $m = n = 1$, it is a scalar quantity.

Definition 8.3 (Square Matrix): An $m \times n$ matrix A is called a square matrix if $m = n$, that is, the number of rows equals the number of columns. The square identity matrix is an $n \times n$ matrix with 1 in its main diagonal and 0 everywhere else. It is usually denoted as I_n.

Definition 8.4 (Trace): The trace of an $n \times n$ square matrix A is the sum of the elements lying along the principal diagonal, that is, $tr(A) = \sum_{i=1}^{n} a_{ii}$.

Definition 8.5 (Diagonal and Triangular Matrix): A diagonal matrix is a square matrix, all of whose elements, except those in the principal diagonal, are zero. An upper triangular matrix is a square matrix in which all the elements below the principal diagonal are zero and a lower triangular matrix is a square matrix in which all the elements above the principal diagonal are zero.

Definition 8.6 (Transpose): The transpose of a matrix A is obtained by interchanging the rows and columns of A and is denoted by A'. For example, if $A = (a_{ij})_{m \times n}$ and $B = (b_{ij})_{n \times m}$, then $B = A'$ if and only if $a_{ij} = b_{ji}$ for all i, j.

Some important properties are listed below:

- $(A')' = A$
- $(A+B)' = A' + B'$
- $(\alpha A)' = \alpha A'$, for any scalar α
- If A and B are two matrices that can be multiplied, then $(AB)' = B'A'$.
- If A is a lower triangular matrix, then A' is an upper triangular matrix.

Definition 8.7 (Conjugate): The conjugate of a matrix A (containing complex numbers) is obtained by replacing the elements of A with their conjugate complex numbers, and is denoted by $\overline{A}$. For example, if $A = (a_{ij})_{m \times n}$ and $B = (b_{ij})_{n \times m}$, then $B = \overline{A}$ if and only if $b_{ij} = \bar{a}_{ij}$ for all i, j.

As before, the following properties are true for a conjugate matrix:

- $\overline{\overline{A}} = A$
- $\overline{A+B} = \overline{A} + \overline{B}$
- $\overline{\alpha A} = \alpha \overline{A}$, for any scalar α
- $\overline{AB} = \overline{A}\,\overline{B}$

> **Useful Tip:** The transpose of the conjugate of a matrix is called the transposed conjugate of A and is denoted by A^*. The conjugate of the transpose is the same as the transpose of the conjugate, that is, $\overline{A}' = \overline{A'} = A^*$. Problems related to transposed conjugate are not commonly encountered at this level.

Definition 8.8: A square matrix $A = (a_{ij})$ is said to be symmetric when $a_{ij} = a_{ij}$ for all i and j. It is called skew-symmetric if $a_{ij} = -a_{ij}$ for all i and j. Hence, all the leading diagonal elements are zero for a skew-symmetric matrix.

Definition 8.9 (Matrix Multiplication): For a scalar α, if $A = (a_{ij})$, then $\alpha A = (\alpha a_{ij})$.

Two matrices can be multiplied only when the number of columns in the first equals the number of rows in the second, called the postfactor. Let A be a matrix of order $m \times n$ and B be another matrix of order $n \times p$. Then, their product is the $n \times p$ matrix C such that

$$\begin{bmatrix} a_{11} & a_{12} & \cdots & a_{1n} \\ a_{21} & a_{22} & \cdots & a_{2n} \\ \vdots & \vdots & \ddots & \vdots \\ a_{m1} & a_{m2} & \cdots & a_{mn} \end{bmatrix}_{m \times n} \times \begin{bmatrix} b_{11} & b_{12} & \cdots & b_{1p} \\ b_{21} & b_{22} & \cdots & b_{2p} \\ \vdots & \vdots & \ddots & \vdots \\ b_{n1} & c_{n2} & \cdots & b_{np} \end{bmatrix}_{n \times p} = \begin{bmatrix} c_{11} & c_{12} & \cdots & c_{1p} \\ c_{21} & c_{22} & \cdots & c_{2p} \\ \vdots & \vdots & \ddots & \vdots \\ c_{m1} & c_{m2} & \cdots & c_{mp} \end{bmatrix}_{m \times p}$$

and $c_{ij} = \sum_{i=1}^{n} a_{ik} b_{kj}$ for $i = 1, \cdots, m$ and $j = 1, \cdots, p$.

The following results are crucial and must be remembered:

Miscellaneous

- Matrix multiplication is not necessarily commutative, that is, AB may or may not be equal to BA. In fact, it is not necessary that both AB and BA are defined. If they are both defined and if $AB = BA$, then the matrices A and B are called commutative matrices. Otherwise, they are called anti-commutative matrices.
- Matrix multiplication is associative and distributive. That is, for three matrices A, B, C of appropriate orders, $(AB)C = A(BC)$ and $(A+B)C = AC + BC$.
- If $AB = 0$ (null matrix), it does not necessarily imply that either A or B is a null matrix.

Definition 8.10 (Determinant): Determinant is a mathematical operation that assigns each square matrix $A_{n \times n}$ with a complex number and is commonly denoted by $|A|$ or

$$\begin{vmatrix} a_{11} & a_{12} & \cdots & a_{1n} \\ a_{21} & a_{22} & \cdots & a_{2n} \\ \vdots & \vdots & \ddots & \vdots \\ a_{n1} & a_{n2} & \cdots & a_{nn} \end{vmatrix}$$

For a 2×2 matrix, the determinant is calculated as

$$\begin{vmatrix} a_{11} & a_{12} \\ a_{21} & a_{22} \end{vmatrix} = a_{11}a_{22} - a_{21}a_{12}$$

Then, the computation of the determinant of a general matrix is carried out recursively as

$$\begin{vmatrix} a_{11} & a_{12} & \cdots & a_{1n} \\ a_{21} & a_{22} & \cdots & a_{2n} \\ \vdots & \vdots & \ddots & \vdots \\ a_{n1} & a_{n2} & \cdots & a_{nn} \end{vmatrix} = \sum_{k=1}^{n} (-1)^{k+1} a_{1k} |M_{1k}|,$$

where M_{ij} is the matrix obtained from A by removing the ith row and the jth column. In general, $|M_{ij}|$ is called the minor of a_{ij} and the cofactor C_{ij} of a_{ij} is defined by $C_{ij} = (-1)^{i+j} |M_{ij}|$.

> **Useful Tip:** Determinants are extremely useful in vector algebra, as you will see in subsequent discussions.

Some important properties of determinants are listed below:

- $|A| = |A'|$
- If any two rows (or columns) of a matrix are interchanged, the resulting determinant is the negative of the original determinant.

- If a constant multiple of a row (or column) is added to another row (or column) of a determinant, the value of the determinant does not change.
- If two rows (or columns) in a matrix have corresponding elements that are equal, the value of the determinant is equal to zero.
- If one row (or column) of a matrix of order $n \times n$ is multiplied by a constant term b, the corresponding determinant is multiplied by b^n.

Definition 8.11 (Singularity): A matrix is called singular if $|A| = 0$ and non-singular otherwise.

Definition 8.12 (Adjoint): Let $A = (a_{ij})$ be a square matrix of order n and let C_{ij} be the cofactor of a_{ij} in A. Then, the transpose of the matrix of cofactors of the elements of A is called the adjoint of A and is denoted by $\text{Adj}(A)$.

Theorem 8.5: Let A be a square matrix of order n. Then

$$A \times \text{Adj}(A) = |A|I_n = \text{Adj}(A) \times A$$

Definition 8.13 (Inverse): A non-singular square matrix of order n is said to be invertible if there exists a square matrix B of the same order such that $AB = I_n = BA$. The inverse of the matrix is given by $A^{-1} = \text{Adj}(A)/|A|$.

One should remember the properties listed below:

- Every invertible matrix has a unique inverse.
- For a square matrix A of order n, $|\text{Adj}(A)| = |A|^{n-1}$.
- $\text{Adj}(\text{Adj}(A)) = |A|^{n-1}A$
- $\text{Adj}(A') = (\text{Adj}(A))'$, which subsequently implies that $(A')^{-1} = (A^{-1})'$.
- If A and B are non-singular square matrices of the same order, then $\text{Adj}(AB) = \text{Adj}(B)\text{Adj}(A)$. In this case, AB is invertible and $(AB)^{-1} = B^{-1}A^{-1}$.

Inverse of a matrix is extremely crucial in solving a system of linear equations. Such a system of m equations in m unknown variables can be written as $Ax = b$, where A is an appropriately chosen $m \times m$ matrix, x is an m-dimensional column vector of the unknown variables, and b is a known m-dimensional column vector. This system has a unique solution if and only if A is invertible, that is, if and only if $|A| = 0$. The corresponding unique solution can be found as $x = A^{-1}b$.

THREE-DIMENSIONAL GEOMETRY AND VECTOR ALGEBRA

In Chapter 6, various properties of two-dimensional coordinate geometry were discussed. Those concepts can be naturally extended to the three-dimensional (3D) case, which relies on three axes, pairwise perpendicular to each other. In the figure on the next page, an

Miscellaneous

example is displayed. Here, OX, OY and OZ represent the three axes, and the coordinates of a point A are given by the distances from the origin along each axis.

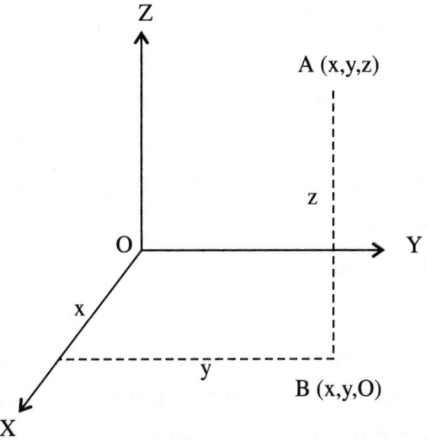

Useful Tip: It is easy to observe that the coordinates of any point on the X-axis is of the form $(x, 0, 0)$, while the coordinates of any point on the YZ-plane is of the form $(0, y, z)$.

The following results are simple extensions of what we learnt earlier in two-dimensional coordinate geometry.

Theorem 8.6: Consider two points $P = (x_1, y_1, z_1)$ and $Q = (x_2, y_2, z_2)$.

- The distance between the points is given by

$$PQ = \sqrt{(x_1 - x_2)^2 + (y_1 - y_2)^2 + (z_1 - z_2)^2}$$

- If the point (x, y, z) divides the line segment PQ internally in the ratio $m : n$, then

$$x = \frac{mx_2 + nx_1}{m + n}, \quad y = \frac{my_2 + ny_1}{m + n}, \quad z = \frac{mz_2 + nz_1}{m + n}$$

- If $R = (x_3, y_3, z_3)$ such that P, Q, R are not collinear, then the centroid of the triangle PQR is given by

$$G = \left(\frac{x_1 + x_2 + x_3}{3}, \frac{y_1 + y_2 + y_3}{3}, \frac{z_1 + z_2 + z_3}{3} \right)$$

Useful Tip: In a similar fashion as above, one can also find out the expressions for circumcentre, incentre and orthocentre of a triangle in the three-dimensional space.

Vectors are commonly defined in a three-dimensional space, so as to better understand the generality of the theory. Let $\mathcal{L}$ be any straight line in the 3D space. It can be given two directions, and a line with one of these directions is called a directed line. If we restrict ourselves to a segment between two points A and B on this directed line, with the direction from A to B, then it is called a directed line segment, or a vector. It is denoted using the notation $\vec{AB}$. The points A and B are called the initial point and the terminal point, respectively. The length of the segment AB is called the magnitude of the vector, and it is typically denoted by $|\vec{AB}|$. If the value of this length is a, the shorthand notation of $\vec{a}$ is also used to indicate the same vector.

Definition 8.14 (Types of Vectors): Following are some important characterizations of vectors:

- **Null vector**: A vector is called a null vector or a zero vector if its initial and terminal points coincide. Denoted as $\vec{0}$, it can be thought to have no definite direction or to have any direction, since it has zero magnitude.

- **Unit vector**: A vector with magnitude 1 is a unit vector. For any vector $\vec{a}$, the vector $\vec{a}/|\vec{a}|$ is a unit vector in the same direction. Unit vectors are typically denoted using the sign $\hat{a}$.

- **Coinitial vectors**: If two or more vectors have the same initial point, they are called coinitial vectors.

- **Collinear vectors**: If two vectors are parallel to the same line, irrespective of their magnitude and direction, then they are collinear vectors.

- **Equal vectors**: Two vectors are said to be equal if they have the same magnitude and direction irrespective of the positions of their initial points.

- **Negative of a vector**: For any vector $\vec{a}$, the vector which has the same magnitude but opposite direction to that of $\vec{a}$ is called the negative of the vector $\vec{a}$, and it is indicated by $-\vec{a}$.

Definition 8.15 (Position Vector and Component Form): If a point P has coordinates (x, y, z), then the vector $\vec{OP}$, where O is the origin, is called the position vector of P. Quite clearly

$$|\vec{OP}| = \sqrt{x^2 + y^2 + z^2}$$

Further, let $\hat{i}, \hat{j}, \hat{k}$ be the unit vectors in the directions of the three axes. Then, the vector $\vec{OP}$ can be written as $x\hat{i} + y\hat{j} + z\hat{k}$. This is called the component form of writing a vector.

Definition 8.16 (Direction Cosine and Direction Ratio): If the magnitude of the position vector of $P = (x, y, z)$ is r, then it can also be indicated by $\vec{r}$. One should note the similarity

Miscellaneous

of this to the polar coordinate system studied earlier. In that same spirit, let α, β, γ be the angles made by $\vec{r}$ with the X-, Y- and Z-axes, respectively. The cosine values of these angles, that is, $\cos\alpha$, $\cos\beta$ and $\cos\gamma$, are called the direction cosines of the vector. Conventionally, ℓ, m, n are used to indicate the direction cosines, and one can obtain

$$\ell = \frac{x}{r}, \quad m = \frac{y}{r}, \quad n = \frac{z}{r}$$

Observe that the coordinates of the point P can also be expressed as $(\ell r, mr, nr)$. The numbers ℓr, mr and nr, which are proportional to the direction cosines, are called the direction ratios of the vector.

Theorem 8.7 (Vector Addition): Consider two vectors $\vec{a}$ and $\vec{b}$. In order to find their sum, position them in such a way that the initial point of the second coincides with the terminal point of the first. Let the new positions of these two vectors be denoted by $\vec{AB} = \vec{a}$ and $\vec{BC} = \vec{b}$. Then, the vector $\vec{AC}$ is the sum of the two vectors. Vector addition is commutative and associative, that is, for any three vectors $\vec{a}$, $\vec{b}$ and $\vec{c}$

$$\vec{a} + \vec{b} = \vec{b} + \vec{a}, \quad (\vec{a} + \vec{b}) + \vec{c} = \vec{a} + (\vec{b} + \vec{c})$$

Theorem 8.8 (Scalar Multiplication of a Vector): Consider a vector $\vec{a}$ and a scalar quantity $\lambda \in \mathbb{R}$. Then, the quantity $\lambda\vec{a}$ is a scalar multiple of $\vec{a}$. It indicates a vector in the same or opposite direction as $\vec{a}$ depending on whether λ is positive or negative, and has magnitude equal to $|\lambda||\vec{a}|$.

Theorem 8.9: Two vectors $\vec{a}$ and $\vec{b}$ are collinear if and only if there exists $\lambda \in \mathbb{R}$ such that $\vec{a} = \lambda \vec{b}$. In the component form, if $\vec{a} = x\hat{i} + y\hat{j} + z\hat{k}$, then

$$\vec{b} = \lambda x\hat{i} + \lambda y\hat{j} + \lambda z\hat{k}$$

> **Useful Tip:** Addition or multiplication can be made more convenient by writing each vector in its component form.

Theorem 8.10: If $P_1 = (x_1, y_1, z_1)$ and $P_2 = (x_2, y_2, z_2)$ are two points in the space, then the vector joining the two points is given by

$$\vec{P_1P_2} = (x_2 - x_1)\hat{i} + (y_2 - y_1)\hat{j} + (z_2 - z_1)\hat{k}$$

Theorem 8.11 (Dot Product): For two non-zero vectors $\vec{a}$ and $\vec{b}$, their scalar product or dot product is given by

$$\vec{a} \cdot \vec{b} = |\vec{a}||\vec{b}|\cos\theta,$$

where θ is the angle between the two vectors. A few important properties of the dot product are listed below:

- Dot product is always a scalar quantity.

- Scalar product is commutative and distributive, that is, for any three vectors $\vec{a}$, $\vec{b}$ and $\vec{c}$

$$\vec{a} \cdot \vec{b} = \vec{b} \cdot \vec{a}, \ \vec{a} \cdot (\vec{b} + \vec{c}) = (\vec{a} \cdot \vec{b}) + (\vec{a} \cdot \vec{c})$$

- For two vectors $\vec{a}$, $\vec{b}$ and for $\lambda \in \mathbb{R}$

$$\left(\lambda \vec{a}\right) \cdot \vec{b} = \lambda \left(\vec{a} \cdot \vec{b}\right) = \vec{a} \cdot \left(\lambda \vec{b}\right)$$

- The dot product of two vectors is zero if and only if they are perpendicular to each other. On the other hand, if two vectors are along the same (or opposite) direction, then their dot product is the simple product (or the negative of the product) of their magnitudes.

- The angle between two non-zero vectors is given by

$$\theta = \cos^{-1}\left(\frac{\vec{a} \cdot \vec{b}}{|\vec{a}||\vec{b}|}\right)$$

Theorem 8.12 (Projection): Consider a vector $\vec{a}$ that makes an angle θ with a given directed line L in the anticlockwise direction. Then, the projection of the vector on the line is another vector $\vec{p}$ with magnitude $|\vec{a}|\cos\theta$, with the direction being the same as (or opposite to) that of L, depending upon whether $\cos\theta$ is positive (or negative). This vector $\vec{p}$ is called the projection vector, and its magnitude is termed the projection of $\vec{a}$ on L. One can infer that the projection of $\vec{a}$ on another vector $\vec{u}$ is $(\vec{a} \cdot \vec{u})/|\vec{u}|$.

Theorem 8.13 (Cross Product): Consider two non-zero vectors $\vec{u}$ and $\vec{v}$. Then, the vector product or cross product of the two vectors is defined as

$$\vec{u} \times \vec{v} = \left(|\vec{u}||\vec{v}|\sin\theta\right)\hat{p},$$

where θ is the angle between the two vectors, and $\hat{p}$ is a unit vector such that the right-handed system rotated from $\vec{u}$ to $\vec{v}$ moves in the direction of $\hat{p}$.

> **Useful Tip:** Cross products are distributive, but non-commutative. The reader is advised to explore other properties of cross products, akin to the ones presented earlier regarding scalar products.

Miscellaneous

One of the most useful ways to calculate the cross product of two vectors is to use the component forms and the concept of determinants. It can be showed that if $\vec{u} = u_1\hat{i} + u_2\hat{j} + u_3\hat{k}$ and $\vec{v} = v_1\hat{i} + v_2\hat{j} + v_3\hat{k}$, then

$$\vec{u} \times \vec{v} = \begin{vmatrix} \hat{i} & \hat{j} & \hat{k} \\ u_1 & u_2 & u_3 \\ v_1 & v_2 & v_3 \end{vmatrix}$$

Theorem 8.14 (Equation of a Line in 3D): Consider a point A in the 3D space such that $\vec{a}$ is the position vector with respect to the origin O. Let $\vec{r}$ be the position vector of a point on the line L that passes through A and is parallel to another vector $\vec{b}$. Then, $\vec{r} = \vec{a} + \lambda \vec{b}$ for some real constant λ. The converse also holds.

From the above, one can also infer that if $A = (x_1, y_1, z_1)$ and $\vec{b} = x_2\hat{i} + y_2\hat{j} + z_2\hat{k}$, then the Cartesian form of the equation of L is

$$\frac{x - x_1}{x_2} = \frac{y - y_1}{y_2} = \frac{z - z_1}{z_2}$$

Further, for two points $A = (x_1, y_1, z_1)$ and $B = (x_2, y_2, z_2)$, the Cartesian form of the equation of the straight line AB is given by

$$\frac{x - x_1}{x_2 - x_1} = \frac{y - y_1}{y_2 - y_1} = \frac{z - z_1}{z_2 - z_1}$$

> **Useful Tip:** It can be more convenient to consider the vector form of a line passing through A and B. If their position vectors are given by $\vec{u}$ and $\vec{v}$, respectively, and if $\vec{r}$ is the position vector of any random point on AB, then $\vec{r} = \vec{u} + \lambda(\vec{v} - \vec{u})$ for some scalar quantity $\lambda \in \mathbb{R}$.

Theorem 8.15 (Angle Between Two Lines): Let L_1 and L_2 be two lines passing through the origin O and with direction ratios x_1, y_1, z_1 and x_2, y_2, z_2, respectively. Let P be a point on L_1 and Q be a point on L_2. If θ is the acute angle between the directed lines OP and OQ, then

$$\cos\theta = \left| \frac{x_1 x_2 + y_1 y_2 + z_1 z_2}{\sqrt{x_1^2 + y_1^2 + z_1^2} \sqrt{x_2^2 + y_2^2 + z_2^2}} \right|$$

Note that the above is in principle the same as the formula obtained using the dot product.

Theorem 8.16 (Coplanar Lines): Two lines given by $\vec{r} = \vec{u_1} + \lambda_1 \vec{v_1}$ and $\vec{r} = \vec{u_2} + \lambda_2 \vec{v_2}$ are coplanar if and only if $(\vec{u_2} - \vec{u_1}) \cdot (\vec{v_1} \times \vec{v_2}) = 0$.

Theorem 8.17 (Distance Between Two Lines): If two lines are intersecting, then the distance between the lines is zero. If two lines are parallel, then their distance can be computed by the perpendicular distance of any point on the first line from the second. However, in 3D geometry, two lines can be neither intersecting nor parallel. They are in fact non-coplanar and are known as skew lines. Let $L_1 : \vec{r} = \vec{u_1} + \lambda_1 \vec{v_1}$ and $L_2 : \vec{r} = \vec{u_2} + \lambda_2 \vec{v_2}$ be two such skew lines. Then, the shortest distance between them is given by

$$d = \left| \frac{(\vec{v_1} \times \vec{v_2}) \cdot (\vec{u_1} - \vec{u_2})}{|\vec{v_1} \times \vec{v_2}|} \right|$$

The equation of the vector corresponding to the above shortest distance is given by $d\hat{\eta}$, where $\hat{\eta}$ is the unit vector whose direction is perpendicular to both $\vec{v_1}$ and $\vec{v_2}$.

In the Cartesian form, if the equations are denoted by

$$L_1 : \frac{x - x_1}{a_1} = \frac{y - y_1}{b_1} = \frac{z - z_1}{c_1},$$

$$L_2 : \frac{x - x_1}{a_1} = \frac{y - y_1}{b_1} = \frac{z - z_1}{c_1},$$

then the shortest distance can be calculated by the determinant of the matrix

$$\frac{1}{\sqrt{(b_1 c_2 - b_2 c_1)^2 + (c_1 a_2 - c_2 a_1)^2 + (a_1 b_2 - a_2 b_1)^2}} \begin{pmatrix} x_2 - x_1 & y_2 - y_1 & z_2 - z_1 \\ a_1 & b_1 & c_1 \\ a_2 & b_2 & c_2 \end{pmatrix}$$

> **Useful Tip:** The above theorem can be directly used to compute the distance between two parallel lines as well. The reader is instructed to find out the simplified expression for that case.

We next turn our attention to planes in 3D space. Observe that a plane is determined uniquely if any one of the following is true:

(i) The normal to the plane and its distance from the origin are known.

(ii) The plane passes through a point and is perpendicular to a given direction.

(iii) The plane passes through three given non-collinear points.

Theorem 8.18 (Equation of a Plane): The aforementioned three cases are presented below:

(i) Suppose that a plane is at a distance d ($d > 0$) from the origin O. Let $\vec{ON}$ be the normal from the origin to the plane such that N is a point on the plane, and let $\hat{\eta}$ be the unit normal vector along $\vec{ON}$. Then, if $\vec{r}$ denotes the position vector of any point on the plane, its equation is given by $\vec{r} \cdot \hat{\eta} = d$.

In the Cartesian form, one can use the direction cosines of $\hat{\eta}$ to find the above equation. If the direction cosines are ℓ, m, n, then the required equation is $\ell x + my + nz = d$.

(ii) Assume that a plane passes through a point $A = (x_1, y_1, z_1)$ with position vector $\vec{a}$ and suppose that it is perpendicular to another vector $\vec{u}$. If $\vec{r}$ is the position vector of any point $P = (x, y, z)$ on the plane, then the equation of the plane is $(\vec{r} - \vec{a}) \cdot \vec{u} = 0$.

If A, B, C are the direction cosines of $\vec{u}$, then the Cartesian form of the equation of the plane is $A(x - x_1) + B(y - y_1) + C(z - z_1) = 0$.

(iii) Let $A = (x_1, y_1, z_1)$, $B = (x_2, y_2, z_2)$, $C = (x_3, y_3, z_3)$ be three non-collinear points whose position vectors are denoted by $\vec{a}$, $\vec{b}$ and $\vec{c}$, respectively. If $\vec{r}$ is the position vector of any point $P = (x, y, z)$ on the plane, then the vector form of the equation of the plane is $(\vec{r} - \vec{a}) \cdot [(\vec{b} - \vec{a}) \times (\vec{c} - \vec{a})] = 0$. The corresponding Cartesian form can be presented using determinants as follows:

$$\begin{vmatrix} x - x_1 & y - y_1 & z - z_1 \\ x_2 - x_1 & y_2 - y_1 & z_2 - z_1 \\ x_3 - x_1 & y_3 - y_1 & z_3 - z_1 \end{vmatrix} = 0$$

Theorem 8.19 (Intercept Form of the Equation of a Plane): If a plane leaves intercepts a, b, c on the three axes, then its equation is given by

$$\frac{x}{a} + \frac{y}{b} + \frac{z}{c} = 1$$

Theorem 8.20 (Angle Between a Line and a Plane): The angle between the line $\vec{r} = \vec{u} + \lambda \vec{v}$ and the plane $\vec{r} \cdot \vec{s} = d$ is

$$\theta = \cos^{-1} \left| \frac{\vec{v} \cdot \vec{s}}{|\vec{v}||\vec{s}|} \right|$$

Theorem 8.21 (Angle Between Two Planes): Consider the planes given by the equations $\vec{r} \cdot \vec{s_1} = d_1$ and $\vec{r} \cdot \vec{s_2} = d_2$. The angle between these planes is defined as the angle between their normals. It can be computed from the formula

$$\theta = \cos^{-1} \left| \frac{\vec{s_1} \cdot \vec{s_2}}{|\vec{s_1}||\vec{s_2}|} \right|$$

If the Cartesian equations of the two planes are $A_1x + B_1y + C_1z + D_1 = 0$ and $A_2x + B_2y + C_2z + D_2 = 0$, then the angle between the planes is

$$\theta = \cos^{-1} \left| \frac{A_1A_2 + B_1B_2 + C_1C_2}{\sqrt{A_1^2 + B_1^2 + C_1^2}\sqrt{A_2^2 + B_2^2 + C_2^2}} \right|$$

Useful Tip: Observe that two planes are parallel if and only if $A_1/A_2 = B_1/B_2 = C_1/C_2$, whereas two planes are perpendicular if and only if $A_1A_2 + B_1B_2 + C_1C_2 = 0$.

Theorem 8.22: Let the equations of two intersecting planes $\mathcal{P}_1$ and $\mathcal{P}_2$ be $\vec{r} \cdot \vec{s_1} = d_1$ and $\vec{r} \cdot \vec{s_2} = d_2$, respectively. Let $\mathcal{P}$ be the plane passing through the line of intersection of the two planes. Then, the vector equation of $\mathcal{P}$ is $\vec{r} \cdot (\vec{s_1} + \lambda \vec{s_2}) = d_1 + \lambda d_2$. If (A_1, B_1, C_1) and (A_2, B_2, C_2) are the direction cosines for the vectors $\vec{s_1}$ and $\vec{s_2}$, then the Cartesian equation of $\mathcal{P}$ is $(A_1x + B_1y + C_1z - d_1) + \lambda(A_2x + B_2y + C_2z - d_2) = 0$.

Theorem 8.23: Consider a point X with position vector $\vec{a}$ and a plane $\mathcal{P}$ with equation $\vec{r} \cdot \hat{\eta} = d$. Then, the distance of A from $\mathcal{P}$ is $|d - \vec{a} \cdot \hat{\eta}|$. In the Cartesian form, if the equation of the plane is $Ax + By + Cz = D$, then the distance of $X = (x_1, y_1, z_1)$ from $\mathcal{P}$ is

$$\left| \frac{Ax_1 + By_1 + Cz_1 - D}{\sqrt{A^2 + B^2 + C^2}} \right|$$

Solved Examples

1. Let $\vec{u}$ and $\vec{v}$ be the position vectors for the points $U = (1,1,1)$ and $V = (1,2,3)$, respectively. Find the unit vector(s) perpendicular to each of the vectors $\vec{u} + \vec{v}$ and $\vec{u} - \vec{v}$.

Solution: Using the concepts of component vectors, we can obtain

$$\vec{u} + \vec{v} = 2\hat{i} + 3\hat{j} + 4\hat{k}, \quad \vec{u} - \vec{v} = -\hat{j} - 2\hat{k}$$

Taking the cross product, we can write

$$(\vec{u} + \vec{v}) \times (\vec{u} - \vec{v}) = \begin{vmatrix} \hat{i} & \hat{j} & \hat{k} \\ 2 & 3 & 4 \\ 0 & -1 & -2 \end{vmatrix} = -2\hat{i} + 4\hat{j} - 2\hat{k}$$

If we denote the above by $\vec{w}$, it is easy to calculate that

$$|\vec{w}| = \sqrt{(-2)^2 + 4^2 + (-2)^2} = \sqrt{24} = 2\sqrt{6},$$

Miscellaneous

which implies that the unit vector is

$$\hat{w} = -\frac{1}{\sqrt{6}}\hat{i} + \frac{2}{\sqrt{6}}\hat{j} - \frac{1}{\sqrt{6}}\hat{k}$$

We can also take the cross product of $\vec{u} - \vec{v}$ and $\vec{u} + \vec{v}$ and obtain the unit vector, which is of the same magnitude and in the opposite direction of $\hat{w}$, that is, the vector $(-\hat{w})$.

2. Show that the points $A = (-2, 3, 5)$, $B = (1, 2, 3)$ and $C = (7, 0, -1)$ are collinear.

Solution: We can use the concepts of vector to solve this. Let $\hat{i}, \hat{j}, \hat{k}$ be the unit vectors in the directions of the three axes. Then, the given coordinates give us the following three vectors:

$$\vec{AB} = 3\hat{i} - \hat{j} - 2\hat{k}, \quad \vec{BC} = 6\hat{i} - 2\hat{j} - 4\hat{k}, \quad \vec{CA} = -9\hat{i} + 3\hat{j} + 6\hat{k}$$

Subsequently, we obtain

$$\left|\vec{AB}\right|^2 = 14, \quad \left|\vec{BC}\right|^2 = 56, \quad \left|\vec{CA}\right|^2 = 126$$

Clearly, $|\vec{AB}| = \sqrt{14}$, while $|\vec{BC}| = 2\sqrt{14}$ and $|\vec{CA}| = 3\sqrt{14}$, which implies that $|\vec{AB}| + |\vec{BC}| = |\vec{CA}|$. Thus, the three points are collinear.

> **Useful Tip:** One can also solve the above by using the fact that three points A, B, C are collinear if and only if the angle between the vectors $\vec{AB}$ and $\vec{BC}$ is either 0 or π.

3. Take the scalar product of the vector $\hat{i} + \hat{j} + \hat{k}$ with a unit vector along the sum of $\vec{u} = 2\hat{i} + 4\hat{j} - 5\hat{k}$ and $\vec{v} = a\hat{i} + 2\hat{j} + 3\hat{k}$. If that scalar product is one, what is the value of a?

Solution: Observe that the sum of the two given vectors is

$$\vec{w} = \vec{u} + \vec{v} = (a+2)\hat{i} + 6\hat{j} - 2\hat{k}$$

Thus, the unit vector along the direction of $\vec{w}$ is

$$\hat{w} = \frac{1}{\sqrt{(a+2)^2 + 40}} [(a+2)\hat{i} + 6\hat{j} - 2\hat{k}]$$

Recall that the dot product of $\hat{i}, \hat{j}$ or $\hat{k}$ with itself is 1; while the dot product of any pair of these unit vectors is 0. Thus, letting $\hat{i} + \hat{j} + \hat{k}$ be denoted by $\vec{z}$, we get

$$\vec{z} \cdot \vec{w} = (a+2) + 6 - 2 = a + 6$$

From the provided condition, we can then write

$$\frac{a+6}{\sqrt{(a+2)^2+40}} = 1 \implies (a+6)^2 = (a+2)^2 + 40 \implies 8a = 8$$

Hence, the value of a is 1.

4. Let $a,b,c,d \in \mathbb{Z}$ such that $ad - bc \neq 0$. If b_1, b_2 are integer multiples of $ad - bc$, prove that there are integers x,y simultaneously satisfying the equations $ax + by = b_1$, $cx + dy = b_2$.

Solution: The given system of equations can be written in matrix form as

$$\begin{bmatrix} a & b \\ c & d \end{bmatrix} \begin{pmatrix} x \\ y \end{pmatrix} = \begin{pmatrix} b_1 \\ b_2 \end{pmatrix}$$

For convenience, let us write the above as $Au = v$. It is easy to observe that $|A| = ad - bc \neq 0$, and therefore, A is an invertible matrix. Clearly, the system has a solution in real numbers, and one can write $u = A^{-1}v$. We further note that there exist integers m,n such that $b_1 = m(ad - bc)$ and $b_2 = n(ad - bc)$. Now, one can calculate the inverse of A as

$$A^{-1} = \frac{1}{ad - bc} \begin{bmatrix} d & -b \\ -c & a \end{bmatrix},$$

which implies that the solution of the given system is

$$u = \frac{1}{ad-bc} \begin{bmatrix} d & -b \\ -c & a \end{bmatrix} \begin{pmatrix} b_1 \\ b_2 \end{pmatrix} = \frac{1}{ad-bc} \begin{pmatrix} db_1 - bb_2 \\ -cb_1 + ab_2 \end{pmatrix} = \begin{pmatrix} dm - bn \\ -cm + an \end{pmatrix}$$

Since all of the terms in the above solution are integers, the proof is completed.

> **Useful Tip:** The above problem describes how the concepts of matrices can sometimes provide a simpler way of solving number theoretic problems. The reader is advised to find a direct solution using the techniques discussed in Chapter 1.

5. Let M_n denote an $n \times n$ matrix such that all diagonal entries are 10, the (i,j)th entry is 3 if $|i - j| = 1$, and all the other entries are zero. We define D_n as the determinant of M_n. If D_n satisfies

$$\sum_{n=1}^{\infty} \frac{1}{8D_n + 1} = \frac{p}{q},$$

where p and q are co-prime positive integers, compute the value of $p + q$.

Miscellaneous 8.17

Solution: Let us write D_n for $n = 1, 2, 3$ as

$$D_1 = |10| = 10, \quad D_2 = \begin{vmatrix} 10 & 3 \\ 3 & 10 \end{vmatrix} = 91, \quad D_3 = \begin{vmatrix} 10 & 3 & 0 \\ 3 & 10 & 3 \\ 0 & 3 & 10 \end{vmatrix}$$

Now, using the recursive definition of determinants, we can rewrite D_3 as

$$D_3 = \begin{vmatrix} 10 & 3 & 0 \\ 3 & 10 & 3 \\ 0 & 3 & 10 \end{vmatrix} = 10 \begin{vmatrix} 10 & 3 \\ 3 & 10 \end{vmatrix} - 3 \begin{vmatrix} 3 & 3 \\ 0 & 10 \end{vmatrix} + 0 \begin{vmatrix} 3 & 10 \\ 0 & 3 \end{vmatrix} = 10D_2 - 9D_1 = 820$$

We observe that the above pattern repeats because the first element in the first row of M_n is always 10, the second element is always 3, and the rest are always 0. Then, the first term directly expands to $10D_{n-1}$. The next term expands to three times the determinant of the matrix formed from omitting the second column and first row from the original matrix. Call this matrix X_n. Note that the first column of X_n is composed entirely of zeros except for the first element, which is a 3. A property of matrices is that the determinant can be expanded over rows or columns (using the recursive definition), and the determinant found will still be the same. Thus, expanding over the first column yields $3D_{n-2}$, since the other elements in the column are all zeros. Subsequently, the $3 \det(X_n)$ expression turns into $9D_{n-2}$. Hence, the equation $D_n = 10D_{n-1} - 9D_{n-2}$ holds for all $n > 2$.

This equation can be rewritten as $D_n = 10(D_{n-1} - D_{n-2}) + D_{n-2}$. This version of the equation involves the difference of successive terms of a recursive sequence. Calculating D_0 backwards from the recursive formula and D_4 from the formula yields $D_0 = 1, D_4 = 7381$. Examining the differences between successive terms, a pattern emerges: $D_0 = 1 = 9^0$, $D_1 - D_0 = 10 - 1 = 9 = 9^1$, $D_2 - D_1 = 91 - 10 = 81 = 9^2$, $D_3 - D_2 = 820 - 91 = 729 = 9^3$, $D_4 - D_3 = 7381 - 820 = 6561 = 9^4$. We can now hypothesize (and prove using the principles of mathematical induction) that

$$D_n = D_0 + 9^1 + 9^2 + \ldots + 9^n = \sum_{i=0}^{n} 9^i = \frac{(1)(9^{n+1} - 1)}{9 - 1} = \frac{9^{n+1} - 1}{8}$$

From the above, the desired sum can be written as

$$\sum_{n=1}^{\infty} \frac{1}{8D_n + 1} = \sum_{n=1}^{\infty} \frac{1}{9^{n+1} - 1 + 1} = \sum_{n=1}^{\infty} \frac{1}{9^{n+1}}$$

The above is an infinite geometric series with first term $1/81$ and common ratio $1/9$. Therefore, the sum is $(1/81)/(1 - 1/9) = 9/(81 \times 8) = 1/72$. It implies that the value of $p + q$ is 73.

6. If $A = \begin{pmatrix} 3 & 1 \\ -4 & -1 \end{pmatrix}$, find the determinant of

$$\lim_{n \to \infty} \frac{1}{n}\left(I + \frac{A^n}{n}\right)^n.$$

Solution: Let us define two column vectors

$$a = \begin{pmatrix} 1 \\ -2 \end{pmatrix}, \quad b = \begin{pmatrix} 2 \\ 1 \end{pmatrix}$$

Then, note that $a^\top b = 0$, that is, a and b are orthogonal. Further, observe that A can be written as $I + ab^\top$. This result will make our calculations easier.

It is straightforward to verify that $(I + pab^\top)(I + qab^\top) = I + (p+q)ab^\top$, which implies that $A^n = I + nab^\top$. Therefore

$$\left(I + \frac{A^n}{n}\right)^n = \left(I + \frac{I + nab^\top}{n}\right)^n = \left(\left(1 + \frac{1}{n}\right)I + ab^\top\right)^n$$

Expanding further, we obtain

$$\left(I + \frac{A^n}{n}\right)^n = \left(1 + \frac{1}{n}\right)^n \left(I + \left(1 + \frac{1}{n}\right)^{-1} ab^\top\right)^n = \left(1 + \frac{1}{n}\right)^n \left(I + \frac{n^2}{n+1} ab^\top\right)$$

The last equality is obtained by using the same property as before. Thus

$$\lim_{n \to \infty} \frac{1}{n}\left(I + \frac{A^n}{n}\right)^n = \lim_{n \to \infty} \left(1 + \frac{1}{n}\right)^n \lim_{n \to \infty} \left(\frac{I}{n} + \frac{n}{n+1} ab^\top\right) = eab^\top = e(A - I)$$

Substituting the values of the matrices, the required determinant can be computed as

$$\begin{vmatrix} 2e & e \\ -4e & -2e \end{vmatrix} = -4e^2 + 4e^2 = 0$$

7. If D_n is the matrix

$$\begin{bmatrix} \frac{1}{x_1 + y_1} & \frac{1}{x_1 + y_2} & \cdots & \frac{1}{x_1 + y_n} \\ \frac{1}{x_2 + y_1} & \frac{1}{x_2 + y_2} & & \frac{1}{x_2 + y_n} \\ \vdots & \vdots & \ddots & \vdots \\ \frac{1}{x_n + y_1} & \frac{1}{x_n + y_2} & \cdots & \frac{1}{x_n + y_n} \end{bmatrix},$$

Miscellaneous 8.19

show that
$$|D_n| = \frac{\prod_{1 \leq i < j \leq n}(x_j - x_i)(y_j - y_i)}{\prod_{1 \leq i, j \leq n}(x_i + y_j)}.$$

Solution: Let us write the entries of D_n with a_{ij} such that $a_{ij} = 1/(x_i + y_j)$. Subtract column 1 from each of columns 2 to n. This leads to the terms

$$a_{ij} \leftarrow \frac{1}{x_i + y_j} - \frac{1}{x_i + y_1} = \frac{(x_i + y_1) - (x_i + y_j)}{(x_i + y_j)(x_i + y_1)} = \left(\frac{y_1 - y_j}{x_i + y_1}\right)\left(\frac{1}{x_i + y_j}\right)$$

From the property of determinants, we know that the multiple of a row added to another row of a matrix does not have any effect on the value of the determinant. Next, we apply the following operations:

(1) Extract the factor $1/(x_i + y_1)$ from each row $1 \leq i \leq n$.

(2) Extract the factor $(y_1 - y_j)$ from each column $1 \leq j \leq n$.

Once again, using the properties of determinants, we can write the following:

$$D_n = \prod_{i=1}^{n}\left(\frac{1}{x_i + y_1}\right) \prod_{j=2}^{n}(y_1 - y_j) \begin{vmatrix} 1 & \frac{1}{x_1 + y_2} & \frac{1}{x_1 + y_3} & \cdots & \frac{1}{x_1 + y_n} \\ 1 & \frac{1}{x_2 + y_2} & \frac{1}{x_2 + y_3} & \cdots & \frac{1}{x_2 + y_n} \\ 1 & \frac{1}{x_3 + y_2} & \frac{1}{x_3 + y_3} & \cdots & \frac{1}{x_3 + y_n} \\ \vdots & \vdots & \vdots & \ddots & \vdots \\ 1 & \frac{1}{x_n + y_2} & \frac{1}{x_n + y_3} & \cdots & \frac{1}{x_n + y_n} \end{vmatrix}$$

Next, subtract row 1 from each of rows 2 to n. Then, column 1 becomes 0 for all but the first row, while columns 2 to n change as follows:

$$a_{ij} \leftarrow \frac{1}{x_i + y_j} - \frac{1}{x_1 + y_j} = \frac{(x_1 + y_j) - (x_i + y_j)}{(x_i + y_j)(x_1 + y_j)} = \left(\frac{x_1 - x_i}{x_1 + y_j}\right)\left(\frac{1}{x_i + y_j}\right)$$

Using similar arguments as before, we can say that this would have no effect on the value of the determinant. Now, consider the following operations:

(1) Extract the factor $(x_1 - x_i)$ from each row $2 \leq i \leq n$.

(2) Extract the factor $1/(x_1 + y_j)$ from each column $2 \leq j \leq n$.

Since each row or column is multiplied by constant terms, we obtain

$$D_n = \prod_{i=1}^{n}\left(\frac{1}{x_i+y_1}\right)\prod_{j=1}^{n}\left(\frac{1}{x_1+y_j}\right)\prod_{i=2}^{n}(x_1-x_i)\prod_{j=2}^{n}(y_1-y_j) \times$$

$$\begin{vmatrix} 1 & 1 & 1 & \cdots & 1 \\ 0 & \dfrac{1}{x_2+y_2} & \dfrac{1}{x_2+y_3} & \cdots & \dfrac{1}{x_2+y_n} \\ 0 & \dfrac{1}{x_3+y_2} & \dfrac{1}{x_3+y_3} & \cdots & \dfrac{1}{x_3+y_n} \\ \vdots & \vdots & \vdots & \ddots & \vdots \\ 0 & \dfrac{1}{x_n+y_2} & \dfrac{1}{x_n+y_3} & \cdots & \dfrac{1}{x_n+y_n} \end{vmatrix}$$

From the law of determinants, with the unit element in what would otherwise be the zero row, and tidying up the products, we get

$$D_n = \frac{\prod_{i=2}^{n}(x_i-x_1)(y_i-y_1)}{\prod_{1\leqslant i,j\leqslant n}(x_i+y_1)(x_1+y_j)}\begin{vmatrix} \dfrac{1}{x_2+y_2} & \dfrac{1}{x_2+y_3} & \cdots & \dfrac{1}{x_2+y_n} \\ \dfrac{1}{x_3+y_2} & \dfrac{1}{x_3+y_3} & \cdots & \dfrac{1}{x_3+y_n} \\ \vdots & \vdots & \ddots & \vdots \\ \dfrac{1}{x_n+y_2} & \dfrac{1}{x_n+y_3} & \cdots & \dfrac{1}{x_n+y_n} \end{vmatrix}$$

We can repeat an identical process for the remaining rows and columns and the result will follow immediately.

> **Useful Tip:** The operations that keep the determinant invariant are used repeatedly in the above problem. One should be careful about how any such operation changes a matrix versus how that affects the determinant.

8. Let $a \neq b$ be two positive real numbers. Define $S_k = \sum_{i=0}^{n} i^k$ for all $0 \leqslant k \leqslant 2n$, where n is an integer greater than 2 (take $0^0 = 1$). Let $a_0, a_1, \ldots, a_n \in \mathbb{R}$ satisfy the equation

$$\begin{pmatrix} S_0 & S_1 & \cdots & S_n \\ S_1 & S_2 & \cdots & S_{n+1} \\ \vdots & \vdots & \ddots & \vdots \\ S_{n-1} & S_n & \cdots & S_{2n-1} \\ S_n & S_{n+1} & \cdots & S_{2n} \end{pmatrix} \begin{pmatrix} a_0 \\ a_1 \\ \vdots \\ a_{n-1} \\ a_n \end{pmatrix} = \begin{pmatrix} a \\ b \\ \vdots \\ b \\ b \end{pmatrix}.$$

Show that

$$a \cdot a_0 + b \cdot \sum_{i=1}^{n} a_i = a^2 - 2ab + 2b^2.$$

Solution: Consider the following expressions

$$A(X) = \sum_{i=0}^{n} a_i X^i, B(X) = \prod_{i=1}^{n}(X-i) = \sum_{i=0}^{n} b_i X^i, C(X) = X\prod_{i=2}^{n}(X-i) = \sum_{i=0}^{n} c_i X^i$$

Then, the given condition is equivalent to $\sum_{i=0}^{n} A(i) = a$ and $\sum_{i=0}^{n} i^k A(i) = b$ for $1 \leqslant k \leqslant n$, and we need to find $(a-b)A(0) + bA(1)$. Let us call it T for convenience.

Note that

$$(a-b)B(0) = \sum_{k=0}^{n} b_k \sum_{i=0}^{n} i^k A(i) = \sum_{i=0}^{n} A(i)B(i) = A(0)B(0),$$

which implies that $A(0) = a-b$. On the other hand

$$bC(1) = \sum_{k=0}^{n} c_k \sum_{i=0}^{n} i^k A(i) = \sum_{i=0}^{n} A(i)C(i) = A(1)C(1),$$

and the above leads to $A(1) = b$. Hence, $T = (a-b)^2 + b^2 = a^2 - 2ab + 2b^2$.

9. Consider the real-valued matrix

$$A = \begin{bmatrix} 1 & 2 & 2 \\ 2 & 1 & -2 \\ a & 2 & b \end{bmatrix}$$

and assume that $AA^\top = 9I_3$. Calculate the value of $C_{22}(A)$. (C is used to denote the cofactor).

Solution: We first note that $A^{-1} = A^\top/9$. On the other hand, using the properties of determinants, from $AA^\top = 9I_3$, we can write $|A|^2 = 729$, which gives $|A| = 27$.

Recall that $A^{-1} = \text{Adj}(A)/|A|$. Here, $\text{Adj}(A)$ denotes the adjoint matrix of A, in which the elements are the cofactors. Thus, we can write $\text{Adj}(A) = 3A^\top$. Therefore, $C_{22}(A)$ (this is the cofactor at the $(2,2)$th position) is 3.

> **Useful Tip:** The above shows a smarter way of using the known properties of determinants and inverses of matrices to solve the problem. One can obviously take a direct approach to first solve for a and b, and then compute the cofactor.

10. If $a^2 + b^2 = 1$, $c^2 + d^2 = 1$, $ac + bd = 0$, show that $a^2 + c^2 = 1$, $b^2 + d^2 = 1$, $ab + cd = 0$.

Solution: Consider the matrix

$$A = \begin{bmatrix} a & b \\ c & d \end{bmatrix}$$

Then

$$AA^T = \begin{bmatrix} a & b \\ c & d \end{bmatrix} \begin{bmatrix} a & c \\ b & d \end{bmatrix} = \begin{bmatrix} a^2+b^2 & ac+bd \\ ac+bd & c^2+d^2 \end{bmatrix} = \begin{bmatrix} 1 & 0 \\ 0 & 1 \end{bmatrix}$$

The above clearly indicates that $A^T = A^{-1}$, and therefore

$$A^T A = \begin{bmatrix} 1 & 0 \\ 0 & 1 \end{bmatrix}$$

We can also show that

$$A^T A = \begin{bmatrix} a & c \\ b & d \end{bmatrix} \begin{bmatrix} a & b \\ c & d \end{bmatrix} = \begin{bmatrix} a^2+c^2 & ab+cd \\ ab+cd & b^2+d^2 \end{bmatrix},$$

and that completes the proof.

> **Useful Tip:** An alternative solution can be worked out by proving that $(a^2+b^2)(c^2+d^2) = 1$, which would subsequently prove the required result.

11. Find the possible real values of a such that the system of equations

$$\begin{aligned} x+y+z &= a, \\ x^2+y^2+z^2 &= 1, \\ xy &= z^2. \end{aligned}$$

has real positive solutions.

Solution: Using the third equation of the given system, we can rewrite the first two equations as

$$(x+y)+z = a, \quad (x+y)^2 - z^2 = 1$$

Since the system has positive solutions, we can infer from the above that $(x+y) - z = 1/a$. This leads to the relations

$$x+y = \frac{a^2+1}{2a}, \quad z = \frac{a^2-1}{2a}$$

For both of the above terms to be positive, we must have $a > 0$ and $a^2 > 1$. We also obtain that

$$x+y = \frac{a^2+1}{2a}, \quad xy = \left(\frac{a^2-1}{2a}\right)^2,$$

which implies that x, y are the roots of the quadratic equation

$$p^2 - \left(\frac{a^2+1}{2a}\right)p + \left(\frac{a^2-1}{2a}\right)^2 = 0$$

Miscellaneous

As x, y are positive real numbers, the discriminant of the above equation must be positive. Therefore
$$\left(\frac{a^2+1}{2a}\right)^2 - 4\left(\frac{a^2-1}{2a}\right)^2 = \frac{(3a^2-1)(3-a^2)}{4a^2} \geqslant 0$$
We have already showed that $a^2 > 1$, which along with the above implies that a^2 lies between 1 and 3, that is, $1 < a < \sqrt{3}$. The corresponding solutions can be worked out in the same way as above.

12. Sketch the set $A \cap B$ in the two-dimensional plane, where
$$A = \left\{z : \left|\frac{z+1}{z-1}\right| \leqslant 1\right\}, B = \{z : |z| - \operatorname{Re} z \leqslant 1\}.$$

Solution: We can treat z as a complex number and consider the points in the Argand plane. Suppose $z \in A \cap B$ and we assume that $z = x + iy$. Since $z \in A$, we get
$$\left|\frac{z+1}{z-1}\right|^2 \leqslant 1 \implies |z+1|^2 \leqslant |z-1|^2 \implies |x+1+iy|^2 \leqslant |x-1+iy|^2$$
The above simplifies to
$$(x+1)^2 + y^2 \leqslant (x-1)^2 + y^2 \implies (x+1)^2 - (x-1)^2 \leqslant 0 \implies 4x \leqslant 0$$
Thus, x is a negative quantity. Now, from B, we get $\sqrt{x^2+y^2} - x \leqslant 1$, implying that
$$x^2 + y^2 \leqslant (x+1)^2 \implies x^2 + y^2 \leqslant x^2 + 2x + 1 \implies y^2 \leqslant 2x + 1$$
The above denotes the inside of the parabola $y^2 = 2x + 1$, and hence, $A \cap B$ is the region inside the parabola where x is negative. This region is denoted in the figure below.

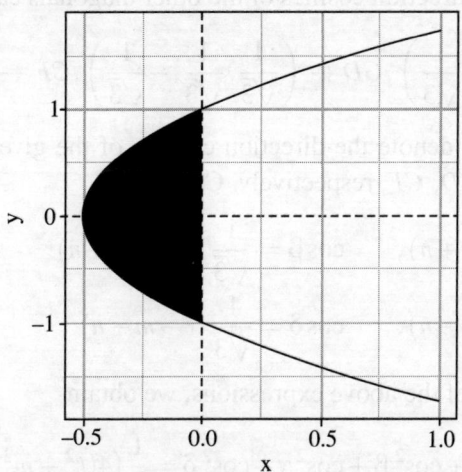

13. If a line makes angles $\alpha, \beta, \gamma, \delta$ with the diagonals of a cube, then show that
$$\cos^2\alpha + \cos^2\beta + \cos^2\gamma + \cos^2\delta = \frac{4}{3}.$$

Solution: A cube has equal length, breadth and width. We present the cube in the following figure. *ABCDEFGO* is the cube, where O is the origin. If we assume that the length of the cube is a units, then the coordinates of the other vertices are $A = (a,a,a)$, $B = (0,a,a)$, $C = (0,a,0)$, $D = (a,a,0)$, $E = (a,0,0)$, $F = (a,0,a)$ and $G = (0,0,a)$.

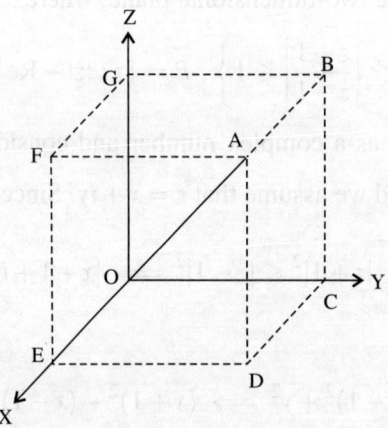

Now, the direction cosines of the diagonal *OA* are given by
$$\left(\frac{a-0}{\sqrt{a^2+a^2+a^2}}, \frac{a-0}{\sqrt{a^2+a^2+a^2}}, \frac{a-0}{\sqrt{a^2+a^2+a^2}}\right) = \left(\frac{1}{\sqrt{3}}, \frac{1}{\sqrt{3}}, \frac{1}{\sqrt{3}}\right)$$

In a similar fashion, the direction cosines of the other diagonals can be obtained as
$$EB \leftarrow \left(-\frac{1}{\sqrt{3}}, \frac{1}{\sqrt{3}}, \frac{1}{\sqrt{3}}\right), GD \leftarrow \left(\frac{1}{\sqrt{3}}, \frac{1}{\sqrt{3}}, -\frac{1}{\sqrt{3}}\right), CF \leftarrow \left(\frac{1}{\sqrt{3}}, -\frac{1}{\sqrt{3}}, \frac{1}{\sqrt{3}}\right)$$

Let us now use ℓ, m, n to denote the direction cosines of the given line that makes angles $\alpha, \beta, \gamma, \delta$ with *OA*, *EB*, *GD*, *CF*, respectively. Clearly
$$\cos\alpha = \frac{1}{\sqrt{3}}(\ell+m+n), \quad \cos\beta = \frac{1}{\sqrt{3}}(-\ell+m+n)$$
$$\cos\gamma = \frac{1}{\sqrt{3}}(\ell+m-n), \quad \cos\delta = \frac{1}{\sqrt{3}}(\ell-m+n)$$

Squaring and adding all of the above expressions, we obtain
$$\cos^2\alpha + \cos^2\beta + \cos^2\gamma + \cos^2\delta = \frac{1}{3}(4(\ell^2+m^2+n^2))$$

Since ℓ, m, n are direction cosines, the sum of their squares is 1, and hence, the required result is proved.

14. Assume that there are two cubes R and S with integer sides of lengths r and s units, respectively. If the difference between the volumes of the two cubes is equal to the difference in their surface areas, then prove that $r = s$.

Solution: Without loss of generality, let us assume $r > s$. The given condition suggests that $r^3 - s^3 = 6(r^2 - s^2)$, which implies

$$(r-s)(r^2 + rs + s^2) = 6(r+s)(r-s) \implies r^2 + rs + s^2 = 6(r+s)$$

The above leads to the quadratic equation

$$r^2 + r(s-6) + (s^2 - 6s) = 0$$

The discriminant of the above equals $(s-6)^2 - 4(s^2 - 6s) = -3s^2 + 12s + 36$, which simplifies to $48 - 3(s-2)^2$ and it must be a perfect square since r is an integer. Hence, the only choice is $(s-2) = 4$, that is, $s = 6$, subsequently yielding $r = 6$. Thus, we obtain a contradiction to our assumption $r > s$ and that completes the proof.

15. Let $y = f(x)$ be a function of x (for $x \neq 0$) such that $\frac{dx}{dy} = 1 - x$. If p, q are integers, show that the value of $\exp(f(p) - f(q))$ is always a rational number.

Solution: Note that $f(x)$ can be written as $\int f'(x) dx$. Then, using the given information, one can also write

$$f(q) - f(p) = \int_p^q \frac{1}{1-x} dx$$

We know that the derivative of the function $f(x) = \log|x|$, for $x \neq 0$, is $1/x$. We can use this to calculate the above integral as

$$\int_p^q \frac{dx}{1-x} = -\int_{p-1}^{q-1} \frac{dz}{z} = -\Big[\ln(z)\Big]_{p-1}^{q-1} = \ln\left(\frac{p-1}{q-1}\right),$$

which subsequently implies that

$$\exp(f(p) - f(q)) = \frac{q-1}{p-1}$$

Since p, q are integers, the above is clearly a rational number.

16. If for all $x \geq 0$,
$$\frac{dy}{dx} = x^{\cos x + \sin x},$$
and if the graph of the function $y = f(x)$ passes through the origin, prove that the value of y at $x = 1$ is between 0.4 and 0.5.

Solution: Let us use $y = f(x)$, which indicates that $f'(x) = x^{\cos x + \sin x}$. Since $f(0) = 0$, we can write
$$f(1) = \int_0^1 x^{\cos x + \sin x} dx$$
Between 0 and 1, it is easy to argue that $1 \leq \cos x + \sin x \leq \sqrt{2}$. Thus,
$$x^{\sqrt{2}} \leq x^{\cos x + \sin x} \leq x \implies \int_0^1 x^{\sqrt{2}} dx \leq f(1) \leq \int_0^1 x \, dx$$
Calculating the integrals on the two sides, we can write
$$\frac{1}{\sqrt{2}+1} \leq f(1) \leq \frac{1}{2} = 0.5$$
Since $\sqrt{2} < 1.5$, one can show that the left bound is greater than $1/2.5 = 0.4$. This completes the proof.

> **Useful Tip:** Finding the lower and upper bounds of a function inside a definite integral can often help in finding the location of the roots.

17. Consider the differential equation $(x^2 + y^2) dy = xy \, dx$, and assume that the corresponding graph passes through $(1, 1)$. Find the point(s) at which the graph cuts the line $y = e$.

Solution: We can rewrite the given equation as
$$x(x \, dy - y \, dx) = -y^2 \, dy \implies \frac{x(y \, dx - x \, dy)}{y^2} = dy \implies \left(\frac{x}{y}\right) d\left(\frac{x}{y}\right) = \frac{dy}{y}$$
Integrating both sides of the above equation, we obtain
$$\frac{1}{2}\left(\frac{x}{y}\right)^2 = \log y + c$$
Since the graph passes through the point $(1, 1)$, c must be equal to $1/2$. Now, if the coordinates of the point at which the graph cuts the line $y = e$ is (h, e), then
$$\frac{h^2}{2e^2} = \log e + \frac{1}{2} \implies h^2 = 3e^2$$

Hence, there are two points and the coordinates are given by $(\pm e\sqrt{3}, e)$.

18. Solve the differential equation $(1+y^2)dx - (\tan^{-1} y - x)dy = 0$.

Solution: The given equation can be rewritten as

$$\frac{dx}{dy} = \frac{\tan^{-1} y - x}{1+y^2} \implies \frac{dx}{dy} + \frac{x}{1+y^2} = \frac{\tan^{-1} y}{1+y^2},$$

which is of the form $dx/dy + P(y)x = Q(y)$. Clearly, we can use the concept of integrating factor. In this case, that would be

$$\text{IF} = \exp\left[\int \frac{dy}{1+y^2}\right] = \exp\left(\tan^{-1} y\right)$$

Thus, the solution to the given equation can be worked out as

$$x \exp\left(\tan^{-1} y\right) = \int \frac{\tan^{-1} y \exp\left(\tan^{-1} y\right)}{1+y^2} dy + c$$

Substituting $z = \tan^{-1} y$, the integral on the right-hand side becomes

$$\int z e^z \, dz = z e^z - e^z = \tan^{-1} y \exp\left(\tan^{-1} y\right) - \exp\left(\tan^{-1} y\right)$$

Finally, the required solution is

$$x \exp\left(\tan^{-1} y\right) = \tan^{-1} y \exp\left(\tan^{-1} y\right) - \exp\left(\tan^{-1} y\right) + c$$

Useful Tip: The above problem displays an interesting way of using the concepts of integrating factor by considering the expression for dx/dy instead of dy/dx.

19. Find the equation of a curve for which the y-intercept of the tangent drawn at (h,k) is proportional to h^3.

Solution: Note that equation of the tangent at (h,k) is of the form

$$y - h = \left.\frac{dy}{dx}\right|_{(h,k)} (x - h)$$

The y-intercept of the tangent can be found by putting $x = 0$ in the above equation, and then, the given condition leads to the differential equation

$$y - x\frac{dy}{dx} \propto x^3 \implies \frac{dy}{dx} - \frac{y}{x} = kx^2,$$

for some real constant k.

We can use the integrating factor (IF) to solve the above. The expression of the IF is $\exp(-\log x) = 1/x$. Using it, we obtain

$$\frac{y}{x} = \int kx\,dx + c = \frac{kx^2}{2} + c$$

Subsequently, the equation of the curve can be written in the form $y = ax^3 + bx$ for some real constants a, b.

20. Suppose a function $y = f(x)$ satisfies $f''(x) = 6(x-1)$. If the line $y = 3x - 5$ is a tangent to the function at the point $(2, 1)$, then find the points at which the graph of the function intersects the x-axis.

Solution: Since $f''(x) = 6(x-1)$, we can obtain

$$f'(x) = \int 6(x-1)\,dx = 3(x-1)^2 + c_1,$$

for some constant c_1. Then, applying the concepts of differential equation again, we can write

$$f(x) = \int \left[3(x-1)^2 + c_1\right] dx = (x-1)^3 + c_1 x + c_2,$$

for some $c_2 \in \mathbb{R}$. Now, the graph of $y = f(x)$ passes through $(2, 1)$, which means that $-1 + 2c_1 + c_2 = 1$. On the other hand, the slope of the tangent at this point is 3, which means that $f'(2) = 3$, and thus, $3 + c_1 = 3$. Solving these two equations, we obtain $c_1 = 0$, $c_2 = 0$. Hence, the function is $f(x) = (x-1)^3$.

Clearly, the function has only one root, and it intersects the x-axis at the point $(1, 0)$.

21. Find all solutions to the ODE $y' - 16y^2 + 8xy = x^2$.

Solution: Note that the given ODE is equivalent to

$$\frac{dy}{dx} = (4y - x)^2$$

Thus, if we introduce a new variable $v = 4y - x$, the above transforms to the ODE

$$\frac{1}{4}\left(\frac{dv}{dx} + 1\right) = v^2 \implies \frac{dv}{4v^2 - 1} = dx$$

Miscellaneous

Integrating both sides, we obtain

$$\frac{1}{4}\int \frac{dv}{v^2 - 1/4} = \int dx \implies \frac{1}{4}\log\left|\frac{v - 1/2}{v + 1/2}\right| = x + c$$

Thus, the solution to the ODE is of the form

$$\left|\frac{v - 1/2}{v + 1/2}\right| = \exp(4x + c)$$

Taking the positive sign of the left side, the above implies

$$4y - x = \frac{1}{1 - \exp(4x+c)} - \frac{1}{2} = \frac{1}{2}\left[\frac{2}{1 - \exp(4x+c)} - 1\right] = -\frac{1}{2}\left[\frac{\exp(4x+c) + 1}{\exp(4x+c) - 1}\right],$$

which is of the form $\coth(-2x+c)/2$. Similarly, if we consider the negative sign in the left-hand side of the previous equation, we can obtain

$$4y - x = \frac{1}{2}\left[\frac{2}{1 + \exp(4x+c)} - 1\right] = -\frac{1}{2}\left[\frac{\exp(4x+c) - 1}{\exp(4x+c) + 1}\right] = -\frac{1}{2}\tanh(2x+c)$$

Combining the above, we can say that the possible solutions are

$$y = \frac{x}{4} - \frac{1}{8}\coth(2x+c), \text{ or } y = \frac{x}{4} - \frac{1}{8}\tanh(2x+c)$$

> **Useful Tip:** Hyperbolic functions are used in the above solution. Interested students may read about them for more knowledge.

22. If

$$\frac{dy}{dx} = \lim_{n \to \infty}\left\{\frac{x}{n+x} + \frac{x}{n+2x} + \ldots + \frac{x}{n+nx}\right\},$$

express y in terms of x.

Solution: Recall the first principle of definite integral, which says that

$$\lim_{n \to \infty} \frac{1}{n}\sum_{r=1}^{n} f(r/n) = \int_0^1 f(t)\, dt$$

Now, the term on the right-hand side of the given equation can be simplified as

$$\lim_{n \to \infty}\left\{\frac{x}{n+x} + \frac{x}{n+2x} + \ldots + \frac{x}{n+nx}\right\} = \lim_{n \to \infty}\sum_{r=1}^{n}\frac{x}{n+rx} = \lim_{n \to \infty}\frac{1}{n}\sum_{r=1}^{n}\frac{x}{1+xr/n}$$

Then, from the aforementioned principle, we can write

$$\frac{dy}{dx} = \int_0^1 \frac{x}{1+tx} \, dt = [\ln(1+tx)]_0^1 = \ln(1+x),$$

where ln is used to indicate natural logarithm. Hence

$$y = \int \ln(1+x) \, dx = (1+x)\ln(1+x) - (1+x) + c$$

23. In epidemiology, the susceptible–infected–recovered (SIR) model is popularly used to understand the spread of an infectious disease, for example COVID-19. In this problem, we consider a very simple version of the SIR model. Assume that the total population remains constant throughout the time, and there is no birth or death. Consider that every infected person can infect every susceptible person at a constant rate of β, and that every infected person can recover at a constant rate γ. Further assume that a recovered person cannot get infected again. If initially 1 person is infected and everyone else is susceptible, write the SIR model as a system of differential equations, and find its solution in terms of the susceptible population.

Solution: Let us use three functions $S(t), I(t), R(t)$ to denote the susceptible, infected and recovered populations, respectively, at time t. We assume that the population has a total of $N+1$ persons. Then, the provided initial condition is $I(0) = 1, R(0) = 0, S(0) = N$.

Since every infected person can infect every susceptible person at a constant rate of β, we can say that $S(t)$ is decreasing at the rate $\beta I(t) S(t)$. Combining it with the information on recovery, we can write the system of differential equations as

$$\frac{dS}{dt} = -\beta IS, \quad \frac{dI}{dt} = \beta IS - \gamma I, \quad \frac{dR}{dt} = \gamma I$$

If we divide the first equation by the third, we get

$$\frac{dS}{dR} = -\frac{\beta S}{\gamma} \implies \frac{dS}{S} = -\frac{\beta \, dR}{\gamma} \implies \log S = -\frac{\beta R}{\gamma} + c$$

Note that initially at time 0, $S = N$ and $R = 0$. Thus, we can write the equation $\log S(t) = -\beta R(t)/\gamma + \log N$, which implies that

$$R(t) = -\frac{\gamma}{\beta} \log \frac{S(t)}{N}$$

On the other hand, from the first and second differential equations in the system, we can write

$$\frac{dI}{dS} = -1 + \frac{\gamma}{\beta S} \implies dI = \left(\frac{\gamma}{\beta S} - 1\right) dS \implies I = \frac{\gamma}{\beta} \log S - S + c$$

Miscellaneous

Initially, $S = N$ and $I = 1$. Therefore, the required solutions are

$$I(t) = 1 + \frac{\gamma}{\beta} \log \frac{S(t)}{N} + N - S(t), \ R(t) = -\frac{\gamma}{\beta} \log \frac{S(t)}{N}$$

24. A function f is defined in such a way that it transforms a sequence of real numbers $s = (s_1, s_2, s_3, \ldots)$ to the sequence $f(s) = (s_2 - s_1, s_3 - s_2, s_4 - s_3, \ldots)$. Assume that all of the terms of the sequence $f(f(s))$ are 2. If $s_2 = s_{100} = 0$, what is the value of s_1?

Solution: Note that f takes the difference of consecutive terms, and its definition points us to the concept of differentiation. Now, since $f(f(s))$ provides a sequence of all 1s, we can consider the differential equation

$$\frac{d^2y}{dx^2} = 2,$$

which signifies that the sequence corresponds to a quadratic function with leading coefficient 1, that is, it should be of the form $s_n = n^2 + bn + c$. Further, we know that two roots of this quadratic are 2 and 100. Thus

$$s_n = (n-2)(n-100) \implies s_1 = 99$$

Useful Tip: The above problem shows a clever use of differential equations. The reader is advised to solve the above using standard techniques of algebra and understand the connection between the two approaches.

---

25. A function $f(x)$ is defined on $[-1, 1]$ such that $f(-1), f(0), f(1) \in [-1, 1]$. If $f'(x)$ is linear for all x, find the maximum possible value of $|f(x)|$.

Solution: Since $f'(x)$ is linear in x, $f(x)$ must be of the form $ax^2 + bx + c$. Let us denote $f(-1), f(0), f(1)$ by u, v, w, respectively. Then, we obtain the system of equations

$$a - b + c = u, \ c = v, \ a + b + c = w,$$

which implies

$$a = \frac{1}{2}(w + u - 2v), b = \frac{1}{2}(w - u), c = v$$

Now, for $x \in [-1, 1]$, we can say that

$$|f(x)| = \frac{1}{2} |(w + u - 2v)x^2 + (w - u)x + 2v|$$

$$= \frac{1}{2} |u(x^2 - x) + v(2 - 2x^2) + w(x^2 + x)|$$

$$\leqslant \frac{1}{2}\left[|u|\,|x^2-x|+|v|\,|2-2x^2|+|w|\,|x^2+x|\right]$$

At this point, note that the absolute value of u, v, w is less than 1. On the other hand, for $|x| \leqslant 1$, if x is positive, $|x^2-x|+|x^2+x| = x-x^2+x^2+x = 2x$. And if x is negative, $|x^2-x|+|x^2+x| = x^2-x-x^2-x = -2x$. Combining all these, we obtain the following inequality:

$$|f(x)| \leqslant \frac{1}{2}\left[|2x|+|2-2x^2|\right] = |x|+1-x^2 = 1+|x|(1-|x|)$$

Using the AM-GM inequality, it is easy to argue that the last term in the above expression is at most $1/4$. Hence, finally, we obtain $|f(x)| \leqslant 5/4$.

26. For some positive constant a, define $f(x) = ax + 1/(x+1)$. Let L and S be, respectively, the largest and smallest value of $f(x)$ for $0 \leqslant x \leqslant 1$. Show that $L - S > 1/12$.

Solution: The values of the function at the end points are $f(0) = 1$ and $f(1) = a + 1/2$. Now, taking the first and second order derivatives of the function, we get

$$f'(x) = a - \frac{1}{(x+1)^2}, \quad f''(x) = \frac{2}{(x+1)^3},$$

which implies that $f''(x)$ is always positive and that $f'(x)$ increases from $(a-1)$ to $(a-1/4)$ as x moves from 0 to 1.

We can now consider the following three cases.

Case 1: $(a \leqslant 1/4)$. It is clear that $f'(x) \leqslant 0$ for all $x \in [0,1]$ in this case. Thus, f is decreasing in the entire interval, which implies that $L = 1$, $S = a + 1/2$. Therefore, $L - S = 1/2 - a \geqslant 1/4 > 1/12$.

Case 2: $(1/4 < a < 1)$. Under this restriction, $f'(x) = 0$ for $x = 1/\sqrt{a} - 1 = a_0$, say. Considering that $f'(x)$ is always increasing, we can infer that $f(x)$ is decreasing in $[0, a_0]$ and increasing in $[a_0, 1]$. Thus, the minimum is attained at $x = a_0$, and the maximum is attained either at 0 or at 1. It subsequently implies that

$$L - S = \max\left\{1, a + \frac{1}{2}\right\} - aa_0 - \frac{1}{a_0+1} = \max\left\{1, a + \frac{1}{2}\right\} - 1 + (1-\sqrt{a})^2$$

If $a < 1/2$, the above indicates $L - S = (1-\sqrt{a})^2 > 3/2 - \sqrt{2}$, which is greater than $1/12$. On the other hand, if $a \geqslant 1/2$, the quantity $L - S$ is equal to $(\sqrt{2a} - 1/\sqrt{2})^2$. Then, a similar calculation as above proves that it is greater than or equal to $1/12$.

Case 3: $(a \geqslant 1)$. As in Case 1, we can argue that f is increasing in the entire interval, and thus, $L - S = a - 1/2 \geqslant 1/2 > 1/12$.

Miscellaneous

27. Let $\alpha, \beta, \gamma \in \mathbb{C}$ such that $|\alpha| = |\beta| = |\gamma| = 1$. If the two lines $x + y + z = 0$ and $\alpha x + \beta y + \gamma z = 0$ intersect at a point other than the origin, then prove that α, β, γ are all equal.

Solution: Based on the given condition, we can find non-zero real numbers a, b, c such that $a + b + c = a\alpha + b\beta + c\gamma = 0$.

Without loss of generality, we can assume that two among a, b, c are positive and the third is negative (if it is the other way round, we can take the negatives of the three numbers and the same proof will follow). So, let us suppose that a, b are positive and c is negative. Using $c = -a - b \neq 0$, we get $a\alpha + b\beta - \gamma(a+b) = 0$, which implies that

$$\left(\frac{a}{a+b}\right)\alpha + \left(\frac{b}{a+b}\right)\beta = \gamma$$

Now, taking absolute values and applying the triangle inequality

$$1 = |\gamma| \leq \left(\frac{a}{a+b}\right)|\alpha| + \left(\frac{b}{a+b}\right)|\beta|$$

However, since both $|\alpha|$ and $|\beta|$ are 1, the right-hand side of the above inequality is also 1. Therefore, equality must hold in the above triangle inequality. It implies that α, β, γ have the same amplitude. They have the same modulus as well. So, we get $\alpha = \beta = \gamma$.

28. Consider two polynomials $p(x)$ and $q(x)$ such that the sum of the coefficients for each of them is equal to σ. If $p(x), q(x)$ satisfy the equation $p(x)^3 - q(x)^3 = p(x^3) - q(x^3)$, prove that there is an integer $\alpha \geq 1$ and a polynomial $r(x)$ with $r(1) \neq 0$ such that $p(x) - q(x) = (x-1)^\alpha r(x)$. Further, show that $\sigma^2 = 3^{\alpha-1}$.

Solution: Since the sum of the coefficients for each of the polynomials is equal to σ, we can say that $p(1) = q(1) = \sigma$. Now, consider the polynomial $h(x) = p(x) - q(x)$. Clearly, $x = 1$ is a root of $h(x)$. So, there exist $\alpha \in \mathbb{N}$ and a polynomial $r(x)$ with $r(1) \neq 0$ such that $h(x) = (x-1)^\alpha r(x)$.

To prove the second part, factorizing the term on the left-hand side of $p(x)^3 - q(x)^3 = p(x^3) - q(x^3)$ and using the above result, we can write

$$(x-1)^\alpha r(x)\{p(x)^2 + p(x)q(x) + q(x)^2\} = (x^3-1)^\alpha r(x^3),$$

which, for $x \neq 1$, further leads to the following:

$$r(x)\{p(x)^2 + p(x)q(x) + q(x)^2\} = (x^2 + x + 1)^\alpha r(x^3)$$

We can now apply the fact that a polynomial is a continuous function. Thus, taking $x \to 1$, we see that the left-hand side of the above equation approaches the value $3\sigma^2 r(1)$ whereas the term on the right-hand side approaches the value $3^\alpha r(1)$. Since both must be equal, we get $\sigma^2 = 3^{\alpha-1}$.

29. Let $X \subset \mathbb{R}^2$ be a set satisfying the following properties:

  (i) If (x_1, y_1) and (x_2, y_2) are any two distinct elements in X, then either $x_1 > x_2$ and $y_1 > y_2$ or $x_1 < x_2$ and $y_1 < y_2$.

  (ii) There are two elements (a_1, b_1) and (a_2, b_2) in X such that for any $(x, y) \in X$,
  $$a_1 \leqslant x \leqslant a_2 \quad \text{and} \quad b_1 \leqslant y \leqslant b_2$$

  (iii) If (x_1, y_1) and (x_2, y_2) are two elements of X, then for all $\lambda \in [0, 1]$,
  $$(\lambda x_1 + (1-\lambda)x_2, \lambda y_1 + (1-\lambda)y_2) \in X$$

Prove that if $(x, y) \in X$, then for some $\lambda \in [0, 1]$,
$$x = \lambda a_1 + (1-\lambda)a_2, \quad y = \lambda b_1 + (1-\lambda)b_2.$$

Solution: From condition (ii), we can say that for any $(x, y) \in X$, there exist $\lambda_x, \lambda_y \in [0, 1]$ such that
$$x = \lambda_x a_1 + (1-\lambda_x)a_2, \quad y = \lambda_y b_1 + (1-\lambda_y)b_2$$

Now we assume that there is a point (x, y) in X for which $\lambda_x \neq \lambda_y$, and without loss of generality, let us assume that $\lambda_x > \lambda_y$. Then, we can find some real number $\delta \in (\lambda_y, \lambda_x)$.

Consider a new point (u, v) such that $u = \delta a_1 + (1-\delta)a_2, v = \delta b_1 + (1-\delta)b_2$. Since δ lies between 0 and 1 (from the way we chose it), using condition (iii), we can say $(u, v) \in X$. Observe that
$$u - x = (\delta a_1 + (1-\delta)a_2) - (\lambda_x a_1 + (1-\lambda_x)a_2) = (\delta - \lambda_x)(a_1 - a_2)$$

Similarly, $v - y = (\delta - \lambda_y)(b_1 - b_2)$. Now, $a_1 < a_2, b_1 < b_2$ and $\lambda_y < \delta < \lambda_x$, and so, we get $u < x, v > y$. However, that cannot be true (because of condition (i)) since both (x, y) and (u, v) are in X. So, we have a contradiction, and hence, λ_x must be equal to λ_y. Therefore, for any $(x, y) \in X$, there exists some $\lambda \in [0, 1]$ such that
$$x = \lambda a_1 + (1-\lambda)a_2, \quad y = \lambda b_1 + (1-\lambda)b_2$$

30. In the figure below, assume that $y = f(x)$ is the graph of a one-to-one continuous function f. For any point P on the graph of $y = 2x^2$, let PA, PB be the horizontal and vertical segments, and assume that the areas OAP and OBP are equal. Find the value of $f(3)$.

Miscellaneous

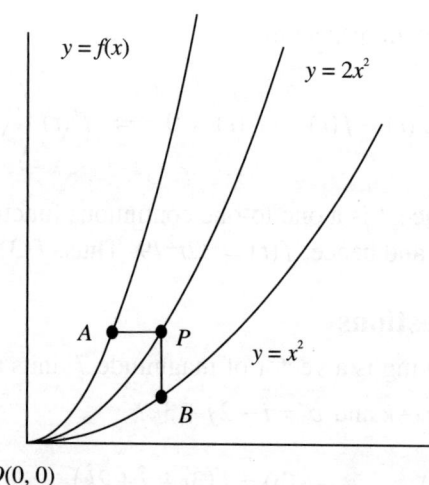

Solution: From the given functions, we can take the following forms for the points A, P and B:

$$A = (t, f(t)), \quad P = \left(\sqrt{\frac{f(t)}{2}}, f(t)\right), \quad B = \left(\sqrt{\frac{f(t)}{2}}, \frac{f(t)}{2}\right)$$

Let us denote the area of a region using the notation [ ]. Consider $T = (t, 0)$ and let PB, when extended, cut the x-axis at S. Then

$$[OAP] = [OAT] + [APST] - [OPS] = \int_0^t f(x)\, dx + f(t)\left(\sqrt{\frac{f(t)}{2}} - t\right) - \int_0^{\sqrt{f(t)/2}} 2x^2\, dx$$

On the other hand, $[OBP] = [OPS] - [OBS]$, which is equal to

$$\int_0^{\sqrt{f(t)/2}} 2x^2\, dx - \int_0^{\sqrt{f(t)/2}} x^2\, dx$$

As we have $[OAP] = [OBP]$, equating the above equations and simplifying, we get

$$\int_0^t f(x)\, dx + f(t)\left(\sqrt{\frac{f(t)}{2}} - t\right) - \left(\frac{f(t)}{2}\right)^{3/2} = 0$$

The above further simplifies to

$$\int_0^t f(x)\, dx - t f(t) + \left(\frac{f(t)}{2}\right)^{3/2} = 0$$

Differentiating the above with respect to t

$$f(t) + \frac{3}{4\sqrt{2}} f'(t) \sqrt{f(t)} - f(t) - tf'(t) = 0 \implies f'(t) \left(\sqrt{f(t)} - \frac{4\sqrt{2}t}{3} \right) = 0,$$

for all real values of t. Since f is a one-to-one continuous function, we can say that $f'(t)$ is not identically equal to 0, and hence, $f(t) = 32t^2/9$. Thus, $f(3) = 32$.

Multiple Choice Questions

1. Which one of the following is a vector of magnitude 7 units and parallel to the resultant of the vectors $\vec{a} = 2\hat{i} + 3\hat{j} - \hat{k}$ and $\vec{b} = \hat{i} - 2\hat{j} + 3\hat{k}$?

(a) $\pm \left(\sqrt{\frac{7}{2}} \right) (3\hat{i} + \hat{j} + 2\hat{k})$ (b) $\pm 7 (3\hat{i} + \hat{j} + 2\hat{k})$

(c) $\pm \sqrt{7} (3\hat{i} + \hat{j} + 2\hat{k})$ (d) None of the foregoing expressions

Solution: (a)

The resultant of the two given vectors is $\vec{r} = 3\hat{i} + \hat{j} + 2\hat{k}$. Clearly, the vector with magnitude 7 and parallel to this resultant vector is

$$\pm 7 \left(\frac{3\hat{i} + \hat{j} + 2\hat{k}}{\sqrt{3^2 + 1^2 + 2^2}} \right) = \pm \left(\sqrt{\frac{7}{2}} \right) (3\hat{i} + \hat{j} + 2\hat{k})$$

2. A cube has four diagonals, connecting opposite vertices. For a unit cube, the angle between an adjacent pair of diagonals is

(a) $30°$ (b) $\cos^{-1} \frac{1}{6}$ (c) $45°$ (d) $\cos^{-1} \frac{1}{3}$

Solution: (d)

For a unit cube, the diagonals can be represented through the concepts of three-dimensional geometry and vector algebra as $(\pm 1, \pm 1, \pm 1)$. Now, without loss of generality, we consider the adjacent pair of diagonals $(1, 1, 1)$ and $(-1, 1, 1)$. If the angle between them is θ, then

$$\cos \theta = \frac{(1,1,1) \cdot (-1,1,1)}{\sqrt{1^2 + 1^2 + 1^2}\sqrt{(-1)^2 + 1^2 + 1^2}} = \frac{1}{3}$$

3. In the three-dimensional plane, consider a pipe A with diameter 0.8 and with its axis passing through the points $(2, 5, 3)$ and $(7, 10, 8)$. There is another pipe B whose axis passes through the points $(0, 6, 3)$ and $(-12, 0, 9)$. Which one of the following is the maximum

possible diameter of B (up to two decimal places) such that the two pipes do not intersect with each other?

(a) 3.25 (b) 2.00 (c) 2.94 (d) 1.96

Solution: (c)

Note that each pipe axis is defined using two points. The vector equation of the axis corresponding to A is

$$\vec{r} = (2,5,3) + \lambda'(5,5,5) = (2,5,3) + \frac{\lambda}{\sqrt{3}}(1,1,1)$$

Similarly, the equation of the axis of the second pipe can be obtained as

$$\vec{r} = (0,6,3) + \frac{\mu}{\sqrt{6}}(-2,-1,1)$$

Thus, the perpendicular to the two axes has direction

$$(1,1,1) \times (-2,-1,1) = \begin{vmatrix} \hat{i} & \hat{j} & \hat{k} \\ 1 & 1 & 1 \\ -2 & -1 & 1 \end{vmatrix} = 2\hat{i} - 3\hat{j} + \hat{k}$$

Clearly, the length of the mutual perpendicular is

$$\{(2,5,3) - (0,6,3)\} \cdot \frac{1}{\sqrt{14}}(2,-3,1) = \sqrt{\frac{7}{2}} = 1.87$$

Hence, the two pipes would not intersect if the radius of B is less than $(1.87 - 0.4) = 1.47$, that is, the maximum possible diameter is 2.94.

4. For a scientific experiment, a group of rabbits are put together in a cage and are allowed to mate without any restriction. If the experiment started with only four rabbits and the size of the group $p(t)$ at time t is growing at a rate of $\frac{p(t)}{2} - 100$, how many rabbits are there at time $t = 100$?

(a) $200 + 196e^{50}$ (b) $200 - 196e^{50}$ (c) $100 + 196e^{50}$ (d) $100 - 196e^{50}$

Solution: (a)

Using the concepts of differential equation, we can write the given conditions as

$$\frac{dp(t)}{dt} = \frac{p(t)}{2} - 100, \ p(0) = 4$$

For convenience, let us write the differential equation as

$$\frac{dp}{p-200} = \frac{dt}{2} \implies \log|p-200| = \frac{t}{2} + c$$

Since at $t = 0$, $p = 4$, we can further argue that $c = \log 196$. Thus, $|p(t) - 200| = 196\exp(t/2)$, and therefore, at $t = 100$, we have $|p(100) - 200| = 196\exp(50)$, which implies that (a) is the correct answer.

5. Suppose f is a periodic function on $[0, \pi/2]$, with $f(0) = 1$ and

$$\int_0^x (f'(t) - \sin 2t)\, dt = \int_x^0 f(t)\tan t\, dt.$$

Which one of the following is true?

(a) Maximum value of f is 1
(b) Minimum value of f is 1
(c) $f(\pi/4) = 1$
(d) $f(\pi/3) = 1$

Solution: (d)

Differentiating the given equation with respect to x on both sides and considering $y = f(x)$, we get

$$f'(x) - \sin 2x = -f(x)\tan x \implies y' + y\tan x = \sin 2x$$

Therefore, the integrating factor (IF) is

$$\exp\left(\int \tan x\, dx\right) = \exp(-\log \cos x) = \sec x$$

Clearly, the solution to the differential equation is

$$y\sec x = \int \sin 2x \sec x\, dx + c = \int 2\sin x\, dx + c \implies y = c\cos x - 2\cos^2 x$$

Using $f(0) = 1$, one may solve the above to get

$$f(x) = 3\cos x - 2\cos^2 x = -2\left(\cos x - \frac{3}{4}\right)^2 + \frac{9}{8}$$

Clearly, the maximum possible value of f is $9/8$, while the minimum value is 0 or less. Also, $f(\pi/3) = 1$, $f(\pi/4) = 3/\sqrt{2} - 1$. Thus, (d) is true.

6. The differential equation
$$\frac{dy}{dx} = \frac{y}{x} + \frac{2\phi(y/x)}{\phi'(y/x)}$$
has the solution (c is arbitrary constant)

(a) $x^2 \phi(y/x) = c$ (b) $y^2 \phi(y/x) = c$ (c) $\phi(y/x) = cy^2$ (d) $\phi(y/x) = cx^2$

Solution: (d)

Letting $y = ux$, we can write $dy/dx = u + x du/dx$, which leads to the differential equation
$$x \frac{du}{dx} = 2 \frac{\phi(u)}{\phi'(u)} \implies \frac{\phi'(u)}{\phi(u)} du = 2 \frac{dx}{x}$$
Evidently, the solution is $\log \phi(u) = \log x^2 + c$, which leads to the answer (d).

7. For three distinct positive constants a, b, c, consider the system of simultaneous equations
$$ax + by = \sqrt{2}, \; bx + cy = \sqrt{3}.$$
Which of the following statements is false?

(a) There exist infinitely many combinations of values for a, b, c such that the above system has infinitely many solutions (x, y).
(b) There exist infinitely many combinations of values for a, b, c such that the above system has unique solutions (x, y).
(c) The above system has no solution if and only if $ac = b^2$.
(d) If the above system has infinitely many solutions, then $2b < a + c$.

Solution: (c)

We can write the system of equations as
$$\begin{bmatrix} a & b \\ b & c \end{bmatrix} \begin{pmatrix} x \\ y \end{pmatrix} = \begin{pmatrix} \sqrt{2} \\ \sqrt{3} \end{pmatrix}$$

Thus, the system has a unique solution if $ac \neq b^2$, which can occur for infinitely many choices of (a, b, c). On the other hand, if $ac = b^2$, then the system has infinitely many solutions if and only if $a/b = b/c = \sqrt{2/3}$, which is equivalent to having $a = r\sqrt{2}, b = r\sqrt{3}$, $c = 3r/\sqrt{2}$ for some positive constant r. Clearly, there are infinitely many such choices, and this shows that option (c) is not necessarily true.

We can also check that for having infinitely many solutions, $a + c$ should be of the form $5r/\sqrt{2}$, whereas $b = r\sqrt{3}$. Since $(2\sqrt{3})^2 = 12 < (5/\sqrt{2})^2 = 12.5$, we can argue that if the above system has infinitely many solutions, then $2b < a + c$.

For the next three questions, the notation A_n (for $n \in \mathbb{N}$) denotes a matrix of order $n \times n$, such that the (i, j)th element is

$$A_n[i, j] = \begin{cases} 0 & \text{if } i \geqslant j, \\ i+j & \text{otherwise.} \end{cases}$$

8. What is the value of $|A_3| - |A_2|$, where $|\cdot|$ is used to indicate the determinant?

(a) 0   (b) 5   (c) $\frac{1}{5}$ (d) 1

Solution: (a)

We note that the matrix A_n is upper-triangular, and thus, the determinant should be equal to the product of the diagonal elements. However, all diagonal entries of the matrix A_n are zeros, and hence, $|A_n| = 0$ for all n.

9. Which one of the following is true about the expression A_n^n?

(a) It is a matrix of all zeros, for any $n \in \mathbb{N}$.
(b) It has zero in exactly $n(n-1)$ positions.
(c) It is a zero matrix for $n > 1$ if and only if n is a prime number.
(d) None of the foregoing statements are necessarily true.

Solution: (a)

It is easy to observe that

$$A_1 = 0, \quad A_2^2 = \begin{bmatrix} 0 & 0 \\ 0 & 0 \end{bmatrix}$$

The above provides the hint that $A_n^n = 0$ for all $n \in \mathbb{N}$. To check this formally, we can rely on mathematical induction. Using $\mathbf{0}$ to indicate a vector of all zeros, note that A_n can be written as

$$A_n = \begin{bmatrix} A_{n-1} & \mathbf{0} \\ \mathbf{c}' & 0 \end{bmatrix},$$

where $\mathbf{c}$ is a vector of positive quantities. Then

$$A_n^2 = \begin{bmatrix} A_{n-1}^2 & \mathbf{0} \\ \mathbf{c}' A_{n-1} & 0 \end{bmatrix}$$

It is now a straightforward exercise to show that A_n^{n-1} is of the form

$$A_n^{n-1} = \begin{bmatrix} A_{n-1}^{n-1} & \mathbf{0} \\ \tilde{\mathbf{c}}' & 0 \end{bmatrix},$$

Miscellaneous

where $\tilde{\mathbf{c}}$ is another vector. Using the induction hypothesis now, we can argue that A_{n-1}^{n-1} is a matrix of all zeros, which implies that A_n^n must be a matrix of all zeros, and thus, it is true for all $n \in \mathbb{N}$.

10. Let $\mathbf{1}_n$ denote the n-dimensional vector that has all terms equal to 1, and let J_n be the $n \times n$ matrix obtained by computing $\mathbf{1}_n \mathbf{1}_n'$. The trace of the matrix $A_n J_n$ is

(a) $n^2 - 1$ (b) $\frac{n(2n-1)}{2}$ (c) $n^2 - n + 1$ (d) $\frac{n^3 - n}{2}$

Solution: (d)

We can use the property that the traces of AB and BA are equal to show that

$$\text{tr}(A_n J_n) = \text{tr}\left(\mathbf{1}_n' A_n \mathbf{1}_n\right) = \mathbf{1}_n' A_n \mathbf{1}_n,$$

which is a scalar quantity. One can now argue that the expression is equal to the sum of all the elements in A_n, which is equal to

$$\begin{aligned}
\sum_{i=1}^{n-1} \sum_{j=i+1}^{n} (i+j) &= \sum_{i=1}^{n-1} \left[i(n-i) + \frac{n(n+1)}{2} - \frac{i(i+1)}{2} \right] \\
&= \frac{n(n+1)(n-1)}{2} + \left(n - \frac{1}{2}\right) \sum_{i=1}^{n-1} i - \frac{3}{2} \sum_{i=1}^{n-1} i^2 \\
&= \frac{n^3 - n}{2} + \frac{n(n-1)(2n-1)}{4} - \frac{n(n-1)(2n-1)}{4} \\
&= \frac{n^3 - n}{2}
\end{aligned}$$

Exercises

1. If a matrix is defined as
$$A = \begin{bmatrix} 0 & 1 \\ 3 & 0 \end{bmatrix},$$
find a column vector x such that $(A^8 + A^6 + A^4 + A^2 + I_2)x = (0,11)^T$.

2. Jon is asked to think of three real numbers such that their sum is 20. He reveals that his first number is four times the sum of the other two, while the second number is seven times the third. Adam says that he knows the product of the three numbers. Can you find that too?

3. Find the angle between any two diagonals of a cube with side 3 units.

4. Find the nature of the triangle formed by $A = (2,-1,1)$, $B = (1,-3,-5)$ and $C = (3,-4,-4)$.

5. Let $\vec{u}, \vec{v}, \vec{w}$ be three vectors such that each one is perpendicular to the sum of the other two. If $|\vec{u}| = 1$, $|\vec{v}| = 2$ and $|\vec{w}| = 3$, find the value of $|\vec{u} + \vec{v} + \vec{w}|$.

6. Compute the area of the parallelogram whose adjacent sides are given by the vectors $\vec{u} = \hat{i} - \hat{j} + 3\hat{k}$ and $\vec{v} = 2\hat{i} - 7\hat{j} + \hat{k}$.

7. Draw the region of points (x,y) in the two-dimensional plane that satisfy $|y| \leqslant |x| \leqslant 1$.

8. A man walking towards a building on which a flagstaff is fixed vertically, observes the angle subtended by the flagstaff to be the greatest when he is at a distance d from the building. If θ is the observed greatest angle, show that the length of the flagstaff is $2d\tan\theta$.

9. Determine the coordinates of the foot of the perpendicular drawn from the point $C = (1,0,3)$ onto the line AB, where $A = (4,7,1)$ and $B = (3,5,3)$.

10. Find the locus of a point, the sum of whose distances from $(1,0,0)$ and $(-1,0,0)$ always remains 4.

11. Describe the curve that satisfies the differential equation $\frac{d^3y}{dx^3} = 0$ and cuts the x-axis at $x = \pm 1$.

12. Find the equation of the curve passing through $(1, \pi/4)$ if the slope of the tangent at any point (h,k) is given by $k/h - \cos^2(k/h)$.

13. Let $P(x)$ be a non-constant polynomial with real coefficients such that for $c,d \in \mathbb{R}$ and for all $n \in \mathbb{N}$,
$$c|n|^3 \leqslant |P(n)| \leqslant d|n|^3.$$

Prove that $P(x)$ has a real root.

14. For a natural number $n > 1$, consider the $(n-1)$ points on the unit circle in a two-dimensional Argand plane, given by $e^{2\pi i k/n}$ for $k = 1, 2, \ldots, n-1$. Prove that the product of the distances of these points from 1 is n.

15. For $n \geqslant 3$, determine all real solutions of the system of n equations:
$$x_1 + x_2 + \ldots + x_{n-1} = \frac{1}{x_n}$$
$$\ldots$$
$$x_1 + x_2 + \ldots + x_{i-1} + x_{i+1} + \ldots + x_n = \frac{1}{x_i}$$
$$\ldots$$
$$x_2 + \ldots + x_{n-1} + x_n = \frac{1}{x_1}$$

16. Determine the coordinates of the point where the line through the points $P = (1, 2, 3)$ and $Q = (6, 5, 4)$ crosses the yz-plane.

17. Suppose a is a complex number such that
$$a^2 + a + \frac{1}{a} + \frac{1}{a^2} + 1 = 0.$$

If m is a positive integer, find the value of
$$a^{2m} + a^m + \frac{1}{a^m} + \frac{1}{a^{2m}}$$

18. Let $f(x) = e^{-x}$ for all $x \geqslant 0$. Consider another function g that is defined as a straight line joining $(k, f(k))$ and $(k+1, f(k+1))$ for every integer $k \geqslant 0$. Calculate the area between the graphs of f and g.

19. Consider a function $y = f(x)$, defined for $x \geqslant 0$ such that
$$\frac{dy}{dx} = \frac{2\sin x - 1}{(x + 2\cos x)^2}.$$

If $f(0) = 1/2$, find the range of the function f.

20. Let f be a twice-differentiable function such that $f'(x) - f'(y) = 2(x - y)$ for all $x, y \in \mathbb{R}$. If $f(0) = 0$ and $f(2020) = 2020$, find the value of $f(2021)$.

Hints

1. Use induction or otherwise to show that for all natural numbers n

$$A^{2n} = \begin{bmatrix} 3^n & 0 \\ 0 & 3^n \end{bmatrix}$$

One can then compute $A^8 + A^6 + A^4 + A^2 + I_2$, and show that x must be $(0, 1/11)^\top$.

2. The given information can be presented using the system

$$\begin{bmatrix} 1 & 1 & 1 \\ 1 & -4 & -4 \\ 0 & 1 & -7 \end{bmatrix} \begin{pmatrix} x \\ y \\ z \end{pmatrix} = \begin{pmatrix} 20 \\ 0 \\ 0 \end{pmatrix}$$

If we use $Au = v$ to denote the above equation, then the above system is solvable if and only if A^{-1} exists. Show that the determinant is 40, which means that the inverse exists. Using the cofactors of the matrix, one can obtain the inverse and find the solution to the above system as

$$\begin{pmatrix} x \\ y \\ z \end{pmatrix} = \frac{1}{40} \begin{bmatrix} 32 & 8 & 0 \\ 7 & -7 & 5 \\ 1 & -1 & -5 \end{bmatrix} \begin{pmatrix} 20 \\ 0 \\ 0 \end{pmatrix} = \begin{pmatrix} 16 \\ 7/2 \\ 1/2 \end{pmatrix}$$

Hence, the product of the three numbers is $xyz = 28$.

3. Let $ABCDEFGO$ be the cube mentioned in the problem such that $O = (0,0,0)$, $A = (3,3,3)$, $B = (0,3,3)$, $C = (0,3,0)$, $D = (3,3,0)$, $E = (3,0,0)$, $F = (3,0,3)$ and $G = (0,0,3)$. Now, the direction cosines of the diagonal OA are given by

$$\left(\frac{3-0}{\sqrt{3^2+3^2+3^2}}, \frac{3-0}{\sqrt{3^2+3^2+3^2}}, \frac{3-0}{\sqrt{3^2+3^2+3^2}} \right) = \left(\frac{1}{\sqrt{3}}, \frac{1}{\sqrt{3}}, \frac{1}{\sqrt{3}} \right)$$

The direction cosines of diagonal EB can be calculated in a similar fashion. Subsequently, one can show that the angle between the two lines is $\cos^{-1}(1/3)$.

4. The concept of vector can be used here. Let $\hat{i}, \hat{j}, \hat{k}$ be the unit vectors along the three axes. Then write $\vec{AB} = -\hat{i} - 2\hat{j} - 6\hat{k}$, $\vec{BC} = 2\hat{i} - \hat{j} + \hat{k}$, $\vec{CA} = -\hat{i} + 3\hat{j} + 5\hat{k}$. Next, calculate the magnitude of the three vectors and show that $|\vec{AB}|^2 = |\vec{BC}|^2 + |\vec{CA}|^2$, which implies that ABC is a right-angled triangle.

5. Since each one of the vectors is perpendicular to the sum of the other two, one can write $\vec{u} \cdot (\vec{v} + \vec{w}) = 0$ (and similarly the others). Then, apply the properties of dot product to argue that

$$\left| \vec{u} + \vec{v} + \vec{w} \right|^2 = \left| \vec{u} \right|^2 + \left| \vec{v} \right|^2 + \left| \vec{w} \right|^2,$$

Miscellaneous 8.45

which leads to the answer $\sqrt{14}$.

6. If $\vec{AB}$ and $\vec{AC}$ are the two vectors $\vec{u}$ and $\vec{v}$, then the magnitude of the length of the perpendicular from C onto AB is given by $\vec{v}\sin\theta$, where θ is the angle between the two vectors in the anticlockwise direction. If D is the foot of this perpendicular, the area of the parallelogram is given by $CD \times AB$. Thus, one can say that the magnitude of the cross product of $\vec{u}$ and $\vec{v}$ is equal to the required area. One can show that it is $\sqrt{450}$.

7. As both x and y have absolute values less than 1, the region is bounded inside a square with end points $(\pm 1, \pm 1)$. Now, $|y| \leq |x|$ implies that $x^2 - y^2 \geq 0$. One can use it to argue that either $y \geq -x, y \leq x$ or $y \leq -x, y \geq x$. The first condition is meaningful when $x > 0$. Thus, $-x \leq y \leq x$. Using similar arguments, one can reflect the first region with respect to the y-axis to obtain the region described by the second condition. This information can then be combined to draw the required region.

8. In the diagram below, AB is the building and it has height b; BF is the flagstaff and let us suppose that its length is h. Now, consider that the angle subtended by the flagstaff is y when a person is at a distance x.

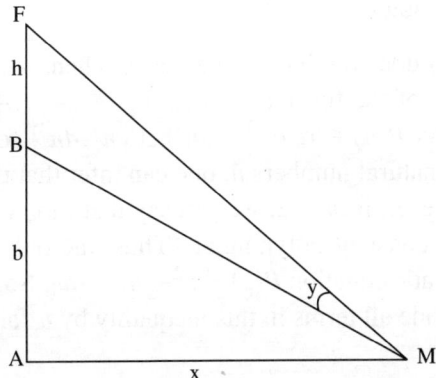

Noting that $y = \angle FMA - \angle BMA$, one can argue that it is maximized when $f(x) = hx/(x^2 + bh + b^2)$ is maximized. It is given that the maximizer is $x = d$. Thus, $f'(d) = 0$, which would imply that $bh^2 + bh = hd^2$. As the observed greatest angle is θ, one can use the above relationship to prove that $h = 2d\tan\theta$.

9. The direction ratios of AB are $(-1, -2, 2)$. Let D be the perpendicular from C onto AB. Assume that D divides the line segment AB in ratio $m : 1$. Then, the coordinates of D are
$$D = \left(\frac{4+3m}{m+1}, \frac{7+5m}{m+1}, \frac{1+3m}{m+1}\right)$$

Now, show that the direction ratios of CD are proportional to $(2m+3, 5m+7, -2)$. Next, use the fact that CD and AB are perpendicular to write $-(2m+3) - 2(5m+7) + 2(-2) = 0$. One can solve it to find out that the coordinates of D are $(5/3, 7/3, 17/3)$.

10. If the coordinates of the moving point are (x,y,z), we can write the equation $\sqrt{(x-1)^2+y^2+z^2} + \sqrt{(x+1)^2+y^2+z^2} = 4$. Simplifying this by taking squares, one can obtain the answer as $3x^2 + 4y^2 + 4z^2 - 12 = 0$.

11. Integrate twice to argue that the equation of the curve is of the form $y = ax^2 + bx + c$ for some real constants a, b, c. Since the curve passes through $(\pm 1, 0)$, the roots of the quadratic equation are ± 1. Hence, $b = 0$ and $c = -a$. Thus, the equation is of the form $y = a(x^2 - 1)$. We can further write this in the form $x^2 = \frac{1}{a}(y+a)$, which describes a parabola whose axis is the same as the y-axis.

12. From the expression of the slope of the tangent, one can write the differential equation as
$$\frac{dy}{dx} = \frac{y}{x} - \cos^2\left(\frac{y}{x}\right)$$
Take $y = vx$ to simplify it to $\sec^2 v \, dv = -dx/x$. Integrating both sides, and using the fact that the curve passes through $(1, \pi/4)$, the equation of the curve can be obtained as $y = x\tan^{-1}(1 - \log x)$.

13. Assume that $P(x)$ does not have a real zero. Then, for some $m \in \mathbb{N} \cup \{0\}$, one can argue that $P(x)$ is of the form $x^{2m} + a_{2m-1}x^{2m-1} + \ldots + a_1 x + a_0$, where the a_is are real constants. As $P(n) \in [-dn^3, -cn^3] \cup [cn^3, dn^3]$ for two positive real numbers $c < d$ and for all natural numbers n, one can infer that the absolute value of $P(n)/n^3$ is bounded. However, if $m \geq 2$, we can say that $\lim_{n \to \infty} P(n)/n^3 = \infty$. On the other hand, P is a non-constant polynomial. Thus, the only possibility is $m = 1$, which leads to the quadratic equation $P(x) = x^2 + a_1 x + a_0$. So, $cn^3 \leq |n^2 + a_1 n + a_0| \leq dn^3$ for all $n \in \mathbb{N}$. Divide all terms in this inequality by n^3 and take $n \to \infty$ to show that it cannot hold.

14. The nth roots of unity are of the form $e^{2\pi\iota k/n}$ for $k = 0, 1, 2, \ldots, n-1$. Denote them by $\alpha_0, \alpha_1, \ldots, \alpha_{n-1}$ and show that
$$\frac{z^n - 1}{z - 1} = \prod_{i=1}^{n-1}(z - \alpha_i)$$

Further, using $\alpha_0 = 1$
$$\sum_{i=0}^{n-1} z^i = \prod_{i=1}^{n-1}(z - \alpha_i)$$

Now, substitute $z = 1$ in the above to complete the proof.

15. Observe that the $(n-i+1)$th equation in the above system has $1/x_i$ in the right-hand side and all but x_i in the left-hand side. Subtract the $(n-i+1)$th equation of the above system from the $(n-j+1)$th equation of the same and show that $x_i x_j = 1$ for all $i,j = 1,2,\ldots,n$. It implies $x_1 = x_2 = \ldots = x_n$. One can easily find all possible solutions from here.

16. The position vectors of the two given points are $P = \hat{i} + 2\hat{j} + 3\hat{k}$ and $Q = 4\hat{i} + 5\hat{j} + 6\hat{k}$, which implies that the equation of the line through P and Q is given by $(1+5\lambda)\hat{i} + (2+3\lambda)\hat{j} + (3+\lambda)\hat{k}$. If S is the point where the line PQ crosses the yz-plane, the position vector of S is of the form $y\hat{j} + z\hat{k}$. It must also satisfy the above equation. Then, show that $\lambda = -1/5$.

17. The given condition gives us the relation $a^4 + a^3 + a^2 + a + 1 = 0$, and so, multiplying by $(a-1)$, we get $a^5 = 1$. Thus, we can say that a is an imaginary fifth root of unity and $a = e^{i2\pi k/5}$, where k is $1, 2, 3$ or 4. Observe that for any such a, the values of a^2, a^3, a^4 are the other three roots. Now, if we write $m = 5k + r$, where r is the remainder if m is divided by 5, then whenever $r \neq 0$, the terms $a^r, a^{2r}, a^{3r}, a^{4r}$ give us a, a^2, a^3, a^4 in some order. One can now show that the value of the given quantity is 4 if m is divisible by 5 and is (-1) otherwise.

18. The area bounded by f can be calculated as $\int_0^\infty e^{-x} dx$, which is equal to 1. On the other hand, the area bounded by the kth segment of $g(x)$ is the area of a trapezium with breadth 1 unit and parallel sides of length e^{-k} and e^{-k-1}. This is equal to $(e^{-k} + e^{-k-1})/2$. Considering the infinite sum of this expression for $k = 0, 1, 2, \ldots, \infty$, show that the total area bounded by $g(x)$ equals $1/2 + 1/(e-1)$. One can also argue that the area between the two graphs is the difference between the integrals of the two functions, evaluated in $[0,\infty)$, and hence, the required answer is $1/(e-1) - 1/2$.

19. Using the function $g(x) = x + 2\cos x$, show that $y = 1/g(x)$. Next, use differential calculus to show that the global minimum of $g(x)$ for all $x \geq 0$ is $5\pi/6 - \sqrt{3}$. As g is continuous, it means that all positive values above this minimum are attainable. Thus, the range of the function f is

$$0 < y \leq \frac{6}{5\pi - 6\sqrt{3}}$$

20. It is given that $f'(x) - f'(y) = 2(x-y)$ for all x, y. Take $x \to y$ and show that $f''(x) = 2$ for all $x \in \mathbb{R}$. Thus, $f(x) = x^2 + c_1 x + c_2$ for some $c_1, c_2 \in \mathbb{R}$. Use the given information to show that $c_2 = 0$, $c_1 = -2019$. Then, the required answer can be obtained as $f(2021) = 2021^2 - 2019 \times 2021 = 4042$.

Appendix
Previous Years' Subjective Questions and Solutions

ISI B.Math and B.Stat Entrance Test (2019)

1. Prove that the positive integer n that cannot be written as the sum of r consecutive positive integers, with $r > 1$, is of the form $n = 2^l$ for some $l \geqslant 0$.

Solution: Assume that an integer n can be written as the sum of r consecutive positive integers $a, a+1, \ldots, a+r-1$. It is equivalent to the following:

$$n = a + (a+1) + \ldots + (a+r-1) = ra + \frac{r(r-1)}{2} = \frac{r(2a+r-1)}{2}$$

We want to prove that n cannot be written as the sum of r consecutive positive integers if and only if n does not have an odd positive divisor > 1.

If part: Assume the converse, which is that there exists a positive integer n with no odd positive divisor > 1, and it can be expressed as

$$n = \frac{r(2a+r-1)}{2}$$

for some positive integers r and a. Since r and $(2a+r-1)$ have different parities, at least one of them must be odd.

Since we assume $r > 1$, it cannot be odd as 1 is the only odd divisor of n. Thus, if $(2a+r-1)$ is odd, then $2a+r-1 = 1$, which is also impossible as $2a+r-1 \geqslant 2 \times 1 + 1 - 1 = 2 > 1$.

Hence, if n does not have any odd positive divisor > 1, then n cannot be written as the sum of r consecutive positive integers.

Only if part: Let us assume that the odd divisor of n is b. Clearly, if $2n/b = c$, then c must be an even positive integer.

If $b < c$, let $r = b$ and $2a + r - 1 = c$, which implies $a = (c + 1 - b)/2$. Obviously, a is a positive integer because $c - b > 0$ and $(c + 1 - b)$ is an even integer. On the other hand, if $b > c$, we can pick $r = c$ and $a = (b + 1 - c)/2$. Here also, a can be easily shown to be a positive integer.

The above confirms that if n has a positive odd divisor > 1, then it can be expressed as the sum of r consecutive positive integers.

Combining the above, n can be written as the sum of r consecutive positive integers if and only if n has an odd positive divisor > 1. In other words, n can be written as the sum of r consecutive positive integers if and only if n is a power of 2.

2. Let $f : (0, \infty) \to \mathbb{R}$ be defined by

$$f(x) = \lim_{n \to \infty} \cos^n \left(\frac{1}{n^x} \right).$$

(a) Show that f has exactly one point of discontinuity.

(b) Evaluate f at its point of discontinuity.

Solution: Let us write $f \sim g$ if and only if $\lim_{x \to 0} f(x)/g(x) = 1$.

For any fixed positive quantity x, $1/n^x \to 0$ as $n \to \infty$, that is, $\cos(1/n^x) \to 1$. Therefore

$$\ln \cos^n \left(\frac{1}{n^x} \right) = n \ln \cos \left(\frac{1}{n^x} \right) \sim n \left(\cos \left(\frac{1}{n^x} \right) - 1 \right) \sim -\left(\frac{n}{2} \right) \left(\frac{1}{n^{2x}} \right) = -\frac{1}{2} n^{1-2x}$$

Thus, if $x < 1/2$, the above term $\to -\infty$, which indicates that $f(x) = 0$. If $x = 1/2$, then the above term is equal to $(-1/2)$ and if $x > 1/2$, then the above converges to 0. Combining the above results, we can write

$$f(x) = \begin{cases} 0 & \text{if } x < \frac{1}{2} \\ \frac{1}{\sqrt{e}} & \text{if } x = \frac{1}{2} \\ 1 & \text{if } x > \frac{1}{2} \end{cases}$$

Obviously, f has exactly one point of discontinuity, and the value of the function at that point is $1/\sqrt{e}$.

3. Let $\Omega = \{z = x + \iota y \in \mathbb{C} : |y| \leqslant 1\}$. If $f(z) = z^2 + 2$, then draw a sketch of

$$f(\Omega) = \{f(z) : z \in \Omega\}.$$

Justify your answer.

Solution: For $z \in \Omega$, we can write
$$f(z) = z^2 + 2 = (x^2 - y^2 + 2) + 2\imath xy$$

Let $u = x^2 - y^2 + 2$, $v = 2xy$. Then, it is easy to show that
$$\frac{v^2}{4} + 1 = x^2 y^2 + 1 \leqslant x^2 + 1 \leqslant x^2 - y^2 + 2 = u,$$

which signifies that the region $f(\Omega)$ must be inside the parabola $y^2 = 4(x-1)$. We can then show that any point (u,v) inside that region corresponds to some $z \in \Omega$.

If $v = 0$, then u must be $\geqslant 1$. If $u < 2$, then let us choose $x = 0$, $y = \sqrt{2-u}$. And if $u \geqslant 2$, then we can choose $x = \sqrt{u-2}$, $y = 0$. In both cases, we obtain a point inside Ω.

Next, if $v \neq 0$, $u \geqslant v^2/4 + 1$, let us choose
$$y = \sqrt{\frac{\sqrt{(u-2)^2 + v^2} - (u-2)}{2}}, \quad x = \frac{v}{2y}$$

From the assumptions, we can write
$$(u-2)^2 < (u-2)^2 + v^2 = u^2 + 4\left(\frac{v^2}{4} + 1 - u\right) \leqslant u^2,$$

which implies that $0 < \sqrt{(u-2)^2 + v^2} - (u-2) \leqslant 2$. This again establishes that the above choice of (x,y) ensures that the point is inside Ω. Hence, we can now conclude that $f(\Omega)$ is the entire region inside the parabola $y^2 = 4(x-1)$. The sketch is displayed below.

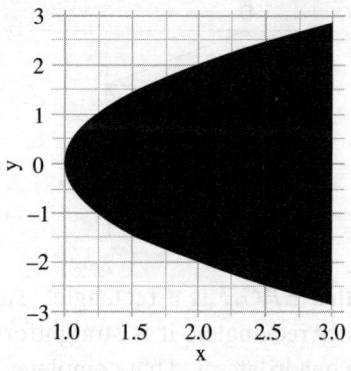

4. Let $f: \mathbb{R} \to \mathbb{R}$ be a twice-differentiable function such that

$$\frac{1}{2y}\int_{x-y}^{x+y} f(t)\,dt = f(x) \qquad \forall\, x \in \mathbb{R}, y > 0.$$

Show that there exist $a, b \in \mathbb{R}$ such that $f(x) = ax + b$ for all $x \in \mathbb{R}$.

Solution: Since f is a continuous and twice-differentiable function, there exists an anti-derivative F such that $F'(x) = f(x)$. Then, the given identity will be

$$F(x+y) - F(x-y) = 2yf(x)$$

Therefore, if we differentiate the above with respect to y by fixing $x \in \mathbb{R}$, we can write $f(x+y) + f(x-y) = 2f(x)$. Differentiating once again with respect to y, we get $f'(x+y) - f'(x-y) = 0$ for all $y > 0$.

Since the above is true for any arbitrarily chosen x, we obtain $f'(x) = f'(x+2y)$ for all $x \in \mathbb{R}$ and for all $y > 0$. This is possible if and only if $f'(x)$ is constant. It subsequently implies that $f(x) = ax + b$ for some real quantities a and b.

5. A subset S of the plane is called convex if given any two points x and y in S, the line segment joining x and y is contained in S. A quadrilateral is called convex if the region enclosed by the edges of the quadrilateral is a convex set. Show that given a convex quadrilateral Q of area 1, there is a rectangle R of area 2 such that Q can be drawn inside R.

Solution: We can prove the result by construction.

Let us assume that $ABCD$ is the convex quadrilateral. Let us draw two lines L_1 and L_2, each parallel to AC, from the vertices B and D, respectively. Next, drop perpendiculars from A onto L_1 and L_2. Since L_1 and L_2 are parallel, these perpendiculars are collinear. Let EF be the line segment formed by the perpendiculars within the lines L_1 and L_2. Similarly, let GH be the line segment formed by the perpendiculars drawn from C onto the lines L_1 and L_2.

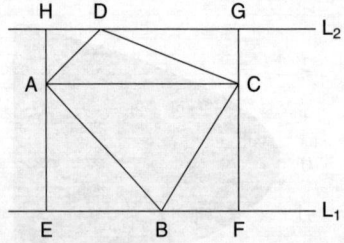

It is clear from construction that $EFGH$ is a rectangle. As ABC and ADC are triangles inscribed within the two smaller rectangles, it is straightforward to show that the area of $EFGH$ is twice the area of the quadrilateral. That completes the proof.

6. For all natural numbers n, let

$$A_n = \sqrt{2-\sqrt{2+\sqrt{2+\cdots+\sqrt{2}}}} \quad (n \text{ many radicals}).$$

(a) Show that for $n \geqslant 2$,

$$A_n = 2\sin\left(\frac{\pi}{2^{n+1}}\right).$$

(b) Hence or otherwise, evaluate the limit $\lim_{n\to\infty} 2^n A_n$.

Solution: First, squaring A_n and readjusting the terms, we note that

$$4 - A_n^2 = \sqrt{2+\sqrt{2+\cdots+\sqrt{2}}} \quad (n-1 \text{ many radicals}),$$

which indicates that

$$A_{n+1} = \sqrt{2-\sqrt{4-A_n^2}}$$

Using this, we can carry out induction on n to prove part (a). It is easy to verify that $A_1 = 2\sin(\pi/4)$. Assume that the result is true for $n = k$. Then, by means of the previous result

$$\begin{aligned}
A_{k+1} &= \sqrt{2-\sqrt{4-4\sin^2\left(\frac{\pi}{2^{k+1}}\right)}} \\
&= \sqrt{2-2\cos\left(\frac{\pi}{2^{k+1}}\right)} \\
&= \sqrt{4\sin^2\left(\frac{\pi}{2^{k+2}}\right)} \\
&= 2\sin\left(\frac{\pi}{2^{k+2}}\right)
\end{aligned}$$

Thus, part (a) is proved. For part (b), we can write

$$\lim_{n\to\infty} 2^n A_n = \lim_{n\to\infty} 2^n \times 2\sin\left(\frac{\pi}{2^{n+1}}\right) = \pi \lim_{n\to\infty} \frac{\sin r_n}{r_n},$$

where $r_n = \pi/2^{n+1} \to 0$ as $n \to \infty$. Then, using the fact $\lim_{x\to 0} \sin x/x = 1$, we can easily argue that the required answer is π.

7. Let f be a polynomial with integer coefficients. Define
$$a_1 = f(0), a_2 = f(a_1) = f(f(0)) \text{ and } a_n = f(a_{n-1}) \text{ for } n \geqslant 3.$$
If there exists a natural number $k \geqslant 3$ such that $a_k = 0$, then prove that either $a_1 = 0$ or $a_2 = 0$.

Solution: It is easy to observe that if $a_1 = 0$, then $a_n = 0$ for all n, which becomes a trivial case for this problem. So, let us assume that $a_1 \neq 0$ and let $K \geqslant 1$ be the smallest integer such that $a_{K+1} = f(a_K) = 0$. Clearly, a_1 is the constant term in the polynomial. It is then straightforward to infer that $a_1 = f(0)$ divides a_2, and that a_1 divides $a_2 - a_1$. Using the assumptions about polynomials and considering the expression of $f(a_K)$, we can also show that a_K divides a_1.

On the other hand, since f is a polynomial with integer coefficients, for integers x, y, $(x-y)$ must divide $f(x) - f(y)$. It automatically implies that $(a_{n+1} - a_n)$ divides $(a_{n+2} - a_{n+1})$, that is, each difference in the sequence divides the next difference. Considering all these divisibility results, we can write
$$|a_1| \leqslant |a_2 - a_1| \leqslant |a_3 - a_2| \leqslant \ldots \leqslant |a_{K+1} - a_K| = |a_K| \leqslant |a_1|$$

Clearly, equality must hold in every step above. From $|a_1| = |a_2 - a_1|$, a_2 must be either $2a_1$ or 0. If it is the former, then we see that a_3 must be $3a_1$, or the sequence would start oscillating between a_1 and $2a_1$, contradicting the assumption that it becomes 0 eventually. Similarly, one can show that a_j must be ja_1 for all $j \leqslant K+1$. However, it implies that $|a_K|$ cannot be equal to $|a_1|$. Hence, we conclude that a_2 must be 0.

8. Consider the following subsets of the plane:
$$C_1 = \left\{(x,y) : x > 0, y = \frac{1}{x}\right\}$$
and
$$C_2 = \left\{(x,y) : x < 0, y = -1 + \frac{1}{x}\right\}.$$
Given any two points $P = (x,y)$ and $Q = (u,v)$ of the plane, their distance $d(P,Q)$ is defined by
$$d(P,Q) = \sqrt{(x-u)^2 + (y-v)^2}.$$
Show that there exist a unique choice of points $P_0 \in C_1$ and $Q_0 \in C_2$ such that
$$d(P_0, Q_0) \leqslant d(P,Q) \quad \forall P \in C_1 \text{ and } Q \in C_2.$$

Solution: The shortest distance between two curves is along their common normal. Now, for the curve described in C_1, we can obtain the slope of the normal at a point (h,k) as (h/k). Since each point is of the form $(r, 1/r)$, the slope of the normal becomes r^2, and thus, the equation of the normal at that point is

$$\frac{y-1/r}{x-r} = r^2 \implies y = r^2 x + \frac{1}{r} - r^3$$

Similarly, at any point of the form $(s, -1+1/s)$ in C_2, the equation of the normal is

$$\frac{y+1-1/s}{x-s} = s^2 \implies y = s^2 x + \frac{1}{s} - 1 - s^3$$

For the shortest distance between C_1 and C_2, the above two normals must be the same straight line. Therefore

$$r^2 = s^2, \quad \frac{1}{r} - r^3 = \frac{1}{s} - 1 - s^3$$

It is easy to note that $r = s$ does not satisfy the second equation. So, the only possibility is $r = -s$. Using this, the second equation becomes

$$\frac{2}{r} - 2r^3 + 1 = 0 \implies 2r^4 - r - 2 = 0$$

Let us call the above four-degree polynomial $p(r)$. It takes the value (-2) at $r = 0$ and becomes positive as $r \to \infty$, indicating that it must have at least one real solution. Hence, there exist points $P_0 \in C_1$ and $Q_0 \in C_2$ such that their distance is the minimum. To prove the uniqueness, we note that $p'(r)$ is monotonic. Thus, $p(r)$ is strictly decreasing for $r < 1/2$, attains its minimum at $r = 1/2$ and is increasing for $r > 1/2$. Evidently, there is a unique $r > 0$ that satisfies the shortest distance requirement.

ISI B.Math and B.Stat Entrance Test (2020)

1. Let ι be a root of the equation $x^2+1=0$ and let ω be a root of the equation $x^2+x+1=0$. Construct a polynomial
$$f(x) = a_0 + a_1 x + \ldots + a_n x^n,$$
where $a_0, a_1, \ldots, a_n$ are all integers such that $f(\iota+\omega) = 0$.

Solution: Note that ω is a complex cube root of unity. Therefore, $\omega + \omega^2 = -1$ and $\omega^3 = 1$. Also, $\omega = \overline{\omega^2}$ and $\omega^2 = \bar{\omega}$.

Now, for a fixed ω, let us consider a polynomial for which $\omega + \iota$, $\omega - \iota$, $\bar{\omega} + \iota$ and $\bar{\omega} - \iota$ are four roots. It is easy to observe that the sum of the four roots is $2(\omega + \bar{\omega}) = -2$. If we take the sum of the products of two roots taken at a time, we get

$$(\omega+\iota)(-1+\bar{\omega}-\iota) + (\omega-\iota)(2\bar{\omega}) + \bar{\omega}^2 - \iota^2 = -\omega - \iota + 1 + \iota\omega^2 - \iota\omega - \iota^2 + 2 - 2\iota\omega^2 + \bar{\omega}^2 - \iota^2,$$

which can be simplified to $5 - \iota(1 + \omega + \omega^2) = 5$.

Next, the sum of the products of three roots taken at a time is

$$(\omega^2 - \iota^2)(2\bar{\omega}) + (\bar{\omega}^2 - \iota^2)(2\omega) = 2\left[\omega^2(\omega^2+1) + \omega(\omega+1)\right] = 4(\omega+\omega^2) = -4$$

Finally, the product of all the roots is $(\omega^2+1)(\omega+1) = 1$. Thus, the expression of the polynomial having the four terms as roots is $x^4 + 2x^3 + 5x^2 + 4x + 1$. Since it has integer coefficients, it completes our proof.

2. Let a be a fixed real number. Consider the equation
$$(x+2)^2(x+7)^2 + a = 0,$$
for $x \in \mathbb{R}$, where $\mathbb{R}$ is the set of real numbers. For what values of a will the equation have exactly one double root?

Solution: It is clear that a must be negative. Let us consider that it is of the form $a = -t^2$, where $t > 0$. Then, we can write $[(x+2)(x+7)]^2 - t^2 = 0$, which implies

$$[(x+2)(x+7) - t][(x+2)(x+7) + t] = 0$$

It is obvious that the two equations $(x+2)(x+7) - t = 0$ and $(x+2)(x+7) + t = 0$ cannot have a common root. Thus, one of these equations must have a double root. As each is a quadratic equation, it subsequently implies that the determinant must be 0. We check that the determinant of the first equation is $81 - 4(14-t) = 25 + 4t$, which is strictly greater than 0. For the second equation, the determinant is $81 - 4(14+t) = 25 - 4t$, which becomes 0 for $t = 25/4$. Hence, the only possible value of a is $-625/16$.

3. Let A and B be variable points on the x-axis and y-axis, respectively, such that the line segment AB is in the first quadrant and of a fixed length $2d$. Let C be the midpoint of AB and P be a point such that

   (a) P and the origin are on opposite sides of AB

   (b) PC is a line segment of length d that is perpendicular to AB

Find the locus of P.

Solution: We use the coordinate system to solve this question. Let O be the origin and assume that $\angle OAB$ is θ. Then, the coordinates of A are $(2d\cos\theta, 0)$ and that of B are $(0, 2d\sin\theta)$. Since C is the midpoint, we can say that the coordinates of C are $(d\cos\theta, d\sin\theta)$.

Let the coordinates of P be (h, k). We know that the slope of AB is $(-\tan\theta)$. Therefore, the slope of PC must be $1/\tan\theta$. It implies

$$\frac{k - d\sin\theta}{h - d\cos\theta} = \frac{\cos\theta}{\sin\theta} \implies \frac{(k - d\sin\theta)^2 + (h - d\cos\theta)^2}{(h - d\cos\theta)^2} = \frac{1}{\sin^2\theta}$$

The numerator in the above expression is equal to d^2. Therefore, $(h - d\cos\theta)^2 = d^2\sin^2\theta$. Using condition (a), one can argue that $h = d\cos\theta + d\sin\theta$. Applying the same technique, we can further show that $k = d\cos\theta + d\sin\theta$, that is, P always lies on the straight line $y = x$.

Now, observe that θ varies from 0 to $\pi/2$. So, the value of $d(\cos\theta + \sin\theta) = \sqrt{2}d\sin(\theta + \pi/4)$ varies from d to $\sqrt{2}d$. Hence, the locus of P is described by a line segment on $y = x$, whose distance from the origin is between $\sqrt{2}d$ and $2d$.

4. Let a real-valued sequence $\{x_n\}_{n\geq 1}$ be such that

$$\lim_{n\to\infty} nx_n = 0.$$

Find all possible real values of t such that $\lim_{n\to\infty} x_n(\log n)^t = 0$.

Solution: We can write the given limit as

$$\lim_{n\to\infty} x_n(\log n)^t = \lim_{n\to\infty} nx_n \frac{(\log n)^t}{n}$$

Clearly, if $t \leq 0$, then using the assumption, we can show that the above limit is 0. Now, for a positive real number t, we write

$$\lim_{n\to\infty} x_n(\log n)^t = \lim_{n\to\infty} nx_n \frac{(\log n)^t}{\exp(\log n)}$$

Considering the expansion of the exponential series, we can argue that for any $t > 0$, e^x grows faster than x^t. Therefore, both of the following hold:

$$\lim_{n \to \infty} nx_n = 0, \ \lim_{n \to \infty} \frac{(\log n)^t}{\exp(\log n)} = 0$$

Hence, $\lim_{n \to \infty} x_n (\log n)^t = 0$ is true for all $t \in \mathbb{R}$.

5. Prove that the largest pentagon (in terms of area) that can be inscribed in a circle of radius 1 is regular (that is, it has equal sides).

Solution: Let O be the centre of the given circle with unit radius. We consider $A_1 A_2 A_3 A_4 A_5$ as a pentagon inscribed inside the circle. Also, for the sake of consistency, let $A_6 = A_1$.

In order to find out the pentagon with the maximum area, it is obvious that O must be inside the pentagon, and therefore, each angle of the form $A_k O A_{k+1}$ must be $\leqslant \pi$. Let us denote these angles as θ_k, for $k = 1, \ldots, 5$.

Now, the area of the pentagon can be written as the sum of the five triangles of the form $A_k O A_{k+1}$, which can be expressed as

$$\Delta = \sum_{i=1}^{5} \frac{1}{2} \times 1^2 \times \sin \theta_i$$

The function $\sin x$ is concave in the interval $(0, \pi)$, and the sum of the angles θ_k is 2π. Clearly, by application of Jensen's inequality, we can say that Δ is maximized when all angles are equal. Therefore, $A_1 A_2 A_3 A_4 A_5$ must be a regular pentagon.

6. Prove that the family of curves

$$\frac{x^2}{a^2 + \lambda} + \frac{y^2}{b^2 + \lambda} = 1$$

satisfies

$$\frac{dy}{dx}(a^2 - b^2) = \left(x + y\frac{dy}{dx}\right)\left(x\frac{dy}{dx} - y\right).$$

Solution: Differentiating the given equation with respect to x

$$\frac{2x}{a^2 + \lambda} + \frac{2y}{b^2 + \lambda}\left(\frac{dy}{dx}\right) = 0$$

Readjusting the terms, we write

$$\left(\frac{dy}{dx}\right)\left(\frac{y(a^2 + \lambda)}{x}\right) = -(b^2 + \lambda)$$

Substituting the expression for $b^2 + \lambda$ in the given equation

$$\frac{x^2}{a^2+\lambda} - \frac{xy^2}{y(a^2+\lambda)}\left(\frac{dy}{dx}\right)^{-1} = 1 \implies a^2+\lambda = \left(x^2\frac{dy}{dx} - xy\right)\left(\frac{dy}{dx}\right)^{-1}$$

Subsequently

$$b^2 + \lambda = -\left(xy\frac{dy}{dx} - y^2\right)$$

Subtracting the two equations above and multiplying by dy/dx on both sides, we get

$$\begin{aligned}\frac{dy}{dx}(a^2 - b^2) &= \left(x^2\frac{dy}{dx} - xy\right) + \left(xy\frac{dy}{dx} - y^2\right)\left(\frac{dy}{dx}\right) \\ &= xy\left(\frac{dy}{dx}\right)^2 + (x^2 - y^2)\left(\frac{dy}{dx}\right) - xy\end{aligned}$$

The above factorizes in the given form and that completes our proof.

7. Consider a right-angled triangle with integer-valued sides $a < b < c$, where a, b, c are pairwise co-prime. Let $d = c - b$. Suppose d divides a. Then

(a) Prove that $d \leqslant 2$.

(b) Find all such triangles (that is, all possible triplets a, b, c) with perimeter less than 100.

Solution:

(a) Because the triangle is right-angled, we can write $a^2 + b^2 = c^2$, which implies $a^2 = (c-b)(c+b) = d(d+2b)$. Subsequently, we can write $(a-d)(a+d) = 2bd$.

From the given conditions, $a = dx$ for some natural number x. Using this, we obtain $(dx-d)(dx+d) = 2bd$, that is, $d(x^2 - 1) = 2b$. As b and c are co-prime, we can argue that d and b are also co-prime. Thus, d must divide 2, and therefore, $d \leqslant 2$.

(b) Next, we focus on the triplets that satisfy $a + b + c \leqslant 100$. Using the result from part (a), we can say that $c = b + 1$ or $c = b + 2$. In the first case, we obtain $a^2 + b^2 = (b+1)^2$, which implies $b = (a^2 - 1)/2$. Since b is an integer, a is odd. We can also say that b must be less than 50, and therefore, $a^2 < 101$, that is, $a < 10$. We can then enumerate the possible triplets as follows: $(3,4,5), (5,12,13), (7,24,25), (9,40,41)$.

Next, under the assumption $c = b + 2$, following a similar procedure as before, we get $b = (a^2/4 - 1)$. Thus, a is even. Also note that

$$a + b + c = a + \frac{a^2}{4} - 1 + \frac{a^2}{4} + 1 = a + \frac{a^2}{2} < 100$$

The above indicates $a^2 + 2a < 200$, that is, $(a+1)^2 < 201$, which is equivalent to $a \leq 13$. Since a is even, we can check that the only possibilities in this set-up are $(8, 15, 17)$ and $(12, 35, 37)$. Hence, all the possible triplets satisfying the given conditions are $(3, 4, 5), (5, 12, 13), (7, 24, 25), (8, 15, 17), (9, 40, 41), (12, 35, 37)$.

8. A finite sequence of numbers $(a_1, \ldots, a_n)$ is said to be alternating if

$$a_1 > a_2, a_2 < a_3, a_3 > a_4, a_4 < a_5, \ldots$$

or

$$a_1 < a_2, a_2 > a_3, a_3 < a_4, a_4 > a_5, \ldots$$

How many alternating sequences of length 5 with distinct real numbers $a_1, \ldots, a_5$ can be formed such that $a_i \in \{1, 2, \ldots, 20\}$ for $i = 1, \ldots, 5$?

Solution: We first note that all numbers in the given set are distinct. We can choose five distinct numbers from this set in $\binom{20}{5}$ ways. Let us assume that $a < b < c < d < e$ are the five numbers chosen. We consider the given two cases separately.

Let us first take $a_1 > a_2, a_2 < a_3, a_3 > a_4, a_4 < a_5$. From the way we selected the numbers, we see that a is bigger than none of the numbers, b is bigger than only a, and e is the biggest. So, a must be either a_2 or a_4. If $a_2 = a$, then a_4 must be either b or c. Now, if a and b occupy these two positions, the other three may be filled in any possible way. On the other hand, if a and c occupy those two positions, then b must be assigned to the number that is a's neighbour.

So, the number of possible configurations of the five numbers is $2 \times 3! + 2 \times 2! = 16$.

Now, if we consider the case of $a_1 < a_2, a_2 > a_3, a_3 < a_4, a_4 > a_5$, the same argument as the previous case may be used, the only difference being that we must first fix the positions of d and e. Hence, here also, the total number of possible configurations is 16.

Hence, the total number of alternating sequences satisfying the given conditions is

$$2 \times 16 \times \binom{20}{5} = 32 \times \binom{20}{5}$$

Appendix: Previous Years' Subjective Questions and Solutions   A.13

ISI B.Math and B.Stat Entrance Test (2021)

1. There are three cities, each of which has exactly the same number of citizens, say n. Every citizen in each city has a total of $n+1$ friends in the other two cities. Show that there exist three people, one from each city, such that they are friends. We assume that friendship is mutual (that is, a symmetric relation).

Solution: Out of $3n$ citizens, suppose citizen A has a maximum number k of acquaintances from one of the other two cities. Also without loss of generality, assume that A is from the first city and A knows k citizens from the second city. Then A must know $(n+1-k)$ citizens from the third city. Observe that $n+1-k \geqslant 1$ since $k \leqslant n$.

Now, consider citizen B from the third city, who knows A. If B knows at least one citizen C from the k acquaintances of A in the second city, then we have the triplet $\{A,B,C\}$ of mutual acquaintances. However, if B knows none of the k acquaintances of A in the second city, then he cannot know more than $(n-k)$ citizens in the second city. And hence, in the first city, he must know more than $n+1-(n-k) = k+1$ citizens, which contradicts the choice of k.

2. Let $f : \mathbb{Z} \to \mathbb{Z}$ be a function satisfying $f(0) \neq 0 = f(1)$. Assume also that f satisfies the two equations below for all integers x, y.

$$f(xy) = f(x) + f(y) - f(x)f(y)$$
$$f(x-y)f(x)f(y) = f(0)f(x)f(y)$$

(i) Determine explicitly the set $\{f(a) : a \in \mathbb{Z}\}$.

(ii) Assuming that there is a non-zero integer a such that $f(a) \neq 0$, prove that the set $\{b : f(b) \neq 0\}$ is infinite.

Solution:

(i) Putting $x = y = 0$ in the first equation, we get

$$f(0) = f(0) + f(0) - f(0)^2, f(0)^2 = f(0)$$

Since $f(0) \neq 0$, $f(0) = 1$. Now, using $y = 0$ in the second equation

$$f(x)^2 f(0) = f(x)f(0)^2, f(x)^2 = f(x)$$

Clearly, either $f(x) = 0$ or $f(x) = 1$. The function f can take only two values 0 and 1 (both values are in the range of f, because $f(0) = 1, f(1) = 0$), that is,

$$\{f(a) : a \in \mathbb{Z}\} = \{0, 1\}$$

(ii) Assume that there exists a non-zero $a \in \mathbb{Z}$ such that $f(a) \neq 0$. Then, clearly $a \neq 1$. We put $x = y = -1$ in the first equation to get

$$0 = f(1) = 2f(-1) - f(-1)^2$$

Hence, it follows that $f(-1) \neq 1$, subsequently implying $f(-1) = 0$ and $a \neq -1$. So, $|a| > 1$. Further, from the first equation, we see that if $f(a) = f(b) = 1$, then

$$f(ab) = f(a) + f(b) - f(a)f(b) = 1$$

Thus, by induction, we can prove that $f(a^k) = 1$ for all $k \geq 1$ and the set $\{b : f(b) \neq 0\}$ is infinite.

3. Prove that every positive rational number can be expressed uniquely as a finite sum of the form
$$a_1 + \frac{a_2}{2!} + \frac{a_3}{3!} + \ldots + \frac{a_n}{n!},$$
where a_n is an integer such that $0 \leq a_n \leq n-1$ for all $n > 1$.

Solution: Let r be a positive rational number. Define $a_1 = [r]$, then $0 \leq r - a_1 < 1$. Let us then define $a_1, \ldots, a_m$ in such a way that

$$0 \leq r - \sum_{k=1}^{m} \frac{a_k}{k!} < \frac{1}{m!}$$

Now define

$$a_{m+1} = \left[(m+1)! \left(r - \sum_{k=1}^{m} \frac{a_k}{k!} \right) \right]$$

Observe that

$$0 \leq (m+1)! \left(r - \sum_{k=1}^{m} \frac{a_k}{k!} \right) < m+1$$

Hence, we must have $a_{m+1} \in \{0, \ldots, m\}$. So, we have defined a sequence of integers $(a_n : n \geq 1)$ such that $a_1 \geq 0, 0 \leq a_n \leq n-1, n > 1$ and for all $n \geq 1$

$$0 \leq r - \sum_{k=1}^{n} \frac{a_k}{k!} < \frac{1}{n!}$$

For a large enough n, we must have $r(n!) \in \mathbb{Z}$, and that makes

$$n! \left(r - \sum_{k=1}^{n} \frac{a_k}{k!} \right) \in [0, 1) \cap \mathbb{Z}$$

This will be only be possible when

$$r = \sum_{k=1}^{n} \frac{a_k}{k!}$$

So, we have proved the existence part. To prove that the representation is unique, assume that there exist two representations

$$\sum_{k=1}^{n} \frac{a_k}{k!} = \sum_{k=1}^{n} \frac{b_k}{k!}$$

with integer coefficients a_k, b_k such that $a_1, b_1 \geqslant 0, a_k, b_k \in \{0, \ldots, k-1\}$ for $k > 1$. Let j denote the first index such that $a_j \neq b_j$. Without loss of generality, we can assume that $a_j < b_j$. Then

$$\frac{a_j}{j!} + \sum_{k=j+1}^{n} \frac{a_k}{k!} = \frac{b_j}{j!} + \sum_{k=j+1}^{n} \frac{b_k}{k!}$$

Now, consider the inequalities

$$\frac{a_j}{j!} + \sum_{k=j+1}^{n} \frac{a_k}{k!} \leqslant \frac{a_j}{j!} + \sum_{k=j+1}^{n} \frac{k-1}{k!}$$

$$= \frac{a_j}{j!} + \sum_{k=j+1}^{n} \frac{1}{(k-1)!} - \sum_{k=j+1}^{n} \frac{1}{k!}$$

$$= \frac{a_j}{j!} + \sum_{k=j+1}^{n} \frac{1}{(k-1)!} - \sum_{k=j+1}^{n} \frac{1}{k!}$$

$$= \frac{a_j}{j!} + \frac{1}{j!} - \frac{1}{n!}$$

$$< \frac{a_j + 1}{j!} \leqslant \frac{b_j}{j!} + \sum_{k=j+1}^{n} \frac{b_k}{k!}$$

Hence, it is impossible to have $\sum_{k=1}^{n} a_k/k! = \sum_{k=1}^{n} b_k/k!$. The contradiction proves the uniqueness of the representation.

4. Let $g : (0, \infty) \to (0, \infty)$ be a differentiable function whose derivative is continuous and such that $g(g(x)) = x$ for all $x > 0$. If g is not the identity function, prove that g must be strictly decreasing.

Solution: Differentiating the relation $g(g(x)) = x$ with respect to x, we get

$$g'(g(x))g'(x) = 1$$

Hence, $g'(x) \neq 0$ for all $x > 0$, thereby suggesting that g' must preserve its sign on $(0, \infty)$. Let us assume that $g'(x) > 0$ for all $x > 0$. Then $g(x)$ is strictly increasing. For some x, we have $g(x) \neq x$, as g is not the identity function. If $g(x) > x$, $g(g(x)) > g(x) > x$, but this contradicts the fact that $g(g(x)) = x$.

On the other hand, if $g(x) < x$, then $g(g(x)) < g(x) < x$, which also contradicts $g(g(x)) = x$.

Since the assumption $g'(x) > 0$ leads us to a contradiction either way, we must have $g'(x) < 0$ for all $x > 0$ and g is strictly decreasing.

5. Let $a_0, a_1, \ldots, a_{19} \in \mathbb{R}$ and

$$P(x) = x^{20} + \sum_{i=0}^{19} a_i x^i, \quad x \in \mathbb{R}.$$

If $P(x) = P(-x)$ for all $x \in \mathbb{R}$, and $P(k) = k^2$ for $k = 0, 1, \ldots, 9$, then find

$$\lim_{x \to 0} \frac{P(x)}{\sin^2 x}.$$

Solution: From the given condition $P(x) = P(-x)$, we can write

$$x^{20} + \sum_{i=0}^{19} a_i x^i = x^{20} + \sum_{i=0}^{19} (-1)^i a_i x^i \implies \sum_{i=0}^{19} (1 - (-1)^i) a_i x^i = 0$$

This means that all coefficients a_i that correspond to odd indices i are equal to zero. So, we can write

$$P(x) = x^{20} + \sum_{i=0}^{9} a_{2i} x^{2i}$$

Now consider a new polynomial $Q(x) = x^{10} + \sum_{i=0}^{9} a_{2i} x^i - x$. By construction

$$Q(k^2) = k^{20} + \sum_{i=0}^{9} a_{2i} k^{2i} - k^2 = P(k) - k^2 = 0, \ 0 \leqslant k \leqslant 9$$

Observe that $(a_2 - 1)$ is the coefficient of x in $Q(x)$. We can work out the 10 roots of the polynomial Q as k^2, for $k = 0, \ldots, 9$, and hence, $Q(x)$ can be factorized as

$$Q(x) = x(x-1)(x-2^2) \ldots (x-9^2)$$

Subsequently, we get $a_0 = 0$ and

$$a_2 - 1 = -\prod_{k=1}^{9} k^2, \ a_2 = 1 - (9!)^2 = -362879$$

Hence, $P(x) = -362879x^2 + \sum_{i=3}^{19} a_i x^i + x^{20}$, which implies that

$$\lim_{x \to 0} \frac{P(x)}{\sin^2 x} = \left(\lim_{x \to 0} \frac{x^2}{\sin^2 x} \right) \left(\lim_{x \to 0} \frac{P(x)}{x^2} \right) = -362879$$

6. If a given equilateral triangle Δ of side length a lies in the union of five equilateral triangles of side length b, show that there exist four equilateral triangles of side length b whose union contains Δ.

Solution: We need to show that $b \geqslant a/2$. On the contrary, assume that $b < a/2$. Consider an equilateral triangle Δ_b of side length b. Note that the distance between any two points in Δ_b is $\leqslant b$. Now consider the equilateral triangle Δ_a of side length a. Observe the following configuration:

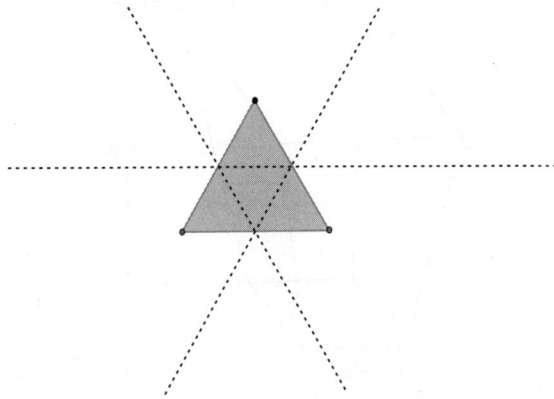

There are six points in the triangle Δ_a with pairwise distances $\geqslant a/2 > b$. Hence, if we have $b < a/2$, then one needs at least six equilateral triangles of side length b to cover an equilateral triangle of side length a. So, we prove that $b \geqslant a/2$. Now, the configuration above gives constructive proof that four equilateral triangles of side length b are enough to cover an equilateral triangle of side length a.

7. Let a, b, c be three real numbers that are roots of a cubic polynomial, and satisfy $a+b+c = 6$ and $ab+bc+ac = 9$. Suppose $a < b < c$. Show that

$$0 < a < 1 < b < 3 < c < 4.$$

Solution: Let the polynomial $P(x)$ have roots a, b, c. Then

$$P(x) = (x-a)(x-b)(x-c) = x^3 - x^2(a+b+c) + x(ab+ac+bc) - abc = x^3 - 6x^2 + 9x - abc$$

Thus, the derivative of $P(x)$ is

$$P'(x) = 3x^2 - 12x + 9 = 3(x-1)(x-3),$$

which signifies that the polynomial P is increasing on $(-\infty, 1]$, decreasing on $[1,3]$, and again increasing on $[3,\infty)$. Therefore, we must have $a < 1 < b < 3 < c$.

Further, $P(3) = 27 - 54 + 27 - abc = -abc < 0$, which implies $abc > 0$ and $a > 0$. On the other hand, $P(1) = 4 - abc > 0$ implies $abc < 4$. We can thus obtain $P(4) = 64 - 24 + 36 - abc = 76 - abc > 72 > 0$, and hence, $c < 4$.

So, we have proved that $0 < a < 1 < b < 3 < c < 4$.

8. A pond has been dug at the Indian Statistical Institute as an inverted truncated pyramid with a square base (see the figure below).

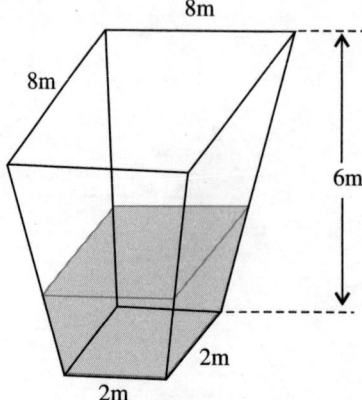

The depth of the pond is 6 m. The square at the bottom has side length 2 m and the top square has side length 8 m. Water is filled in at the rate of 19/3 cubic metres per hour. At what rate is the water level rising exactly 1 hour after the water began filling the pond?

Solution: Let us denote $V(t)$ as the volume of the water t hours after the water started to fill the pond. Then $V(t) = 19t/3$ (in cubic metres). Now, let $h(t)$ be the level of the water and $a(t)$ be the side of the square at the top of the water t hours after the water started to fill the pond.

Now we extend the truncated pyramid to obtain a non-truncated pyramid and let x be the height of the added part.

Similarity of two triangles implies

$$\frac{x}{x+h(t)} = \frac{2}{a(t)}, \quad \frac{x+h(t)}{x+6} = \frac{a(t)}{8}$$

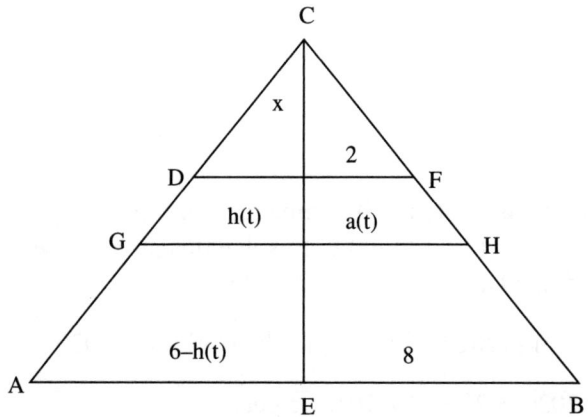

Multiplying the two equations above, we find

$$\frac{x}{x+6} = \frac{1}{4}, \ x = 2, \ a(t) = h(t) + 2$$

Now, subtracting the volume of the pyramid CGH and CDF, we get

$$V(t) = \left(\frac{h(t)+2}{3}\right) a(t)^2 - \frac{2}{3} \times 4 = \frac{1}{3}\left((h(t)+2)^3 - 8\right),$$

which implies

$$V'(t) = (h(t)+2)^2 h'(t)$$

Thus, $h'(1)$ would give us the water level rising exactly 1 hour after the water began filling the pond and we find

$$h'(1) = \frac{V'(1)}{(h(1)+2)^2} = \frac{V'(1)}{(3V(1)+8)^{2/3}} = \frac{19/3}{9} = \frac{19}{27} \text{ (metres per hour)}.$$

CMI BSc. Mathematics Entrance Test (2019)

1. For a natural number m, define $\Phi_1(m)$ to be the number of divisors of m and for $k \geqslant 2$ define $\Phi_k(m) = \Phi_1(\Phi_{k-1}(m))$. For example, $\Phi_2(12) = \Phi_1(6) = 4$. Find the minimum k such that $\Phi_k(2019^{2019}) = 2$.

Solution: If a number n is written in its prime factorized form as $n = p_1^{\alpha_1} \ldots p_k^{\alpha_k}$, then its number of divisors is $(\alpha_1 + 1) \ldots (\alpha_k + 1)$. To solve this problem, we need to consider the prime factorization of 2019 and that is 3×673. Thus

$$\Phi_1\left(2019^{2019}\right) = \Phi_1\left(3^{2019} 673^{2019}\right) = 2020^2$$

Once again, writing $2020 = 2^2 \times 5^2 \times 101$, we get

$$\Phi_2\left(2019^{2019}\right) = \Phi_1\left(2^2 \times 5^2 \times 101\right) = 3^2 \times 2 \implies \Phi_3\left(2019^{2019}\right) = 3 \times 2$$

Since $\Phi_1(3 \times 2) = 2^2$ and $\Phi_1(2^2) = 3$, we can write that

$$\Phi_5\left(2019^{2019}\right) = 3,$$

which is a prime number, thereby implying that the required value of k is 6.

2. Let f be a real-valued continuous function defined on $\mathbb{R}$ such that $f'(\tan^2 \theta) = \cos 2\theta + \tan \theta \sin 2\theta$ for all real numbers θ. If $f(0) = -\cos \frac{\pi}{12}$, find $f(1)$.

Solution: The given expression for $f'(\tan^2 \theta)$ can be simplified as $2\cos^2 \theta - 1 + \tan \theta \times 2\sin \theta \cos \theta$, which is in fact equal to 1. Now, substituting $y = \tan^2 \theta$, we get $f'(y) = 1$, that is, $f(y) = y + c$ for some real constant c. Using the value of $f(0)$, one can obtain $c = -\cos \frac{\pi}{12}$, and thus, $f(1) = 1 - \cos \frac{\pi}{12}$.

3. You have a piece of land close to a river, running straight. You are required to cut off a rectangular portion of the land, with the river forming one of the sides of the rectangle, so your fence will have three sides to it. You only have 60 metres of fencing. Find the maximum area that you can enclose.

Solution: Assume that the length and width of the rectangular land are x and y, respectively, with y being on the side of the river. Then, we need to maximize xy, under the restriction $2x + y = 60$.

Taking $y = 60 - 2x$, we get the area as $60x - 2x^2$. Let us call it $f(x)$. Then, $f'(x) = 60 - 4x$ and $f''(x) = -4$, signifying that the function attains its maximum at $x = 15$. It implies that $y = 30$, and therefore, the maximum area that can be enclosed is equal to 450 square metres.

4. Calculate the sum

$$S = 1 + 111 + 11111 + \ldots + \underbrace{11 \ldots 1}_{2k+1}.$$

Solution: The rth term in the given sum, for $1 \leq r \leq k+1$, can be written as

$$1 + 10 + 10^2 + \ldots + 10^{2r-1} = \frac{10^{2r-1} - 1}{9} = \frac{100^r - 10}{90}$$

Thus, the required sum is

$$\frac{1}{90} \sum_{r=1}^{k+1} [100^r - 10] = \frac{1}{90} \left[\frac{100(100^{k+1} - 1)}{99} - 10(k+1) \right] = \frac{(10^{2k+3} - 99k - 109)}{9 \times 99}$$

5. You are given an 8×8 chessboard. If two distinct squares are chosen uniformly at random, find the probability that two rooks placed on these squares attack each other. Recall that a rook can move either horizontally or vertically, in a straight line.

Solution: Two rooks placed on the chessboard would attack each other (we call it 'favourable condition' below) if the two chosen squares share either a common row or a common column. Now, the first square can be chosen randomly from any of the available 64 squares. Then, to allow the 'favourable condition', the second square must be chosen from among the 15 squares that share either a column or a row with the first. Thus, the total number of possible choices for the 'favourable condition' is 64×14, whereas the total possible choices without any restriction is 64×63. Hence, the required probability is $14/63 = 2/9$.

6. For how many natural numbers n is $n^6 + n^4 + 1$ a square of a natural number?

Solution: If n is odd, because any perfect square is 1 (mod 8), we can say that $n^6 + n^4 + 1 \equiv 3 \pmod 8$, and thus, it cannot be a perfect square. Let us now take $n = 2k$ and write

$$n^6 + n^4 + 1 = (2k)^6 + 2 \times (2k)^3 \times k + k^2 + (1 - k^2) \leq [(2k)^3 + k]^2,$$

with equality holding if and only if $k = 1$. On the other hand, note that

$$[(2k)^3 + k - 1]^2 = (2k)^6 + 2 \times (2k)^3 \times (k-1) + (k-1)^2 = (n^6 + n^4 + 1) - (16k^3 - k^2 + 2k)$$

Since $k \geq 1$, it is evident that $n^6 + n^4 + 1 > [(2k)^3 + k - 1]^2$. Thus, the only possibility of $n^6 + n^4 + 1$ being a square is to have $k = 1$. Hence, only for $n = 2$ is the given term a square of a natural number.

7. A broken calculator has all its 10 digit keys and two operation keys intact. Let us call these operation keys A and B. When the calculator displays a number n, pressing A changes the display to $n + 1$. When the calculator displays a number n, pressing B changes the display to $2n$. For example, if the number 3 is displayed, then the key strokes $ABBA$ change the display in the following steps $3 \to 4 \to 8 \to 16 \to 17$. If 1 appears on the display, what is the least number of key strokes required to obtain 260 on the display?

Solution: Assume that x number of A operations and y number of B operations are required to obtain 260 from 1. Since each A operation adds 1, and each B operation doubles the number, we can say that the least number one can obtain by x number of A operations and y number of B operations is $2^y + x$. Therefore, $2^y + x \leqslant 260$, which implies that $y \leqslant 8$. Since 260 is not a perfect power of 2, we can also say that $x \geqslant 1$. Now, if all operations were B (which leads to the maximum possible number on the display), then we would have obtained 2^{x+y}, which must be greater than 260. It further implies that $x + y \geqslant 9$.

Now, observe that a possible sequence is $1 \to 2 \to 4 \to 8 \to 16 \to 32 \to 64 \to 65 \to 130 \to 160$, which indicates $x + y = 9$. Hence, a minimum of 9 strokes are required to obtain 260 on the display. The corresponding sequences are *ABBBBBABB* or *BBBBBBABB*.

8. Let $\pi = \pi_1 \pi_2 \ldots \pi_n$ be a permutation of the numbers $1, 2, \ldots, n$. We say π has its first ascent at position $k < n$ if $\pi_1 > \ldots > \pi_k$ and $\pi_k < \pi_{k+1}$. If $\pi_1 > \ldots > \pi_n$, we say π has its first ascent in position n. For example, when $n = 4$, the permutation 2134 has its first ascent at position 2. Find the number of permutations that have their first ascent at position k.

Solution: Let S_k denote the set of permutations that have their first ascent at position $r \geqslant k$. Then, we are interested in the number $|S_k| - |S_{k+1}|$. For each permutation of S_k, we can say that the first k numbers are in strictly decreasing sequence. This can happen in $\binom{n}{k}(n-k)!$ ways. Hence, the required answer is

$$\binom{n}{k}(n-k)! - \binom{n}{k+1}(n-k-1)!$$

9. Consider $f : \mathbb{R} \times \mathbb{R} \to \mathbb{R}$ defined as follows:

$$f(a,b) = \lim_{n \to \infty} \frac{1}{n} \log_e \left[e^{na} + e^{nb} \right].$$

Find out if the following statements are True or False:

(a) f is not onto, that is, the range of f is not all of $\mathbb{R}$.

(b) For every a, the function $x \to f(a,x)$ is continuous everywhere.

(c) For every b, the function $x \to f(x,b)$ is differentiable everywhere.

(d) We have $f(0,x) = x$ for all $x \geqslant 0$.

Solution: We can simplify the expression of f by using L'Hospital's rule

$$f(a,b) = \lim_{n \to \infty} \frac{ae^{na} + be^{nb}}{e^{na} + e^{nb}} = \max\{a,b\}$$

(a) It is clear that $f(a,b)$ would take all real values, and so f is onto.

(b) For a given a, the function $g(x) = f(a,x)$ can be written as

$$g(x) = \begin{cases} a & \text{for } x \leqslant a \\ x & \text{for } x > a \end{cases}$$

Thus, g is continuous everywhere.

(c) In a similar fashion as above, we can write

$$h(x) = f(x,b) = \begin{cases} b & \text{for } x \leqslant b \\ x & \text{for } x > b \end{cases}$$

Thus, at $x = b$, we can argue that the right derivative of h is 1 whereas the left derivative of h is 0. Hence, h is not differentiable everywhere.

(d) It is easy to see from the above that $f(0,x) = x$ for all $x \geqslant 0$.

Therefore, the above statements are, respectively, False, True, False, True.

10. Find out if the following statements are True or False:

(a) There is no continuous function $f : \mathbb{R} \to \mathbb{R}$ for which $\int_0^1 f(x)(1 - f(x)) \, dx < 1/4$.

(b) There is only one continuous function $f : \mathbb{R} \to \mathbb{R}$ for which $\int_0^1 f(x)(1 - f(x)) \, dx = 1/4$.

(c) There are infinitely many continuous functions $f : \mathbb{R} \to \mathbb{R}$ for which $\int_0^1 f(x)(1 - f(x)) \, dx = 1/4$.

Solution: Consider that $f(x)$ is strictly non-negative in the interval $[0,1]$. Then, applying the AM-GM inequality, we can argue that $f(x)(1 - f(x)) \leqslant 1/4$ for all $x \in [0,1]$, where equality holds if and only if $f(x)$ is identically equal to $1/2$ in that interval. Clearly, there are infinitely many continuous functions f that take positive values within the interval $[0,1]$, and for them, $\int_0^1 f(x)(1 - f(x)) \, dx < 1/4$. Similarly, one can define f in infinitely many ways such that it is continuous everywhere, and takes the value $1/2$ in $[0,1]$. For all these functions, $\int_0^1 f(x)(1 - f(x)) \, dx = 1/4$.

Hence, the given statements are, respectively, False, False and True.

11. For a natural number n denoted by $\text{Map}(n)$, the set of all functions $f : \{1, 2, \ldots, n\} \to \{1, 2, \ldots, n\}$. For $f, g \in \text{Map}(n)$, $f \circ g$ denotes the function in $\text{Map}(n)$ that sends x to $f(g(x))$.

(a) Let $f \in \text{Map}(n)$. If for all $x \in \{1, 2, \ldots, n\}$, $f(x) \neq x$, show that $f \circ f \neq f$.

(b) Count the number of functions $f \in \text{Map}(n)$ such that $f \circ f = f$.

Solution:

(a) Let us assume that $f \circ f = f$. Then, denoting $y = f(x)$, we can write $f(y) = y$, which is a contradiction since for all $x \in \{1, 2, \ldots, n\}$, $f(x) \neq x$. Thus, $f \circ f \neq f$.

(b) From the previous part, we can argue that if $f \circ f = f$, then there must be at least one x such that $f(x) = x$. We call these fixed points. If there are exactly k fixed points, then each of the other $n - k$ numbers must be mapped to one of these k fixed points, and hence, the number of such functions is $\binom{n}{k} k^{n-k}$. Since k can be any number between 1 and n, our required answer is

$$\sum_{k=1}^{n} \binom{n}{k} k^{n-k}$$

12. (a) Count the number of roots ω of the equation $z^{2019} - 1 = 0$ over complex numbers that satisfy $|\omega + 1| \geq \sqrt{2 + \sqrt{2}}$.

(b) Find all real numbers x that satisfy following equation:

$$\frac{8^x + 27^x}{12^x + 18^x} = \frac{7}{6}.$$

Solution:

(a) A root of the equation $z^{2019} - 1 = 0$ is of the form $\exp(\iota 2\pi k/2019)$, where $k \in \{0, 1, \ldots, 2018\}$. Thus, the given condition implies that

$$\left| e^{\iota 2\pi k/2019} + 1 \right|^2 = \left| 1 + \cos\left(\frac{2\pi k}{2019}\right) + \iota \sin\left(\frac{2\pi k}{2019}\right) \right|^2$$

$$= \left(1 + \cos\left(\frac{2\pi k}{2019}\right) \right)^2 + \sin^2\left(\frac{2\pi k}{2019}\right)$$

$$= 2 + 2\cos\left(\frac{2\pi k}{2019}\right)$$

$$\geq 2 + \sqrt{2}$$

Thus, k must satisfy

$$\cos\left(\frac{2\pi k}{2019}\right) \geq \frac{1}{\sqrt{2}} \implies \left|\frac{2\pi k}{2019}\right| \leq \frac{\pi}{4} \implies |k| \leq \frac{2019}{8} < 253$$

Hence, there are 505 possible choices for k.

(b) Let us write $2^x = u$ and $3^x = v$. Then, the given equation can be rewritten as

$$\frac{u^3 + v^3}{u^2 v + uv^2} = \frac{7}{6} \implies \frac{(u+v)(u^2 - uv + v^2)}{uv(u+v)} = \frac{7}{6},$$

which leads to the equation $6u^2 - 13uv + 6v^2 = 0$. This can be factorized as $(2u - 3v)(3u - 2v) = 0$, which is equivalent to the solution set

$$\frac{2^x}{3^x} \in \left\{\frac{2}{3}, \frac{3}{2}\right\}$$

Clearly, the solutions are $x = \pm 1$.

13. Evaluate $\int_0^\infty (1+x^2)^{-(m+1)} dx$, where m is a natural number.

Solution: Substituting $x = \tan\theta$, we get

$$\int_0^{\frac{\pi}{2}} (\sec^2\theta)^{-m} d\theta = \int_0^{\frac{\pi}{2}} (\cos\theta)^{2m} d\theta$$

Let us denote the above by I_m. We are going to use the Wallis formula, which works as follows:

$$\begin{aligned} I_m &= \int_0^{\frac{\pi}{2}} (\cos^2 x)(\cos^{2m-2} x) dx \\ &= \int_0^{\frac{\pi}{2}} \cos^{2m-2} x \, dx - \int_0^{\frac{\pi}{2}} (\sin^2 x)(\cos^{2m-2} x) dx \\ &= I_{m-1} - \int_0^{\frac{\pi}{2}} \sin x (\cos^{2m-2} x \sin x) dx \end{aligned}$$

Note that the anti-derivative of $\cos^{2m-2} x \sin x$ is $(-\cos^{2m-1} x)/(2m-1)$. Thus, using integration by parts for the second term of the above, we get

$$\int_0^{\frac{\pi}{2}} \sin x (\cos^{2m-2} x \sin x) dx = \left[\frac{\sin x \cos^{2m-1} x}{1-2m}\right]_0^{\frac{\pi}{2}} + \int_0^{\frac{\pi}{2}} \frac{\cos x \cos^{2m-1} x}{2m-1} dx = \frac{I_m}{2m-1}$$

Therefore, the integral follows the recursive relation

$$I_m \left(1 + \frac{1}{2m-1}\right) = I_{m-1} \implies I_m = \frac{(2m-1)}{2m} I_{m-1}$$

Since $I_0 = \pi/2$, it is straightforward to infer that

$$I_m = \frac{(2m-1)}{2m} \cdot \frac{(2m-3)}{(2m-2)} \cdots \frac{1}{2} \cdot \frac{\pi}{2} = \frac{(2m)!}{2^{2m}(m!)^2} \cdot \frac{\pi}{2}$$

14. Let $ABCD$ be a parallelogram. Let O be a point in its interior such that $\angle AOB + \angle DOC = 180°$. Show that $\angle ODC = \angle OBC$.

Solution: Assume, without loss of generality, that the sides AB and DC are along the x-axis and the line $y = b$. Also assume that the sides AD and BC are along the lines $y = mx$ and $y = mx - a$. Clearly, the vertices of the parallelogram are $A = (0,0)$, $B = (a/m, 0)$, $C = ((a+b)/m, b)$, $D = (b/m, b)$. Let us also consider that the coordinates of O are (h,k).

Our aim is to find a point P such that $AOBP$ is a cyclic quadrilateral. Note that the slopes of the lines DO and CO are $(b-k)/(b/m-h)$ and $(b-k)/(a/m+b/m-h)$, respectively. Subsequently, the equation of a line parallel to DO and passing through A can be found as

$$\frac{y}{x} = \frac{b-k}{b/m-h}$$

On the other hand, the equation of a line parallel to CO and passing through B can be found as

$$\frac{y}{x-a/m} = \frac{b-k}{a/m+b/m-h}$$

Thus, the point of intersection of these two lines should satisfy

$$\frac{x}{b/m-h} = \frac{x-a/m}{a/m+b/m-h} \implies \frac{xa}{m} = -\frac{a}{m}\left(\frac{b}{m}-h\right) \implies x = h - \frac{b}{m},$$

which implies that the coordinates of the point of intersection (let us call it P) are $(h-b/m, k-b)$. Therefore, the slope of the line OP is

$$\frac{k-b-k}{h-b/m-h} = m,$$

which is the same as the slope of AD and BC.

Observing that $DO \parallel AP$, $CO \parallel BP$, $OP \parallel BC$ and $\angle AOB + \angle DOC = 180°$, it is straightforward to infer that $AOBP$ is a cyclic quadrilateral. Using the fact that a chord makes equal angles with any point on the circumference, we write $\angle PAB = \angle POB$. However, $OP \parallel BC$ indicates that $\angle POB$ and $\angle OBC$ are alternate angles, and therefore, $\angle PAB = \angle OBC$.

Next, using $DO \parallel AP$ and $AB \parallel DC$, it is easy to show that $\angle PAB = \angle ODC$, and hence, $\angle ODC = \angle OBC$.

15. Three positive real numbers x, y, z satisfy

$$\begin{aligned} x^2 + y^2 &= 3^2, \\ y^2 + yz + z^2 &= 4^2, \\ x^2 + \sqrt{3}xz + z^2 &= 5^2. \end{aligned}$$

Find the value of $2xy + xz + \sqrt{3}yz$.

Solution: Observing that all of the given equations are similar to the cosine formula for triangles, we first construct a triangle ABC such that $AB = 3$, $BC = 4$, $CA = 5$. It is clear that ABC is a right-angled triangle with the right angle at B.

Next, let us take a point P inside the triangle such that $AP = x$, $BP = y$ and $\angle APB = 90°$. The first equation ensures that such a point exists. We also observe that if $CP = z$, then the second equation is of the form $BP^2 + CP^2 - 2(BP)(CP)(-1/2) = BC^2$, which implies that $\angle BPC$ must be $120°$. Similarly, from the third equation, we can argue that $\angle CPA = 150°$.

Using the above, $2xy + xz + \sqrt{3}yz$ can be written as

$$4\left[\frac{1}{2}(AP)(BP) + \frac{1}{2}(AP)(CP)\sin\angle CPA + \frac{1}{2}(BP)(CP)\sin\angle BPC\right],$$

which is clearly 4 times the total area of the triangles APB, BPC and CPA. Since they combine to form the triangle ABC, we can easily conclude that the required answer is $4 \times 6 = 24$.

16. (a) Compute $\frac{d}{dx}\left[\int_0^{e^x} \log(t)\cos^4(t)dt\right]$.

   (b) For $x > 0$, define $F(x) = \int_1^x t\log(t)dt$.

      i. Determine the open interval(s) (if any) where $F(x)$ is decreasing and the open interval(s) (if any) where $F(x)$ is increasing.

      ii. Determine all the local minima of $F(x)$ (if any) and the local maxima of $F(x)$ (if any).

Solution:

(a) We can use the Leibniz formula to obtain

$$\frac{d}{dx}\left[\int_0^{e^x} \log(t)\cos^4(t)dt\right] = e^x\left[\log(e^x)\cos^4(e^x)\right] = xe^x\cos^4(e^x)$$

(b) Once again, the Leibniz formula can be used to indicate

$$F'(x) = x\log x \implies F''(x) = 1 + \log x$$

Clearly, $F'(x) = 0$ only for $x = 1$. It is positive for $x > 1$ and negative for $x < 1$. Also, $F''(x) > 0$ for all $x > 1/e$ and is < 0 otherwise. Thus, $F(x)$ is increasing in $(1, \infty)$ and is decreasing in $(0, 1)$. It has only one local minima, at $x = 1$, and the corresponding value is 0.

CMI BSc. Mathematics Entrance Test (2020)

1. Each student in a small school must be a member of at least one of three school clubs. It is known that each club has 35 members. It is not known how many students are members of two of the three clubs, but it is known that exactly 10 students are members of all three clubs. What is the largest possible total number of students in the school? What is the smallest possible total number of students in the school?

Solution: We call the three clubs A, B, C. Let a, b, c be the number of people who are in only A, B and C. Let x, y, z be the number of people who are in $A \cap B \cap C^c$, $A^c \cap B \cap C$ and $A \cap B^c \cap C$. Since exactly 10 students are members of all three clubs, we can write the equations
$$a + x + z = 25, \ b + x + y = 25, \ c + y + z = 25$$
Now, if n is the total number of students, then $n = a + b + c + x + y + z + 10$. Thus, we can write $n = 85 - (x + y + z)$, and we need to find the maximum and minimum possible values for $x + y + z$. It is easy to note that the minimum is attained when $x = y = z = 0$ and the maximum is attained when $a = 0, b = 0, c = 0$, that is, if $x + y + z = 37.5$. Since x, y, z must be integers, it is straightforward to infer that $0 \leqslant x + y + z \leqslant 37$. Hence, the minimum and maximum values of n are 48 and 85, respectively.

2. Let P be the plane containing the vectors $(6, 6, 9)$ and $(7, 8, 10)$. Find a unit vector that is perpendicular to $(2, -3, 4)$ and that lies in the plane P. (Note: All vectors are considered as line segments starting at the origin $(0, 0, 0)$. In particular, the origin lies in the plane P).

Solution: Any vector in the plane P is of the form $v = (6\hat{i} + 6\hat{j} + 9\hat{k}) + \lambda(7\hat{i} + 8\hat{j} + 10\hat{k})$. Since it is perpendicular to $w = 2\hat{i} - 3\hat{j} + 4\hat{k}$, we can say that the dot product of v and w is 0. Thus
$$2(6 + 7\lambda) - 3(6 + 8\lambda) + 4(9 + 10\lambda) = 0 \implies 30\lambda + 30 = 0$$
Clearly, $\lambda = -1$, and the corresponding vector is $-\hat{i} - 2\hat{j} - \hat{k}$, which implies that the required unit vector is $-\frac{1}{\sqrt{6}}(1, 2, 1)$.

3. Calculate the following two definite integrals.
$$\int_1^{e^2} \ln|x| \, dx \quad \text{and} \quad \int_{-1}^1 \frac{\ln|x|}{|x|} \, dx.$$

Solution: For the first integral, we can follow integration by parts and write
$$\int_1^{e^2} \ln|x| \, dx = \left[x \ln x - x\right]_1^{e^2} = e^2 \ln e^2 - e^2 + 1 = e^2 + 1$$

In the case of the second integral, letting $g(x) = \ln|x|/|x|$, we can say that $g(x)$ is discontinuous at 0. Also, note that the anti-derivative of $g(x)$ is $(\ln|x|)^2/2$. Since $\lim_{x \to 0} \ln|x| = -\infty$, one can argue that the definite integral of $g(x)$ in both $(-1,0)$ and $(0,1)$ is $-\infty$.

4. A fair die is thrown 100 times in succession. Find the probabilities of the following events:

   (i) 4 is the outcome of one or more of the first three throws.

   (ii) Exactly two of the last four throws give an outcome divisible by 3 (that is, outcome 3 or 6).

Solution: Since it is a fair die, the probability of every number is $1/6$.

   (i) The probability that 4 is not the outcome of any of the first three throws is $(5/6)^3$. Thus, 4 is the outcome of one or more of the first three throws with probability $1 - 125/216 = 91/216$.

   (ii) The probability that exactly two of the last four throws give an outcome divisible by 3 is $\binom{4}{2}(1/3)^2(2/3)^2 = 8/27$.

5. Consider the following functions and identify, for each, if they have (i) a horizontal asymptote, (ii) a vertical asymptote, (iii) a removable discontinuity.

$$f(x) = \frac{x^3}{x^2 - x}, \quad g(x) = \frac{x^2 - x}{x^3}, \quad h(x) = \frac{x^3 - x}{x^3 + x}.$$

Solution: A function of the form $p(x)/q(x)$, where both $p(x)$ and $q(x)$ are polynomials, has a horizontal asymptote if the degree of $q(x)$ is $\geq$ the degree of $p(x)$. Clearly, g and h have horizontal asymptotes while f does not. On the other hand, a vertical asymptote may exist at points that are zeros of the denominator.

For $f(x)$, we note that it is not defined at $x = 0, 1$. Now

$$\lim_{x \to 0} f(x) = 0, \quad \lim_{x \to 1} f(x) = 1$$

Thus, f has a vertical asymptote and has removal discontinuities.

Next, observe that $g(x)$ is undefined at 0 and $\lim_{x \to 0} g(x) = -\infty$, which signifies that there is a vertical asymptote but the discontinuity is not removable.

Finally, $h(x)$ is not defined at $x = 0$ and we can write $\lim_{x \to 0} h(x) = 1$. Obviously, there is a removable discontinuity and no vertical asymptote.

6. Recall the function arctan(x), also denoted as $\tan^{-1}(x)$. Complete the sentence: arctan(20202019) + arctan(20202021) _____ 2 arctan(20202020), because in the relevant region, the graph of $y = \arctan(x)$ _____ .

Fill in the first blank with one of the following: is less than / is equal to / is greater than. Fill in the second blank with a single correct reason consisting of one of the following phrases: is bounded / is continuous / has positive first derivative / has negative first derivative / has positive second derivative / has negative second derivative / has an inflection point.

Solution: For $y = \arctan(x)$, $y' = 1/(1+x^2)$ and $y'' = -2x/(1+x^2)^2$. Clearly, for all positive x, the second order derivative is negative and the first order derivative is positive. Therefore, the function is increasing and is convex, which further signifies that $\arctan(20202019) + \arctan(20202021) < 2\arctan(20202020)$. Hence, the two blanks should be filled in by the terms "is less than" and "has negative second derivative".

7. The polynomial $p(x) = 10x^{400} + ax^{399} + bx^{398} + 3x + 15$, where a, b are real constants, is given to be divisible by $x^2 - 1$.

   (i) If you can, find the values of a and b. If it is not possible to derive them, state why.

   (ii) If you can, find the sum of reciprocals of all 400 (complex) roots of $p(x)$. If it is not possible to derive them, state why.

Solution:

(i) $p(x)$ is divisible by $x^2 - 1$. Thus, $p(1) = p(-1) = 0$, which implies that $10 + a + b + 3 + 15 = 10 - a + b - 3 + 15 = 0$. Clearly, $a + b = -28$, $a - b = 22$. Solving these two equations, we can write $a = -3, b = -25$.

(ii) Let $\alpha_1, \ldots, \alpha_{400}$ be the roots of $p(x)$. Then

$$\sum_{i=1}^{400} \frac{1}{\alpha} = \frac{\sum_{i=1}^{400} \text{Product of all roots except } \alpha_i}{\prod_{i=1}^{400} \alpha_i}$$

It is easy to argue that the numerator is $-3/10$ while the denominator is $15/10$. Thus, the sum of reciprocals of all 400 (complex) roots is $-1/5$.

8. For a positive integer n, let $D(n)$ be the number of positive integer divisors of n. For example, $D(6) = 4$ because 6 has four divisors, namely, 1, 2, 3 and 6. Find the number of $n \leqslant 60$ such that $D(n) = 6$.

Solution: If the prime factorization of n is $p_1^{\alpha_1} \ldots p_k^{\alpha_k}$, then the number of divisors is $D(n) = (\alpha_1 + 1) \ldots (\alpha_k + 1)$. Since $D(n) = 6$, one can argue that n must be of the form $p_1 p_2^2$ or p_1^5. In the first case, the possible choices of (p_1, p_2) are

$$(2,3), (2,5), (2,7), (2,11), (2,13), (3,2), (3,5), (5,2)$$

In the second case, there is only one possible choice of $p_1 = 2$. Hence, in total, there are 9 choices of $n \leqslant 60$ such that $D(n) = 6$.

9. Notice that the quadratic polynomial $p(x) = 1 + x + x(x-1)/2$ satisfies $p(j) = 2^j$ for $j = 0, 1, 2$. A polynomial $q(x)$ of degree 7 satisfies $q(j) = 2^j$ for $j = 0, 1, 2, 3, 4, 5, 6, 7$. Find the value of $q(10)$.

Solution: Recall that the sum of $\binom{n}{i}$, for $i = 0, 1, \ldots, n$, is 2^n. Then, based on the given condition, we can write $q(x)$ as $\sum_{j=0}^{7} \binom{x}{j}$, where $\binom{x}{j}$ is defined to be 0 whenever $x < j$. It is easy to see that $q(j) = 2^j$ for all $j = 0, 1, 2, 3, 4, 5, 6, 7$ and that $q(x)$ is a 7-degree polynomial. Subsequently, we can obtain

$$q(10) = \sum_{j=0}^{7} \binom{10}{j} = 2^{10} - \binom{10}{8} - \binom{10}{9} - \binom{10}{10} = 1024 - 45 - 10 - 1 = 968$$

10. Note that $25 \times 16 - 19 \times 21 = 1$. Using this or otherwise, find positive integers a, b and c, all $\leqslant 475 = 25 \times 19$, such that

- a is $1 \pmod{19}$ and $0 \pmod{25}$,
- b is $0 \pmod{19}$ and $1 \pmod{25}$, and
- c is $4 \pmod{19}$ and $10 \pmod{25}$.

Solution: We note that 25 and 19 are relatively prime. Let $M = 19 \times 25$, $d_1 = M/19 = 25$, $d_2 = M/25 = 19$. Using the Chinese Remainder Theorem, a number K would leave remainder r_1 when divided by 19 and remainder r_2 when divided by 25 if

$$K \equiv d_1 s_1 r_1 + d_2 s_2 r_2 \pmod{M},$$

such that $d_1 s_1 \equiv 1 \pmod{19}$ and $d_2 s_2 \equiv 1 \pmod{25}$. From the given information, we can then write $s_1 = 16$, $s_2 = -21$.

Therefore, a, b, c must satisfy

$$a \equiv 400 \pmod{475}, \ b \equiv -399 \pmod{475}, \ c \equiv -2390 \pmod{475}$$

Since we want positive integers less than 475, the required solutions are $a = 400$, $b = 76$, $c = 460$.

11. Suppose A, B, C, D are points on a circle such that AC and BD are diameters of that circle. Suppose $AB = 12$ and $BC = 5$. Let P be a point on the arc of the circle from A to B (the arc that does not contain points C and D). Let the distances of P from A, B, C and D be a, b, c, d,

respectively. Find the values of $\frac{a+b}{c+d}$ and $\frac{a-b}{d-c}$. You may assume $d \neq c$ so the second ratio makes sense.

Solution: $ABCD$ is a cyclic quadrilateral, with AC and BD being diameters. Thus, all angles of the quadrilateral are essentially angles in a semicircle. Therefore, all angles are $90°$, indicating that $ABCD$ is a rectangle. We can write $AB = CD = 12$, $BC = AD = 5$, $AC = BD = \sqrt{12^2 + 5^2} = 13$.

Next, we use the fact that $PADB$ is a cyclic quadrilateral and use Ptolemy's Theorem to write
$$(PD)(AB) = (PA)(BD) + (PB)(AD) \implies 12d = 13a + 5b$$

Similarly, from $PACB$, we obtain the equation $12c = 5a + 13b$. Adding and subtracting these two equations, we get

$$\frac{a+b}{c+d} = \frac{12}{18} = \frac{2}{3}, \quad \frac{a-b}{d-c} = \frac{12}{8} = \frac{3}{2}$$

12. Let $z = e^{2\pi i/n}$, where $n \geq 2$ is a positive integer, $\imath^2 = -1$ and the real number $2\pi/n$ can also be considered as an angle in radians.

(i) Show that $\sum_{k=0}^{n-1} z^k = 0$.

(ii) Show that $\sum_{k=0}^{8} \cos(40k+1)° = 0$, that is,
$$\cos(1°) + \cos(41°) + \ldots + \cos(281°) + \cos(321°) = 0.$$

Solution: Consider the polynomial $x^n - 1 = 0$. We know that z^k, for $k = 0, 1, \ldots, n-1$, are roots of this polynomial.

(i) Since the sum of the roots of a polynomial is given by the ratio of the coefficient of the first degree term to the same of the highest degree term, we can say that the sum of the roots of the polynomial $x^n - 1 = 0$ is 0. That completes the proof of this part.

(ii) Let us use $n = 9$ in the result of the first part. Using De Moivre's Theorem and the fact that $1° = 2\pi/360$ radians, we can write

$$\sum_{k=0}^{8} \left[\cos\left(\frac{2\pi k}{9}\right) + \imath \sin\left(\frac{2\pi k}{9}\right)\right] = 0 \implies \sum_{k=0}^{8} [\cos(40k)° + \imath \sin(40k)°] = 0$$

If we multiply the above equation by $\cos 1° + \imath \sin 1°$, then the kth term becomes

$$\cos(40k)° \cos 1° - \sin(40k)° \sin 1° + \imath [\cos 1° \sin(40k)° + \sin 1° \cos(40k)°]$$

Since the real part of the above is $\cos(40k+1)°$, using the previous relationship, it is now straightforward to argue that the given sum is 0.

13. A spider starts at the origin and runs in the first quadrant along the graph of $y = x^3$ at a constant speed of 10 units/second. The speed is measured along the length of the curve $y = x^3$. The formula for the curve length along the graph of $y = f(x)$ from $x = a$ to $x = b$ is $\ell = \int_a^b \sqrt{1 + f'(x)^2}\, dx$. As the spider runs, it spins out a thread that is always maintained in a straight line connecting the spider with the origin. What is the rate in units/second at which the thread is elongating when the spider is at $(1/2, 1/8)$?

Solution: Let us assume that at time t, the spider is at the point (u, u^3), while the length of the thread joining it to the origin (along a straight line) is s. Then, $s^2 = u^2 + u^6$. Let the length of the curve along $y = x^3$ from the origin till (u, u^3) be denoted by ℓ. The information given in this problem is as follows:

$$\frac{d\ell}{dt} = 10, \quad \ell = \int_0^u \sqrt{1 + 9x^4}\, dx$$

We need to find the value of ds/dt at $u = 1/2$. It is easy to observe that at $u = 1/2$

$$s = \sqrt{\left(\frac{1}{2}\right)^2 + \left(\frac{1}{2}\right)^6} = \frac{\sqrt{17}}{8}, \quad 2s\frac{ds}{dt} = 2u\frac{du}{dt} + 6u^5\frac{du}{dt} \implies \frac{ds}{dt} = \frac{19}{4\sqrt{17}}\frac{du}{dt}$$

Next, using the fundamental theorem of calculus, at $u = 1/2$

$$\frac{d\ell}{dt} = \sqrt{1 + 9u^4}\frac{du}{dt} \implies \left.\frac{du}{dt}\right|_{u=\frac{1}{2}} = \frac{4}{5} \times \frac{d\ell}{dt} = 8 \implies \left.\frac{d\ell}{dt}\right|_{u=\frac{1}{2}} = \frac{38}{\sqrt{17}}$$

14. In this problem, we are interested in a real-valued function f satisfying two conditions: at each x in its domain, f is continuous and $f(x^2) = f(x)^2$. Prove the following independent statements about such functions.

   (i) There is a unique function f with domain $[0, 1]$ and $f(0) \neq 0$.

   (ii) If the domain of such f is $(0, \infty)$, then ($f(x) = 0$ for every x) OR ($f(x) \neq 0$ for every x).

   (iii) There are infinitely many functions f with domain $(0, \infty)$ such that $\int_0^\infty f(x)\, dx < 1$.

Solution: For all three parts, we need to consider functions that are continuous in non-negative real numbers. Since $f(x^2) = f(x)^2$, we can also write $f(x^{2^m}) = f(x)^{2^m}$ for all $m \in \mathbb{N}$.

(i) For the domain $[0,1]$, using the given condition, we can write $f(0) = f(0)^2$. Since $f(0) \neq 0$, we get $f(0) = 1$. Now, for every x in the domain, $x^n \to 0$ as $n \to \infty$. Using the continuity property, we can say that $f(x^{2^m}) \to f(0)$ as $m \to \infty$. Then, the given condition suggests that as $m \to \infty$, $f(x)^{2^m} \to 1$ for all x in the domain. This is only possible if f is a constant function, taking value 1 everywhere.

(ii) For all positive x, we can take $\sqrt{x}$ and get $f(\sqrt{x}) = \sqrt{f(x)}$, thereby proving that $f(x)$ is positive for all real positive x. Now, assume that there are real numbers $a, b \in (0, \infty)$, such that $f(a) = 0, f(b) > 0$. Following the earlier technique, we can take repeated square roots to obtain

$$f\left(a^{2^{-n}}\right) = f(a)^{2^{-n}} \to 0, \ f\left(b^{2^{-n}}\right) = f(b)^{2^{-n}} \to 1$$

However, in both cases, because of the continuity of the function, the terms should converge to $f(0)$, and it cannot be both 0 and 1. Hence, $f(x)$ is either 0 for all x or non-zero for all x.

(iii) We wish to find functions with domain $(0, \infty)$ such that $\int_0^\infty f(x)\,dx < 1$. To that end, let us define a function of the form

$$f(x) = \begin{cases} x^p & \text{for } x < 1 \\ 1 & \text{for } x = 1 \\ x^q & \text{for } x > 1 \end{cases}$$

where p, q are integers. Then, note that the function is continuous and defined for all $x \in (0, \infty)$. Further, the given condition is equivalent to

$$\int_0^1 x^p\,dx + \int_1^\infty x^q\,dx = \left[\frac{x^{p+1}}{p+1}\right]_0^1 + \left[\frac{x^{q+1}}{q+1}\right]_1^\infty < 1$$

Now, if we choose p and q such that $p+1 > 0$ and $q+1 < 0$, then the above inequality can be rewritten as

$$\frac{1}{p+1} - \frac{1}{q+1} < 1$$

It is evident that one can choose p and q satisfying the above conditions in infinitely many ways. Hence, there are infinitely many functions with domain $(0, \infty)$ such that $\int_0^\infty f(x)\,dx < 1$.

15. Consider polynomials $p(x)$ with the following property, called (†):

    (†) if r is a root of $p(x)$, then $r^2 - 4$ is also a root of $p(x)$.

(i) We want to find every quadratic polynomial of the form $p(x) = x^2 + bx + c$ such that $p(x)$ has two distinct roots, integer coefficients and property (†). Prove that there are exactly two such polynomials.

(ii) It is also true that there are exactly two cubic polynomials of the form $p(x) = x^3 + ax^2 + bx + c$ with the property (†) such that $p(x)$ shares no root with the polynomials you found in part (i). Explain fully how you will prove this along with the method to find the polynomials, but do not try to explicitly find the polynomials.

Solution:

(i) Assume that the polynomial $p(x)$ has two roots α, β. Based on the given conditions, $\alpha^2 - 4$ and $\beta^2 - 4$ must be roots of $p(x)$. So, $\alpha^2 - 4 = \alpha$ or $\alpha^2 - 4 = \beta$. In the first case, α must be a root of $x^2 - x - 4 = 0$, which allows two real roots. If we call the second root β, then $\beta^2 - 4 = \beta$, thereby establishing that this polynomial satisfies all the required properties.

We now turn our attention to the condition $\alpha^2 - 4 = \beta$, which further requires $\beta^2 - 4 = \alpha$. Thus, α, β must be roots of the polynomial $(x^2 - 4)^2 - 4 - x = 0$. We can simplify and factorize the polynomial as

$$x^4 - 8x^2 - x + 12 = (x^2 - x - 4)(x^2 + x - 3)$$

Clearly, there are exactly two polynomials, namely, $(x^2 - x - 4)$ and $(x^2 + x - 3)$, which satisfy the required conditions.

(ii) Consider that the three roots of the cubic polynomial are α, β, γ. If we denote $g(x) = x^2 - 4$, then we can see that $g(\alpha) \neq \alpha$; otherwise it would be a root of the polynomial found in part (i). Similarly, if $g(\alpha) = \beta$ and $g(\beta) = \alpha$, then they would be the roots of $x^2 + x - 3$, which is again not allowed. Thus, α, β, γ must be distinct and must satisfy $g(\alpha) = \beta$, $g(\beta) = \gamma$ and $g(\gamma) = \alpha$.

Next, using similar techniques as before, we can argue that these values should be roots of the polynomial $((x^2 - 4)^2 - 4)^2 - 4 - x = 0$. It is easy to see that $x^2 - x - 4$ is a factor of this polynomial. Since the roots must be different from the roots of $x^2 - x - 4$, we can divide the previous polynomial by $x^2 - x - 4$ and obtain a six-degree polynomial. This six-degree polynomial can be factorized into two cubic polynomials, thereby providing the required solutions.

16. For sets S and T, a relation from S to T is just a subset R of $S \times T$. If (x, y) is in R, we say that x is related to y. Answer the following. Part (i) is independent of parts (ii) and (iii).

(i) A relation R from S to S is called antisymmetric if it satisfies the following condition: if (a,b) is in R, then (b,a) must NOT be in R. For $S = \{1,2,\ldots,k\}$, how many antisymmetric relations are there from S to S?

(ii) Write a recurrence equation for $f(k,n)$ = the number of non-crossing relations from $\{1,2,\ldots,k\}$ to $\{1,2,\ldots,n\}$ that have no isolated elements in either set. (See below for the definitions of the two terms and their visual meaning. Drawing pictures may be useful). Your recurrence should have only a fixed number of terms on the RHS.

(iii) Using your recurrence in (ii) or otherwise, find a formula for $f(3,n)$.

Definition 1: We say that a relation from S to T has no isolated elements if each s in S is related to some T in T and if for each T in T, some s in S is related to T.

Definition 2: We say that a relation R from $S = \{1,2,\ldots,k\}$ to $S = \{1,2,\ldots,n\}$ is non-crossing if the following never takes place: (i,x) and (j,y) are both in R with $i < j$ but $x > y$.

Visual meaning: One can visualise a relation R as being very similar to a function. List 1 to k as dots arranged vertically in increasing order on the left and list 1 to n on the right. For each (s,t) in R, draw a straight line segment from s on the left to T on the right. In this situation, where one wants to avoid non-crossing relations, the segments connecting i with x and j with y would cross. Having no isolated elements also has an obvious visual meaning.

Solution:

(i) Consider the set $S \times S$. Because of the antisymmetric property, we can say that all terms of the form (j,j) cannot be in R. Next, all other terms of S are divided into $k(k-1)/2$ pairs of the form $\{(k_1,k_2),(k_2,k_1)\}$. It is clear that only one pair or no pair can be in the relation R. Thus, there are three possible choices for every pair. Therefore, there are $3^{k(k-1)/2}$ antisymmetric relations from S to S.

(ii) We can look at the image of k and argue that it must be related to n, or else it would not be non-crossing. Now, there are three possibilities: (a) k is related to $n-1$ as well, (b) k is not related to anyone else, $k-1$ is related to n, (c) k is not related to anyone else, $k-1$ is not related to n but is related to $n-1$.

In the above three cases, the number of relations are $f(k,n-1)$, $f(k-1,n)$ and $f(k-1,n-1)$, respectively. Since the three cases are disjoint and exhaustively describe all relations from $\{1,2,\ldots,k\}$ to $\{1,2,\ldots,n\}$, the recurrence relation can be written as

$$f(k,n) = f(k,n-1) + f(k-1,n) + f(k-1,n-1)$$

(iii) Using the recurrence from part (ii), we can write

$$f(3,n) = f(3,n-1) + f(2,n) + f(2,n-1)$$

Also, for $k=2$, another use of the recurrence indicates

$$f(2,n) = f(2,n-1) + f(1,n) + f(1,n-1) = f(2,n-1) + 2,$$

which is essentially an arithmetic progression. This has the solution $f(2,n) = 2(n-1) + f(2,1) = 2n - 1$. Plugging it back in the previous equation, $f(3,n) = f(3,n-1) + 4(n-1)$. Therefore

$$f(3,n) = f(3,1) + \sum_{k=1}^{n-1} 4k = 1 + 4 \times \frac{n(n-1)}{2} = 2n^2 - 2n + 1$$

CMI BSc. Mathematics Entrance Test (2021)

1. Solve the following two independent problems:

   (i) Let f be a function from domain S to codomain T. Let g be another function from domain T to codomain U. For each of the blanks below, find out which one of the four options listed underneath is true. (It is not necessary that each choice is true exactly once).

   If $g \circ f$ is one-to-one, then f _____ and g _____
   If $g \circ f$ is onto, then f _____ and g _____

   Option A: Must be one-to-one and must be onto.

   Option B: Must be one-to-one but need not be onto.

   Option C: Need not be one-to-one but must be onto.

   Option D: Need not be one-to-one and need not be onto.

   (ii) In the given figure, $ABCD$ is a square. Points X and Y, respectively on sides BC and CD, are such that X lies on the circle with diameter AY. What is the area of the square $ABCD$ if $AX = 4$ and $AY = 5$? (The figure is schematic and not to scale).

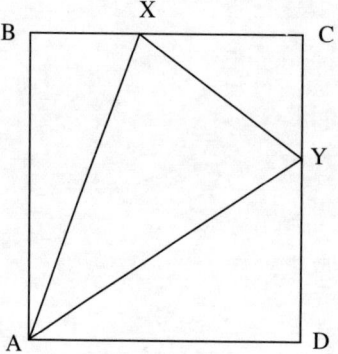

Solution:

(i) To solve this problem, let us define $h(x) = g \circ f(x) = g(f(x))$. The function $h : S \to U$ is one-to-one if $h(x_1) = h(x_2)$ implies $x_1 = x_2$, whereas h is onto if for every $y \in U$, there is $x \in S$ such that $h(x) = y$.

First, we assume that h is one-to-one. Then, $h(x_1) = h(x_2)$ implies $x_1 = x_2$. Thus, if $x_1 \neq x_2$, then $g(f(x_1)) \neq g(f(x_2))$, which ensures that $f(x_1)$ cannot be equal to $f(x_2)$. Clearly, f must be one-to-one. We also notice that only that restriction on f is sufficient to ensure that h is one-to-one. Hence, f need not be onto and g need not be either one-to-one or onto.

Next, when h is onto, we can say that for every $y \in U$, there exists $x \in S$ such that $g(f(x)) = y$. It clearly shows that for every $y \in U$, there exists $t \in T$ (which is equal to $f(x)$) such that $g(t) = y$, thereby proving that g must be onto. Once again, we notice that g need not be one-to-one. Also, no restriction on f is required as well.

Combining the above, we can say that the four blanks can be filled by options B, D, D and C, respectively.

(ii) Our aim is to find the quantity AB^2. Since X, A, Y lie on a circle that has AY as a diameter, we can easily say that AXY must be a right angle. Then, by the Pythagorean Theorem, $AX^2 + XY^2 = AY^2$, which implies that $XY = 3$.

Next, observing that $\angle AXB + \angle CXY = 90°$, we can say that $\angle CYX = \angle AXB$. Thus, the triangles ABX and XCY are similar. Subsequently, we can write $AB/CX = AX/XY = 4/3$, that is, $AB = (4/3)(CX)$. As $AB = BC$, it further implies $AB = (4/3)(AB - BX)$. From these, one can write $BX = AB/4$. Then, applying the Pythagorean Theorem once again for triangle ABX, we write $AB^2 + BX^2 = AX^2$, which indicates $AB^2 + AB^2/16 = 16$. Solving it, we get the area of the square as $AB^2 = 256/17$.

2. Solve the following two independent problems:

   (i) A mother and her two daughters participate in a game show. At first, the mother tosses a fair coin.

   Case 1: If the result is heads, then all three win individual prizes and the game ends.

   Case 2: If the result is tails, then each daughter separately throws a fair die and wins a prize if the result of her throw is 5 or 6. (Note that in case 2, there are two independent throws involved and whether each daughter gets a prize or not is unaffected by the other daughter's throw).

   (a) Suppose the first daughter did not win a prize. What is the probability that the second daughter also did not win a prize?

   (b) Suppose the first daughter won a prize. What is the probability that the second daughter also won a prize?

   (ii) Prove or disprove each of the following statements:

   (a) $2^{40} > 20!$

   (b) $1 - \frac{1}{x} \leqslant \ln x \leqslant x - 1$ for all $x > 0$

Solution:

(i) Let us use X to denote the outcome of the first toss (that is, 1 or 0 depending on whether it was heads or tails) and Y_1 and Y_2 to denote the outcome of the daughters' dice throws. For part (a), since the first daughter did not win a prize, the first toss was tails. We can compute the probability as

$$P[(X=0) \cap (Y_2 \notin \{5,6\}) \mid (X=0) \cap (Y_1 \notin \{5,6\})]$$

As X, Y_1, Y_2 are independent, the above reduces to $P[Y_2 \notin \{5,6\}]$. Now, because the dice are fair, the required value is $4/6 = 2/3$.

For part (b), let F and S indicate the events of the first and the second daughter winning a prize. It is easy to see that $F = (X=1) \cup ((X=0) \cap (Y_1 \in \{5,6\}))$ and $S = (X=1) \cup ((X=0) \cap (Y_2 \in \{5,6\}))$. Thus, $F \cap S = (X=1) \cup ((X=0) \cap (Y_1, Y_2 \in \{5,6\}))$. We can use the independence assumption to compute the probability

$$P(S \mid F) = \frac{P(S \cap F)}{P(F)} = \frac{P(X=1) + P(X=0)P(Y_1, Y_2 \in \{5,6\})}{P(X=1) + P(X=0)P(Y_1 \in \{5,6\})}$$

Since the coin and the die are fair, the above simplifies to

$$\frac{(1/2) + (1/2)(2/6)^2}{(1/2) + (1/2)(2/6)} = \frac{1 + 1/9}{1 + 1/3} = \frac{5}{6}$$

(ii) For part (a), let us first calculate the highest power of 2 that divides 20!. It can be computed as ($[\cdot]$ represents greatest integer function)

$$\left[\frac{20}{2}\right] + \left[\frac{20}{2^2}\right] + \left[\frac{20}{2^3}\right] + \left[\frac{20}{2^4}\right] = 10 + 5 + 2 + 1 = 18$$

In a similar fashion, we can proceed and obtain the prime factorization of 20! and write

$$\frac{20!}{2^{40}} = \frac{3^8 \times 5^4 \times 7^2 \times 11 \times 13 \times 17 \times 19}{2^{22}}$$

We observe that $3^2 > 2^3$ and $5 > 2^2$, that is, $3^8 \times 5^4 > 2^{20}$. Subsequently, one can argue that $20!/2^{40} > 1$, and hence, statement (a) is disproved.

For solving part (b), consider the function $f(x) = x - 1 - \ln x$. Since $f'(x) = 1 - 1/x$ and $f''(x) = 1/x^2$, we can say that $f(x)$ has a minima at $x = 1$. It is easy to verify that this is a global minima, and thus, $f(x) \geq f(1) = 0$, which implies $\ln x \leq x - 1$ for all $x > 0$. For the other inequality, let us substitute $x = 1/y$ to get $\ln(1/y) \leq 1/y - 1$, which is equivalent to $1 - 1/x \leq \ln x$. Hence, statement (b) is proved.

3. You are supposed to create a seven-character-long password for your mobile device.

   (i) How many seven-character passwords can be formed from 10 digits and 26 letters? (Only lowercase letters are taken throughout the problem). Repeats are allowed, for example, 0001a1a is a valid password.

   (ii) How many of the passwords contain at least one of the 26 letters and at least one of the 10 digits? Write your answer in the form: (Answer to part (i)) − (something).

   (iii) How many of the passwords contain at least one of the 5 vowels, at least one of the 21 consonants and at least one of the 10 digits? Extend your method for part (ii) to write a formula and explain your reasoning.

   (iv) Now suppose that in addition to the lowercase letters and digits, you can also use 12 special characters. How many seven-character passwords are there that contain at least one of the 5 vowels, at least one of the 21 consonants, at least one of the 10 digits and at least one of the 12 special characters? Write the final formula analogous to your answer to part (iii).

Solution:

   (i) For every character, there are 36 choices in total, since repetition is allowed. Thus, there are a total of 36^7 possible passwords.

   (ii) If a password consists of only letters and no digits, there are 26 choices for every position. So, there are 26^7 passwords that contain no digits. Similarly, there are 10^7 passwords that contain no letters. Hence, the total number of passwords that contain at least one of the 26 letters and at least one of the 10 digits is $36^7 - (26^7 + 10^7)$.

   (iii) We can use the principle of include-exclusion (PIE) here. Let V be the set of passwords that contain at least one vowel. Similarly, C and D are used to denote the sets of passwords containing at least one consonant and at least one digit, respectively. Our aim is to find out the cardinality of the set $(V \cap C \cap D)$. Note that $|V \cap C \cap D| = 36^7 - |V^c \cup C^c \cup D^c|$. Using PIE, the second term can be written as

   $$|V^c| + |C^c| + |D^c| - [|V^c \cap C^c| + |C^c \cap D^c| + |D^c \cap V^c|] + |V^c \cap C^c \cap D^c|$$

   We can argue that $|V^c|$ is 31^7, since for every character in the password, there are 31 choices (21 consonants and 10 digits). Proceeding in a similar way, we can show that

   $$|V \cap C \cap D| = 36^7 - |V^c \cup C^c \cup D^c| = 36^7 - [(31^7 + 15^7 + 26^7) - (10^7 + 5^7 + 21^7)]$$

   (iv) The above idea can be directly extended here, by using PIE for four sets. We shall obtain the answer as

$$48^7 - [(43^7 + 27^7 + 38^7 + 36^7) - (22^7 + 33^7 + 26^7 + 15^7 + 17^7 + 31^7) + (5^7 + 10^7 + 12^7 + 21^7)]$$

4. Show that there is no polynomial $p(x)$ for which $\cos(\theta) = p(\sin\theta)$ for all angles θ in some non-empty interval.

Solution: Let Θ be an open interval such that $\cos(\theta) = p(\sin\theta)$ for all $\theta \in \Theta$. Let us take $z = \sin\theta$. Then, $p(z)^2 = \cos^2\theta = 1 - \sin^2\theta = 1 - z^2$. Since the image set $\{\sin\theta : \theta \in \Theta\}$ is also an open interval, we get $p(z)^2 = 1 - z^2$ for all z in some open interval. Considering that $p(z)$ is a polynomial, it subsequently implies that there exists another polynomial $q(z)$ such that $q(z) = 0$ for all z in an open interval. However, that is possible if and only if $q(z)$ is a zero polynomial. Equivalently, $p(z)^2 = 1 - z^2$ for all real z, but that is impossible since the leading coefficient of the square of a polynomial cannot be -1. That completes our proof.

5. Define a function f as follows: $f(0) = 0$ and, for any $x > 0$,

$$f(x) = \lim_{L \to \infty} \int_{\frac{1}{x}}^{L} \frac{1}{t^2} \cos t \, dt \quad \left(\text{or the improper integral} \int_{\frac{1}{x}}^{\infty} \frac{1}{t^2} \cos t \, dt \right).$$

(i) Show that the definition makes sense for any $x > 0$ by justifying why the limit in the definition exists, that is, why the improper integral converges.

(ii) Find $f'(1/\pi)$ if it exists. Clearly indicate the basic result(s) you are using.

(iii) Find $\lim_{h \to 0+} \frac{f(h) - f(0)}{h}$, that is, the right-hand derivative of f at $x = 0$. We can take the limit only from the right-hand side because $f(x)$ is undefined for negative values of x.

Solution:

(i) For the given improper integral, we can use the fact that $|\cos t| \leq 1$ to argue that

$$|f(x)| \leq \int_{\frac{1}{x}}^{\infty} \frac{1}{t^2} dt = \left[-\frac{1}{t} \right]_{\frac{1}{x}}^{\infty} = x$$

Thus, the improper integral converges.

(ii) Using the fundamental theorem of calculus, we can write

$$f'(x) = -\frac{1}{1/x^2} \cos\left(\frac{1}{x}\right)\left(-\frac{1}{x^2}\right) = \cos\left(\frac{1}{x}\right)$$

Clearly, $f'(1/\pi) = \cos\pi = -1$.

(iii) Using the definition of f and integrating by parts

$$\lim_{h \to 0+} \frac{f(h) - f(0)}{h} = \lim_{h \to 0+} \frac{1}{h} \int_{\frac{1}{h}}^{\infty} \frac{1}{t^2} \cos t \, dt = \lim_{h \to 0+} \frac{1}{h} \left(\left[\frac{\sin t}{t^2} \right]_{\frac{1}{h}}^{\infty} + \int_{\frac{1}{h}}^{\infty} \frac{2 \sin t}{t^3} \, dt \right)$$

The first term in the right-hand side expression of the above equation can be simplified to $\lim_{h \to 0+}(-h)\sin(1/h)$. Since $|\sin t| \leq 1$, this limit is 0. On the other hand, using the same fact in the second term

$$\left| \frac{1}{h} \int_{\frac{1}{h}}^{\infty} \frac{2 \sin t}{t^3} \, dt \right| \leq \frac{1}{h} \int_{\frac{1}{h}}^{\infty} \frac{2}{t^3} \, dt = \frac{1}{h} \left[-\frac{1}{t^2} \right]_{\frac{1}{h}}^{\infty} = h$$

Therefore, as $h \to 0+$, the second term also goes to 0, thereby implying that the desired limit is 0.

6. n and k are positive integers, not necessarily distinct. You are given two stacks of cards with a number written on each card, as follows:

- Stack A has n cards. On each card, a number from the set $\{1, \ldots, k\}$ is written.
- Stack B has k cards. On each card, a number from the set $\{1, \ldots, n\}$ is written.

Numbers may repeat in either stack. Using this, you play a game by constructing a sequence $t_0, t_1, t_2, \ldots$ of integers as follows. Set $t_0 = 0$. For $j > 0$, there are two cases:

- If $t_j \leq 0$, draw the top card of stack A. Set $t_{j+1} = tj+$ the number written on this card.
- If $t_j > 0$, draw the top card of stack B. Set $t_{j+1} = tj-$ the number written on this card.

In either case, discard the taken card and continue. The game ends when you try to draw from an empty stack. Example: Let $n = 5, k = 3$, stack A $= 1, 3, 2, 3, 2$ and stack B $= 2, 5, 1$. You can check that the game ends with the sequence $0, 1, -1, 2, -3, -1, 2, 1$ (and with one card from stack A left unused).

(i) Prove that for every j, we have $-n+1 \leq t_j \leq k$.

(ii) Prove that there are at least two distinct indices i and j such that $t_i = t_j$.

(iii) Using the previous parts or otherwise, prove that there is a non-empty subset of cards in stack A and another subset of cards in stack B such that the sum of numbers in both the subsets is the same.

Solution:

(i) We can use the principles of mathematical induction on j to prove this. Note that for $j = 0$, the result trivially holds. Let us assume that $-n+1 \leq t_r \leq k$ for some $r > 0$. If

$t_r \leqslant 0$, then $t_{r+1} = t_r+$ the number written on a card from stack A, which means that the number is from the set $\{1,\ldots,k\}$. Thus, $t_{r+1} \leqslant t_r + k \leqslant k$, while it is obviously greater than $-n+1$. On the other hand, if $t_r > 0$, then t_{r+1} is obtained by subtracting some number of the set $\{1,\ldots,n\}$ from t_r. Since the maximum one can subtract is n, it is easy to argue that $t_{r+1} > t_r - n > -n$. Hence, by induction, the result follows.

(ii) Suppose that the game ended when we tried to draw a card from an empty stack A. This means that by that time, all n cards from stack A have been drawn and this would have been the $(n+1)$th time we are trying to draw a card from stack A. It subsequently means that there are $(n+1)$ instances of t_j which are all $\leqslant 0$. However, $t_j \geqslant -n+1 = -(n-1)$, and thus, there are only n values that are $\leqslant 0$. Hence, by the Pigeonhole Principle, there are two distinct indices i and j such that $t_i = t_j$. A similar proof can be written if we assume that the game ended when we tried to draw a card from an empty stack B.

(iii) From part (ii), let $i < j$ be two numbers such that $t_i = t_j$. Consider the set of cards drawn during the turns $i+1, \ldots, j$. Let A_{ij} and B_{ij} be the subsets indicating cards from stack A and stack B, respectively. Because the numbers written on cards from stack A are added and the numbers written on cards from stack B are subtracted, it is easy to conclude that the sum of the numbers of cards in A_{ij} is equal to the sum of the numbers of cards in B_{ij}.